A BRITI
IN ZUL

A BRITISH LION IN ZULULAND

Sir Garnet Wolseley in South Africa

WILLIAM WRIGHT

AMBERLEY

First published 2017

Amberley Publishing
The Hill, Stroud
Gloucestershire, GL5 4EP

www.amberley-books.com

ISBN 978 1 4456 6548 1 (hardback)
ISBN 978 1 4456 6549 8 (ebook)

British Library Cataloguing in Publication Data.
A catalogue record for this book is available from the British Library.

Typesetting and Origination by Amberley Publishing.
Printed in the UK.

CONTENTS

MAPS

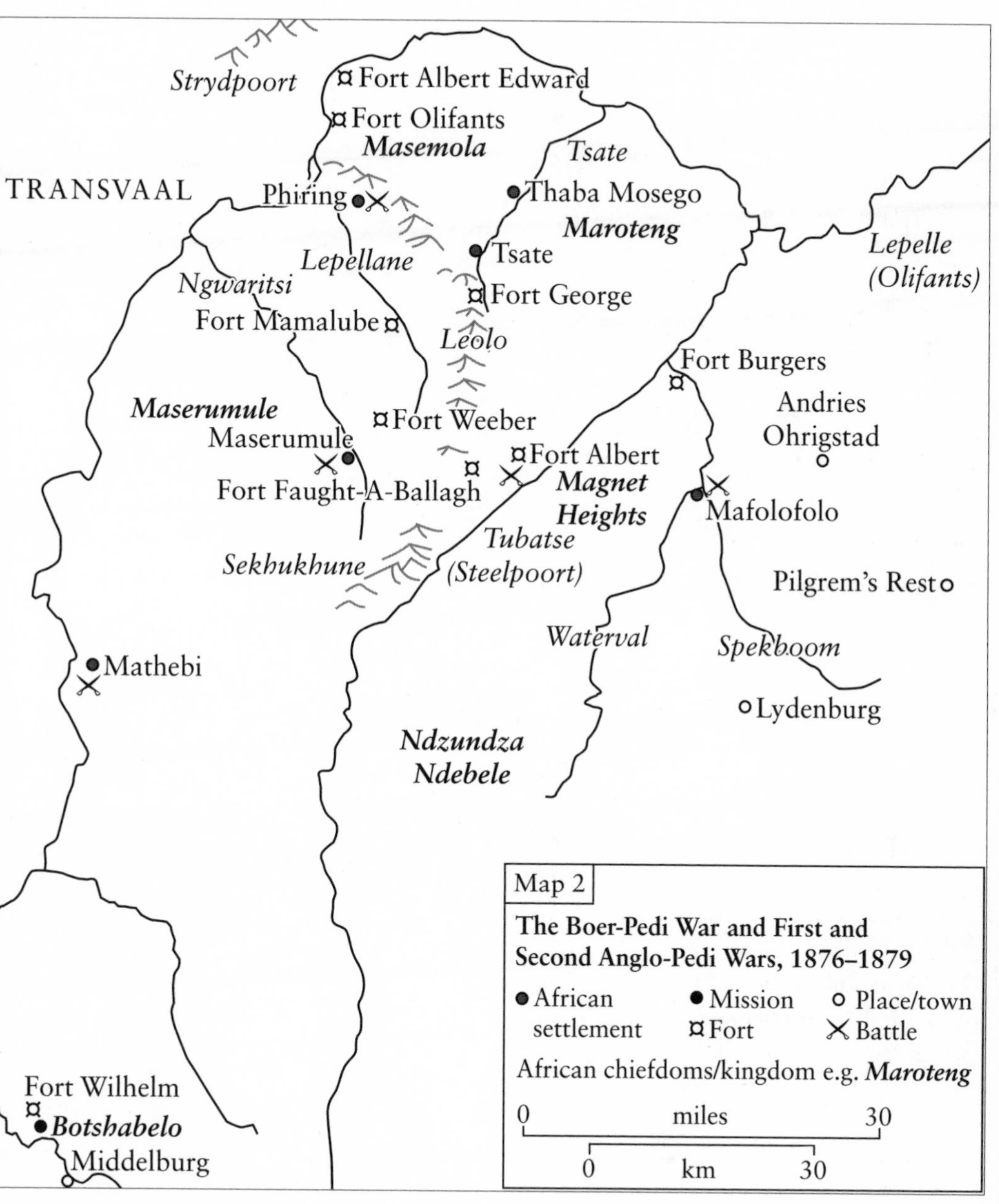
Strydpoort
Fort Albert Edward
Fort Olifants
Masemola
Tsate
TRANSVAAL
Phiring
Thaba Mosego
Maroteng
Tsate
Lepellane
Lepelle
(Olifants)
Ngwaritsi
Fort George
Fort Mamalube
Leolo
Fort Burgers
Andries
Ohrigstad
Maserumule
Fort Weeber
Maserumule
Fort Albert
Fort Faught-A-Ballagh
Magnet
Heights
Mafolofolo
Tubatse
Sekhukhune
(Steelpoort)
Pilgrem's Rest
Waterval
Spekboom
Mathebi
Lydenburg
Ndzundza
Ndebele
Map 2
The Boer-Pedi War and First and
Second Anglo-Pedi Wars, 1876–1879
African
settlement
Mission
Place/town
Fort
Battle
African chiefdoms/kingdom e.g. Maroteng
0
miles
30
0
km
30
Fort Wilhelm
Botshabelo
Middelburg

Ntombe Caves
Ntombe Drift
SWAZI KINGDOM
Luneburg
Ntombe
The Disputed Territory
Phongolo
Bivane
Utrecht
Khambula
ebaQulusini
Mkhuze
Hlobane
Transvaal Territory
Hlobane
Ngome Forest
kwaDwasa
Conference Hill
Prince Imperial killed
Ncome
Landman's Drift
Black Mfolozi
Dundee
Nhlazatsche
Nquthu
oNdini
White Mfolozi
kwaSogekle
Zungeni
Ulundi
kwaMbonambi
Isandlwana
Babanango
kwaNodwengu
Mfolozi
Rorke's Drift
esiKlebheni
Helpmekaar
Siphezi
Mthonjaneni
Mzinyathi
ZULU KINGDOM
emaNgweni
Nkandla Forest
Mhathuze
oNdini
Port Durnford
Fort Eshowe
Fort Cherry
Nyezane
Nyezane
COLONY OF NATAL
Middle Drift
Matigulu
Gingindlovu
Greytown
Thukela
Fort Pearson
Map 6
The Anglo-Zulu War, 1879
African settlement
Mission
Place/town
Fort
Battle
0 miles 20
0 km 20

PREFACE

In the three months between late August and late November 1879 the two most warlike and dangerous potentates in southern Africa were captured, their kingdoms destroyed, the military prowess of their armies and states blown to the winds.

One man was responsible for this, one Englishman tasked with restoring national honour after a string of costly and humiliating defeats, mistakes and fiascos. His name was Garnet Wolseley. He is largely forgotten today despite a statue on Horse Guards Parade and a tomb in St Paul's Cathedral. Yet the mid-Victorians thought him the master of irregular colonial warfare, so much so that he was satirised on the stage by Gilbert and Sullivan as the very model 'of a modern major-general'. His skills as a soldier and ability, as Disraeli said, to 'not only succeed but succeed quickly' helped create a new term in the English language, 'All Sir Garnet', meaning ready and in apple-pie order.

In May 1879, after a series of disasters in a war against the Zulu kingdom that was forced on the British government, a conflict planned without prior knowledge in London by the country's man-on-the-spot, Sir Bartle Frere (in concert with his military commander, General Lord Chelmsford), the Prime Minister finally thought enough was enough. He sent out Wolseley with wide powers to end the war, capture the Zulu king, settle the country – and do it all cheaply and without annexation.

Before Sir Garnet could take charge Lord Chelmsford managed to bring the Zulus to battle near the royal kraal, thus saving his reputation and ending the war. Most books on the events of 1879 end with this, the Battle of Ulundi. The whole affair was over – or was it?

This book examines 1879 through the eyes of Wolseley, using his personal journal and hundreds of his letters. My special focus is that period after Ulundi. This began with an eight-week-long 'king hunt' as Cetshwayo was pursued across Zululand. Much to their credit, his people refused to give him up. Desultory fighting continued and the last British soldier did not die in action until sixty-five days after the Ulundi battle.

Wolseley then carried out a reorganisation of Zululand. This rushed settlement has been decried ever since. It was controversial at the time and still remains so. Failings in the scheme were one cause of a disastrous civil war that rocked Zululand a few years later. It is impossible to defend the indefensible, but I have tried to examine every document of Wolseley's I could find, to see what was in his mind when he made his plans. Who really guided him? What did he hope to achieve for the Zulu people? Were his aims Machiavellian or benign?

After Zululand Sir Garnet set off for the newly acquired British territory of the Transvaal, where he hoped to deal with some rumblings of Boer discontent and return home by Christmas. Trouble was unfortunately looming, with the powerful Bapedi tribe in the eastern Transvaal under a remarkably cunning leader called Sekhukhune. From their extraordinary mountain fastnesses the Bapedi had seen off Swazi and Zulu invaders as well as two white armies, one of them British. A chain of events now led Wolseley into a war he did not want. It ended on 28 November 1879 in a long and bloody battle, the only offensive one waged by the British in that year's long succession of military encounters. Some defenders then hid on a last redoubt called the 'Fighting Kopje' and took four more days to surrender.

This book presents what I think is the fullest account so far published of the Second Anglo-Pedi War. I have also toured the battlefield, tucked away in a remote corner of South Africa.

The book introduces a large and colourful cast of characters – British, Boer, Pedi and Zulu. I have tried to tell their story in a narrative style and to let the original participants speak for themselves where possible. Any lapses in style or mistakes in Bapedi or Zulu terminology, or choice of spellings (is it Sekhukhune, Sekukuni, Secocoeni and so on) are down to me and I apologise if I have introduced any errors. My sources are listed at the end of the book. I also undertook two field trips to South Africa. I hope the reader thinks the efforts worthwhile.

General Wolseley was a prolific correspondent; he wrote numerous letters daily to public and private figures, not to mention his large family and especially his wife. In Zululand he also kept a daily journal to put down his thoughts. This is in the National Archives but was published with scholarly notes in South Africa in 1979. The book is now out of print and a rare find. I have used the journal as a template to expand on our knowledge of Wolseley's actions. Along the way I have read over 600 of his letters in British and overseas institutions. The general's letters to his wife are particularly revealing and sometimes quite shocking.

Two theses were of especial help in steering a path on Transvaal affairs: Kenneth Smith's pioneering study of the Bapedi–Boer War of 1876 and the British ones of 1878–79, and Bridget Theron-Bushell's in-depth examination of Owen Lanyon's time as an administrator in South Africa. Very recently the doyen of South African military historians, John Laband, has written some chapters on the Bapedi campaigns that were also most useful. Any person researching this period owes a special debt to these historians.

Among those persons holding copyright I must first thank HM the Queen for permission to quote from the letters of HRH the Duke of Cambridge, Queen Victoria's cousin. At Hove the library team were helpful as ever, and Mark Bunt was a godsend in preparing in advance all the Wolseley letters I needed to see. He even dragged down some scrapbooks from the attic. My time at Hove was wet and windy as only an English seaside town can be when out of season. My thanks to Mary Nimmo for giving me a slap-up breakfast every day before I trudged off into the storms.

In South Africa the staff at the Campbell Collections (formerly the Killie Campbell Africana Library) in Durban, the kwaZulu Natal Records Office in Pietermaritzburg and the National Archives in Pretoria all gave up their time for my odd enquiries. The director of the Lydenburg Museum was friendly to a stranger calling without an appointment, while my hosts even offered to put me in touch with the Bapedi paramount chief. A final thank you to my guide at Tsate in South Africa, whose name I have sadly misplaced, but who will never be forgotten.

A book of this kind is a collaborative effort. While I take all responsibility for any errors I must first thank Krisztina Elias who assisted, as she has on all my previous books, with the illustrations and indexing. Finally, sincere thanks must go to Shaun Barrington for his encouragement and support.

William Wright
Budapest

PROLOGUE

CHRISTMASTIDE 1878 – CYPRUS AND SOUTH AFRICA

I fear we are in for (if not already in) a war with the Zulus.
Sir Robert Herbert

It was Christmas Eve and Garnet Joseph Wolseley was in high spirits. On the previous afternoon the first commander-in-chief and high commissioner of the newly acquired British island of Cyprus had been reunited with his wife and daughter after an absence of five months. Louisa Wolseley had felt unwell for most of the sea voyage, but on the morning of 24 December she and six-year-old Frances came ashore at Larnaca, beneath arches decorated with colourful flowers as a crowd of well dressed local women handed out bouquets. Bells were rung, and despite a strong wind another large crowd awaited the visitors outside Nicosia later that morning with more addresses, greetings and floral tributes. Upon arrival at the newly constructed Government House it was found that the previous night's gale had smashed many of the windows. 'Altogether the house did not look very habitable,' admitted Sir Garnet in his journal. 'However, we had a good luncheon and must make up our minds to "bivouac" in a half-finished and almost totally unfurnished house for some time to come.' The British Empire's latest island possession was the result of skilful diplomacy by Foreign Secretary Lord Salisbury and Prime Minister Lord Beaconsfield at the Congress of Berlin held during that summer. A year earlier the Russian Tsar, embroiled in yet another war with the Turks, had threatened to march his troops into Constantinople. Sabre-rattling war fever gripped the British nation, long seen as the champion of the Ottoman Empire. 'We've fought the Bear before, and while Britons shall be true, the Russians shall not have Constantinople,' chanted the music hall crowds. Within the Cabinet it was Salisbury who pushed hardest for 'some territorial re-arrangement', such as Crete or the Dardanelles, where Britain might have a strong Mediterranean base from which it could protect its own and Ottoman interests in the Near East. On 3 March 1878 the Russo-Turkish War ended with a treaty signing at San Stefano. Its provisions, all bad news for the Turks, included the creation of a large, pro-Russian Slav state of Bulgaria, which would dominate the Balkans. Lord Salisbury, realizing that the Russians would be able to 'menace the balance of power in the Aegean' and wield vast influence over Turkey (both unacceptable to British interests), suggested at a meeting on 27 March several possible measures including the occupation of Cyprus. He was supported by the Prime Minister. Both men agreed that the island provided an ideal operational base for the British Navy if Turkey continued to decline. Danger of a second war with Russia seemed very real and a fleet was sent towards Constantinople, spending six months anchored in nearby waters.

In May a draft Anglo-Turkish agreement, called the 'Cyprus Convention', was agreed by the Sultan; it accepted British suzerainty over the island. On 13 June, in the gilded salons of Berlin's Radziwell Palace, the diplomats of Europe's great nations sat down to try and cool the call to arms. The Cyprus provision, one of the conference's main secrets, was made public in the British newspapers on 8 July and was included in a treaty signed five days later. Six days earlier the Sultan had issued his firman (edict) and that same day a British naval squadron had sailed into Cypriot waters and taken formal control. The Union Jack was hoisted at Larnaca for the first time on 11 July 1878.

Early on the morning of Monday 8 July, Sir Garnet Wolseley, along with Lady Louisa and toddler Frances, had set out to spend a lazy English summer's day on a boat belonging to George Greaves, one of the general's celebrated circle of bright officers. It was during luncheon, as the hero of the Ashanti War and rising War Office star was tucking into a salad at Datchet, that a telegram arrived from Fricke, his butler, saying that an urgent letter awaited him at home. Wolseley left abruptly, leaving his family on the boat, and found – not to his surprise, one suspects – that he was required to call immediately on the Secretary of State for War. He knew that Parliament would hear of the Cyprus acquisition that afternoon, although the whole affair was a state secret until then. Sir Garnet had already been asked and had accepted the post of commander-in-chief and high commissioner, another secret that duly ruffled the feathers of Wolseley's superior at the War Office, Prince George, Duke of Cambridge, the reactionary C-in-C of the British Army.

Wolseley had been a thorn in the flesh of Cambridge and his clique of 'old school' officers for several years. Vexed that he had not been let in on the Cyprus secret, a 'barely civil' Cambridge now proceeded to lecture Sir Garnet on his duties, while the younger man tried as politely as possible to hide his irritation. Seeing the radical upstart shunted off to a backwater island like Cyprus ought to have delighted the duke, but, as Wolseley noted, 'That I should be selected for work by a minister or cabinet, without his being even consulted, was indeed a bitter pill for him to swallow.'[2]

The Foreign Secretary asked if Wolseley could depart 'at once'. He assented but pointed out that no preparations had been made for the trip or his new command. Astonishingly, he managed to complete everything in time to catch the 7.40 a.m. train from

Charing Cross on Saturday 13 July – less than four days later. This was all the more remarkable in that he assembled a fine team of officers to assist him despite many hours being 'squandered' by the Duke of Cambridge as he insisted on talking over what Wolseley termed 'frivolities'. Sir Garnet's personal situation was also strained; he had to find time to say farewell to his aged mother, make plans to sell his London home and its contents, organise his own kit, stores and servants, and part company with his daughter and 'Loo', his beloved 'rumpterfoozle' and soulmate. Sir Garnet was given a free hand by HM Govt in selecting his team, much to Prince George's displeasure. Hugh McCalmont and Lord Gifford, two of his favourite fighting soldiers, were taken as aides, while a third warrior, the stentorian Baker Russell, went as his military secretary; the bright Robert Biddulph would command the British artillery, and Dr Anthony Home VC, an old Ashanti War friend, would be principal medical officer. Two womanisers, the conceited George Greaves and the brilliant Henry Brackenbury, both colleagues since West Africa days, were selected as chief of staff and quartermaster-general; the team was completed by the grandly named James Charlemagne Dormer, who had worked alongside Sir Garnet in the Indian Mutiny and the Second China War and now became his assistant adjutant-general (AAG). A new face, St Leger Herbert, went as the general's private secretary.

From Calais the Cyprus team travelled via Brindisi to Malta, where Sir Garnet took charge of three British battalions who would accompany him on HMS *Himalaya* and three Indian battalions who were to follow a few days later. Early on the morning of Monday 22 July the British party arrived at Larnaca. Wolseley's reaction to the place was shared by all his officers, for they agreed with him when he wrote, 'I never saw a filthier spot … a pesthouse of dirt and fever.'[3] Until his arrival Sir Garnet, like the British public, had fallen for the government's propaganda. Lord Salisbury had told him that Cyprus was 'a land flowing with plenty, a land of orange and myrtle groves, interspersed with picturesque-looking oriental cities, abounding in palatial residences'.[4] The reality was somewhat different. 'I find that none exist,' wrote Wolseley of his expected palaces, 'and that for years to come the Governor and all his officers will have to content themselves with huts and bell-tents, and rough it in a manner unknown to Indians, and that in a climate which for at least two-thirds of the year is nearly tropical.'[5]

It soon became apparent to the new rulers that while the Turks were suspicious of them, waiting to see what taxes their masters would levy, the Greek population welcomed them ecstatically as fellow Christians. Sir Garnet sensed right away that the Greek community's goodwill was based on a hope that British rule might lead towards enosis rather than a long-term desire to be governed from London.

By his third week, as the fierce heat of August took hold, Wolseley was writing to his wife that his workload was already heavy: 'Minutes to be written upon every subject under heaven – petitions from peasants, declaring they have been beaten and ill-treated by the police, or someone else, and a thousand other things, one after another, until my poor brain goes round like a humming-top.' Nicosia, where he was renting a house, was 'a filthy hole ... The sanitary arrangements here are dreadful ... Fleas and bugs abound.' He complained that on one occasion his trousers beneath the knees 'were literally covered with a mass of jumping fleas'. He had decided to have the island explored 'to discover a good site for a large encampment'. Meantime he was proposing to spend the summer in a bell tent. His personal effects had arrived, but all the jams, blacking and mustard had merged into a mass and his saddles were missing, while 'horse flies drive my old horse really wild'.[6]

'Cyprus is the key to Western Asia,' declared Lord Beaconsfield grandiloquently. Wolseley was not so sure; he would have preferred almost any Aegean island or a spot on the Dardanelles coast to the fever-ridden, hot and dusty land he was tasked with governing; but, as in everything he ever attempted, Sir Garnet set to work with gusto. Roads were improved, refuse swept away, trees planted to improve the landscape and act as windbreaks (over 20,000 eucalyptus trees around Nicosia alone), revenue experts began dismantling the unjust Ottoman tax system and a scientific mapping of the whole island and its resources was proposed. By 10 September the high commissioner was writing in his journal that Larnaca had changed and 'now it is a really go-ahead thriving place'.

August had seen temperatures rise to 110°F (43°C) in Wolseley's tent. Plagues of locusts arrived and almost one-fifth of the troops went down with fever. To everyone's joy and relief, dark clouds bringing much-needed rain and cooler temperatures finally appeared in the third week of September. Any doubts by now that the general had about Cyprus were reserved for his private journal and his letters to Louisa and politicians such as Salisbury. A natural leader of men, Sir Garnet worked to promote a jaunty *esprit de corps* among his officers. The wife of one described him as 'cheerful and genial as if in the midst of a London season'.[7] He told them all that Cyprus had a great future and even called the climate 'simply delightful'. When George Greaves complained of hardships Wolseley reprimanded him in a letter: 'I confess I don't think so: we have had champagne every day and ice most of the hot days since we landed.' His staff were not convinced by this bonhomie; Hugh McCalmont noted that 'nobody but a born idiot would stop in such a place if he could live out of it'.[8]

On orders to survey the island and prepare a detailed map, a sandy-haired young subaltern arrived on 13 September. His name was Herbert Kitchener. Unfortunately he and the general got off on the wrong foot after Wolseley heard that the mapping might take up to three years and would be a scholarly model of its kind. Extremely irritated, he made it clear that what was needed was a quick revenue survey. He also objected to Kitchener's operations being under Foreign Office control. Archeological studies and such were not important, he reminded the offended young officer, who protested to the Foreign Secretary. If Wolseley found the surveyor 'annoyingly bumptious', Kitchener, in turn, wrote home that the general was 'very agreeable and pleasant, though I don't like his manner much or that of his staff'. Kitchener complained that Wolseley and his team had 'come with English ideas in everything and a scorn for native habits or knowledge of the country. The result is fatal – they work hard and do nothing absolutely except make mistakes, absurd laws etc. that have to be counter-ordered. All is in fact chaos.'[9] Wolseley repeatedly told Salisbury that he needed land surveyors, 'not scientific engineers with exalted ideas', and the Foreign Secretary was forced to admit that 'the requisitions of Lieutenant Kitchener and his survey staff ... have created some consternation at the Treasury'.[10]

With the coming of cooler weather, and as Wolseley's team settled into their work routines, so inexorably improvements took shape. A decent camping ground was found and a sanatorium was created in the Troodos Mountains. Work also began on constructing Government House. This had been shipped out from England and was a Colonial Office kit, assembled in sections and designed for use in the Malayan jungle. McCalmont described it as 'a great big wooden barrack of a place'. Along with several of his fellow officers, war-hungry McCalmont was hoping to escape from the backwater that was Cyprus and see some campaigning. In Afghanistan that autumn three British columns were marching towards Kabul, while, as McCalmont noted, 'We, moreover, learnt from the newspapers that a struggle with the Zulus was about to take place' in southern Africa.[11] Two of his old friends from Ashanti War days – Redvers Buller and Evelyn Wood – had seen action in a recent campaign against the Xhosa nation and were currently serving on the South African frontier.

All along the Natal–Zululand border that Christmastide, a British army including McCalmont's old chums was hunkering down and praying for the weather to improve. The rains had come late that year, finally breaking in the middle of December, a ferocious torrent that made a mockery of the South African summer. On a good day the noon heat was replaced by ominous grey clouds that soon gave way to sudden electrical storms followed by the heavy beat of raindrops, flattening the coarse veldt grass, pounding the dust into a greasy soup of red mud that ran in streams down the hillsides. Roads were soon churned up as wagons, oxen, horses and men laboured on their journeys. Officers and other ranks who had served in India recalled the monsoons as the rain fell, sometimes unbroken for thirty-six hours.

War clouds every bit as forbidding as the physical ones loomed on the horizon and were fast approaching, as an ultimatum delivered to the Zulu king, Cetshwayo, was due to expire on 11 January 1879. This war was the brainchild of one man who saw it as a necessity to extend and protect British interests in South Africa. Sir Henry Bartle Edward Frere was the sixty-three-year-old, silver-haired high commissioner who had arrived at the Cape nineteen months previously, tasked by the Colonial Secretary, Lord Carnarvon, with the creation of a South African confederation of states. A nervous man, known to his friends as 'Twitters', Carnarvon had successfully fathered confederation in Canada and predicted that a similar arrangement in southern Africa 'would greatly improve and cheapen the administration of affairs in almost every branch and greatly lessen the probability of a demand for aid in the shape of Imperial money or troops'.[12] His parliamentary under-secretary got to the nub of the matter more directly when he told the House of Lords that 'confederation will involve, we hope, self-defence, which will remove the liability under which we labour of spending our blood and our money upon these wretched kaffir quarrels in South Africa'.[13]

Sir Bartle Frere seemed to everyone in the Conservative government to be the ideal man for the job. He was a statesman through and through: aged nineteen he had left his large and happy family in England to begin a career in the Indian Civil Service, a tough upward path that led him into the ranks of the pro-consuls of the Raj. He had toiled for years in various outposts before being made Chief Commissioner of Sind, then held that blistering desert province and its troublesome tribes under a tight rein during the Great Rebellion of 1857–59. At age forty-seven he was a reforming Governor of Bombay, improving the city's sanitation and openly entertaining Indians in his own home. In 1872 he was chosen to undertake a mission to Zanzibar to negotiate the end of the slave trade. When the Sultan refused to agree to British demands Frere ordered a blockade by warships. This went way beyond his Foreign Office instructions, but it was successful, and the Sultan, backing down, agreed to abolish the trade. Queen Victoria was delighted and made him a Privy Councillor. Such an honour sat lightly on the shoulders of a man who was already President of the Royal Asiatic and Geographical Societies. Asked to mastermind the Prince of Wales's trip to India in 1875, Frere once again pulled it off with aplomb.

Carnarvon outlined his plans to Frere. He replied somewhat condescendingly: 'I should not have cared for the ordinary current duties of Governor of the Cape, but a special duty I should look upon in a different light.'[14] It was agreed by Parliament that Sir Bartle would get an additional £2,000 above his governor's salary and have the joint powers of high commissioner and commander-in-chief for southern Africa. Two days before his departure Frere dined with his sovereign at Windsor. She always had a soft spot for him, especially since he had steered her boy Bertie safely across India, and had elevated his knighthood to a baronetcy in consequence. In her diary, Queen Victoria noted how Frere's 'conciliatory disposition, great experience & knowledge of native character & wild races, as well as his prudence, are calculated to do great good'.[15] The queen's views were not echoed by her private secretary, Sir Henry Ponsonby, who found Lady Frere to be 'rather superior', and dismissed Sir Bartle as 'rather twaddling', a 'dear old patapouf'. Neither the queen nor her courtier were accurate in their assessments; Frere's military secretary in South Africa, Captain Henry Hallam Parr, found him to be 'gentle and kindly' on the surface, yet also a man of 'courage, iron will and exceptionally steady nerves' who 'read most men like an open book'.[16] Frere clearly had a strong personality shot through with charm; the Lutheran missionary Hans Schreuder came away from just one meeting declaring him 'about the most splendid man I have ever met'.[17] The Zanzibar mission had shown how Frere was a man used to making up his own mind on important issues and willing to act without first consulting HM Govt. Now, as he set sail, he saw confederation, in the words of historian John Laband, as 'nothing less than a Christian duty and moral objective, which would bring the myriad benefits of British civilization to all the peoples of southern Africa'.[18]

Barely a fortnight after arriving at the Cape an item of news, four days old, reached Frere; it was so unexpected that he blurted out, 'Good heavens! What will they say in England?' This was the annexation of the Dutch-Boer South African Republic (ZAR) of the Transvaal, which had taken place on 12 April, a bloodless coup masterminded by Sir Theophilus Shepstone, long-time expert on all matters of native policy and Carnarvon's appointed 'special commissioner' for the Transvaal. We will examine the affairs of the ZAR and its inhabitants in a later chapter. For the time being, Shepstone's reasoning requires some explanation. Born in England but brought up at the Cape from the age of three, he spoke several native dialects and saw himself as a benevolent paterfamilias to many tribes including the Zulus; they called him 'Somtsewu', as did the Swazi, roughly translated as 'father of the white man'. He was Secretary of Native Affairs from the 1840s. As the years rolled by Shepstone became increasingly arrogant about his knowledge of native matters; he knew better than the tribes or chiefs and he knew what was best for them. Inscrutable to many, with an ability of seeming vague when it suited him, a journalist at the time of annexation described him as 'a crafty-looking and silent man who never used an unnecessary word or gesture'.[19] Frere was to call Shepstone 'shrewd, observant, silent, self-controlled, immobile'. Expansionist in outlook, Sir Theophilus came to believe that the fledgling ZAR, whose independence had been guaranteed by the 1852 Sand River Convention, was incapable of administering its own affairs. The republic was said to be bankrupt with less than £10 in the Treasury, its Boer inhabitants, almost all farmers who preferred to be left alone on their farms, argued incessantly among themselves that a large non-Boer population of immigrant miners and tradespeople would welcome the stability of British rule and, most serious of all, the locals had been bested in a short, savage war against the Bapedi tribe under its wily chief, Sekhukhune. To Shepstone, it was now plain that it was in the best interests of the inhabitants if Great Britain controlled the Transvaal. The Boer-Bapedi war was the final straw in the bankruptcy and collapse of the ZAR, argued Shepstone, and this 'pinnacle of peril', as he termed it, 'had sent the thrilling intelligence through all the immense masses of natives between the Zambezi on the north and the Cape Colony on the South that the relative positions of the white and black man had been seriously changed; and had prompted the thought that the supremacy of barbarism was no longer hopeless provided only that the effort be well planned and simultaneously executed.'[20]

Shepstone's new obsession of a 'black conspiracy' (it seems to have particularly taken hold of him after he was insulted by a group of Zulu dignitaries), a great rising that might upset all plans for white advancement in southern Africa, soon influenced Frere. Both men realized that the biggest native danger was the Zulu nation. 'Cetewayo is the most formidable as he is the most hostile,' wrote Sir Theophilus, adding, 'He can, it is believed, send 30,000 soldiers into the field; his men are under the strictest discipline, embodied in regiments in every way well organized; most are provided with firearms, a large proportion of which are of a superior description.'[21]

From the month of his arrival Frere's hopes of fully implementing Carnarvon's plans for confederation started to fall apart: the Boers were soon loudly demanding their independence; boundary disputes between the Transvaal and Zululand rumbled on ominously as Afrikaner farmers continued to make claims on native territory; the Cape Government under Premier John Molteno 'not only did not share Frere's imperial vision, but was morbidly suspicious of British interference in the newly self-governing colony's affairs.'[22] Frere hit back in typical style; an outbreak of violence at a native wedding feast gave him a pretext for launching a ninth war against the Xhosa frontier tribes. When Molteno complained of the handling of affairs and tried to interfere in the military conduct of operations, Sir Bartle dismissed the ministry and replaced it with one sympathetic to his aims. Damian O'Connor, one of Frere's biographers, explains what happened next:

> His conviction that the administration of South Africa was incompetent was a major stepping stone towards his disobedience because it convinced him that South Africa was vulnerable to an internal threat, represented by the actual and potential threat of Xhosa and Boer revolts, at the same time as an immediate external threat from Russia existed. It also fundamentally undermined his confidence in the judgement of 'men on the spot' and forced him to cast around for alternatives. From the middle of the Xhosa revolt onwards, Frere felt that he needed to take much more personal control of affairs if the dual aims of defence and confederation were to be achieved, and he went back to his Indian experience to justify his taking command.[23]

In January 1878, to Frere's surprise, Lord Carnarvon resigned as Colonial Secretary and was replaced by Sir Michael Hicks Beach, strikingly handsome and aloof, known as 'Black Michael' for his biting tongue. Two months later affable but ineffective General Cunynghame was recalled as commander of troops at the Cape, Natal and Transvaal. His replacement in March was fifty-one years old, the Eton-educated Lieutenant-General Sir Frederic Thesiger. Frere and Thesiger had known one another at Bombay in the 1860s, the new commander being well liked, the perfect gentleman, interested in the welfare of ordinary soldiers, a tall figure with a spade beard, hair carefully parted in the centre, soft-spoken, and with cool, impeccable manners. On 31 May the Ngquika chief, Sandile, tried to break out of the Buffalo River valley with his bodyguard, but was mortally wounded in a firefight with colonial troops. With Sandile died the spirit of revolt. Some 3,680 amaXhosa warriors had been killed in this brutal war, almost half their nation's fighting force. Less than 200 had been taken prisoner. British casualties had been just 60 white and 133 African troops killed. Thesiger, an old school soldier who liked old school tactics, was left with a low opinion of black Africans and white colonials as warriors, coupled with an excessively high regard for his red-coated regulars. Peace in August 1878 saw Frere dictate harsh terms that involved the expulsion of most of the Xhosa from their ancestral lands. He also forbade any Africans under Cape rule from owning firearms. This law applied not just to the defeated Xhosa but also to the Mfengu, who had supplied many of the colonial native troops.

Colonists and missionaries agreed with Frere and Shepstone that the Zulu power must next be broken. 'No rational being believes in the struggle with that military nation being postponed much longer,'[24] wrote a commentator on the Xhosa war. Norman Macleod, the British agent in Swaziland, expressed the colonial viewpoint most forcibly when he stated, 'My opinion is that unless we thrash the Zulus ... we shall lose what prestige we ever had. All eyes, native eyes, are on the Zulus & ourselves now ... I believe the only chance of settling S. Africa once and for all is to lick the Zulus now right or wrong, justly or unjustly.'[25]

Writing to London, Frere collated and inflated a mix of arguments and incidents all intended to underline the Zulu menace. In this task he was supported by Shepstone. Both men portrayed the Zulu military system (*amabutho*) as a 'frightfully efficient man-slaying war machine' ruled by an 'unscrupulous and extremely ambitious savage'. King Cetshwayo was, they concluded, the inspiration of black aims to overthrow the white man in South Africa. Peace and security made the downfall of the amaZulu a necessity. In Britain HM Govt was slow to accept where all these arguments were leading; Premier Disraeli was obsessed by Russian designs on Turkey and Afghanistan, while Hicks Beach for several months showed no inclination to do or say very much at all.

In February 1878 a Commission had been appointed to inquire into the Transvaal-Zululand boundary disputes. It reported to Frere in July and, perhaps surprisingly, ruled emphatically in favour of the Zulus. Sir Bartle tried to pick holes in the document. On 10 September, as he and Thesiger – now raised to the peerage in succession to his father as Lord Chelmsford – made their plans, HM Govt was asked for reinforcements. News of this at the Colonial Office caused the Permanent Under-Secretary for the Colonies, Sir R. G. Herbert, to write with a sigh: 'I fear we are in for (if not already in) a war with the Zulus.'[26] His superior, Hicks Beach, started to wake up; he at first agreed to send out only special service officers to the Cape and told Frere of his confident hope that 'by the exercise of prudence and by meeting the Zulus in a spirit of forbearance and reasonable compromise, it will be possible to avert the very serious evil of a war with Cetewayo'.[27] The Prime Minister felt all the disturbances at the Cape were the fault of Carnarvon and Shepstone:

> If anything annoys me more than another, it is our Cape affairs, where every day brings forward a new blunder of Twitters. The man he swore by was Sir T. Shepstone, whom he looked upon as heaven-born for the object in view ... We sent him out entirely for Twitters' sake, and he has managed to quarrel with Eng., Dutch, and Zulus ... but not before he has brought on, I fear, a new war.[28]

Frere, meanwhile, whipped up the war fever and denounced 'the demon king, Cetewayo ... an ignorant and blood-thirsty despot, with a most overweening idea of his own importance ...' Inflating the Zulu army by a third over Shepstone's earlier figure (so that it now numbered 'at least 40,000 men'), these savages were 'ready and eager at any moment to execute in their ancient fashion of extermination, whatever the caprice or anger of the despot may dictate.'[29] By now Hicks Beach was well aware that if war came about he would get some of the blame for not controlling Frere, but as he told the Prime Minister on 3 November,

> I cannot really control him without a telegraph (I don't know that I could with one). I feel it is as likely as not that he is at war with the Zulus at the present moment; and if his forces should prove to be inadequate, or the Transvaal Boers should take the opportunity to rise, he will be in a great difficulty and we shall be blamed for not supporting him.[30]

So it was that further requests for reinforcements were approved by HM Govt in November 1878.

What of the Zulus in all these machinations? Their king, Cetshwayo, was frankly confused and frustrated by the actions of white officials who had in the past seemed to curry favour with him and now made threats of war. In an appeal for moderation he asked: 'What have I done or said to the Great House of England ... What have I done to the Great White Chief?'[31] Two years earlier in a rebuke to Sir Henry Bulwer, Governor of Natal, Cetshwayo had stated his position:

> Why does the Governor of Natal speak to me about my laws? Do I go to Natal and dictate to him about his laws? ... while wishing to be friends with the English I do not agree to give my people over to be governed by laws sent to me by them. He is Governor of Natal, and I am Governor here.[32]

There was one authority figure in the white community prepared to befriend and stand up for Cetshwayo. John William Colenso, Bishop of Natal, was a radical prelate who had upset conventional Victorian church leaders decades earlier by suggesting the Pentateuch was mainly fables and not the literal word of God. This heresy saw him excommunicated by the Anglican hierarchy and ostracised by many of his flock. Colenso visited the Zulus when he first arrived in Natal in 1854. Over the years, and supported by three highly intelligent daughters and a loving wife, the bishop had grown to distrust the settlers and government officials as he increasingly championed Cetshwayo and his people. By June 1878 the bishop was highly suspicious of Shepstone's 'crafty under-scheming' and told a friend, 'I greatly fear that something will be done to provoke a war with Ketchwayo.'[33] He was still hopeful that Frere would not prove to be such a cad as Shepstone, since Sir Bartle 'has always been *remarkably* friendly in his manner towards me. I have sometimes almost thought too much so, as if he wished to secure my approval or at least my *silence* for his plans.'[34]

On the morning of 11 December 1878 a delegation of fourteen Zulu dignitaries and their attendants arrived by the banks of the fast-flowing and muddy Thukela River swollen by the rains. On the far side, their border with Natal Colony, waited a group of

British officials and a small body of troops. The *indunas* (advisers, ambassadors, or military commanders) led by Vumandaba kaNthathi, a trusted attendant of the king, were ferried across and invited to squat under the shade of a tarpaulin stretched across a clump of fig trees near the water's edge. The results of the boundary commission were read to them in English by John Wesley Shepstone, a younger brother of Sir Theophilus and the Acting Secretary for Native Affairs, his words being translated into Zulu by F. B. Fynney, the local border agent. This rigmarole took some time and the Zulus muttered their approval of the commission's findings, which were largely in their favour. The meeting broke for lunch, the Zulus being offered cow and sweet water, but to their surprise at 2.30 p.m. they were asked to sit down again and listen to a supplement that Frere had drafted. This sting in the tail, a long and complex document, made the boundary award conditional. It contained thirteen key demands with a whole set of rambling justifications – Cetshwayo had not kept his 1873 coronation promise to introduce laws 'for the better treatment of the Zulu people', the amabutho system was 'destroying the country', families could not live 'in peace and quiet', and the Zulu king's army made it 'impossible for his neighbours to feel secure ...' So Frere now insisted on the abolition of the present military system to be replaced by one sanctioned by a Council of Chiefs and British officials; a British Resident was to stay in Zululand and enforce all regulations; missionaries and converts were to be allowed to return and Zulu males, contrary to tradition, to be allowed to marry at will. Sir Bartle had calculated that the amabutho changes alone would deprive the Zulu king of most of his power and he would be forced to resist. Cetshwayo was given thirty days to comply or find himself at war with Great Britain.

Vumandaba and the other Zulu functionaries were aghast and took their time returning to the royal *amakhanda* at Ulundi (oNdini) with this awful news (although Cetshwayo must have heard the gist of things within hours of the meeting breaking up). The ultimatum came also as a nasty shock to Bishop Colenso, who was hoping 'for better things from Sir B.F'. When he got the news the prelate was apoplectic with rage. Two days before Christmas he told a friend:

> The dishonesty of the whole affair is so palpable – the delaying of the award until he had got together all his forces – announcing it without the slightest intimation to the Zulu king that he was giving with one hand what he took away with the other – & then leaving the poor Zulus & their friends, especially after my interview with him, in the enjoyment of a fool's paradise, because we trusted in the word & good faith of an English Gentleman ...[35]

The ultimatum had been endorsed by Sir Henry Bulwer, a more prudent man than Frere, who quickly admitted it was 'the worst thing I ever did in my life'.[36] Sir Bartle had no such qualms and used the time-lag in communications with England to bolster his plans. In a letter to HM Govt dated 8 December he wrote of the boundary award but deliberately omitted any mention of the ultimatum. Meanwhile in London, the Colonial Secretary wrote on the very same day that the Zulus received the ultimatum – this letter did not arrive in South Africa until after the war had started – wanting more details of a strange document he had seen of Frere's to Shepstone talking of 'an ultimatum' and 'final proposals'. A nervous Hicks Beach complained: 'I really do not know at all what you contemplate in this direction, nor do I see the necessity for such an ultimatum ... we entirely deprecate the idea of entering on a Zulu war in order to settle the Zulu question.'[37] Nothing could have been plainer but by the time he received it Sir Bartle had cast the die.

On 23 December, knowing that his letter would take about a month to reach England, Sir Bartle confessed to Hicks Beach that he intended to invade Zululand and that Chelmsford would lead forces to converge on the royal kraal. He added a limp justification for his action, saying that it was inevitable 'long before I, or Bulwer, or even Sir Garnet Wolseley came here'.[38] That Christmas Day in England was not a relaxing holiday for 'Black Michael', now made aware from other sources of parts of Frere's ultimatum. He angrily wrote to his recalcitrant governor:

> When I first came to the Colonial Office I told you you might rely on my support: and so you may. But (bearing in mind all I written to you against the Zulu war, at the instance, remember, of the Cabinet) I think you will see how awkward a position you may have placed me in by making demands of this nature without my knowledge or sanction ... Cetewayo may very possibly prefer fighting to accepting them, and then, if the Cabinet should not be satisfied that you were right in making them, it will be too late to draw back, and we shall find ourselves involved in this war against our will.[39]

By the middle of December troops had began assembling along the Natal-Zululand border as Lord Chelmsford's invasion plans took shape. As early as July 1878 the general had told Shepstone, 'If we have to fight the Zulus ... They must be thoroughly crushed to make them believe in our superiority ...'[40] On 24 August he compiled a memorandum entitled the 'Invasion of Zululand' with five (later reduced to three) columns converging on Ulundi. This division of forces went against conventional military wisdom but Chelmsford had used the same strategy against the Xhosa (where it had been signally unsuccessful). John Laband has explained:

> Chelmsford hoped to move with greater speed with smaller columns, and to have more forage at the disposal of each. Moreover, the presence of a number of supporting columns

> would engross more of the enemy's territory, reduce the chance of their being outflanked, and discourage Zulu counter-thrusts against the British frontiers.[41]

His No. 1 Column, under Colonel Pearson, would advance across the Lower Thukela and protect the coastal plain. No. 3 Column, under Colonel Glyn, would enter Zululand near Rorke's Drift and safeguard central Natal, while No. 4 Column, under Colonel Wood, aimed to protect the Transvaal as it moved across the Blood (Ncome) River to the north. The general later broke up his No. 2 Column, under Colonel Durnford, to help support his No. 3 Column. Finally, his No. 5 Column, under Colonel Rowlands, a commander who had been unsuccessful that September–October in operations against Sekhukhune of the Bapedi, was held back in a defensive role watching Transvaal Boers, potentially duplicitous Pedi and even equivocal Swazi on the northern flank. In all, Chelmsford was committing a total of 17,177 officers and men, imperial and colonial, Africans and white men.[42]

Chelmsford put the greatest trust in his British regulars, especially two battalions of the 24th Foot accompanying No. 3 Column. The 1st Battalion had been in South Africa since 1875 and the 2nd had arrived in February 1878. Both battalions were acclimatised to conditions on the veldt and composed of experienced and, in many cases, battle-hardened men. Colonel Pearson had with him the 2nd Battalion HM 3rd Foot, and Wood was leading his own regiment, the 90th Light Infantry. Various other imperial units were spread around including batteries of Royal Artillery and No. 1 Column even had a naval brigade. The largest part of Chelmsford's army was his colonial units, including three battalions of the newly raised Natal Native Contingent who were under Durnford's command. White colonials had also eagerly signed up for action – and through a sense of patriotism – to swell the ranks of mounted corps, such as the ruffianly Frontier Light

Horse, commanded by Major Redvers Buller, (operating with No. 4 Column) and the prestigious Natal Mounted Police, led by Major John Dartnell (part of No. 3 Column).

In the last days of December every waking moment provided new headaches for Chelmsford. Biggest of these were the transport and commissariat problems for so many columns operating in enemy territory. The quest for forage and transport combined with the need to supplement what imperial troops he had with white colonial volunteers and native auxiliaries, along with countless matters concerning the different commands, officers and men, kept his lordship busy, especially so since he was very bad at delegating. Nevertheless, at the year's close, as he toured the frontier Chelmsford felt his army was 'in good health and spirits'. On New Year's Day 1879, in words that now contain a gentle irony, he wrote to Frere:

> I feel it would be almost mockery in your present position to wish you a happy new year ... I have every confidence in those under my command ... Our cause will be a good one, in spite of all the Colenso party may say, and I hope to be able to convince them all before many weeks are over that for a savage, as for a child, timely severity is greater kindness than mistaken leniency ...[43]

Sitting in their tents along the Natal-Zululand border Lord Chelmsford's officers and men agreed with him. Everyone knew the ultimatum to Cetshwayo was simply the pretext for a fight. 'It asks so much that he cannot, even if his wishes, give in,' wrote Lieutenant Curling, Royal Artillery, 'The only thing the natives understand is force ... so the only thing to be done is to take all their cattle, burn all their huts and kill a few thousand of them ...'[44]

Christmas dinner was a mixed affair made worse by the bad weather; the incessant rains had brought chills and pneumonia as well as infected sores on feet chafed by sodden boots. Dysentery had also started to rear its ugly head. That Christmastide, in the opinion of Corporal Brown, 2/24th, was 'the worst one I ever had in all my born days'. A splendid example of that special breed – the ever-grumbling Tommy Atkins – Brown wrote to his wife back home in Dover that the battalion marched eleven miles on Christmas morning before receiving 'a dinner that was not fit for a dog to eat – at least, the meat we had, dogs would not eat it'. Sleep was 'on the ground wet through without anything to put under or over us', while the rain fell in torrents. Corporal Brown rounded off his festive epistle with some personal moans: 'It is not any use you asking me for money until this is over, for we cannot get anything at all; and you talk about being teetotal, I am forced to be for I cannot get anything here whatever neither for love nor money.'[45] The 1/24th men, already stationed at Helmakaar, the lonely outpost on the upland not far from Rorke's Drift, ate boiled beef and biscuit that Christmas Day, although after a night of rain the sun deigned to shine on them. Colonial troops were also having a bad time; the Natal Mounted Police were responsible for the payment and procurement of their own commissariat, so one can imagine their misery when a wagonload of luxuries including their Christmas puddings was swept away in the fast-flowing Mooi River, along with six oxen.

There were comforts for some soldiers amid the rain. 'I have succeeded in managing splendidly for Xmas dinners for the men,' declared Lt-Colonel Arthur Harness, Royal Artillery, stationed further north at Greytown. 'The officers have given them a quart of beer each, a goose to every ten men and plum puddings.'[46] The Natal volunteer units stationed nearby at Potspruit did best of all – the ladies of Greytown sent them so much goose, roast beef, plum puddings and candied fruit that enough remained for breakfast on Boxing Day. The camp had sing-songs, football and horse racing. Pearson's No. 1 Column also seem to have had a festive Christmas.

The good folk of Durban had sent the officers 'cases of champagne and huge plum puddings', while the Naval Brigade from H.M.S. *Active* feasted on a dinner of roast and canned meat followed by a monster plum pudding cooked by Gunner John Carroll of the Royal Marine Artillery. This repast was washed down with 'plenty of English ale' made possible by a generous advance in pay from the ship's commander. The afternoon's entertainment for officers was a splendidly drunken buck hunt. 'No buck was killed,' wrote Lieutenant Thomas Main R.E., 'and none of the skirmishers was shot, which was fortunate as the firing became fast and furious regardless of the position of the beaters.'[47]

Further north, on the Transvaal-Zululand frontier, Colonel Evelyn Wood had a surprise visitor ride into camp on Christmas Eve. This was Sir Theophilus Shepstone, who stayed for three days and gave his host some lectures about the Zulus. A leading member of Wolseley's ring of bright officers, Wood was also notoriously accident prone, and a hypochondriac to boot. There was much to do, and Wood was up on Christmas Eve at 6.30 a.m. inspecting mounted infantry, 'and a more ragged crew perhaps was never got together except the professional beggars on a stage'.[48] After breakfast, he visited the lines of the 90th Light Infantry and found that 'every man's boots were unsatisfactory'. The local townspeople at nearby Utrecht came with complaints about their meagre defences, while officers argued over transport problems, and expected Wood to arbitrate. On Christmas Day in rode Major Redvers Buller from his camp, about ten miles distant, to attend the communion service. Over the New Year a complaining Wood suffered from what he called 'swollen glands', but on 3 January he led his No. 4 Column to the banks of the Blood River ready for the ultimatum's expiry and the invasion of Zululand.

Thousands of miles around the globe on Cyprus some of the officers pining for active service or some escape from ennui received a Christmas present when Sir Garnet Wolseley agreed to let several of them start for home on Boxing Day. The gales continued and the general noted on 30 December:

> A large wooden house with by no means well-fitting doors and windows, lofty rooms and heaps of windows, no stoves or fireplaces, perched on a rocky hill, where it enjoys every blast of wind is not the pleasantest of residences in the chilly weather. The house is so large that the absence of furniture makes it look dreary to an appalling degree.[49]

He went on to complain that the place was freezing except for large copper braziers burning charcoal 'which just heat one's fingers enough to enable one to write in the early morning before breakfast'.

Wolseley always ended his yearly journals and pocket diaries with comments on past events coupled with some crystal ball gazing. 'So ends this year upon my career in Cyprus,' he wrote on New Year's Eve, 'where shall I be this day 12 months, it is hard to say. I hope not here ...' He mused about more wars in Afghanistan and South Africa and recalled that on his visit to Natal in 1875 he had taken 'notes in preparation for an invasion of Cetewayo's territory'. Back then every colonist knew that a war with the Zulu king 'must come off sooner or later'. Reflecting on Cetshwayo, as he warmed himself no doubt by a brazier, Wolseley wrote his last sentence for 1878 – indeed the last one in his Cyprus journal – 'With his 40,000 men armed with fire-arms he will be no mean enemy.'[50]

PART ONE

THE ZULUS

I

A TERRIBLE DISASTER

I could describe the battlefield to you, but the sooner I get it off my mind the better.

Private William Meredith

Fear looms unseen but it is a palpable entity. You cannot feel it, smell it or touch it. Yet ask any soldier who has ever been placed in harm's way – fear makes the heart beat faster, sweat run longer and thicker, one's bowels feel looser and sleep is made impossible. Ultimately it can destroy the fragile courage and cohesive discipline required of each individual soldier – things necessary for an army's survival – just as surely as a .303 Martini Henry bullet or the steel tip of an assegai piercing the heart. Fear was in Lord Chelmsford's army on that dreadful night of 22 January 1879.

The day had started normally enough, not so very different from all the others since the expiry of the British ultimatum to the Zulus on 11 January. Chelmsford might have commented that things were going swimmingly with all his columns invading Zululand from various directions. The Zulus, according to a local trader, Cornelius Vijn, had decided that the British demands would only lead to further ones and, as some warriors told him, 'it was better to fight at once, since it evidently must come to that'.[1] Cetshwayo had decided on a strictly defensive policy: the sovereign British territories of Natal and Transvaal were not to be attacked, but once inside his borders the invading armies were to be met and repulsed. In early January the regiments gathered at oNdini to be ritually cleansed for war by the witch doctors (*izangoma*). Addressing thousands of his warriors Cetshwayo is supposed to have said: 'I have not gone over the seas to look for the white men, yet they have come into my country ... What shall I do?' The amabutho replied as if in one voice: 'We shall go and eat up the white men and finish them off. They are not going to take you while we are here. They must take us first.'[2]

The British Centre Column, nominally commanded by Brevet-Colonel Glyn of the 24th Foot, but in reality led by Chelmsford, entered Zululand shortly after the sound of reveille at 2 a.m. on 11 January. The starting-off point was Rorke's Drift on the Natal side of the Buffalo (today Mzinyathi) River. It was a foggy morning and as the mist cleared the 'only Zulu in sight was a solitary herdsman, who watched in astonishment as a foreign army emerged from the fog,' notes Ian Knight, 'the Natal Volunteers Corps set off gleefully to rob him of his charges.'[3] Next day a minor skirmish convinced Tommies and officers alike that the war ought to be a walkover. 'It is thought we shall not meet a Zulu army for some time,'[4] commented Lt-Colonel John North Crealock, Chelmsford's military secretary.

Rain continued to make a rapid advance impossible as the passage of men, carts, guns and animals churned up the sodden ground. Struggling up a mimosa-clad valley the Centre Column reached the shadow of Isandlwana, ten miles from Rorke's Drift, on 20 January. Here, under the eastern flank of this impressive hill, was a strange sphinx-shaped outcrop that many soldiers noticed bore a remarkable resemblance to the badge of the 24th Foot. Chelmsford decided to make a temporary camp. He did not intend to stay there long, and when Glyn plucked up the courage to suggest 'some protection was required', the general pooh-poohed the idea, saying, 'It is not worthwhile, it will take too much time, and besides the wagons are most of them going back at once to Rorke's Drift.'[5] Chelmsford thus chose to ignore his own 'Regulations for Field Forces in South Africa, 1878', which specified how camps in enemy territory should be 'partially entrenched on all sides', with animals safely kept in a wagon-laager. Several old hands had warned the general shortly before the campaign based on their experiences of Zulu warfare. One of these was the respected Afrikaner, Paul Kruger, who lectured on 'the absolute necessity of laagering his wagons every evening and always at the approach of the enemy'. Kruger added ominously in his gravel tones that if these precautions were omitted, 'one evening it will be fatal'.[6]

Lord Chelmsford must have smiled to himself at these words of gloom. He was a professional soldier who hardly needed advice from a colonial, and worse, a grubby Boer farmer. His army was in good spirits and, as he told Sir Bartle Frere in a letter from Isandlwana on 21 January, the whole country round about 'was deserted'. A local border agent, John Fannin, sent intelligence of a large impi, but the general thought this report was 'alarmist', a colonial response by a man 'who sees danger when there really is none'. Convinced that the main Zulu army was somewhere in the Mangeni Valley to the east, Chelmsford decided to split his force in two, and advanced around 3 a.m. on 22 January, leaving at Isandlwana a garrison of five companies of the 1/24th, one of the 2/24th, some colonial troops and four companies of the 1/3rd Natal Native Contingent (NNC) with two 7-pounder guns. The Isandlwana garrison seemed sufficiently large to cope with any enemy attack, especially after the general ordered up Brevet Colonel Anthony Durnford from Rorke's Drift with the available men of No 2 Column – a total of sixty-seven officers and 1,707 men (half of whom were Africans).

No one at the camp expected an attack. Even the sight of Zulus on the hills to the east later that morning did not alarm the officers unduly, one of whom later wrote that they 'never dreamed they would come on'. Indeed, the Zulus had not intended to attack that day as the signs were not propitious, but a party of colonial mounted troops stumbled by accident on the main Zulu army quietly sitting on its haunches in the Ngwebeni Valley. Like a nest of disturbed bees the Zulus poured over the lip of the escarpment and made for the British camp. During this advance the main *impi* deployed its classic chest and horns formation and almost succeeded in enveloping their enemy. The British furthest out on the veldt tried doggedly to fall back on the main camp from their exposed forward positions, but the Zulus were hard on their heels. Nervous, frightened, two companies of the barely trained NNC in the British centre broke and ran. Within minutes the Zulus were exploiting this gap and pouring into the camp. Now, at last, they could do what they did best – show their skill at close-quarter combat. The camp was thick with smoke and dust, the loud sounds as bullets whizzed about, the screams of dying men and animals, and the shouts of 'Usutu' as the amabutho drove their assegais into the red men's chests.

This terrible drama was not for some time apparent to Lord Chelmsford or his staff. While breakfasting he received a cryptic message from Brevet Lt-Colonel Pulleine, sent about 8.05 a.m., reporting that the enemy were advancing on the camp. Chelmsford received this news, notes historian Ian Knight, 'with a calm bordering on indifference'. About 9 a.m. a mounted police orderly brought the news that 'the camp is being surrounded and attacked'. Still unruffled, the general then sent his naval aide to climb a peak and see if he could view the camp through his powerful telescope. Not waiting for an answer, Chelmsford set off on a scouting expedition and 'the unpredictability of his movements meant that for hours urgent messages concerning the unfolding battle at Isandlwana failed to find him'.[7]

Chelmsford's staff were as relaxed as their chief; John Crealock was heard to exclaim, 'How very amusing. Actually attacking our camp! Most amusing.' Not long after 1.15 p.m., using his field glasses from a hill north of his Mangeni campsite, the general peered towards Isandlwana. It was difficult to make out much, but the tents were visible, and Chelmsford concluded that they would have been struck if a serious attack had taken place. An hour or so later he decided to return to his main camp and investigate. The general and his small escort jogged along slowly. Around 3 p.m. and some four and a half miles from Isandlwana they were suddenly confronted by a shattered man on a spent horse. This was Commandant Rupert Lonsdale of the 3rd NNC who blurted out, 'The Zulus have the camp!' For a moment his lordship stared back in disbelief, then Chelmsford replied, 'But I left over 1,000 men to guard the camp.'

It took over three hours for soldiers, scattered in patrols and across the Mangeni Valley, to receive the dreadful news and reach their general. Trooper Fred Symons of the Natal Carbineers, who waited alongside Chelmsford, lamented 'watching the sacking of the camp. My head, and my heart, ached, too with the thought of how the survivors must be willing us to their help, for survivors there must have been when first we came to our present position, and how they must have cursed us for the delay.'[8] It was nearing the end of a lovely summer's day, the sun sinking behind Isandlwana, as the troops gathered around their chief, close to the twinkling banks of the Nxibongo stream. The three-hour delay had finally brought home to the general the tragedy he had ignored. He looked gloomy and one soldier thought him 'very near crying'. There are various versions of what he told his assembled officers and men, but according to a senior staff officer, it ran: 'Men, the enemy have taken our camp. Many of our friends must have lost their lives in defending it. There is nothing left for us now but to fight our way through – and mind, we must fight hard, for we will have to fight for our lives. I know you and I know I can depend on you.'[9] There were cheers and shouts of 'Alright sir, we'll do it.' Chelmsford added grimly: 'No man must retire.' The men formed up as the sun started to slip fast below the horizon. They moved off along the line of the wagon road with four guns, two ambulances and a ration wagon. On either side were six companies of 2/24th in two equal wings moving by fours. The men marched from the left of companies, at company intervals, so they could form a line quickly if attacked. The 1/3rd NNC in three ranks marched on the left, the 2/3rd on the right. On the flanks were the volunteers and mounted infantry while the Natal Mounted Police formed a rearguard.

Hope spurred on Chelmsford's soldiers as they set off jauntily along the dusty track; hope that they would find survivors, perhaps in groups or singly, men who had somehow fought off the Zulus; hope that at the very least there would still be wounded men clinging to survival. A total massacre seemed improbable and unthinkable. Before the last light vanished the troops saw to the right of Isandlwana 'dense masses' of Zulus moving away with cattle and wagons.

It was now dark, a moonless night. The first thing many soldiers noticed as they approached the camp was that the long grass was completely flattened as if a giant steamroller had swept over it. Along the way fear had started to trickle through the ranks as cursing men and neighing horses fell into dongas or stumbled over rocks. Already nervous, the NNC made matters worse by crowding inwards as if seeking protection from an imaginary foe. One of their officers, Lieutenant Henry Harford, wrote in his journal:

> Had it not been for the seriousness of the situation, the manner in which my lot of the N.N.C. had to be driven along would have been amusing. A two-deep line formation was not at all to their liking, all were in a most mortal funk, nothing on earth could make those who were armed with rifles keep their place in the front rank, and all the curses showered on them by their officers could not prevent them from closing in and mixing up in clumps.[10]

As the column passed over the ground rushed by the Zulu left horn, Fred Symons and his comrades riding to the left of the track began to notice their mounts 'move aside for something peculiar that we could not discern in the dim light; these objects were dead Zulus lying face downwards and their shields on their backs.'[11]

At about 7.45 p.m. and half a mile from Isandlwana the general halted his forces and the volunteers dismounted in skirmishing order. Two small fires burned brightly in camp, their flames distantly silhouetting a jumble of wagons outlined on the nek below the hill suggesting a barricade of sorts. The 2/24th now formed line and fixed bayonets, while the guns of Brevet Lt-Colonel Arthur Harness fired some rounds towards the nek, but there was no reply. After the first discharge of the cannon the fires in camp were quickly extinguished, noted Trooper Symons, 'the Zulus being wiser in that respect than our NNC ... It was a pretty sight to see the bright flash of the gun and the graceful curve of the shell as it passed like a meteor through the air, to fall and rebound over the nek. Sometimes the shell would strike Isandlwana and bring down rocks with a crash. Some went into the valley beyond.'[12] Major Wilsone Black, 2/24th, was then ordered off with the left wing of his battalion and 1/3rd NNC to take and occupy the stony hill to the south of the nek while the remainder of the force halted about 300 yards from the camp. With Black went young Lieutenant Henry Mainwaring, who later described how after 'stumbling over rocks, debris of the camp and a few bodies, we at length gained the top of the kopje, and then by a cheer we signalled the remainder of the force to advance'.[13] 'Such cheering I never heard,' recalled Trooper Symons, 'and with lighter hearts we advanced towards the nek.'[14]

It turned out that there were few Zulus hiding in the shadows apart from some drunks. Lieutenant John Maxwell of the NNC found a party of eight or ten Zulus sprawled among some wagons. He called for help from some men of the 24th. 'They mounted the wagons and put the bayonet through them,' he noted laconically.

Amidst all the awful detritus of battle on the stony nek, where some of the fiercest fighting had taken place just a few hours earlier, Lord Chelmsford decided his men should bivouac for the night. A hollow square was formed with the three right-wing companies of the 2/24th forming a two-deep line across the nek, with the artillery and mounted troops in a second line sixty yards behind and facing the rear. Black's men occupied the stony hill while on the right the 2/3rd NNC were positioned in quarter column just below the foot of Isandlwana.

It was to be a night none of those present would ever forget. In his journal Lieutenant Harford wrote:

> The night was pitch dark and the stench, which was mostly from the smashed-up contents of the Royal Army Medical Corps wagon containing all manner of chemicals, within a few yards of us, was truly awful. As soon as the bivouac had settled down – and by this time the Zulus had begun to light fires and could be seen moving about on the ridge just across the valley, barring our line of retreat to Rorke's Drift – Lord Chelmsford himself took a look round to see how things were going. On coming across to us he had many questions to ask concerning the Contingent, and stayed talking for some time, among other things asking me what I thought the Zulus would do, whether they would attack us or not, and I told him that I felt pretty certain that they would as soon as it was daylight.[15]

Later in the night the general returned when he heard that the NNC 'had disappeared as if by magic', noted Harford, 'Curiously no-one had noticed them as they squatted gently and gradually sliding down the hill into the valley like a huge landslide ...' He 'bolted' down, stumbling over clumps of them and 'literally drove them back to the square'. A furious Chelmsford personally placed two men of the 24th as sentries 'with orders to bayonet the first Native that attempted to move from his position'.

Despite the darkness Harford also managed to find his old tent. Everything had gone but next to it 'lay the bodies of two artillery men, disembowelled and terribly mutilated', whilst nearby he saw two wagon masters, 'with their faces blackened'. Passing the hospital wagon, where dozens of broken bottles gave off an 'abominable' stench, Harford saw, lying face downwards, the body of Surgeon-Major Shepherd, the Centre Column's P.M.O. He had been 'stabbed in the neck, but his body had not been mutilated'. During the night Harford chatted several times with Major Cornelius Clery, principal staff officer to Glyn. This led them at one point to rest on a comfortable-looking tarpaulin before realising it was uncommonly soft and they were clearly sitting on a dead body. The two men rose, horrified at the thought of who might lay beneath them, but they decided not to investigate further. 'Under the circumstances of the moment,' wrote Harford, 'with dead all around one, we had no stomach for curiosity.'[16]

The Zulus had smashed up or carried off the contents of the commissariat wagons so Harford could find nothing to eat for himself or his men. Far luckier was another NNC officer, George Hamilton Browne, whose 'trusty Irish servant', an acting senior sergeant with the corps, 'was a past master in the art of looting'. He went scavenging and found bully beef and biscuits, a bottle of brandy, a bottle of port and a large packet of tobacco. Wilsone Black joined Browne and the pair smoked and quaffed the port as they watched and remarked on flashes in the sky in the direction of Rorke's Drift.

Soon, scores of Zulu camp fires could be spotted on the hills. Some soldiers were so tired after the long day's marching (more than thirty miles) that they fell fast asleep, but for most it was an uncomfortably chilly night, sleep made impossible by false alarms, NNC panics, the squeals of injured mules and the shout, far off, of an occasional drunken Zulu. Captain Henry Hallam Parr, a staff officer, wrote:

> The first part of the night was very black and dark, but about one a.m. the sky cleared and the stars shone out, and I received orders to serve out the rations of biscuit and tinned meat we luckily had with us. It was disagreeable work moving about inside the square; in the dark it was difficult to walk without stumbling over the dead and the debris of all kinds with which the ground was strewn. After the regulars and volunteers had drawn their rations, the officers and non-commissioned officers of the Natal Contingent came for theirs.[17]

The stench of death hung in the heavy, still air. A half-century later Sam Jones of the Natal Mounted Rifles would say: 'I can still smell it at times. Some things remind me of it, as for instance a sweet potato that has been cooked when it is just beginning to go bad. And when I smell such things I become quite ill.'[18]

While some men slept and others thought of the morrow, the horror that lay around them made itself felt: Lt-Colonel Henry Degacher, 2/24th, almost rode over the body of his dead brother, Captain William Degacher, 1/24th. 'I did not feel it much,' he admitted later, 'for I never expected to see daylight and said to myself, "Old Boy, I shall be with you in half an hour."'[19] A nightmarish moment occurred to Trooper Symons when he asked a shape on the ground, 'Got a drink in your water bottle mate?' Thinking the man was asleep, Symons felt for his water flask – and put his hand into the man's disembowelled guts. Equally gruesome was an incident when Lieutenant Maxwell of the NNC tripped and rolled downhill. 'A dive it was,' he recalled, 'for I found myself with my hands in the inside of what turned out to be the body of a 24th man, and my heels uphill.'[20] At the rear of the square Trooper

Clarke of the Natal Mounted Police was in charge of thirty horses for part of the night. 'There were the corpses of four men of the 24th Regiment in the ring,' he later recalled, 'and others under the horses' legs, which caused the animals to surge to and fro so that it was almost impossible to control them. At one time we were on top of the adjoining ring which brought curses down on my head. I was not sorry to be relieved.'[21]

Any hope of survivors was dispelled in the light of first dawn. 'Ah, those red soldiers at Isandlwana,' a Zulu later told Captain Parr, 'how few they were, and how they fought! They fell like stones, each man in his place.' For now the awful horror was revealed – lying in front of the camp, amidst the wagons, on the nek and the track towards the river and Rorke's Drift lay the bodies of 52 white officers, 739 white troops, 67 white NCOs of the NNC and 471 black soldiers. The 24th Foot alone had lost 21 officers and 578 other ranks – 16 officers and 408 men just from the 1st Battalion. Later, as reports trickled in, the army was to learn of the harrowing escapes of 85 known white survivors (36 from the regular army). Among the dead were Colonel Anthony Durnford – soon to be made a scapegoat for the debacle. He had led a gallant stand with some of his men in the wagon park fighting with knives and fists when their ammunition ran out. Lt-Colonel Pulleine of the 1/24th had been speared in his tent in the act of firing a pistol at his assailant. A third victim of the tragedy, whose death added a grim note of irony, was Captain George Shepstone, the twenty-nine-year-old son of one of the war's architects (Sir Theophilus had three sons, all of whom volunteered for service in the war). George died near a rocky outcrop below the southern peak of Isandlwana. A Zulu boy later recounted: 'He fought bravely. He killed our people. The others feared to approach him. Suddenly there dashed in our brother Umtweni before he could load and killed him.'[22]

More than 1,000 Zulus had died in the battle, countless more had crawled away to have their wounds tended by friends, witch-doctors and in some cases their own families. Many must have died of these horrific injuries or would carry the scars for the rest of their lives.

What shocked Chelmsford's troops was the state of their comrades' bodies; most of them had been disembowelled, some had been decapitated and in other cases body parts were missing. The fact that the disembowelling was part of a ritual known as *qaqa*, allowing the man's spirit to escape, else it might haunt his killer, would have been of little comfort to his comrades even if they had been aware of this ethnological symbolism, any more than the realisation that body parts were added to Zulu ritual medicines and sprinkled on warriors by the *izinyaga* in the belief that if they came from brave men extra strength and courage might be theirs in the next battle.

The sights on that dawn morning did not seem to speak much of religion, symbolism or honouring the dead. The first thing some men noticed was how 'we had literally been lying in blood, for we were peeling cakes of it and mud from our mackintoshes'.[23] A vivid picture was drawn by Major 'Maori' Browne of the NNC, a man who was often loose with facts, but for once can be believed:

> My God, in the grey dawn it was a sight! In their mad rush into the camp the Zulus had killed everything. Horses had been stabbed at their picket lines. Splendid spans of oxen were lying dead in their yokes, mules lay dead in their harness and even dogs were lying stabbed among the tents. Ripped open sacks of rice, flour, meal and sugar lay everywhere. They had even in their savage rage thrust their assegais into tins of bully beef, butter and jam. Among all the debris, singly and in heaps, or rather in groups of two or three, lay the ripped and mutilated bodies of the gallant 24, showing how, when their formation was broken, they had stood it out, and fought back to back or in groups until they had been run over and destroyed. That they had fought to the last gasp could be seen

> by the number of dead Zulus who lay everywhere in amongst them, the bayonet wounds on their bodies telling of the fierce, though short combat, that had taken place after the right horn of the Zulus had swept round the hill. I had just time to get to the door of my tent, inside of which I saw my old setter dog, dead with an assegai thrust through her. My two spare horses were also lying killed at their picket rope, with my Totty groom dead between them.[24]

Atrocity stories later circulated, though modern historians such as Ian Knight have warned against taking this 'evidence' at face value. Yet there were so many references to dead drummer boys that it seems reasonable to assume that some teens in the camp met ugly deaths. Private Sweeney, 2/24th, wrote to his Oldham newspaper of two drummers and five band boys, aged about fourteen years, 'butchered most awfully indeed. One little chap named M'Every, they hung up by the chin to a hook.'[25] Another 2nd Battalion man, Private William Meredith, wrote to his brother and sister at Pontypool: 'I could describe the battlefield to you, but the sooner I get it out of my mind the better. It was a pity to see about 800 white men lying on the field cut up to pieces and stripped naked. Even the little boys that we had in the band, they were hung up on hooks and opened like sheep.'[26] Captain Penn Symons noted how, 'Most of the bodies were more or less stripped. One little Band Boy of the 2/24th, a mere child, was hung up by his heels to the tail of an ox wagon, and his throat cut. Even the dogs and goats about the camp, and the horses and mules tied to the picket ropes were butchered.'[27]

One professional war correspondent, Charles Norris-Newman of the London *Standard* and *Natal Times*, accompanied Chelmsford's column:

> The corpses of our poor soldiers, white and natives, lay thick upon the ground in clusters, together with dead and mutilated

> horses, oxen and mules, shot and stabbed in every position and manner; and the whole intermingled with the contents of the Commissariat wagons ... The dead bodies of the men lay as they had fallen, but mostly only with their boots and shirts on, or perhaps a pair of trousers or remnant of a coat, with just sufficient means of recognition to determine to which branch of the Service they had belonged. In many instances they lay with sixty or seventy empty cartridge cases surrounding them, thus showing they had fought to the very last ...[28]

Lord Chelmsford had the good sense to realise that it was wisest to get his force away from the sights of Isandlwana as early as possible. They moved off at daybreak as quickly as time permitted with few officers allowed to search about the camp. Heading along the track towards Rorke's Drift, where the general must have been expecting to encounter another catastrophe, the omens were not good; a large Zulu impi passed by (the worn-out remains of the attacking force) at relatively close distance. Both sides moved on and chose not to fight, though some NNC wildly fired a few shots at their foes and a lone Zulu charged the enemy ranks. A well-aimed bullet dropped him to the red earth.

Great was the relief of Chelmsford and all his men when they reached the former mission station to find it charred and blackened but basically intact. Its garrison of eight officers and 131 men (including thirty-five listed as sick soldiers) had fought off an impi of 3–4,000 warriors (at a loss of 350 or more Zulu dead to just seventeen of the defenders), and won for themselves everlasting fame.

Now, at last, Chelmsford had a few hours free to put pen to paper. He wrote to Frere on 23 January that 'No 3 Column has maintained a terrible disaster ...' The bravery of the Zulus, he confessed, was the subject of 'much astonishment'. The next day the general left for Helpmekaar, twelve miles away, and on the 25th raced to Pietermaritzburg in a pony and trap. The rum thing about this journey was that his staff followed 'slowly' on horseback, while he was accompanied only by his intensely loyal military secretary, John Crealock. The pair thus had twenty-four hours to privately discuss the battle and see if they could find a scapegoat for the disaster: the weak NNC were at fault; Glyn's dispositions were at fault; above everything else, Durnford's defence of the camp was at fault. The historian Ian Knight has written: 'Over the following months Crealock would work hard behind the scenes to ensure the blame for the disaster fell anywhere but upon him or his chief.'[29]

To Colonel Frederick Stanley, Secretary of State for War in Lord Beaconsfield's Conservative Government, a telegram was despatched on 27 January starting with those famous words immortalised in the film, *Zulu:* 'I regret to have to report a very disastrous engagement which took place on the 22nd instant between the Zulus and a portion of No 3 Column ... The former came down in overwhelming numbers and in spite of the gallant resistance ... completely overwhelmed them.'[30] Next day Chelmsford met with Frere for a long talk. The High Commissioner had first received news of the battle on the morning of 24 January. His first inclination had been to arrest the messengers, so fantastic did the disaster sound. During that same Black Friday, as word of the massacre spread like wildfire among the populace, consternation followed by panic set in; soon the air was noisy with carpenters nailing boards across doors and windows, workmen sinking wells, labourers constructing vedettes and barricades. Matters at Durban were, if anything, worse than Pietermaritzburg, and a columnist accused the locals of behaving like 'raving lunatics'. Bishop Colenso, who with his family were literally the only people in Natal with a good word for the Zulus, admitted that in the immediate weeks after Isandlwana '"Extermination" is the cry ...' When Sir Henry Bulwer called for a day of prayer on 12 March in consequence of the battle the bishop castigated the authorities from his pulpit, using as the text for his sermon, 'And what doth the Lord require of thee, but to do justly, and to love mercy, and walk humbly with thy God.'

Shocked by how worn out Chelmsford looked, well aware that HM Govt would blame him for the war and terrible loss of life, Sir Bartle Frere fired off a letter to Hicks Beach on 29 January in which he argued that the Zulus had threatened 'a raid to destroy this town or Durban ...' He tried to soft-soap the government with news that the colonial spirit of 'self-defence is good', but added, 'you should send out not less than two brigades' to fight the Zulus. Frere even had the temerity to tell his Whitehall masters that 'you need not be in the least alarmed at the expense' since the Zulus could be taxed heavily once the war was over. Frere, won over by Chelmsford's explanations for the Isandlwana defeat, was already referring by 3 February to 'poor Durnford's disaster', while on the 10th he bluntly told the Queen in a letter that the general's orders to Pulleine 'were not obeyed owing apparently to Colonel Durnford ...'

Natal, indeed all of South Africa, was in shock. One of those in deepest mourning was Sir Theophilus Shepstone. He had feuded with Durnford for years over native policy and could now blame him for young George's death. The colonel had failed, he wrote just two days after the battle, because if the troops had 'taken the simple precaution of turning their wagons in a defensive laager, the catastrophe would not have happened'.[31]

While Frere's intelligence and long experience as a pro-consul – not to mention huge ego – kept him calm, the pressures of command were telling badly on Chelmsford. He now seemed strangely aged to his staff, a dazed man who confessed to Evelyn Wood, his No 4 Column Commander, that he was 'fairly puzzled' about how to proceed with operations and wished only to find a way 'with honour out of this beastly country'. He had convened a Court of Inquiry after Isandlwana that sat on 27–29 January under

Arthur Harness as its president. A limp institution, the court did not give an opinion, declined to question or interrogate witnesses and, as Harness told his brother in a letter, he 'recorded or rejected nearly what I liked …' Colonel Crealock, as several historians including Adrian Greaves have pointed out, 'gave false evidence stating that he had ordered Durnford, on behalf of Chelmsford, to take command of the camp; this persuasive evidence totally exonerated Chelmsford.'[32]

Fortunately, the general had what he termed 'a gleam of sunshine' in the notable victory of Rorke's Drift. It was in his own interest that this defence should be played up to the hilt so that aspects of Isandlwana might become cobwebbed. For the mission station's defenders – the general reduced them to a gallant band of just sixty or so – he personally pushed for recognition of their achievement with the granting of an unprecedented eleven Victoria Crosses. The awards were popular in an army that appreciated when its officers and men got public recognition for their deeds. There is no question that his lordship's soldiers generally liked him for the gentleman he was, but the view was not universal. Lieutenant Robert Fell of the 90th Light Infantry, who had been in South Africa since 1878, wrote in a letter home to his family: 'Chelmsford was certainly to blame for the Disaster at Isandlwana – and though it is high treason to say so – he must have known the Zulu Army was on the march – he made no attempt to laager and split up his force …'[33]

It was in the early hours of 28 January that the official telegram conveying news of Isandlwana left Cape Town aboard the steamer, *Asiatic*. Without the direct telegraphic communication that would probably have prevented the war, the news had to be conveyed by ship to Cape Verde, from whence it was relayed via Madeira and Lisbon to London. 'At Cape Verde the *Reuters* correspondent aboard the steamer bribed the telegraph operator to send his message before Sir Bartle Frere's official despatch, hence *Reuters* in London was slightly ahead of officialdom in breaking the news.'[34] So it was, twenty-five days after the battle, in the dead of night on 11–12 February 1879 that a messenger knocked at the door of Hicks Beach's house in Portman Square. The shock he felt on opening the envelope was to reverberate across the country as politicians, the military establishment and ordinary people digested the news. In the succeeding days and weeks, as more dismal details – including the long roll call of the dead – arrived, not just in communiqués to HM Govt but also in letters from soldiers serving in South Africa, it seemed as if a flock of black crows had dropped out of the sky into a graveyard.

Only three days earlier, on Saturday 8 February, *The Graphic* illustrated newspaper had told its readers: 'The Zulu War has begun.' The editorial accepted that 'Cetewayo is not altogether in the wrong', but went on to conclude that 'a feeble resistance is expected ...' News of Isandlwana saw a quick change in the jingoistic rhetoric; now, while the Zulus were of course 'savages', they were also 'well-drilled (and as our loss has proved) well-led', their strength and generalship having been 'greatly undervalued'. *The Daily News*, organ of the lower middle classes, grimly reminded its readers: 'British treasure and blood would now be expended on a scale the authors of the war had not contemplated, and burdens, heavy in all cases and ruinous in many, will be inflicted on struggling industries, and all for what? Lord Beaconsfield's answer is awaited.'[35]

Privately the Prime Minister found the news so 'agitating' that his health suffered a relapse. This was probably psychosomatic, noted his biographer, Robert Blake, 'and he was sunk in a mood of depression and irritation for several weeks'.[36] The Queen was told immediately by 'Dizzy' that 'the Cabinet met, and have sent five regiments of Infantry instead of the three asked for by Lord Chelmsford, and all the Cavalry, and Artillery, and stores which he requested'.[37] The Prime Minister also told Victoria bluntly how the disaster 'will change everything, reduce our Continental influence, and embarrass our finances'. He rose in the House of Lords on 13 February and, in one of his typically masterful displays, told fellow peers that Isandlwana was 'a military disaster, a terrible military disaster, but I think I may say it was, it is no more. It is not a military defeat which arises from the falling energies or resources of the country, but it arises accidentally ...' Adroitly the Prime Minister chose to dwell not on the reasons for the disaster but moved swiftly on to the 'exhibition of heroic valour' demonstrated at Rorke's Drift. This, he concluded, had proved 'the stamina of the English soldiery has not diminished or deteriorated [cheers]'.[38]

Once Beaconsfield recovered some of his old composure his mood blackened towards the men he saw as the architects of an unnecessary war that had thrown his foreign policy into jeopardy 'by this inopportune call on British reserves, while the cost was all too likely to damage the national finances already in an unsatisfactory state because of the economic and agricultural depression'.[39]

What was to be done? The government was angrier with Frere than Chelmsford since they could not judge the latter man's military abilities. The Prime Minister had also a decade earlier kicked the general's father out of his Cabinet as an incompetent lord chancellor. It would be distressing to have to brand the son as an incompetent general; given time, he might retrieve what he had lost. Beaconsfield told the Queen that the feelings in the Cabinet against both Frere and Chelmsford required 'considerable private handling', but no censure would be directed towards the general, while Frere would simply receive a rebuke and continue in his post. Her Majesty, who loyally supported both men, was most relieved.

'Black Michael' approached the prickly Frere with some cunning. He sent a personal letter – 'what I say is for yourself alone' – ahead of the official censure despatch. Matters were so alarming, wrote Hicks Beach, that he almost had to choose between 'resigning and consenting to supersede or recall you ... I attach the greatest importance to your continuance in South Africa ... I rely on you ... to help me ...'[40] The use of such a private letter made it impossible for Frere to allude to it publicly. It was, as Frere's modern biographer has written, 'rank moral blackmail'. HM Govt also made plain that any annexation of Zululand was not on the cards and the Transvaal question was to be delayed until after the defeat of the Zulus. Indeed, as constitutional historian C. W. de Kiewiet wrote, 'Isandlwana marks a definite turning point in British South Africa policy.' Confederation was now to 'slip down the arduous path it had steeply trodden, back again finally to abandonment and non-interference.'[41] Hicks Beach's letter arrived on 18 April while Frere was visiting Boer malcontents at Pretoria. After digesting its contents he wrote sarcastically and with a degree of self-pity that 'it is pleasant that the government is not likely to defend me or anyone else'.[42] He replied to Hicks Beach that his choice had been 'simple' – risking a Zulu war 'at once or something far worse – a Zulu War a few months later, preceded by a Boer rebellion'. Sir Bartle made it clear that he was offended, but Hicks Beach's trick worked; 'I will not desert my post'[43] declared the High Commissioner. His ego was restored and his self-pity washed away by a stream of messages of support from various South African dignitaries, old friends in India, some home politicians, the Prince of Wales and especially the Queen.

It looked for a few weeks as if Lord Chelmsford had slipped off the hook of public outrage, but on 17 March his letter to the Secretary of State for War of 8 February was published. It triggered an explosion in the Press. 'No such appeal to the Authorities in England for dismissal ... had ever before been addressed to them by a General in the field commanding Her Majesty's troops,'[44] declared the *Standard* newspaper. The general had a wide range of influential friends in society who sprang to his defence. Even the Zulu War historian, Donald Morris, has written, 'The accusation was unfair. Chelmsford was depressed and discouraged when he wrote home ...

He was in the midst of a serious quarrel with Sir Henry Bulwer which took up much of his time ... He was a substantive major-general with the local rank of lieutenant-general and the next senior man to him in Southern Africa was Glyn who had been a colonel since 1872.'[45] All this was true but they remain excuses; Chelmsford had clearly written that he wanted a more senior officer in command, and in life, generally, one must reap what one sows.

The British public could not understand why, after such a failure as Isandlwana, his lordship did not prosecute the war energetically? 'The British army may be likened to the children of Israel wandering aimlessly in the wilderness,' wrote one columnist. Meantime, news reached England of No. 1 Column besieged at Ekowe, the nightmarish flight from Hlobane by Wood's No. 4 Column troops, the massacre at Intombi Drift – a seemingly endless stream of disasters and deaths. Letter-writers to the newspapers had a field-day. One crackpot blamed Isandlwana on the 'unmilitary and perverted education of British army officers' and 'competitive examinations in Chaucer and Spenser' that made them weak. Several critics demanded that England 'leave the colonists to make their own terms with the Zulus'.

Punch's famous cartoon of 1 March, drawn by John Teniel, showed a Zulu chalking on a blackboard in front of John Bull the words, 'Do not despise your enemy.' More brutal was a cartoon one week later in *Fun* by Gordon Thomson showing Chelmsford in the mode of a little boy, a dunce's cap on his head, as Mrs Dizzy said to her 'pet': 'Did he get himself into a nasty mess? And did they say unpleasant things about him? Never mind, my dear, here are some more soldiers to play with.' One wit wrote:

England's in a pretty mess
Out in Zululand,
The blunders of our General there,
None can understand.

Stanzas in the same vein were interspersed with a chorus (a parody of a famous 1878 music hall song):

> We don't want to fight
> But by Jingo if we do,
> We've got the men,
> We've got the ships,
> We've got the money too.
> Lord Chelmsford is the man,
> To skedaddle if he can,
> And leave our men to be
> Slaughtered by the Zooloos.[46]

In Parliament the general's name simply would not fade away. It was clear that the debate as to his ability to successfully prosecute the war was rising inexorably towards boiling point. On 14 March a back-bencher declared there was 'a prima facie case of incompetence' against Chelmsford. He accused him of 'a great deal of want of discretion, if not of military misconduct and incapacity'. A fortnight later the fiery Liberal front-bencher, Sir Charles Dilke, bluntly attacked 'a General upon whose head rests the blood of these men until he has been tried and acquitted'. Despite howls of protest from the government benches, Sir Charles went for the general's jugular:

> Lord Chelmsford blames Colonel Durnford for not having fortified the camp. Why, he was there 48 hours himself with the whole of his ammunition for the campaign, and during all those 48 hours he never made the slightest attempt to do what he says Colonel Durnford should have done in 4 hours. The other day I asked a distinguished General his opinion about Lord Chelmsford's conduct and his answer was – 'It is to me perfectly incomprehensible. He seems to have left the camp with all his ammunition and to have gone fiddling

> about looking for a parade ground with a hostile army of 30 thousand men on his flank.' After the disaster we find him flying for his life.[47]

Dilke's attack was cruel and ill-informed but it showed how some people were thinking. The government was also being made to feel extremely uncomfortable; Sir William Harcourt, a Liberal front-bencher not known for his wit, had perhaps his finest hour when he ridiculed the Censure Document. He read out an imaginary letter from Hicks Beach: 'Dear Sir Bartle Frere, I cannot think you are right. Indeed, I think you are very wrong; but after all you know better than I do. I hope you won't do what you are going to do; but if you do I hope it turns out very well.'[48] This speech had MPs rolling in the aisles, much to the discomfort of Lord Beaconsfield, who liked to think he was Parliament's chief wit.

The Cabinet did not need Harcourt's jibes. As March and April drifted into May their mood was one of extreme annoyance with both Chelmsford and Frere. One of their main critics was the ever-realistic Lord Salisbury, who later told a friend, 'Bartle Frere should have been recalled as soon as news of his ultimatum reached England. We should then have escaped in appearance, as well as in reality, the responsibility of the Zulu War. So thought the majority of the Cabinet, so thought Dizzy himself.'[49] Within a month of news of Isandlwana reaching Britain the sagelike Salisbury told the Prime Minister that defending Frere was 'a waste of political capital'. In April Lord Beaconsfield admitted 'alarm' at Frere's persistence in vindicating his conduct. By May the Prime Minister, watching the drift of events in South Africa, decided something had to be done. 'The news from the Cape very unsatisfactory,' he wrote on 8 May to Lady Chesterfield, 'Chelmsford wanting more force, tho' he does nothing with the 15,000 men he has. He seems cowed and confused.'[50]

Exasperation finally boiled over at Cabinet meetings held on three successive days from 19 to 21 May. Salisbury and others were furious that no news had been received from Frere or Chelmsford for some time while war costs were rising alarmingly. Only five members of the Cabinet, including Hicks Beach and Colonel Stanley, supported Chelmsford but, as Beaconsfield told the Queen, the government 'were left in a state of great darkness, and that no one seemed clearly to understand what we are aiming at, and what terms could satisfactorily conclude the war'. He warned Her Majesty that 'the prevalent, not to say unanimous opinion seemed to be, that without superseding either Sir Bartle or Lord Chelmsford, a "dictator" should be sent out, intimately acquainted with the views and policy of yr. Majesty's Government, who should be able to conclude peace, when the fitting opportunity occurred, and effect a general settlement …'[51]

The Prime Minister had decided already on the man, though he knew the choice would not please his Sovereign. It had to be a person who understood something of South Africa's complex affairs, someone sufficiently skilled in the arts of diplomacy who could woo distrustful Cape politicians and rebellious Boers, a soldier who moreover could combine his civil duties with those of a military supremo. Beaconsfield had on his lips the name of a man who had delighted HM Govt by enforcing the Pax Britannica in other parts of Africa and won over South Africans with his champagne and sherry diplomacy just four years earlier, an energetic, cheery figure considered by some to be a rising military genius – even if the Royal Family loathed him. On 23 May the Prime Minister told Queen Victoria that the Cabinet had agreed to send 'Sir Garnet Wolseley to be yr. Majesty's High Commissioner, and Commander-in-Chief for Natal, Transvaal, and territories adjacent, including Zululand, and to have within that area supreme civil and military authority …' Lord Chelmsford, he added, 'will become second-in-command'.[52]

2

ALL SIR GARNET

They are determined to send Garnet Wolseley to the Cape!

Lady Geraldine Somerset

One fine morning in late spring 1879 two youths were strolling down Fleet Street, Torquay, when their attention was caught by a large crowd listening to a speaker on an improvised rostrum under the branches of a large oak tree. 'Lord Chelmsford has proved incapable of the task he has undertaken of subduing the Zulus and should never have been entrusted with the job,' declared the man to loud murmurs of approval from his audience. 'Thank God, Sir Garnet Wolseley is under orders to go out to the Cape,' concluded the orator, 'He will soon settle "Cechywhale"!'[1]

Let us pause to examine this man, Wolseley, hated by the Royal Family, popular with the masses, and also admired by so adroit a politician as Disraeli. The Prime Minister's decision, moreover, elicited a universal sigh of relief in the popular press. 'A General of almost unrivalled military experience among British officers,' declared *The Graphic*, 'who had already studied on the spot the South African problem, and who had the merit – a great merit in the eyes of soldiers – of having always been lucky.'[2]

Sir Garnet's great luck was to hold out for another six years, but in 1879, almost at the apex of his popularity, he really was the best soldier who could be sent to Zululand. No rival stood in his path in popular esteem (Frederick Roberts, soon to fill this role was, in 1879, just setting forth in Afghanistan to garner fame), while Wolseley had already proved himself a thoroughly professional master of the colonial small ear having led an expedition against Metis rebels in western Canada and defeated the bloodthirsty Ashanti on the Gold Coast of Africa. Critics then (and now) might note his character defects – egotism, bombast, pride, and these just for starters – but he was also hard-working, intelligent, interested in every aspect of his profession and willing to help the careers of other like-minded progressive military thinkers. His life was dedicated to one thing besides his own personal ambition (which was admittedly vast), and that was to pull the British Army up by its boot straps if necessary from the state he witnessed in Burma, the Crimea and India in the 1850s, to one of maximum modern efficiency. Little wonder that he bruised the egos of old-school officers along the way, or upset Queen Victoria, who always viewed army reform with suspicion.

Wolseley was born on 4 June 1833 into that remarkable social group who supplied so many Victorian officers, the Anglo-Irish gentry. Several of the Garnet ring's members were to come from the same background including Butler, Colley and McCalmont. Unlike his friends, however, Wolseley's family were relatively poor and this upbringing would affect him for the rest of his life. In his autobiography (and even in a ghosted biography of 1878), Wolseley studiously avoided any reference to his childhood, yet his later behaviour, as any clinical psychiatrist can attest, was rooted in those early years.

Garnet's father was an impecunious major of the King's Own Borderers who married late in life, quickly fathered four sons and three daughters and died when his eldest child, the subject of this book, was just seven years old. His widow, Frances, the daughter of pious Protestants, was left to struggle on his army pension. Until his father's death young Garnet Joseph and his siblings lived in a Queen

Anne country house on the outskirts of Dublin, but it is unclear if the family continued to rent this place from Frances's parents. So poor were the family that Garnet was educated partly on his mother's knee and at a local day-school. He was excluded from the cloisters and fine education at Eton where Brackenbury and McCalmont were pupils, or like Edric Gifford who was sent to Harrow; he would not know of English preparatory school life like Colley, or even see the scholastic world of an Irish Jesuit-run boarding school as enjoyed by William Butler. The shame Wolseley felt at his poor education and upbringing, coupled with a corresponding need to prove superior in all things, would burn in him throughout his career. From his earliest days in the army there was also a necessity to care for his mother, brothers and sisters. These financial responsibilities – and it is to Wolseley's great credit that he did all he could for his extended family, including two brothers constantly in debt and a spinster sister, as well as paying most of his mother's bills – meant that he constantly strived for wealth and greatness, yet, when wealth and greatness were achieved, he still thought himself far from rich and worried that he might die poor. People with these kinds of psychological problems often develop a chip-on-the-shoulder mentality. So it was with Garnet; and his meteoric rise in the army bred, not surprisingly, an ego and conceit of outlandish proportions.

At fourteen Garnet was forced by poverty to leave school and take a job as a draughtsman in a land surveyor's office. Letters to Horse Guards begging for a commission without purchase (in view of his father's twenty-nine years in the army) went unanswered. It was not until March 1852, five years after starting work and rather to everyone's surprise, that Wolseley was gazetted an ensign in the 12th Foot. Within a month he had transferred to the 80th Foot, then getting ready to embark for the Second Burmese War. The lure of the East meant for a poor ensign such as Wolseley the chance of active service and possible promotion alongside the ever-present dangers of death from disease or war. In his first two years in the army Garnet would see Cape Town and Calcutta, men who had been tortured to death by Burmese dacoits, lead his first charge and get his first wound. Commanding a small band of men to death or glory was, as he later wrote, 'a supremely delightful moment ... The blood seems to boil, the brain to be on fire.' His wound was painful: 'I tried to stop the bleeding with my left hand, and remember well seeing the blood squirting in jets through the fingers of my pipe-clayed gloves.'[3] Wolseley was enthralled by the glory of battle – 'there can be nothing else in the world like it, or that can approach its inspiration, its intense sense of pride' – but the act of killing did not excite him, it 'gave me a rather unpleasant sensation ...'

During his first charge a fellow officer was killed but Garnet somehow survived despite a gingall bullet, 'the size of a small orange', shattering his left thigh. His luck held out also in the Crimea where he started the war as a lieutenant with the 90th Light Infantry in 1854. He survived being blasted by a shell that killed his comrades, split open his jaw and left cheek and blinded him permanently in the right eye. He rose to captain's rank and got a plum appointment as Deputy Assistant Quartermaster-General under General Airey. Staff appointments led him ever upwards; he served under fiery Major-General Sir Hope Grant in both the Indian Mutiny 1857–58 and China War 1860 as his Quartermaster-General. On 11 January 1862, just two months short of his first ten years in the army, Wolseley was gazetted Assistant-Quartermaster-General to the British Army in Canada. He was by now a major in his regiment and an acting brevet lieutenant-colonel, a remarkable rise from obscurity based solely on merit.

Ever ambitious, Wolseley spent most of the 1860s based in Canada and feared that his career would stagnate in peacetime soldiering. He visited both Confederate and Union armies during the American Civil War and tried to learn from the mistakes of McClellan and other generals. Robert E. Lee, Wolseley later wrote, was one of the two greatest men he ever met (the other was his old Crimean War friend, Charles Gordon). Just as Airey and Hope Grant had become lifelong friends and sponsors in the Crimea and India, so in Canada the rising Wolseley was taken under the wing of General Sir John Michel, commanding the British Army in North America, a wise old bird who had fought the Xhosa in South Africa and rebels in India, and was an acknowledged master of irregular warfare. In 1866, Michel, who considered Wolseley to be 'excellent and talented and energetic', sent him to Ontario to advise a locally inept commander on how best to tackle the threat of invasion across the United States border from Irish Fenians intent on ousting the British from Canada. Luckily, this war scare quickly fizzled out.

On leave in Ireland in 1868 Garnet at last married; seven years earlier he had met eighteen-year-old Louisa Erskine, an attractive blonde (she prided herself on having the same height and figure as the Venus de Milo), probably illegitimate, who was brought up as the niece and ward of her actual father. She had been living with her grandmother since infancy in Ireland. Wolseley had kept an Indian mistress during the Mutiny – 'she answers all the purposes of a wife without giving any of the bother',[4] he told his brother, Richard ('Dick') – but now admitted being 'dreadfully in love' with Louisa, though he told his sister, Matilda, 'I shall never marry to live in poverty and as that lady is as poor as I am there is not much chance of her being Mrs Garnet Junior.'[5] With a change of mind but not heart, the couple got married on his birthday. Their union was to be an intensely happy one, the pair having a seemingly special bond, their innermost thoughts shared in letters they wrote to one another almost daily when apart.

With 'Loo' in tow, Garnet returned to Canada where, in his spare time, he completed his *Soldier's Pocket-Book for Field Service*, a compendium on everything from tactics to caring for elephants, from military law to recipes for Irish stew. The book gave Wolseley his first real chance to promote army reforms. Cocked hats at the Horse Guards took note and feathers were ruffled. Wolseley was now a full colonel but he still yearned to 'become at least known if not famous'. The historian, Adrian Preston, the general's chief modern critic, while praising 'his enormous capacity for logistical detail' contained in the *Soldier's Pocket-Book*, concludes that it had 'no deep or permanent influence upon military thought or practice'. This may be so, but the book was widely read, critically praised and went through several editions. It was also absolutely *not* intended for armchair military theorists but, as Wolseley wrote, consisted of 'simple remedies such as any fool of an officer could avail himself of' on a colonial campaign. Preston has lambasted the general for his 'ordinariness of mind, the clumsiness of style and intellect, the absence of rigorous analysis and the inability to push an argument to its logical conclusions that was to become characteristic of much of his later writing ...'[6] Yet Sir Garnet never claimed to be a leading military thinker, simply a man set on army reform. His early campaigns, especially in the Crimea, enabled him to see enough of bad soldiering to last all his days. 'All my sympathy was with the Rank and File,' he wrote half a century later, 'My heart was daily rent as I saw the privates die around me because they had not the means of even buying the offal which my servant purchased weekly for himself and me.'[7] He was irritated by an officer-class who 'fought well, and had nobly led their men straight, but yet they lacked the manliness to bear for any length of time the hardships and discomfits the men experienced daily'. Above all else, Wolseley learned to despise politicians, who sent men to die in stupid, far-off wars under appalling conditions. Ministers of War, he felt, generally 'know as much about war and soldiers as I do of abstruse theology'.[8] Inspiring the rank and file, educating its officer-corps to be more professional soldiers and defending his cherished British Army from political knavery became hallmarks of Wolseley's life. In Canada he was also lucky to serve with three important military thinkers: Henry Havelock, son of the famous Indian Mutiny general, propounded theories on the novel use of 'mounted infantry'; George

Denison, a native Canadian, published in 1868 his *Modern Cavalry*, a sensational and seminal work; and Patrick MacDougall, who had authored *Modern Warfare And Modern Artillery*, and in 1873 would become head of the British Army's first properly constituted Intelligence Department. These friends and reformers all helped shape Wolseley's views as he reached middle age.

The chance for an independent command came in 1870 when settlers in the Red River district of Manitoba rose in revolt under the charismatic leadership of Louis Riel, a mixed-race Metis trader. They established a 'Republic of the North-West' at Fort Garry and murdered a minor government official. Hastily, Wolseley was told to assemble a force and take charge of an expedition to restore authority. His army of less than 1,000 British troops supported by Canadians used trains, steamers, canoes and their feet to cover the 1,200 miles to remote Fort Garry. Not a man went sick or was lost. On arrival they found Riel had already fled, but Wolseley's bloodless little expedition, costing only £100,000, was hugely popular and made him a hero in Canada and Britain.

The Red River Expedition enabled Wolseley to put some of his theories to the test while assembling a team of keen, progressive officers around him. Faces who were to reappear in Zululand included an obscure officer of the 60th Rifles with intellectual tendencies called Redvers Buller, a piano virtuoso who had been a 'wet bob' at Eton by the name of Hugh McCalmont and a thirty-one-year-old Irishman, William Butler, who cheekily surprised Wolseley after having entered Fort Garry and interviewed Riel, by turning up in a canoe paddled by Iroquois Indians, leaving the commander to utter, 'Where on earth have you dropped from?'

This tiny Canadian victory was overshadowed in Europe by the Franco-Prussian War. The speed with which the Prussian eagle brought the French cockerel to its knees shocked the British Army. Warfare, so long the prerogative of gentlemen, had been turned, or so it seemed, into an exact science. Reform of the army had been on the backburner for years, ever since the Crimean War had highlighted many defects, but now it seemed essential, and Prime Minister Gladstone selected Edward Cardwell, 'a thoughtful and coldly methodical politician', to tackle a host of issues. Around him the War Minister gathered a team of like-minded reformers led by Lord Northbrook as Under-Secretary and including Captain Evelyn Baring, Major Robert Biddulph and the new Assistant-Adjutant-General, Sir Garnet Wolseley, freshly knighted after Red River (an honour that Adrian Preston admits came with 'distinct advantages and definite compensations'). The team had their hands full, but set to work abolishing the purchase of commissions, introducing short-service enlistment for soldiers, forming an army reserve, ending flogging in peacetime, withdrawing Imperial troops from self-governing dominions, improving education for the ordinary Tommy, instituting a retirement system that gave younger officers a better chance of promotion, moving the Horse Guards staff to the War Office in Pall Mall, and bringing the C-in-C more closely under the control of the War Minister.

Although Wolseley certainly became known as the face of 'the young Army school of reform', it is misleading to give him too much credit since several of Cardwell's measures were formulated in the War Office Act of 1870 and Wolseley did not take up his post until May 1871 during the big debate on the purchase of commissions. He did not really enter the fray until 1872 when Cardwell pushed forward with his short service reforms; their aim was to limit enlistment for six years in the colours, then six in the newly established army reserve. It was hoped these reforms would save costs, improve recruitment and enable the army to fight anywhere in the world at short notice. Early estimates suggested that 32,000 extra recruits would have to be found annually (Wolseley was to spend much of his time at the War Office over the next thirty years dealing with a recurring manpower crisis).

Sir Garnet's principal reform work in 1871–73 was connected with the 1872 Localisation Act linking two battalions, one serving at home and one abroad. Great Britain had to be divided into sixty-six military districts and Wolseley served on the committee to decide the division. Cardwell hoped that 'ties of kindred and locality' would draw men to the colours and attract a better class of recruit. Old school officers rose en masse to denounce the reform as they 'feared that the loss of their traditional battalion numbers and facings would jeopardise *esprit de corps*'.[9] Single-battalion regiments were forced to merge (only the Queen's Own Cameron Highlanders escaped this fate), and the shot-gun marriages and consequent uniform changes were not popular, nor complete by 1879.

The Cardwellites were met head-on by the traditional officers to whom all this change was poppycock. They were led by HRH Prince George, Duke of Cambridge, the Queen's cousin, who had commanded the British Army since 1856. Prince George was irascible, deeply conservative, suspicious of anything new and felt that an institution approved of by the Duke of Wellington did not need any tinkering. He deeply resented politicians trying to meddle with his authority. His blimpish looks – stout chest, white mutton-chop whiskers, saggy jowls and pink bald dome – made HRH seem the perfect choleric old soldier. Indeed, his parade-ground speeches were the stuff of legend. In Hyde Park he once told the Grenadiers: 'In all my experience of reviews in England, Ireland, or the Continent of Europe I have never witnessed such a damnable exhibition of incompetence as has been shown by the Grenadier Guards today. When the "Cease Fire" sounded the 1st Battalion was firing at the Serpentine, the 2nd Battalion was firing at the Marble Arch and God Almighty knows where the 3rd Battalion was firing. I don't!'[10] At Sandhurst on another occasion he began a speech to the officer cadets with the attention-grabbing address, 'You dirty little bastards!'

The duke was no fool and his opposition to reform sprang from a deep-rooted love of the Army and its traditions. It was a reaction based on fear that the reformers would undermine or damage an institution he was proud to serve and which had a noble history.

Wolseley, as the decades rolled by, would grow fond of Prince George and admit that he had deliberately goaded the old school officer corps: 'As a reformer, I was impatient and in a hurry; my nature would not brook the sapping of a regular siege: I wanted to assault the place at once, and I did so.'[11] Cambridge resented everything the reformers stood for and in February 1879, after a day spent at Aldershot inspecting troops en route for Zululand, his feelings were expressed forcibly to his mother:

> Every day shows more the abomination of idiotic Cardwell's system!! Every regiment for service having to be brought up to its full numbers by 300 or 400 volunteers from other regiments, destroying all *esprit de corps* and solidity, starting on a campaign and then not knowing each other, not the officers, their men, not one another's names!! The *idiocy* of the English constitution taking an ignorant *civilian,* a stupid *lawyer* full of theories to organize the Army!!![12]

In 1871 and 1872 Wolseley gained further experience in the practical side of war serving on staff in large-scale manoeuvres. Cambridge thought deficiencies in the first year were much improved by the second. Wolseley chose to disagree and went so far as to publish an article that dared to say 'the great majority of generals and brigadiers employed this year were not the men to whose care the lives of soldiers could be entrusted in war'.[13] In 1871 Sir Garnet had also entered a military essay competition; he did not win but was pleased that the victor, Lieutenant John Maurice, had quoted from the *Soldier's Pocket-Book*. He thought this 'not only a compliment but a good advertisement for the *great* work ...'

India beckoned again when a new Viceroy, Lord Northbrook, invited Sir Garnet to serve as his military secretary, but with Louisa now pregnant, he declined. A daughter, Frances, was born in September 1872. Four months later a large army of Ashanti warriors crossed the Prah river, entered the Gold Coast Protectorate and threatened to sweep the British and their possessions into the sea. The Colonial Secretary, Lord Kimberley, and the War Secretary, Edward Cardwell, needed to address this threat. On 1 August 1873 Wolseley submitted a plan 'for going to Coomassie with about 1,400 English soldiers, making our way up the rivers which I know exist there'.[14] A similar scheme drawn up by a naval commander, John Glover, using native troops via the Volta River to operate on the flanks and rear of the Ashantis had, in the eyes of the politicians, the twin virtues of low costs and minor risks. It was accepted and Wolseley's Red River style operation was rejected (he never forgave Glover). Sir Garnet next suggested that he be appointed Governor of the Gold Coast so that, with a staff of special service officers, he could train 20,000 Africans to drive the Ashantis from the Protectorate and then push two battalions of British troops, via staging posts, to the enemy capital, destroying both it and their army. On 13 August 1873 Wolseley's scheme was accepted by the two ministers without consulting Parliament (which was in recess).

There is not scope in this book for a detailed study of the Ashanti Expedition, but Wolseley's war, fought between September 1873 and March 1874, was a huge success. He returned home to the thanks of both houses of Parliament, a grant of £25,000 a year, promotion to the rank of major-general, decorations including the KCB and honorary degrees from Oxford and Cambridge. Not bad rewards for a day-school boy who was just turning forty.

Wolseley's expedition had been a new kind of war with the Press firmly in tow. William Russell of *The Times* had set a trend as he followed the troops in the Crimea and Indian Mutiny campaigns. A few more reporters including George Henty, later author of numerous adventure stories for boys, and the explorer, Henry Morton Stanley, recorded Napier's expedition to Abyssinia in 1868. Now Henty and Stanley, along with at least six others, sweated their way through the jungle and ushered in a golden age of war correspondents. John Maurice authored an account and Henry Brackenbury, who had acted as Wolseley's military secretary, was given free access to all his papers and penned in only six weeks a two-volume 795-page semi-official history of the Ashanti War, a Herculean effort that made the writer quite ill. The book was highly acclaimed and further enhanced Sir Garnet's name.

Among the papers loaned to Brackenbury was Wolseley's own journal of events. He had been in the habit of daily writing up his campaign experiences since a young man but almost all of this early material was destroyed in a warehouse fire. Ashanti marks the start of the Wolseley journals that have remained a vibrant source of information for scholars and all have been published. The exception is his 1882 Egyptian War journal, wrongly supposed by Preston not to have been written, but it appears destroyed or lost, perhaps misplaced amid his vast collection of papers split up on his death and still surfacing in odd places; his pocket diaries turned up in Scotland and a large quantity of material was formerly with the Royal United Service Institution, but is now in Canada. It is in his journals and personal letters that Wolseley was most critical of others; they reveal his conceit, dislikes and bitterness to an astonishing degree. Yet it is all too easy to forget that these writings were never meant for public consumption. Adrian Preston, who edited Wolseley's South African and Sudan journals, has noted that the 'decisive, iron-willed, charming and tactful' general loved by his staff 'stands in almost incredible contrast to the apprehensive, querulous, bombastic, vain and uncharitable'[15] man who inhabits many pages of his confidential writings. Preston observes, quite rightly I think, that Wolseley's barbs 'were an inverse reflection of the self-control and flattery he exercised' dealing with dull colonial officials, crafty politicians and stupid soldiers who did not share his views on reform. Trying to seem tough, calm or cheerful in stressful situations meant that acrimony and frustration beneath the surface built up to intolerable levels – and his escape mechanism was to set his immediate thoughts down on paper.

The most important aspect of the Ashanti War in connection with Wolseley's South African campaigns of 1879 was the team he assembled. They formed the nucleus of his famous 'ring' of officers, and in addition this time to Buller, Butler and McCalmont were the selfish yet brilliant Henry Brackenbury; energetic intellectual George Colley; kind-hearted, disorganized and eccentric military theorist, John Maurice; tough, accident-prone Evelyn Wood; along with two officers who did not claim to be brainy, but were full of pluck, Edric Gifford and Baker Russell. The 'Garnet ring' was to come in for much criticism later, be riven by its own internal feuds and see a fight develop with the circle of officers who gathered around Frederick Roberts in the 1880s and 1890s. But that was in the future; in 1874 Wolseley's band all showed outstanding merit – as administrators, experts, warriors or all-round professional soldiers.

On his return to England it looked for a time as if Wolseley might go out to India as adjutant-general. Cambridge got quite excited at the prospect, but Lord Napier, C-in-C, India, disliked Sir Garnet intensely so the move never happened. Instead he was attached to the War Office as Inspector-General of the Auxiliary Forces. Here he threw himself energetically into reforming the militia and volunteers. Eight months later this work was interrupted by a request from the new Colonial Secretary, Lord Carnarvon, asking Wolseley to go out to Natal on a six-month contract as chief administrator of the fledgling colony. Obsessed with his scheme to promote confederation as a panacea in South Africa, Henry Molyneux Herbert, 4th Earl of Carnarvon – 'Twitters' to his friends – tasked Sir Garnet with making sure Natal was brought into line with other British interests in the region. The colonists had to be made to abandon several of their constitutional privileges, particularly control of their finances, granted to them by Royal Charter in 1856. Quite why Wolseley was chosen remains a mystery, although it must be assumed that Carnarvon thought a popular hero might be the best man to sugar his confederation cake in Natal; and the Duke of Cambridge, anxious to remove his reform-mad underling from England, insisted to the Secretary of State that Wolseley was the man for the job.

The role of civilian administrator along with a load of political baggage was not to Wolseley's liking, but he always considered himself a State servant, and so was ready to do his duty. But how to tackle the dull Natal colonists? Sir Garnet always thought of himself as English, not Irish, yet this Dublin boy could, if required, turn on the Gaelic charm like a gas lamp. He devised a policy of 'champagne and sherry diplomacy' to woo Natal, a seemingly endless round of balls, fetes, race meetings and dinners. It worked a treat. 'He frightens these small folk with his amazing energy and decision,' chuckled his Natal colonial secretary.[16] After a meal with Wolseley one mayor gasped that he felt as though he had been put 'through a cullender'. He landed at Durban on 29 March 1875 and departed on 3 September. During this period he successfully managed to get the Natal Constitution modified, an act which gave the colony 'for good or ill ... an influence in the politics of imperial defence out of all proportion to its intrinsic strategic importance'.[17]

Touring Natal with a staff that included Butler, Brackenbury, Colley and Gifford, Sir Garnet met for the first time and formed an opinion of many persons he would meet again four years later including Sir Henry Bulwer, Bishop Colenso, John Dunn and Sir Theophilus Shepstone. While in Natal the conditions across the frontier in Zululand were a frequent topic for debate. At this stage Wolseley was influenced heavily by Shepstone and he respected the older man's long dealings with the native tribes. In his letters and journal he thus followed the line of the Secretary for Native Affairs that the barbarity of Cetshwayo's reign was a 'disgrace to humanity'. Wolseley hoped for a war between the Zulus and the Boers, since it might destroy Cetshwayo while also weakening the Transvaal financially and making its inhabitants possibly more amenable to Carnarvon's confederation scheme. Shepstone told Wolseley that

1,000 British soldiers would be enough to defeat the Zulus, an estimate he, in turn, quoted in a letter to Carnarvon. This grave error possibly encouraged the sanguine attitude of the Colonial Office when the Zulu War loomed. During his travels Wolseley met several Zulus and thought them a people superior to the Boers: 'The pure low Zulu, although very low down in the order of humanity as regards the arts and sciences, has many fine traits about him, and he is an acute reasoner and indeed I may say that he is a philosopher.'[18]

Back in London and relieved to be home, Sir Garnet returned to his War Office duties. He was then offered a seat on the India Council to give advice on the Cardwell reforms in India. The war scare engendered by events in the Balkans led to an announcement in February 1878 that Lord Napier of Magdala would lead an expeditionary force that might be sent to fight Russia. The public enthusiastically accepted Wolseley as his second-in-command. Behind closed doors there was little affection between the two men; they had served together in India and China, it was true, but Napier, an old school officer, thought Wolseley was insolent to those in higher authority. This was, in fact, the case, as he maliciously opined that his lordship could not read a map and did not know the Dardanelles from the Bosphorus.

That summer the Congress of Berlin ended the talk of war. Not long after, as described in the prologue, Wolseley was sent as first British administrator to Cyprus. The war correspondent, Archibald Forbes, a tough old boot who had reported on the Franco-Prussian and Balkan Wars, accompanied the general and his staff. The team had been hurriedly assembled, yet they 'met, blended and set to work in the saloon carriage between Dover and Calais, as if … they had been co-operating for years, wrote Forbes, 'While they settled minor points of detail their chief slept serenely, easy in the perfect assurance, based on experience, that his subordinates would deal with these as he would desire they would be dealt with.'[19]

With dramatic events taking place in Afghanistan during the autumn of 1878 and dark clouds forming over Zululand it was not surprising that these two theatres of war were on everyone's lips at Government House, Cyprus. During a ride in the pine forests of Mount Olympus on 23 January 1879, scouting the site for a sanatorium, all the talk was of war, but Wolseley summed up his own position: 'I have put my hand to the Cypriot plough and must hold it until the furrow is finished.' Sir Garnet's comrade, Major William Butler, was a house guest in Cyprus for a few weeks and he recorded this remark in his autobiography, adding: 'But at that moment when we were cantering along the track that early morning the remnants of Lord Chelmsford's main column on invasion were moving out of the wrecked camp at Isandula [sic] in Zululand, and the commotion which was to follow the disaster was destined to move us all to South Africa a few months later.'[20] In a letter to his mother, dated 26 January, Sir Garnet recalled the same few days in the mountains rather differently: 'To walk a long distance over hard frozen snow ... after all the baking I have endured during the past hot season was a really enjoyable sensation.' Next day, matters of personal finance worried him as always; he told sister Matilda that 'as long as I am in Cyprus I shall be well-off' and this rare sense of well-being made providing for his mother 'an intense pleasure', but at the same time younger brother Fred, who had a stupid habit of investing in bad schemes, had written asking for a loan of £3,000 (about £250,000 in today's money). Sir Garnet agreed to the request and told his wiser brother Dick, an army surgeon, that Fred now owed him £8,500 and 'that damned fool, George', youngest of the clan and a spendthrift officer, had borrowed a further £1,800. He worried what would happen to all the family, including himself, if his health ever broke down. Despite these fears he assured his mother, 'You only have to write to me at any time for money ... please afford me the satisfaction of feeling that I can be of some little use to you.'[21]

According to Hugh McCalmont his chief 'never said a word' about Isandlwana, although 'I knew that he also was pining to be at this new seat of war.'[22] News of the disaster did not reach Cyprus until 18 February. That same day Wolseley fired off a letter to Lord Salisbury at the Foreign Office. With a mixture of cunning and tact he did not suggest openly that he should supersede Chelmsford, yet he clearly intended to cultivate the idea in Salisbury's mind. He wrote as an expert on Zululand and advised that military operations should not be undertaken before the start of May and ought to cease by 10 September. He warned that if the war was conducted 'in Horse Guards practice the result may be a failure'. Then he dropped into his memo something he knew would make economy-minded politicians like Salisbury sit up and think – the war was going to be very costly. Taking a swipe at Napier's Abyssinian Expedition, which cost £9,500,000, Sir Garnet said:

> To carry on a war as we did in Abyssinia with an utterly reckless disregard to public expenditure is a simple process for the General employed, but it is an unwarrantable extravagance … of course when it is a question between failure and success, England can never pay too much to avoid the former, but she may, I think, pay too highly to secure the latter.[23]

Eight days later an impatient Wolseley offered his services to the War Office. 'If required I could at any time reach Natal from Cyprus sooner than anyone could get there from England,' he told Cambridge, 'and as I know the people and country well, I think I might be of use.'[24] The letter went unanswered. With his old comrades Wolseley was outspoken in pointing a finger of blame; he told John Maurice in a February letter that he was 'lost in astonishment at the folly of the Government allowing the command to fall into Crealock's hands and I have now made up my mind that nothing short of a miracle can possibly save the Government. They will be wrecked on the Zulu rock ...'[25]

Ignored by the authorities, Wolseley told his mother on 4 March, 'This Cape news is deplorable. I have been longing to receive a telegram ordering me there, but I fear I am doomed to civil work in Cyprus.'[26] By the end of the month Hugh McCalmont noted, 'Sir Garnet has been living on the hope for the last few days of being sent to Natal, and I think the anxiety is almost too much for him sometimes.'[27] March passed into April and Wolseley was forced to accept his quiet posting. A lawn tennis match for a prize of 100 cigars continued his run of ill-luck; Sir Garnet, a keen player, lost seven games to twelve to McCalmont, a complete novice at the sport. He admitted in a letter to his mother on 23 April that 'hope has died in me of being sent to the Cape'. Gloomily he predicted, 'The Zulu War will be a long one that will most probably kill the present Government in the end.'[28]

To relax his nerves Wolseley went off on a picnic on Sunday 27 April amid the green hills of Kyrenia, their peaks crowned with ethereal castles. One can imagine his joy on returning from the romantic hills to find a cypher telegram which requested him to return to London and report to the War Office. The naval dispatch boat placed at his disposal was appropriately named the *Surprise*. Next morning Sir Garnet replied that he would leave on 12 May. 'I had a sneaking hope that I might never have to return to Cyprus,' he wrote, 'but I tried to dissuade myself from building on this hope,' since 'Loo' 'was quite confident ... we should never go back there'.[29] The Wolseleys had all their belongings packed away, the bulk to follow after them. Temporarily, George Greaves was placed in command of the island. At 4.20 a.m. on 12 May Sir Garnet, Louisa, Hugh McCalmont and Arthur Creagh (the general's young nephew and acting ADC, son of his sister, Matilda) set off on horseback, the servants and Frances following in a carriage. At Larnaca the party boarded HMS *Salamis* to Brindisi, then travelled overland to Paris and, after 48 hours rest, leaving his wife and child to follow on, Wolseley took the boat-train for London, arriving on the morning of 21 May.

That May the whole country seemed focused on the Zulu War, and not just in the newspapers and Parliament: the Prince and Princess of Wales had attended a concert on 7 May at the Gaiety Theatre in aid of the Isandlwana Fund (it raised about £40,000 by today's standards); a large-scale military extravaganza was held at the Albert Hall on the 12th also attended by the Prince of Wales in aid of the Zulu War Relief Fund; the Duke of Cambridge was patron of a morning concert on 15 May to raise funds for widows and orphans of those who fell at Isandlwana and Rorke's Drift; the great Baptist minister, Charles Haddon Spurgeon, preached at the Metropolitan Tabernacle, and even made the Zulus the subject of one of his May sermons. Similar events were taking place up and down the country.

The official reason for Sir Garnet's recall was that he had been chosen to serve on a committee intended to evaluate the short service system and its relation to small wars such as the one in Zululand. Wolseley confessed in his journal to 'an inkling' that this might happen before he had left Cyprus, but he clearly hoped that while in London he might be asked to go out to South Africa. Within hours he was at the Foreign Office talking with Salisbury and that evening dined at the home of Sir Stafford Northcote, Chancellor of the Exchequer. Here Sir Garnet met once again his nemesis, the Duke of Cambridge, who was 'very cordial and very tipsy'. It was, by all accounts, a socially relaxed evening, and Wolseley was teased about his Cyprus sun tan.

Next morning Sir Garnet went to see Colonel Stanley at the War Office, but found him delayed at a Cabinet meeting. While waiting to see the Secretary-of-State he had a long discussion of current events with a man he disliked very much: Sir Charles Ellice, Adjutant-General, one of the Duke's old cronies and a man viewed by Wolseley as his rival for the plum of C-in-C, India, an appointment due for renewal in 1881. Ellice gossiped that he thought Sir Garnet ought to be sent to South Africa and that HMG was that day trying to decide whether to send him or Lord Napier. Displaying his usual conceit, Wolseley replied that, 'If that is the case, I am the man, for they will never send old Napier.' Matters turned to the disasters in Zululand, and on being asked his opinion Sir Garnet bluntly stated that Lord Chelmsford was 'unfit for such an important command' and if it had been up to him the general would have been recalled 'at once' after Isandlwana. Sir Charles then intimated that he and others at Horse Guards 'had backed up the Duke in backing up Chelmsford,' Wolseley wrote later, 'and he gave me to understand that it was entirely Horse Guards influences that had saved him from being recalled.'[30]

When Wolseley saw Stanley the truth came out at last: he was told in the 'strictest confidence' that it had been decided in Cabinet that morning to send him to Natal 'with full civil and military powers'. He was to go 'at once' if possible, but the matter was to stay top secret until the Prime Minister personally discussed it with him. When the Duke of Cambridge barged in during the middle of their conversation, Stanley and Wolseley changed the subject. Prince George was to be kept in the dark.

Heading towards the telegraph office to cable 'Loo' the great news, a very cheerful Wolseley bumped into Monty Corry, the Prime Minister's young and energetic private secretary, who had just been to his lodgings looking for him. Lord Beaconsfield wanted to see Wolseley immediately and so the pair drove hurriedly to Downing Street. In a letter to his brother, Dick, written next day, Sir Garnet explained:

> I had a long interview with Lord Beaconsfield yesterday but he did not tell me what was in store for me. I believe he knew I was in the secret but made no allusion to it, confining himself to pumping me & compliments & asking my advice & opinion etc etc. This etiquette is for nothing to be said until the Queen's orders have been obtained & she is in Scotland,

> so a messenger had I presume to be sent to her there & an answer may not be obtained for another 24 hours.[31]

At last, on 23 May, Sir Garnet was reunited with his wife and daughter, but as the family no longer had a London house they were forced to stay in a West End hotel. Wolseley had already telegraphed 'Loo' that 'my desire had been fulfilled' but, as he told brother Dick, he had left all his campaign kit in Cyprus, 'so now I have to fit myself out afresh. The expense is heavy but it cannot be helped.'[32]

That morning Sir Garnet finally had to face the Duke of Cambridge to discuss military affairs. The duke still knew nothing about Wolseley's new appointment and one can imagine how Sir Garnet must have felt knowing that at any minute the news might leak out. To make matters worse, Cambridge began by asking him why Chelmsford might have embarked on such a faulty plan of campaign. Wolseley was at his most diplomatic in replying as he explained in his journal: 'The subject was a delicate one as I knew … & it was not my business to find fault with the strategy or tactics of a commander who had been selected by the C. in C.'[33] (This journal entry is representative of Wolseley's Janus-like qualities since he had, in fact, both privately to family and friends, publicly to people like Salisbury and Ellice, been finding fault with Chelmsford ever since news of Isandlwana).

Moving on to what Cambridge still thought was Wolseley's reason for returning home, the duke lambasted him with a furious attack on the short service system. Cardwell's reforms, he declared, had left the army 'utterly inefficient', and he lectured Sir Garnet with some glee: 'My good man, the short service system has broken down and we must alter the law so that we may in future keep men with the colours for eight years …' When finally given a chance to reply Wolseley went into attack mode:

> You, sir, tell me the army is completely inefficient at this present moment; you know you have already a small but very

> efficient reserve, and yet you would propose measures for breaking it up. If your proposals are accepted what will be the result, why, if next year we have a real war thrust upon us, we shall have neither Army nor Reserve. The responsibility for such a condition of things will be very great for it may destroy the nation.[34]

The two men parted, thought Sir Garnet, on 'fairly good terms', though he was riled, as always, by Cambridge's constant abuse of Cardwell's system, '& declaring it has broken down when ... it has never been fairly and honestly tried, and tried it can never be as long as the present authorities are at the Horse Gds'. That night he dined with a small elite party – Salisbury, Stanley, their wives and the Prime Minister – but still 'Dizzy' made no mention at all of a South African appointment.

Though Cambridge and Wolseley did not know it, that same afternoon Lord Beaconsfield had informed the Queen of Wolseley's new command. The result for a few days was to be a rearguard action fought by Queen Victoria on behalf of Chelmsford and Frere against a Prime Minister who stubbornly held on to his position. Beaconsfield's 'startling telegram', as the Queen called it, arrived at Balmoral while she was out for a drive. She telegraphed on her return: 'I will not withhold my *sanction* though I cannot *approve* it.' The measure would, Her Majesty argued, 'lead to the immediate resignation of both Sir Bartle Frere & Ld. Chelmsford. This I would deeply deplore ...' Guessing that the Cabinet had ignored the views of her favourite cousin, she asked, 'Has the Commander-in-Chief been consulted?' Finally: 'Why is Sir Garnet Wolseley considered the most fit person? He is not likely to be conciliatory.'[35]

To placate his Sovereign the Prime Minister wrote a long letter on 23 May explaining in more detail his decision to send Sir Garnet to the Cape: the Cabinet, he argued, were alarmed by recent despatches suggesting 'dissensions' between Bulwer and

Chelmsford, 'private information' suggested that 'several members of the staff were not on speaking terms' and the 'disheartened condition of the troops' was approaching 'demoralization'. 'Dizzy' tried to soothe the Queen's temper by pointing out that neither Chelmsford nor Frere were being recalled. Colonel Stanley, backing up his chief, also wrote the same day telling Her Majesty that Chelmsford was 'vague in his demands, admits his want of knowledge of the Zulu country & apparently is on bad terms with the Colonial Government.'[36] These two letters arrived on the Queen's breakfast table in the red despatch boxes on 24 May – Her Majesty's 60th birthday. She had by now contacted Cambridge and her ill-temper continued as she condemned the Government for its reliance 'on information derived from private sources, a course which I never think desirable ...'

The Queen's irritations were amplified at St James's Palace that day when the Duke of Cambridge in a choleric rage talked over the news with his mother and their friend, Lady Geraldine Somerset. The Wolseley cat was now out of the bag. Lady Geraldine in her diary noted how the duke 'plainly saw that they are determined to send Wolseley out to the Cape!! We had a long discussion about him and the *danger* of him! and his being at the bottom of the whole Cardwell system!!'[37]

Sunday 26 May passed and Sir Garnet still had not received any confirmation from Whitehall. He started to have his own doubts: 'Knowing Dizzy to be such a Courtier I was afraid he might give way if the Queen strongly objected to my superseding Chelmsford & I know I am represented to Her as a fiend who should be kept down if possible.'[38] It was during the afternoon of 26 May that Wolseley finally got his marching orders. Summoned to Downing Street, he arrived late (having had to change his clothes after a Royal Levee), and found the Prime Minister 'rather cross'. Explaining that Sir Garnet would have supreme command in South Africa, Beaconsfield asked how soon he could leave?

Wolseley replied that he would go whenever the Prime Minister wished and the pair agreed on 29 May. Beaconsfield immediately set off for the House of Lords to tell Parliament (Northcote doing the same in the Commons).

The new South African supremo was thus given barely seventy-two hours to make his preparations. He was delighted to see the next morning that the press was full of compliments. *Punch* was typical of the mood with a piece of doggerel:

> When Wolseley's mentioned, Wellesley's brought to mind;
> Two men, two names, of answerable kind;
> Call to the front, like Wellesley, good at need,
> Go Wolseley, and like Wellesley, greatly speed.[39]

The above verse might have tickled Sir Garnet with its allusions to Wellington, but the comparison between his beloved Iron Duke and the arch-reformer would have brought on a stroke if read by Cambridge! The C-in-C met Wolseley on the morning of 27 May and the duke was very put out to find that the general had already cabled India for the services of a damned ring member, Colonel George Colley, as his chief of staff. The duke had hoped Wolseley might accept Major-General Hugh Clifford V.C., an old Crimean War veteran who was already serving in South Africa, a man he considered a safe pair of hands (Wolseley had served under Clifford twenty-five years earlier and respected him, but Colley was almost his ideal soldier).

The Queen continued to try and create difficulties. Her temper, or so it seemed, had actually worsened. Colonel Stanley was forced to telegraph her about Wolseley's letter of service making him a full general (so that he could outrank Chelmsford). In reply the Secretary-of-State for War 'got a sharp rap over the knuckles from Her Majesty for making these arrangements in such a hurry'.[40] Queen Victoria had already protested Wolseley's appointment in a telegram to Beaconsfield and also in a long letter defending both Chelmsford and Frere. The Prime Minister had to choose his words carefully in reply, but told Her Majesty that the Cabinet unanimously adhered to its earlier decisions. They also urged 'the appointment of Sir G. Wolseley instead of Lord Napier; among other grounds, on his local experience of the scene of war ... It was with much difficulty that Lord Beaconsfield secured the arrangement that Sir Bartle Frere should remain as High Commissioner of the Cape Colony & its dependencies ... No one upheld Lord Chelmsford.'[41] The Queen's normal good humour was restored somewhat by a letter from Hicks Beach pointing out that it was Frere himself who had requested a new general with both civil and military powers. After reading this letter the Queen noted in her diary on 28 May, 'Lord Chelmsford seems not to be up to the mark.' Disraeli felt exhausted by six major Cabinet meetings in eight days alongside the difficulties of dealing with his Sovereign. 'Sir Garnet Wolseley goes to S. Africa and goes tomorrow night,' he told Lady Chesterfield on 28 May, 'though between ourselves the Horse Guards are furious, the Princes all raging and every mediocrity as jealous as if we had prevented him from conquering the world.'[42]

It was true that the Cabinet had discussed sending Lord Napier of Magdala out to South Africa with Wolseley as his deputy. This was certainly what the Duke of Cambridge wanted. Napier himself was not keen to go and strongly objected to 'taking away part of the authority' of his much respected old India friend, Frere. Nor did he wish to supersede Chelmsford who had been his Adjutant-General in India (ironically the post once considered for Wolseley). According to his biographer, Napier opined that, 'it was not fair to supersede a General on a first reverse'.[43]

Sir Garnet started his last day in Britain by rising early and attending to his correspondence. He had not been able to get down to Eastbourne and say farewell to his mother, but now wrote to say, 'I am at least spared the great pain I always experience in bidding you goodbye.'[44] These partings before each of Garnet's campaigns had special significance for mother and son; both found the experience an emotional one, and as the future general shipped out of harbour in 1854 heading to the Crimea he never forgot the sight of his mother quietly sobbing on the quayside. He told her that grandson Arthur Creagh, a twenty-four-year-old subaltern in the Royal Artillery, had lost all his money on the journey through Italy. The boy was 'stupid' and Sir Garnet had told his sister Matilda in a letter six days previously to 'wake him up'. Arthur was now with him and would go out to South Africa as an ADC. He hoped the campaign might turn him into 'a polished gentleman' after the raffish crowd he had mixed with in India. Combining his typical mix of criticism and good humour, Wolseley admitted that Arthur was 'the best tempered young fellow I have ever met', though 'Loo' thought him 'plain lazy'.

At Gloucester House the new South African commander took his leave of the C-in-C. It was not a pleasant meeting; Cambridge was not at all happy with the free hand Stanley had given Wolseley in choosing his staff as well as the men he had asked for as special service officers. Parting from Louisa at their Hanover Square hotel was, as always, a great strain. 'Each time I say good bye to her takes off at least a year from the time I am to be in this world … the strain is so great upon my heart,'[45] he wrote in his journal.

Most of his staff and special service officers had also assembled at Paddington on the evening of 29 May to take a special overnight train to their ship at Dartmouth. Hugh McCalmont had rushed home to Ireland, quickly packed his things, and was now there with the others. 'We got a great send-off,' he recalled. 'There were swarms of people of note on the platform … Sir Michael Hicks Beach, the Colonial Secretary, travelled in the saloon carriage with the Chief as far as Didcot, and as we steamed out of the station there was great cheering and hat-waving.'[46] There were big crowds on platforms even up to 2 a.m. Sir Garnet tried to snatch some sleep in his private carriage but in the saloon car a boisterous crowd of officers led by McCalmont, who was a capital practical joker, hit upon the idea of dressing up one of the special service officers, Major Henry Bushman, 9th Lancers, in a helmet and with a pillow under his cloak to give him the appearance of an enormous stomach. Sword drawn and bowing, Bushman was cheered by the crowds who mistook him for Wolseley, much to his comrades' amusement. Encouraged by this adoration, Bushman plucked up the courage at one station to stick his head out of the window and make a speech promising to sort out the Zulus and reduce the tax on tobacco! McCalmont 'never laughed so much ... What Sir Garnet was thinking of all this time I don't know, but no one could have slept within half a mile of our carriage.'[47]

Wolseley actually listened to much of the cheering but as usual at the start of one of his campaigns his egotism was marbled by self-doubt. He found adoration 'all very flattering', but realised that 'popularity is easily obtained, easily lost and should be taken at its face value'.[48]

While Wolseley tried to rest and his staff made high cockalorum in their carriage we might, for a moment, take final stock of our man. He is forty-five years old, happily married with a six-year-old daughter. Friends generally think him handsome with clean-cut features, five foot nine with prematurely greying hair and a chestnut moustache. Most people note his 'penetrating blue eyes' though he is blind in the right one. In public his persona is invariably all smiles and charm; Evelyn Wood thought his chief characteristics were 'a cheery optimism and his pleasant, unpretentious manners ...' Elizabeth Butler, the military artist and wife of William Butler, then serving in Natal, said that as a child she had met Charles Dickens and only ever heard one man use the same distinct and hearty laugh – Garnet Wolseley. George Greaves at the time of the Ashanti War described him as 'a man free from nerves, with clear, penetrating, observant blue eyes, light frame and brisk, active step' with a 'strong but suave voice ...' Wolseley has his critics, not least the old school officers led by the Duke of Cambridge who have labelled him 'that cocksure young bookworm', conceited, pushy and reform-mad. The truth is that the new Zulu War commander is a mass of contradictions: a snob who is self-made and claims to hate snobs; a courageous man who fears he would faint at the sight of a flogging; an egotist but not a noisy braggart; a man willing to give interviews and write articles yet calls war correspondents 'those newly invented curses to armies, who eat the rations of fighting men and do no work at all ...';[49] a determined army reformer, but one who considers himself a Tory and a 'Jingo of the Jingoes'; a fellow of immense charm, seemingly sure of himself, who manages to control his psychological stresses only by pouring out his innermost thoughts on paper in confidential journals where application of the pen rather than the sword can free his mind of jealousies and recriminations – real and imagined – hurt pride, spite, fear and boastful plans. Perhaps it is Sir Garnet's detached manner, or an effortless superiority concerning military facts and figures that have prevented any deep cult of personality developing in the way it would around Frederick Roberts, whose mystique and fame would soon grow to eclipse Wolseley's. But those who work closely with him simply adore the man despite all his faults. 'The best and most brilliant brain I have ever met in the British Army,' is William Butler's estimation, adding that he was 'the only man I ever met in the army on whom command sat so easily and fitly that neither he nor the men he commanded had ever to think about it ...'[50]

This, then, is the man setting out to supersede Chelmsford in South Africa. Hicks Beach had given him a letter setting forth his final instructions. The most important passage read:

> There appears some reason to hope that the evidence which has been given of the power of Her Majesty's forces may have disposed the Zulus to submission. And it will be your

> first duty on arrival ... to encourage any *bona fide* proposals which may afford a reasonable prospect of a satisfactory peace ... You will carefully bear in mind that the object of Her Majesty's Government is not to add to the extent of the British possessions adjoining Zululand, but to relieve them from the danger to which they have hitherto been exposed ... The detailed arrangements by which that policy may best be carried into effect can only be properly matured by you after full consideration of the circumstances which may exist on your arrival in Natal.[51]

Wolseley thus had complete authority to negotiate a peace settlement. The British Government expected him to do this as soon as possible and Zululand was not to be annexed (thus finally ending any dreams of a South African Confederation), though how the country was to be divided or settled was left for him to work out.

No doubt while tossing these thoughts around in his head Sir Garnet was disturbed from his slumber in the middle of the night by a farcical situation when a retired general, Sir William Olpherts, clambered aboard the train and begged to be allowed to join the expedition. He was known throughout the army as 'Hellfire Jack' because of his strong language and hot temper. Wolseley had served with 'Billy' Olpherts at the Siege of Lucknow where the eccentric campaigner had won a Victoria Cross. It was not until Captain Dunn of the SS *Edinburgh Castle* talked with old Billy that he was finally prevented from boarding the ship. Sir Garnet felt rather sorry because Olpherts, while 'a madman', was also 'the bravest of the brave', the kind of man, mused Wolseley, who would have been of much use as a captain in his forthcoming campaign but was of no value at all as a lieutenant-general.

At noon on 30 May the *Edinburgh Castle* steamed out of Dartmouth harbour, 'black with people, all cheering like mad'. Just before departure Wolseley dashed off a very personal letter to Louisa, the contents of which demonstrate his own sensitivity: 'What a brave little woman you are and how *manfully* you bore up all yesterday & indeed may I say ever since the news arrived that I was to leave for the Cape. My own throat & eyes were very full as I said goodbye to you & I had to stay in the little dining-room a little before appearing before the public downstairs ... Tell Frances that I hope to bring home a lock of Cetewayo's hair which I shall put in a locket for her.'[52]

Four days later it was Sir Garnet's birthday and the couple's twelfth wedding anniversary. He wrote to Louisa, 'I am 46 years old today – what an old buffer.' The voyage had so far been a nasty one, 'the ship rolling about like a dolphin'. Despite some early feelings of sea-sickness he was quite well, helped by having his cabin on the main deck, 'which is very pleasant'. That same day, 4 June, Wolseley told his brother Dick in a letter that the Duke of Cambridge was 'furious' at his appointment:

> It was he, and those about him, who kept Lord C. in his place, as they knew that if he was recalled I was to have been sent to replace him & anything's better than that. They positively hate me & persuaded the Queen that I am a low Radical who wishes to upset everything. Anyone who opposes H.R.H. she regards as a rebel – foolish old man! He might do so much good, for he is very clever and has a position that no C-in-C coming after him can ever hope to occupy.

Bluntly the new supremo told his brother that Chelmsford's plan of campaign 'was opposed to every principle of war and the manner in which he proceeded to carry it out was in defiance of every rule and precaution which the youngest Ensign is grounded in'. The future lay uncertain. 'God knows I may possibly do as badly,' concluded Sir Garnet, 'I cannot, however, do worse.'[53]

3

GENERALS IN THE KITCHEN

Too many cooks spoil the pudding.

Lieutenant Henry Curling

While Sir Garnet, his staff and special service officers were being tossed about like corks in the stormy waters of the Bay of Biscay, an event was taking place in a muddy donga in Zululand that was to cement opinion (if any more proof were needed) that the war truly was, as journalist Archibald Forbes termed it, 'miserable and luckless'. On the afternoon of 1 June, while out scouting with a small patrol, the Prince Imperial of France, twenty-three-year-old Napoleon Eugene Louis Jean Joseph Bonaparte, heir to a great dynasty and name, sole son and heir of the late Emperor Napoleon III and the Empress Eugenie, was killed fighting Zulus. He died bravely facing his foes, firing his revolver before being speared to death. Matters were made worse by the fact that the officer commanding the patrol, Lieutenant Jaheel Carey, 98th Regiment, had apparently ridden off leaving the young Frenchman to his fate.

A staff officer found Lord Chelmsford in 'a state of absolute despair' after he got the news. Back in Britain the press and society went into hysterics; bad enough that the last of the Napoleonic line should die in a British colonial war, but he did so wearing the uniform of the Royal Artillery (ostensibly the Prince was simply an 'observer' in South Africa, but he had pestered the Duke of Cambridge who asked Chelmsford to find him some duties to perform, nothing too hazardous of course). The Prime Minister was appalled; referring harshly to the Prince Imperial as 'that little abortion', Beaconsfield was 'mystified' how a 'mere traveller' was allowed on such an 'adventure'. 'I did all I could to stop his going,' a pained Disraeli told one of his correspondents. Then, thinking of the Queen and her bosom friend, the boy's mother, he added, 'But what can you do when you have to deal with two obstinate women?'[1] The Foreign Secretary, Lord Salisbury, had recently told another Cabinet member, 'Oh! that Bartle Frere, I should like to construct for him a gibbet.' Now he wrote to Beaconsfield of the Prince Imperial tragedy, 'I am puzzled as you are. Every way it seems to me a mistake.'[2]

During that first week of June this latest South African tragedy was unknown to everyone outside South Africa. It was to be another nail in the coffin of Chelmsford's generalship. Indeed, when he got the news, the Duke of Cambridge seemed more appalled by the loss of 'the poor dear gallant young fellow' than he was by the disaster at Isandlwana. Painfully unaware of how things were proceeding in Zululand, Sir Garnet spent his time aboard ship reading Parliamentary bluebooks and starting a journal, which he commenced at Madeira. The voyage gave him ample time to observe the foibles of his officers. His impatience to get to the seat of war meant that Wolseley recorded their idiosyncrasies with a caustic eye.

Travelling aboard the *Edinburgh Castle* with the general were twelve military men – four staff officers and eight special service officers. The civilians on board were his private secretary, a manservant and one war correspondent. The officers were led by brevet-Lieutenant-Colonel Henry Brackenbury who had served Wolseley in the same capacity as military secretary in the Ashanti War and acted as his private secretary during the 1875 Natal trip.

No pen portrait of Brackenbury can equal that of Joseph Lehmann who described him thus:

> In uniform he appeared to be a businessman in disguise. In or out of uniform, he was ugly: with a pasty yellow face, an unkempt black moustache, and bulbous nose, which Lady Wolseley – who detested him – described as looking like a squashed strawberry. She and others were annoyed by the disgusting way he had of clearing his throat loudly. His sonorous, informing voice was clothed in the comical 'haw-haw' accent of the Victorian 'swell' – a lisp, usually affected, sometimes real, by which 'r's' were pronounced as 'w's'. Hence 'Brack' would describe the Rifles as 'weahwing gween jackets'. Out of his mouth his own name became 'Whackenbaywe'. His lisping conversation was interspersed with a hectoring or exclamatory 'haw, haw'.[3]

Wolseley once described 'Brack' as 'the cleverest man in the British Army' and Sir Henry's biographer has called him 'the thinking man's soldier'. Some contemporaries found him to be 'arrogant' and 'sarcastic'; the gossipy Ian Hamilton, a soldier with a penchant for making cruel remarks, called him 'the most competent administrator in our Army', but added that 'he hated live soldiers ... He had never worked with soldiers; never kept in touch with them; always tried to keep out of cannon-shot range of them ...'[4] Brackenbury's fame rests comfortably on army reform, so it would be wrong to read too much into Hamilton's spite; he had seen his fair share of fighting as a twenty-year-old officer serving with the Saugor Field Force during the Indian Mutiny. The gruesome sight of good soldiers killed by sun-stroke, as a result of inadequate equipment, haunted Brackenbury for the rest of his career and helps explain his zeal as a reforming organiser. On the way to Kumasi in 1874 he was one of two officers who led the frontal assault on the Ashantis at Essaman and he stood beside Wolseley in the thick of it at the hard-fought battle at Amoaful. Now in Zululand Sir Garnet would make full use of this intellectual powerhouse who, as one of his assistants in the intelligence branch wrote a few years later, had an 'almost uncanny power of getting at the root of a complicated matter in a word or a question or two ...'[5]

Three ADCs accompanied Wolseley: one was his twenty-four-year-old happy-go-lucky nephew, Lieutenant Arthur Gethin Creagh R.A.; another was Captain E. L. Braithwaite, Highland Light Infantry; and the third was a longtime ring member, brevet-Major Hugh McCalmont. A great practical joker, scion of a rich Irish landowning family, McCalmont shines as a perfect example of the rich, brave, but none-too-bright officers who formed the backbone of the mid-Victorian army. He once set off a naval maroon rocket under a table while the Queen's military-minded son, the Duke of Connaught, was playing whist (the explosion destroyed the table, broke windows and a mirror and filled the room with smoke). Since McCalmont was also with Connaught when their boat sank going over Maidstone Weir, everyone having to swim to shore (he also once accidentally hit the royal prince in the face with an orange), one suspects Prince Arthur was rather glad to get away from his company. As a youth Hugh was delighted when he was rejected as too dim for university. He bought himself a cornetcy in the 9th Lancers and spent much time riding to hounds. Bored by such pursuits, he duly found his way to Canada in 1870 and presented himself to Wolseley with a letter of introduction from Sir Hope Grant. Sir Garnet was amused to read this wiry scamp had been his old commander's accompanist on the piano when Grant played his cello! McCalmont's Eton wet bob skills were put to use in the campaign and he was given the signal honour of bringing home the Red River despatches. He only got so far as St Paul, Minnesota when, by his own admission, he made 'a bad blunder' and dropped the important documents into a United States mailbox. The C-in-C, Canada, was furious and Wolseley none too pleased either. His punishment was to be passed over for promotion; by the time of the Cyprus expedition Sir Garnet had forgiven him. Now in South Africa McCalmont was praying he might see some fighting, since witnessing real warfare, apart from a visit to the Russo-Turkish War, had so far eluded him.

The special service officers were Major Henry Bushman, 9th Lancers, Captain Francis Doyle, a son of one of Wolseley's old Canadian comrades, Captain John Maurice, Royal Artillery (R.A.), Captain A. M. Patterson, 16th Regiment, Major Baker Russell, 13th Hussars, Major Webber, Royal Engineers, Major the Hon. Henry Wood, 10th Hussars, and Captain Arthur Yeatman-Biggs R.A. Of this bunch the stand-outs were Bushman, Maurice, Russell and Yeatman-Biggs. It was Bushman who had been the joker on the first night of the expedition impersonating Wolseley; he had been in his regiment for twenty years and was just due for promotion if he stayed at home, but managed to convince his commanding officer to grant him two months leave.

Bushman's long regimental association was rivalled by big, burly Baker Russell, one of Sir Garnet's favourite fighting soldiers, who had joined the 13th Hussars in 1862 and would be linked so closely with them as commander that as their fame grew as a light cavalry regiment, they became known throughout the British Army as 'the Baker's dozen'. Robert Baden-Powell, who served as a junior officer in the 13th Hussars, described Russell as 'the beau ideal of a fighting leader'. He had been born in Australia in 1837 and first saw action during the Indian Mutiny. In Ashanti a frustrated Wolseley exclaimed that Russell was 'rather impetuous & does not obey orders as strictly as I should like when he is near the enemy', but he admired the man's fighting skills.[6] On a parade ground Russell bawled out his orders in a voice that could have waken the dead. Indeed, with his fierce eyes and a huge moustache he much resembled a grumpy old wild boar; famous for his hatred of red tape, a War Office clerk once rejected one of his expense forms as the distance was measured 'as the crow flies', to which Russell in a stentorian voice thundered back, 'I do not ride a crow, sir! I ride a horse!' He cared little for the drill-book and had an instinctive soldier's eye for where his men should be in a fight. Russell used to tell his officers that it was a cavalryman's duty 'to look smart in peace and to get killed in war'.

John Frederick Maurice was the thirty-eight-year-old son of social reformer John Denison Maurice. It was his essay on field manoeuvres that had won him a special prize at the Staff College and got him noticed by Wolseley. Four years later he was invited to serve as his private secretary in West Africa. Sir Garnet thought him 'the worst man of business I ever had to deal with. He is like a woman, never on time,'but he found the studious eccentric to also be 'a real good fellow' who nursed him through a bout of malaria.[7]

Two years younger than Maurice was Arthur Godolphin Yeatman-Biggs. His father was a Wiltshire landowner who had hoped his boy would become a lawyer, but Arthur opted instead, like Maurice and Creagh, for the Royal Artillery. He joined in 1860, the youngest officer in the Queen's service, and within months was wounded in China at the storming of the Taku Forts. He remained in China for another two years, fighting Chinese rebels, befriending Wolseley's hero, 'Chinese' Gordon. Peacetime soldiering had occupied Yeatman-Biggs ever since and now he was thirsting to prove himself.

Completing the team was a smooth-faced, Canadian-born civilian, Algernon St Leger Herbert. This twenty-eight-year-old, known as 'Sankey' to his friends, was a likeable young man described by Brackenbury as 'handsome as a young Greek god'. He was the son of a naval commander and a grandson of the 1st Earl of Carnarvon (the Permanent Under-Secretary-of-State at the Colonial Office, Sir Robert Herbert, was also his uncle). From 1875–78 'Sankey' had been private secretary to the Governor-General of Canada, Lord Dufferin, then acted as Wolseley's secretary on Cyprus. A scholar of Wadham College, Oxford, Herbert fancied himself as a writer and represented *The Times* as a correspondent in South Africa.

The most important component of Wolseley's ring as far as the general was concerned did not sail with him because he was travelling from India. This was George Colley, whom Wolseley wanted as his second-in-command, but was forced to accept only as chief of staff. The argument over Colley's appointment began even before the ship had sailed. General Horsford, the duke's military secretary, had written on 29 May to say that Colley could only be designated a 'Colonel on the Staff'. A furious Wolseley wrote straightaway to Stanley apologising 'that I have to begin my campaign with a complaint ... I am no sooner "got rid of" than the arrangement to which I understood H.R.H. had no objection that Col. Colley was to be given the rank of Brig. Genl. has been upset.' Sir Garnet insisted he was 'not working for my private ends in asking for this rank ...' He was willing to accept (he added with a note of sarcasm) the duke's 'superior wisdom in this matter', but since Colley would have to deal with a 'dearth of generals' in South Africa, it would 'be desirable to push him up the ladder'.[8] Next Sir Garnet sent Horsford a flea in his ear: he called the letter he had received 'a mistake' and said he could not accept a lower rank for Colley than brigadier-general. To make his point plainly he concluded, 'I am very very sorry that it has been decided to depart from the arrangements which I understood yesterday H.R.H. raised no objection to; and that the decision was not communicated to me before I left town.'[9] With Stanley's backing Wolseley was able to secure for Colley the temporary rank of brigadier-general but lost the battle to have him confirmed as second in command. Cambridge would not budge from his belief that Major-General Sir Henry Clifford V.C. ought to be. He defended his view with the words that 'no army could stand these sorts of preferences without entirely dampening the energies of senior officers.'[10] The issue was still unresolved at the end of June when Wolseley wrote to the duke, 'I cannot say too much for the earnest zeal of General Clifford ... he should be given a commission as second-in-command to succeed me in the event of my being shot; that is always supposing that H.M.Government is not disposed to promote Colonel Colley to that position.'[11]

In Ashanti no man had impressed Wolseley quite so much as thirty-nine-year-old Colley. He had passed out of the Staff College in just ten months instead of the usual two years and with the highest marks ever awarded; he wrote the influential 1875 article on 'Army' for the *Encyclopaedia Britannica*; Evelyn Wood said he was 'the best instructed soldier I ever met', while others whispered the words 'genius'. Colley had been lecturing at the Staff College when Wolseley asked him to join his West African expedition. 'What should we have done without Colley,' Sir Garnet told a war correspondent. 'He brought order out of chaos.' Back home, Colley was probably the only officer who could call this pestilential campaign 'fun and a pleasant three months trip'. He served with Wolseley on his 1875 Natal trip, then went out to India as military secretary to the expansionist Viceroy, Lord Lytton. Critics of the Forward Policy that resulted in a second war with Afghanistan breaking out in 1878 saw Colley as the *éminence grise* and 'real military mentor' of events. He made enemies; the C-in-C, India, Sir Frederick Haines, thought him 'a greatly over-rated man'. Over-rated or not, Wolseley had written asking for Colley's services in Zululand. 'Accept gratefully; leave in three days,' he cabled back.

Finally, bringing up the rear of Wolseley's entourage in more ways than one was Fricke, his long-suffering and deeply loyal manservant. Never referred to by any other name but his surname, Fricke was by his master's side throughout several campaigns and was quite willing to buckle a swash. His down-to-earth remarks and minor eccentricities helped the general through his gloomiest moments.

The *Edinburgh Castle* stopped briefly at Madeira for supplies. Wolseley and everyone else stepped briefly ashore. The party included the only passenger on the ship who was not directly there with the general; William Russell, known to everyone as 'Billy', was the genial, hard-drinking war correspondent who had been a legend ever since he sent his first despatches home from the Crimean War. He was now portly and not the hard-working journalist who had enthralled the world with his descriptions of the Indian Mutiny and American Civil War. Missing the first six months of the Zulu War, Billy Russell now wanted to make up for lost time and was under contract to the *Daily Telegraph*. Wolseley had known this first British media celebrity for twenty-five years. He loved his fund of amusing stories but rather resented the way Russell expected every regimental mess to keep him in food and drink.

At Madeira they all found no news from the Cape except a report that Chelmsford intended to advance into Zululand on 21 May. 'The campaign as far as the heavy fighting is concerned must be over by the time I can reach Durban,' concluded a gloomy Wolseley. In a letter to Louisa he argued that his mission 'will resolve itself into embarking the troops for England and endeavouring to settle matters with the Boers in the Transvaal'.[12]

Small, managing just 270 horsepower, the *Edinburgh Castle* was at the mercy of Atlantic headwinds. Sir Garnet confessed in a letter to his 'little sandpiper' that he missed her 'beyond all my powers of description'. He told Louisa that during the early part of the voyage Baker Russell had an attack of fever, an old reminder of his days in India: 'I am glad he has had his attack here and not in Natal.' Brackenbury had the same 'putty nose & bilious complexion' that Louisa disliked so much, but 'he is a great comfort to me' and 'such a real fellow with such a truly loyal soul ... as his mind never seems to be at rest for a moment & his brain is always in a ferment'. To amuse his wife Wolseley wrote a very vivid description of life aboard ship:

> There are two girls of the school age, 4 rate type, on board with their father, one of whom is very larky indeed and gives her respected parent I should say many an uncomfortable quarter of an hour – Herbert has taken her up & devotes himself to her. She is just the sort of creature he can do & say what he likes to so she suits him admirably & it is rather amusing watching his dishonourable courtship. Brackenbury's liver is out of order as usual with him on board ship & his complexion in consequence is of a yellowish green tint. Maurice is all effervescence. Captain Doyle sits for hours with his mouth open & a foolish expression on his countenance reading the 'Soldiers Pocket Book': McCalmont plays upon the ship's piano every day; it is very much out of tune, is a miserably poor instrument & the C in the middle of the notes is dumb. At times he also plays upon a harmonium which is in his cabin, but he is so lazy that he will not blow up the bellows sufficiently to make himself heard. Billy Russell of Times notoriety is the life and soul of the party, his memory is wonderful and his stories are inimitable ... Baker Russell is very nice & very sober.[13]

Wolseley usually played a rubber or two of whist after dinner and went to bed at 10 p.m. He was anxious, as he told Louisa, to get to Cape Town and 'hear what old Billy Bartle, as you call him, has to say for himself'.

In truth, Sir Garnet admitted to 'a great admiration for Frere', but felt 'he was wrong in bringing on this Zulu war when he did', in view of the very serious one already taking place in Afghanistan. A Zulu War was 'bound to come off sooner or later, but we ought to have chosen a more propitious time for it, when we were free from complications elsewhere.' In Wolseley's opinion Frere's desire to accomplish his confederation mission and win a peerage had blinded him to all other considerations. Sir Bartle had also ignored the huge costs of waging war and it was his 'utter disregard for financial considerations that makes him a dangerous man in power'.[14]

In his journal Sir Garnet admitted that each mile nearer South Africa made his brain act like a steam engine at high pressure. 'I keep thinking as one does at chess, if my adversary moves his Castle, or his Bishop, or his Queen. I shall do so and so and so etc., etc., etc.' Wolseley realised that in this Zulu War, 'I shall not have time to act on my own plans or alter Chelmsford's arrangements.' In the Red River Expedition and the Ashanti War he had been able to organize things down to the smallest detail, but in Zululand he would have to work with plans, generals and staff chosen by others. Even some of the equipment was not to his liking (a demand for the Elcho sword bayonet was disregarded).

On Sunday 22 June Sir Garnet noted in his journal that Major Webber had delivered interesting lectures on the electric telegraph and a new marvel called the telephone. A day earlier Maurice had given a dreary talk on the causes of the Zulu War, 'but, then, the subject was a difficult one ...' Wolseley's ears were recovering from some 'awful concerts' led by McCalmont. 'How one longs to fly from the ship that has been one's prison house for so long,' he wrote in the journal.

That blessed release came at 7.30 p.m. the next night when the *Edinburgh Castle* at last dropped anchor in Table Bay. A small boat came alongside and several on the ship yelled out, 'Is the war over?' 'No' came the reply and everyone on deck cheered up. Then came a shout, 'The Prince Imperial was killed some weeks ago.' Wolseley told Louisa that he thought immediately of the Empress Eugenie – 'She has nothing now to live for – poor woman.'

On reaching Government House, with Brackenbury and Herbert in tow, Sir Garnet found the place in a party mood as Frere had just finished holding a levee. Until late that night the old proconsul and the new civil and military supremo sat up burning the midnight oil in the governor's study. Wolseley's mind was set whirling with so much information that he could not sleep at all (a rare occurrence for a man who normally slept like a top even on campaign). Frere made it plain he thought the government was 'weak-kneed & cowardly' (in Wolseley's words). And what of Frere's military views? Did he set the ball rolling down on Chelmsford? No doubt he was diplomatic but by now one suspects he was losing faith in his general's talents. A guest at Government House shortly before Wolseley arrived was Captain the Hon. Fitzwilliam Elliot, 93rd Foot. He was making his way to join General Crealock's column as a special service officer but, as a brother of the Earl of Minto, he was important enough to be accorded the VIP treatment. During his stay he detected a new mood towards Chelmsford. 'I believe Frere has little confidence in him,' he wrote in a letter home, 'that is the impression the staff here have given me and of course in giving it to me they know, probably wish, that I won't keep it to myself. No one seems to expect the war to end this year.'[15]

Wolseley has of course been accused by some historians of conducting a smear campaign against Chelmsford. 'He clearly wished to give the authorities in England the impression that Chelmsford's campaign was teetering on the edge of disaster,' wrote Donald Morris, one of many who raised this point.[16] There can be no question as to the substance of what Wolseley wrote but malicious intent cannot be proven; he cannot be blamed for repeating what he heard from highly respected men such as Henry Bulwer, Henry Clifford, Evelyn Wood and even Bartle Frere. These men had strong reservations about the war as the new supremo Wolseley had to inform his Whitehall masters. Furthermore, Sir Garnet's comments in his public and personal correspondence are mirrored in his highly confidential journal; there can be no question that as a serious student of warfare he thought Chelmsford was a hapless general and out of his depth.

Dashing off a letter to his wife on 24 June, Wolseley wrote 'I hear sad accounts of affairs in our Columns under Crealock & Lord C., so I am hurrying to the front as fast as I can.' Sketching some first impressions that same day, he wrote, 'There seems no directing head in Zululand, everyone seems to act on his own hook & staff arrangements there seem to be none.'[17] He had received a 'peculiar' telegram from Clifford imputing blame and finding fault with Chelmsford's arrangements along the Line of Communications. He could not understand Chelmsford's plan, or why he had stopped Clifford's command at the Natal-Zululand border. 'He appears to have snubbed Wood by breaking up his command,' noted Wolseley. Reports indicated that Chelmsford 'is care-worn and will be very glad to be relieved', and was very much under the influence of his military secretary, John North Crealock. 'That offensive snob is his ruin,' wrote Sir Garnet in his journal.

After luncheon on the 24th with the cream of Cape society, a volunteer cavalry escort and an honour guard led by Frere and the Cape Premier, J. W. Sprigg, guided Wolseley to the quay. A salute was fired and the locals cheered as the general and his staff steamed off in the SS *Dunkeld* for Natal. In his cabin Sir Garnet put his latest thoughts down on paper:

> I confess that the more I look at the job before me & think over it, the less I like it. Chelmsford's force, as far as I can gather consists of 5640 Infry. & 2100 cavalry with 3200 horses & mules & 10,632 oxen to feed. I presume he has about 500 large & heavy ox wagons which would alone occupy at least twelve miles of road: I do not see how he could ever fight a successful battle with such an amount of impediments. Indeed I should not be the least surprised to hear when I get to Durban that he had met with a serious check if not another disaster ... Crealock & Chelmsford are operating on independent lines & are not in communication

> with one another. Nothing could be more unpromising or more fraught with danger than the existing condition. Of course a happy stroke of good fortune might possibly end the war at any moment, but I confess I can see no probability of it under present circumstances with a demoralized army the men of which in all ranks are thoroughly sick of the war & have lost all confidence apparently in their leaders. It is very, very probable that I shall find myself forced to postpone all operations until January which would create a bad impression at home politically speaking & would be a fearful disappointment to the Ministry: however they have only themselves to blame for not having sent me out here three months ago. Delay will embolden the enemy & might possibly lead to rebellion amongst the natives in many districts between Zululand and Cape Town.[18]

Lord Chelmsford had received the horrifying news that he was being superseded in command just one week earlier. The official telegram, coming on the heels of the Prince Imperial's death, must have left him thinking 'the fates had conspired against him, that he would never be given the chance to erase properly the stain of Isandlwana'.[19] The telegram said his lordship should not view the appointment of a more senior officer as a 'censure on yourself', yet made it plain that 'you will, as in ordinary course of service, submit and subordinate your plans to his control'. About this time Chelmsford also received a telegram from his brother, Lord Justice Thesiger: 'For God's sake do something! Wolseley supersedes you.'[20]

What Chelmsford had been doing for several laborious weeks was drawing his main No. 2 Division and that of General Henry Hope Crealock's No. 1 Division ever closer to Cetshwayo's kraal at oNdini. This manoeuvre had been taken at a snail's pace, especially by Crealock's column, who were known as 'the crawlers'. Wolseley's apprehensions were voiced by many under Chelmsford's command. 'We do not know where the Zulu Army is and until it is defeated we are in a very ticklish position,' wrote Lieutenant Henry Curling R.A., 'Our baggage columns are longer than ever ... You would hardly believe it possible but we do not know the road and are wandering with the greatest uncertainty as to where we shall go ... too many cooks spoil the pudding and we have no less than five Generals (including two Brigadiers) with us.'[21]

Delays in receiving and responding to communications were to cause much misunderstanding and ill-feeling between Chelmsford and Wolseley. As soon as he arrived at Cape Town a telegram was despatched from Sir Garnet asking for the latest news. This did not reach Chelmsford until 28 June, and his detailed reply took a further three days to get back to Wolseley – in other words, one week to deal with a question and an answer. It was impossible for Sir Garnet to control events in this fashion, as he very well knew, but it made him vexed and irritable. There was a telegraph link with General Crealock and Wolseley ordered both of the field commanders to 'report in every instance to me and I must stop this system of everyone communicating direct with the Authorities at home'. He noted that Chelmsford has been told that 'all communications regarding peace must be made to me'. Sir Garnet was under no illusions that making the various generals respond to him would be an easy task. He noted: 'I shall have some trouble making the team pull together and answer to the one whip.'

On board the *Dunkeld* the general sat in his cabin and wrote to the Secretary of State for War:

> I am still in the dark as to what Chelmsford's plans are or why he is operating in two columns about 80 miles apart without inter-communication of any sort. In fact, one might be destroyed without the other knowing anything about it for many days ... I see nothing else for it but to draw back the troops to near the Natal frontier, and to wait there until

> the climate will again allow us to begin operations ... Now all ranks seem to be down on their luck whilst the Enemy's self-confidence has probably increased by seeing week after week elapse without any attack being made upon him. From all sides I hear abuse of Lt-Col. Crealock, who seems to have an influence over Chelmsford, and to use it badly, whilst he continues to rub everyone up the wrong way.[22]

At Port Elizabeth a report reached Wolseley from Clifford that 'Zulus have crossed the Tugela River into Natal near Fort Buckingham'. This seemed to him a mere 'flank diversion'. This raid of 25 June was made by two small impis who later combined into a fighting unit of some 500 warriors and caused havoc and a few deaths among friendly natives living near the Middle Drift. Cetshwayo got the blame for this attack but historians have since concluded that 'the raid was a retaliatory blow of purely local initiative ...'[23] 'I find that everything in the army is in a hopeless condition of Jumble,' Sir Garnet wrote to his wife that day, 'the troops out of heart & without any confidence in their leaders – I confess to you my dear little woman that I never embarked on any enterprise before with the gloomy feelings I entertain at present, for I know that the Home Govt looks to me to finish the war quickly ...'[24]

At 7 a.m. on Saturday 28 June, to frenzied cheers of welcome along a quayside decorated with bunting, every floating vessel in the harbour being similarly en fete with flags from stem to stern, Sir Garnet came ashore at Durban. His friend from Red River and Ashanti days, Major William Butler (currently Clifford's A.A.G., Assistant Adjutant General, dealing with endless problems of transport and supply), was waiting to meet him. The pair breakfasted together and Butler, always a man of strong opinions, told his old chief of what he termed in his autobiography as 'confusion' and 'chaos'. After speeches of welcome, Wolseley set off by train for the colonial capital of Pietermaritzburg. Halfway the party disembarked and mounted a four-horse trap. In this conveyance they galloped into the driveway of the governor's residence before Sir Henry Bulwer had finished buttoning up his uniform.

Once sworn in as the chief civil and military authority in Natal, Sir Garnet was able to hear in detail how the war was progressing from two very important sources – Bulwer, the lieutenant-governor who had presided over Natal affairs since Wolseley's departure in 1875, and Clifford, the general in charge of forces in Natal and Lines of Communication as far as the Zululand frontier. Sir Garnet had met Bulwer briefly in August 1875 and recorded him as 'a nice fellow', his very fair reddish hair giving the forty-six-year-old bachelor 'a youthful air'. A career diplomat, Sir Henry had administered Labuan and Borneo before being posted to Natal. Tough, brave Clifford had been Wolseley's superior for a time in the Quartermaster-General's department in the Crimea. He had won a Victoria Cross at Inkerman leading a charge, killing one of the enemy with his sword, disabling another, saving a soldier's life and recapturing three guns. This was his second tour of duty in South Africa; he had seen service during the Seventh and Eighth Xhosa Wars while at the Cape from 1847 to 1854. Later war service in China had led him to being appointed an aide to the Duke of Cambridge in 1875. Clifford was a rare man as someone both the reactionary Cambridge and progressive Wolseley held in respect.

By the time of Sir Garnet's arrival, matters between Bulwer and Chelmsford had reached such a low that it was their unsatisfactory relationship, more than any other single issue, that had led to the general's supercession. Shortly before the war began Bulwer had written that his lordship was 'a good general officer', but 'not very pleasant to deal with in official matters'. The general had similarly described the lieutenant-governor as 'essentially a small mind [that] cannot take a full grasp of the situation ...' Bulwer had made strong objections to the formation of the Natal Native Contingents and did not approve of natives being armed in the war since there was the potential for later rebellion. He also disapproved of the general's policy of implementing cross-border raids since he thought, wisely as it turned out, that they might lead to Zulu reprisals. By April 1879 Chelmsford was complaining to Cambridge that Bulwer 'has thrown every obstacle in my way'. Now, talking with Wolseley, Sir Henry made it plain that Chelmsford was 'very much inflated by the idea of his ability as a general ... That his [Bulwer's] opinions and views were pooh-poohed & that in the end he was barely treated with even ordinary civility.' Bulwer did not mince his words:

> He declared that Bartle Frere had forced on the war which was quite unnecessary. That Bartle Frere, Chelmsford & Col. Crealock came to Natal last autumn fully determined upon making this war: that Chelmsford was, of the three, the least anxious for it ... He regarded the annexation of the Transvaal as a great mistake & the real origin of all the evils & misfortune that fallen to our lot, as he regarded young Crealock as the origin of all poor Chelmsford's mistakes ... That Chelmsford was now endeavouring to 'rush it' so that he might gain some victory ... [25]

The other person to give Wolseley a clear impression that things were now at a deplorable level was Major-General Clifford, who had also fallen out of favour with Chelmsford. The fact that his powers were restricted to Natal irked Clifford enormously. Out of spite he misrepresented some of Chelmsford's actions to the authorities. While realizing that Clifford was extremely efficient, the Duke of Cambridge had found it necessary to reprimand him for criticizing a senior officer. At the time Wolseley arrived matters were approaching boiling point; Chelmsford had written on 2 July that Clifford was 'ignorant of the situation of the forces under my command and very foolish'. Some modern historians have described Clifford's actions as 'dictatorial'. The animosity between the two generals grew partly out of their very differing natures and approach to work. Bulwer thought Clifford was making himself ill through over-work and wrote, 'I like him, but I think he is a little bit of a Jesuit,'[26] a reference not just to the man's stern work ethic, but also his staunch Roman Catholicism (Clifford attended regular mass and daily prayers and one of his sisters was a nun). His deputy, William Butler, another Catholic, wrote that 'of all the generals I have been brought into contact with, none possessed a personality more lovable, none had a higher courage, a larger sense of public duty, or a greater aptitude for untiring toil.'[27] The workaholic Clifford was thus a very different fish from the refined Chelmsford who, according to his rival, 'moves in a very narrow world of his own, as I have told him, shut off by Crealock from many who would give him good sound advice …' Now Clifford told Wolseley (as related in Sir Garnet's journal):

> Crealock with 1st Division has been pottering about for the last two days evidently afraid to advance. He has no dash and judging from his past history is very careful of his own hide & not likely to expose his valuable person to any dangers. He advanced at last to his present position only when he heard of my early arrival. Chelmsford has been pushing on well ahead also since he heard I was likely soon to be on the spot and to supersede him. He has apparently cut himself off from his base in order to prevent my communicating with him. No one knows where he is at the moment but he & his evil genius, that arch-snob young Crealock are now doing all they know to do something brilliant before I can join the troops in the field.[28]

Wolseley came to the conclusion that Clifford was 'working like a slave to try and evolve order out of the existing chaos'.[29]

On the afternoon of 28 June, around the time that Sir Garnet was being greeted by Bulwer, a small, mud-splattered patrol led by Captain Herbert Stewart, Brigade-major of the Cavalry Brigade, spurred their sweating English horses onto the Mathonjaneni Heights and into the Headquarters Camp. The place was one of 'extraordinary confusion' as word had just come in of a large Zulu army just five miles away. 'Everyone laagering for bare life,' wrote Guy Dawnay, one of the riders, 'and Crealock telling them they only had thirty minutes to do it in, or all were as good as dead.'[30] Stewart carried with him Wolseley's original request for a situation report. Lord Chelmsford immediately penned a lengthy reply indicating that he was within striking distance of Ulundi (oNdini) and intended to hasten on with ten days provisions and without tents.

It would be three days before Sir Garnet got Chelmsford's letter. On 30 June, Lieutenant James Douglas, chief signalling officer, 2nd Division, accompanied by Corporal Cotter, 17th Lancers, rode twenty miles to Fort Evelyn to deliver the general's reply to Wolseley via the heliograph. Refusing to wait until daybreak the pair set off back that night and had the bad luck to blunder into a Zulu impi, who killed them. That same day, as Chelmsford's soldiers moved off in the direction of oNdini, back in Natal Sir Garnet was firing off another missive: 'Concentrate your force immediately and keep it so concentrated. Undertake no serious operation with detached bodies of troops. Acknowledge receipt of this message at once and flash back your latest news. I am astonished at not hearing daily from you.'[31]

Sir Garnet had decided he must somehow hasten on to the front. Before leaving Pietermaritzburg he issued a slew of orders: Clifford was now given command of all the columns in Zululand to the base; supplies accumulating at Durban and Landsman's Drift were to be hurried on to the front; a supply base for Crealock's column was to be created at Port Durnford; and a corps of 4,000 native carriers were to be formed working from Fort Tenedos on the Lower Tugela.

Zulu messengers who had arrived at General Crealock's camp asking for the British troops to halt were, in Wolseley's opinion, simply a 'subterfuge' and 'similar in character to those which I constantly received from the King of Ashanti when he was engaged in collecting his army to oppose me'. A message via Fort Pearson was heliographed to tell the Zulu messengers, 'I alone have the power to make peace. All the other generals are under my orders.'[32]

In letters to his main correspondents, Stanley and Cambridge, Sir Garnet gave his latest impressions: he told the Secretary-of-State for War that he was in 'absolute ignorance' of Chelmsford's plans and 'indignant and anxious' for General Crealock. In his 30 June letter to the duke he was able to work in some sly digs in favour of short service and his ring of officers: 'It is no question of young soldiers, but of bad leading. Had a man like Evelyn Wood been in command here, or a man like Colonel Colley, or many others whom I could name, the war would have been over by this.' Waxing lyrical, Wolseley referred to Clifford as 'a bright object in the clouds of confusion that reign supreme in this military chaos'.[33] He told Cambridge that 'the two regiments of Cavalry have ceased to exist as a Brigade. The men are too big and heavy for service here.' Crealock was 'so slow that he is not likely to meet the enemy'. On a brighter note, the Zulu peace overtures now convinced Wolseley 'that Cetewayo is now anxious to end the war'. Once peace was achieved Sir Garnet made clear that he would hurriedly embark as many troops as he could, retaining only enough to 'make a demonstration of strength in the Transvaal'. The sick and wounded seemed to be doing well, but the Principal Medical Officer, Surgeon-General Woolfryes, was 'an old woman'.[34]

Sir Garnet had visited the local hospitals on the 30th offering a kind word to some of the 100 or so soldiers suffering mainly from eye infections, though none so badly as poor Major Robert Hackett, 90th Light Infantry, who had been shot through the head at Kambula and was now permanently blind in both eyes.

Wolseley felt very sorry for him and saddened to see a promising career cut short. In the afternoon he had met many of the Natal native chiefs who had been summoned to see him. It was an amiable meeting; he was very complimentary to them and offered £1.10.0 a month for every native who would be a carrier plus free rations and a blanket. The war might be ended quickly if the chiefs gave their support, Wolseley pointed out, but 'Her Majesty would go on fighting for ever if necessary ...'

At the end of a long day Sir Garnet knew he was in a quandary; he had been six days in South Africa but still did not know precisely what was happening at the seat of war, though a message sent from General Marshall at Landman's Drift told him that the army was nine miles from Ulundi, the Zulus estimated at 10,000 warriors. Wolseley had hoped to make an overland dash via Rorke's Drift using horses purchased at the Cape but the beasts had still not arrived. Rightly or wrongly, he now decided to rush down to Durban, take ship eastwards up the coast to Port Durnford, about 60 miles from Ulundi, meet up with Crealock's column and push forward to the front. The reader might well ask why Wolseley did not just set off overland from Pietermaritzburg sooner, say on the 29th or morning of 30 June, but history is littered with such questions. According to Guy Dawnay, who rode to Landman's Drift via Rorke's Drift on 30 June, it took him twelve hours non-stop riding 'from within sight of Ulundi to Natal'. If Wolseley had left a day earlier with a large cavalry escort, doing ten to twelve hard hours in the saddle each day, he probably would have got to the front in a pretty exhausted state after three days. The unfortunate deaths of Lieutenant Douglas and Corporal Cotter illustrate, however, the dangers – Zululand was so disturbed, with regiments marching to join their king at oNdini, that there is no way of knowing if such an epic ride might have courted disaster. It would also have been a tough journey; on the night of the 30th Herbert Stewart's horse stumbled in a hole and broke both her knees, the rider being badly shaken. Sir Garnet well knew that he had been sent to South Africa to end a war, not become another casualty of it.

On the morning of 1 July Wolseley rose early and breakfasted in the dark. He knew that a reply to his first telegram was on its way from Chelmsford but an hour after eating it had still not arrived. Arrangements were made to forward on the message, and the general and his staff set off at a gallop for Durban. On the train section the driver pushed his locomotive so hard as it whirled around curves, ascents and descents that he won a wager and set a speed record. They got to Durban ten minutes to noon, had a meal with William Butler, and boarded HMS *Shah* at 4 p.m. A large crowd watched the embarkation. Chelmsford's letter arrived just before departure. On a calm and pleasant sea and to a seventeen-gun salute Wolseley now set off up the coast. Port Durnford was reached at 7.30 a.m. the next morning but a heavy surf made landing impossible. The general was forced to stare at the sandhills on shore and the soldiers waiting to greet him, everyone on board 'hating the ship, the sea & all belonging to it ...' Sir Garnet's mood was not improved by a series of messages he got from General Crealock. Attempting to ingratiate himself, he had sent word: 'I have got two milch cows for your Excellency.' Sir Garnet was not impressed and ignored a man whom he truly loathed. Perhaps wondering why he had not had a reply, Henry Crealock then heliographed: 'I have a marquee for your Excellency.' The suggestion that he needed such a luxury infuriated Wolseley, who fired back: 'All marquees should be at the base: send it back!'[35]

Next day, 3 July, things got even worse; various attempts were made to get Wolseley and his party ashore, but the sea got rougher and rougher. Thirteen of them were battened down in the hold of a small boat when the tow rope broke and they were adrift near the breaking rollers. A message had come from shore saying they ought not to attempt to land. The transport officer asked the general if he wished to attempt it. 'It is a naval business regarding which I have no responsibility and am no judge,' replied Sir Garnet.[36] So the order was given to return to the *Shah*. The ship's captain warned Wolseley that he needed to put out to sea since his ship was almost scraping its bottom in such shallow water. Reluctantly the general told him to return to Durban. It had all been a fiasco. He now knew he had to get to the front overland. A headwind and high seas delayed the return until late on 4 July. By now several of Wolseley's entourage had been sick, all were in 'very bad humour' and most of the glasses and plates were lying smashed on the dining room floor.

Though Wolseley did not know it, that same morning, as his ship pitched and tossed with crockery flying around, the Zulu War had reached its inevitable bloody climax at Ulundi. Lord Chelmsford had led his 2nd Division down from the Mthonjaneni Heights towards oNdini on 30 June within hours of receiving Sir Garnet's first telegram. The advance was led by Evelyn Wood's flying column of experienced troops with Major-General Edward Newdigate's 2nd Division men following behind. They passed into a landscape of lush, tall green grass and bushes aflame with scarlet flowers as the army moved towards the Mahalabathini Plain, torching homesteads (*amakhanda*) and vast stores of mealies along the way. Lord Chelmsford had no intention of letting Wolseley steal his victory; the Zulu War had been for its general six months filled with heartache and worry, but he had tried to learn from his mistakes and he felt victory was at hand. Officers under his command sympathised and they also wanted to prove themselves worthy. 'Under our chief we had waited, worked and fought,' wrote one of them, 'and it was hard on him as on us to see another come, hot-haste at the eleventh hour, to snatch victory, all ready prepared at hand.'[37] One of the general's staff officers, Captain William Molyneux, wrote that Wolseley's demand that the 2nd Division should somehow link up with 'Crealock's Crawlers' 'made us all laugh, considering that the Chief had been unsuccessfully plying General Clifford to find out where Crealock was'.[38]

By the night of 3 July it was apparent to both the Zulus and the British that a battle would take place on the next day. Earlier on the 3rd scouting parties led by Redvers Buller had encountered the enemy and there had been actions of Victoria Cross-winning heroism. 'It was a most successful affair,' wrote Molyneux. 'He had noted an excellent position for the next day's fight: he had shown us where the Zulus were in force, and that they were posted in horseshoe form ready for us to enter the trap; and he had returned when nearly surrounded by many thousand men, with a very small loss indeed.'[39] Chelmsford had received Sir Garnet's sharp telegram of 1 July during the day; he replied giving his proposed movements on the 4th.

That night British troops lay encamped on the opposite bank of the White Mfolozi (Umfolozi) River from oNdini. Sleep was made impossible for most of the men by the noise of the Zulu amabutho being doctored and the dancing and singing of their war songs. According to Zulus who were there, all of Cetshwayo's regiments were represented. The historian, John Laband, has noted, poignantly, how 'never again would the gathered manhood of the Zulu kingdom join in ... the sacred ballads honouring the mighty deeds of the ancestors and great warriors of the past, for the coming day would see them scattered in final defeat.'[40]

The Tommies, naturally enough, found the whole experience quite 'hideous'. Sergeant Edward Jervis, 90th Light Infantry, wrote later to his mother: 'That night was full moon, and ... the Zulus could be heard yelling like demons ... we could see their fires plainly. I could not sleep, so I lay awake thinking of home, and you, old Ted and Dick ... and wondering if I should be alive the next night.'[41] Another man in the same regiment, Bandsman Joseph Banks, said the yelling 'made many a man's hair stand on end. I never heard the like before and never wish to hear again.'[42] An NCO of the 17th Lancers, sleeping outside the laager, described the noise as 'something awful'; he was scared the Zulus might attack and easily stampede the horses: 'You may guess we did not sleep much after.' War correspondent Charles Fripp described the Zulu chants as 'infernal', yet found the thousands of voices 'sonorous' as the song grew louder and louder until 'one could hear the higher voices prevail over the resonant roar of the bass ...'[43] Fripp was one of the lucky few; he went back to sleep.

Around 3.45 a.m. the soldiers were roused from their uneasy slumbers. Men of the 90th breakfasted on hot coffee and biscuits, but an NCO of the 17th Lancers complained of being sent to fight 'without any coffee or anything else'. By 5 a.m. the men were being formed up into columns preparatory to crossing the river. A bogus reveille was sounded fifteen minutes later to deceive the enemy, but the Zulus had disappeared and everything on their side of the Mfolozi lay ominously silent.

It was a cold dawn, 'everything clouded in a thick white mist', noted Molyneux. 'I can tell you we felt anything but comfortable,' wrote a trooper. The soldiers and horses began splashing across the twelve-inch-deep river. Left behind to guard the entrenched camp were 622 white and black troops including five disappointed companies of the 1st/24th. Wild guava, pomegranate and scented bushes gave off sweet smells as they were crushed by the horses' hooves, noted a cavalry officer, with bees humming among the perfumed dolichos as the sun rose. Marching into battle were 4,166 white and 958 black soldiers with twelve artillery pieces and two Gatling guns. It was the largest imperial force that had ever been marshalled against a native tribe in southern Africa.

The Zulus did not oppose the crossing. Their plan was 'to allow the British into the plain, and force them to fight in the open, so they could be destroyed as at Isandlwana.'[44] British participants could never agree on the size of the Zulu army that was soon to go into battle (war correspondent Archibald Forbes suggested as few as 10,000, a Lieutenant Hotham ventured 30,000). John Laband, an authority on the battle, has suggested 'between 15,000 and 20,000 strong, with 5,000 in reserve' (very similar to eye-witness

Charles Norris-Newman), but the exact figure will never be known. King Cetshwayo was not present having left oNdini the night previous for his kwaMbonambi *ikhanda* (military kraal), but look-outs were posted to bring him news. The king's brother, Ziwedu kwaMpande, watched the battle from a nearby hill. With him were several other of his relatives and generals, but who they were is disputed.

Once across the Mfolozi, Buller's irregular horsemen moved forward, while the infantry marched for about two miles from the drift when an order rang out to form a square. This fighting formation – actually a huge oblong or parallelogram – was composed of infantry in four ranks (two kneeling and two standing during a battle), with artillery at three of the four corners and at intervals along the long sides, two Gatlings dead centre at the front. Five companies of the 80th Regiment protected that face of the square; eight companies of the 90th Light Infantry and four companies of the 94th Regiment occupied the left face; the opposite wall was held by eight companies of the 1/13th Regiment and four companies of the 58th Regiment; the rear face by two companies of the 2/21st Royal Scots Fusiliers and two companies of the 94th Regiment. In the centre of the square rode Chelmsford and his staff and space was made for a field hospital, the nervous, huddled mass of the Natal Native Contingent and the war correspondents.

With the band of the 1/13th playing martial airs and Colours of the various regiments uncased and held high (the last major battle in which British troops fought and died under their Colours), the square pushed on through the tall grass and bushes. On nearing the kwaNodwengu royal kraal the general's voice suddenly rang out ordering the square to half-right turn. This was, perhaps surprisingly in view of the circumstances, very well performed. The front of the square now faced oNdini. An advance was made for another ten minutes until the square reached the spot selected by Buller on the previous day as the perfect place for the battle.

Here the ground sloped away for several hundred metres on every side giving a perfect field of fire. In addition it was 'uncommanded from any point and there was little bush for cover, only the long grass.'[45] In the distance was the vast oNdini complex, 'looking like monstrous bee hives', thought Trooper Turnham, 17th Lancers. Evelyn Wood asked the general if he wished to entrench, but Chelmsford replied, 'No, they will be satisfied if we beat them fairly in the open. We have been called ant-bears long enough.'[46]

To provoke the Zulus a deserted ikhanda was torched by the Natal Native Horse. Watching the smoke rising in the sky the Zulu army at last stirred into action. The first warrior was sighted just after 8 a.m. and within fifteen minutes or so the amabutho were moving inexorably forward in the long grass. The colonial mounted irregulars now engaged them and amid the firing traded insults. Zulus taunted the Edendale and Sotho black troops saying such things as 'Gallop on, but we will overtake you. We are going to kill every one of the white men.'[47] A British officer at this point was struck by what could be termed the technicolour of it all – 'The surrounding green hills, and the skirmishing cavalry, and the red square and the black Zulus.'[48]

All the cavalry, both the irregular units and imperial troops, were next ordered inside the square just before 9 a.m. as the artillery 'opened fire on the enemy at two thousand yards or more', wrote Arthur Harness, 'from all sides, and the Zulus came on very pluckily, in small groups, taking wonderful advantage of cover'.[49] A special service officer, Lieutenant Jervis, was also impressed how the Zulus advanced 'in beautiful order, covered by skirmishers, apparently in one long continuous line about four deep, with intervals between the different regiments – not in the dense irregular crowds we had been led to expect'.[48] Jervis was impressed how the Zulu fighting formation of the buffalo developed as the horns came to 'surround us with their largest force in our rear to cut off our retreat: it was a grand sight'.[50]

The rear right corner of the square, held by the 58th and 21st Regiments, faced a major attack as the Zulu horns contracted. This was the sharpest fight but all sides were under attack and bullets came thick and fast. Chelmsford had insisted on officers remaining on horseback and three of them were hit in the same minute while talking together (luckily, two were contusions from spent balls and the other man was only slightly wounded). The Zulus fired their guns too high, which saved most of the mounted officers from injury, but all kinds of slugs were dropping into the centre of the square. Through the smoke the hoarse cries of the indunas could be heard urging on their men. Stuck in the middle of the square, Guy Dawnay recalled:

> My horse, with many others was, at first, out of his mind with the row, but wonderfully soon got used to it ... Newdigate was as if the bullets were butterflies ... the only real thick mass I ever saw attacking appeared opposite our corner, about 130 yards off ... our fire didn't check them the least; nearer they came – 100 yards, 80 yards – still rushing on, a thick black mass. Lord Chelmsford came galloping up, telling the 58th and 21st to fire faster; Newdigate pulled out his revolver. The nine-pounder crashed through them again and again, but at that short distance the canister did not burst. Everyone thought it would be hand to hand in another minute when at 60 yards, the mass faltered, wavered and withered away.[51]

There is some dispute about how close the Zulus actually got but the general consensus of opinion was expressed by a staff officer present, Major Francis Grenfell, who wrote: 'At no point did *any large numbers* [my italics] of men get within thirty yards of the square ...' The same officer also noted one induna who got as close as eighteen yards. Grenfell paced this out after the action and did the same thing on a return visit two years later, 'and came to my old friend, a splendid skeleton, his bones perfectly white, his flesh eaten away by the white ants'.[52] Grenfell, not a callous man in most respects but a man of his time, popped the head into a bag and kept it at home in his cabinet of curiosities.

In the middle of the square the irrepressible war artist, Melton Prior, sketched busily away. His description of the battle remains one of the most vivid:

> The air seemed alive with the whistling of bullets and slugs and pieces of cooking-pot legs fired from elephant guns as they came banging in amongst us from all directions. Our artillery practice was very fine, but it failed to daunt the Zulus. The rockets must have astonished them a good deal, for they did us. I saw one fired, and watched its triumphal progress amongst the enemy, until, catching a corner of a hut, it suddenly altered its direction, then striking the ground, it once more deviated from its proper course, and came straight back at us, luckily missing our square by a quarter of a yard. My faith in rockets and tubes has considerably weakened ever since ... I have since read various statements as to how near the enemy got to our square, and it is often stated that twenty or thirty paces was the closest, but I can say that I personally went out and reached the nearest one in nine paces, so their onslaught was pretty determined ... [53]

The courage of the Zulus was beyond praise. They faced a terrible fire yet charged and re-charged. There are no records of how many bullets were fired by the colonial mounted troops, but British regulars used some 35,000 rounds, along with 130 rounds fired by the seven pounders and 68 by the nine pounders, together with three rockets. The Gatlings jammed repeatedly yet Wood later claimed to have counted sixty dead in front of them. The battle was general for about thirty minutes from 8.45 a.m. but the Zulu attack seemed to falter by 9.15 a.m. Some British soldiers started cheering, others taunted the enemy with shouts of 'Come on, you black devils.' A lance-corporal of the 58th was in the act of cheering when a bullet killed him outright, passing through his open mouth and coming out at the back of his head.

Cavalry troopers in the square were having a 'fearful' time, noted C. M. Turnham of 'C' Troop, 17th Lancers, as 'it was a job to keep our horses quiet, they were getting shot and we had a job to keep them from making a confusion ...' At one point a bullet came 'hissing through my horse's mane twisting it into a tight plait and then through my cloak. Had I been in the saddle I should have got my bullet but it was not to be that time thank God ...'[54]

Judging it was now time to use his cavalry, Chelmsford shouted out, 'Now Colonel Lowe – the Lancers!' To loud cheers from the infantry Drury-Lowe led forward five troops of the 17th Lancers and twenty-four men of the King's Dragoon Guards. The Zulus made a final rush and the cavalry dismounted. A few minutes later the general waved his helmet and yelled, 'Go at them, Lowe!' Captain Edmund Wyatt-Edgell was shot dead leading out his dragoons, Lieutenant and Acting-Adjutant Herbert Jenkins jaw was shattered by a bullet, and even Drury-Lowe was hit in the back by a spent bullet, causing him to fall off his horse (his second-in-command, Major Samuel Boulderson, took over) but he returned to the fray. A young trooper of the Frontier Light Horse, George Mossop, watched in awe:

> On their great imported horses they sat bolt upright, their long lances held perfectly erect, the lance heads glittering in the sunshine. They formed into line. In one movement the lances dropped to the right side of the horses' necks, a long level of poles, stretching out a distance in front of the horses, the steel heads pointing straight at the mass of retreating Zulus. As the

> big horses bounded forward and thundered into them, each lance point pierced the Zulu in front of it; the man fell, and as the horse passed on beyond him the lance was withdrawn, lifted and thrust forward into another Zulu in front.[55]

An even more vivid account was written the same day by a participant, Guy Dawnay, who described what the action felt like:

> The first man I reached turned round with shield in left hand and assegaies and gun in right, and I found my long heavy Life Guard sword given me by H. do well. It cut clean half down the shield, hit something hard, and caught the Zulu on the neck I think, though I don't think deeply; anyhow, down he went, and the next minute a lance was through him. I let an old man go, and got to an Inkhela, who had just stopped to fire a minute before, changed my cut and dodged his shield, and caught him through the headring, and he fell in a heap. Another threw himself down out of reach in the grass only to receive a lance, and then I chased three into a donga, tried to give one the point, but he dodged in front of my horse, the back of the sword only grazing him; but my horse knocked him down and went clean over him; he had his assegaies all ready, and I wonder he didn't hit me, and still more the horse. One of the other three threw at me from the other side of the donga; but it took me a little out of my way to get out of it, and I couldn't come up with him, my horse like all the others being blown. The Lancers did well. I know each man I had anything to do with had a lance through him before he could move, whether wounded or not.[56]

Watching from the safety of the square was awestruck Private Tucker, 58th Regiment, who observed in a letter home that the cavalry cut down the Zulus 'like grass before the scythe'. Trooper

Turnham wrote of 'lancing them by hundreds'. The battle was over. Across the plain lay some 1,500 Zulu dead, while thousands more crawled away to nurse their wounds or die later. Only two Zulu prisoners were taken alive on 4 July, which gives some idea of the slaughter. British losses were a trifling three officers and ten other ranks killed, and one officer and sixty-nine men wounded. Before the dusty, throat-parched red soldiers could take rest and refreshment, they watched huge flames and columns of smoke fill the sky as the whole of the oNdini complex was set ablaze, 'a dense mass of flames seven miles in length', wrote an observer. The site held some 1,000–1,400 huts with the king's special homestead, known as his *isigodlo*, at the top. Now all was set to the torch. Lord Chelmsford must have felt a deep sense of relief and joy. Guy Dawnay noted that the difference in the general's appearance before and after the fight 'was something to see'. One of his officers voiced the feelings of many when he wrote: '*I am so glad for Lord C.* He has quite taken the wind out of Sir G. W.'s sails.'[57] Sergeant O'Callaghan of the 58th spoke for the rankers when he told his folks back home that Chelmsford was 'an able general, and a cool, brave and determined leader ...'[58]

The Zulus would continue to fight if their king demanded it, but most of them seemed to sense that this had been the last great battle. One warrior said a short time later, 'The army is now thoroughly beaten, and as we were beaten in the open, it will not reassemble or fight again.'[59]

Being first with the news was now the main thing for the war correspondents. Determined to scoop his rivals, Alexander Forbes, 'a great, strong, coarse-looking man', was correspondent for the *Daily News*. This ex-cavalry trooper had witnessed many wars and he now asked Chelmsford if he might send back his account of the battle with the official despatch rider. When the general pointed out he was not sending despatches until the next day, Forbes snappily replied, 'Then, sir, I will start at once.' He also agreed to carry Melton Prior's sketches for the *Illustrated London News*. Forbes later wrote:

> I think on the whole I was sorry I had spoken the moment I had spoken. It was already dusk. I had been in the saddle almost without food from five o'clock in the morning. All my horses had been worn out and were no longer fresh. My first stage (to our standing camp on the ridge) would consist of some fourteen miles through thick bush and broken ground, and in close proximity to the military kraals burnt on the 28 ult ... Many men tried to dissuade me ... The night was just falling as I rode up the steep rugged track from the laager ... There was no road, only a confusion of wagon-tracks ... Behind me seethed the Gehenna of the blazing Ulundi and other kraals fired that day.[60]

Despite the Press calling this 'The Ride of Death' it was, of course, the same journey that Dawnay, Stewart and other despatch riders had done frequently. Ironically, Chelmsford changed his mind a short time after Forbes left camp and Guy Dawnay was sent off that night after dinner with the official despatches. Meantime, Forbes, out in front, got to Landman's Drift between 2–3 p.m. on the 5th having used six horses and ridden the 110 miles in twenty hours. He pushed on to Pietermaritzburg, an additional 175 miles, using a buggy and horses and was there by the evening of 6 July. He then travelled on to Durban and posted Prior's drawings, so that both correspondents got their scoops.

Sir Garnet, accompanied by Braithwaite, Herbert, Maurice, Billy Russell and Fricke had at last got back on land and by 7 p.m. on 5 July had reached Fort Pearson on the south bank of the Tugela River. Here several telegrams awaited him, including one from Forbes reporting the Ulundi victory and saying the cavalry had cut the Zulus 'into mincemeat'. Wolseley at once sent the news to the men in camp and 'heard cheers of delight from the tents.' He telegraphed congratulations to Chelmsford and thanked Forbes for the great news. In his journal Sir Garnet concluded his entry: 'A fine day.'

Rain poured from forbidding grey skies all through 7 July and it was after dark when Wolseley finally reached General Crealock's column between Fort Durnford and Fort Napoleon. 'He came out to meet us,' wrote Sir Garnet. 'Just the same vain swaggering snob he has always been.' The two men had served together as junior officers in the 90th Light Infantry during the Siege of Sebastopol. 'His manner to the men, as it always was in the 90th, is most offensive,' continued Wolseley in his journal, 'I hate hearing him speak to soldiers as he addresses them as if they were dogs, not men – most of them are more men than he is a man.'[61] For once it seems Wolseley was not exaggerating; hardly a soldier had much good to say of Henry Hope Crealock and another general concluded that he was 'not strong and never much on a horse,' with an aptitude only for writing 'long letters and keeping an office in apple pie order ...'[62] For months Crealock had led his troops at a snail's pace until they were the laughing-stock of the entire army. To make matters worse, the general, who was described by Clifford as 'rather too easy-going', had begun dressing 'like a guest at an artist's ball', wearing a sombrero with a long peacock feather or a turban; his personal hen house had been trundled through the bush so that Crealock could enjoy fresh eggs with his breakfast and he had demanded – and got despite objections – a small herd of milch cows.

With the raindrops pelting down heavily, Wolseley strode forward to meet Crealock with the damning words, 'How do you do, sir. You might as well have been marching between Wimbledon and Aldershot as what you have been doing here.'[63] Sir Garnet ran into Fitzwilliam Elliot who complained of the boring weeks he had spent serving under Crealock. Sir Garnet replied, as Elliot reported in a letter home, 'I should have thought not of what the column should or could have done, but rather by what sort of man it is commanded.' A shocked Elliot noted: 'These are strong words for the C-in-C to use.'[64]

It rained all that night and most of the next day. Yeatman-Biggs, 'a first-rate officer whom I shall hold on to in future' noted Wolseley, turned up with the baggage. The 'white chief' of Zululand, John Dunn, arrived in camp and the general sat in his tent and quizzed this man who fascinated him so much about Zulu affairs. Next morning the sun shone forth and Sir Garnet rode down to the beach to watch stores being unloaded. To his annoyance a telegram was received from Chelmsford saying he was moving south towards St Pauls. Despite having written, 'A hasty occupation of the country I now occupy seems to me advisable at the present moment, and I await your further instructions before carrying it out,' his lordship had sent his telegram the slow route via Landman's Drift and had certainly not stopped his southward retreat to await instructions. This latest telegram sparked off another controversy that has caused dispute ever since – did Wolseley approve of Chelmsford moving his army away from the oNdini area? In the words of Joseph Lehmann: 'Chelmsford tried to fix the blame for his hasty retreat on Wolseley by claiming that he gave him no instructions before the battle on how to act in the event of a victory ...'[65] In his excellent *Kingdom In Crisis* the historian John Laband seems to suggest that the retreat was 'desirable' and that Wolseley 'recognized' this fact because 'Chelmsford's victory was a decisive one'. In his *The Destruction Of The Zulu Kingdom* Jeff Guy does not accept this argument; he says that the conventional view 'is a distorted one ... the battle of Ulundi, like the campaign itself, was a failure.'[66] Bishop Colenso, who often had his finger on the pulse of Zulu feelings, wrote of the battle: 'The burning of Ulundi & other kraals means nothing in Zulu eyes, as I hear from natives. And there is no clear evidence as yet that the loss of so many warriors ... has broken the spirit of the natives.'[67] An examination of Wolseley's correspondence – public and private – together with his journal would seem to suggest that from the very outset he disapproved of a full withdrawal from the oNdini area. As the weeks went by, and Cetshwayo still refused to submit, then this matter took on an even greater seriousness. It is true that Sir Garnet had not been clear on how Chelmsford should proceed if he won a victory, but just five days after the battle he wrote in his journal: 'I sent him a messenger with a duplicate copy of the orders I sent him yesterday desiring him to *leave Wood's column in the neighbourhood of Emtonjaneni ... as I am anxious to maintain the forward position the troops now occupy as long as I can possibly feed them there* [my italics]. This is very desirable for political reasons.'[68] The next ten days saw this argument hotting up. So much so that Wolseley on 20 July wrote to Stanley, enclosing all his correspondence on the subject, since 'I hear Chelmsford is giving out that he left the neighbourhood of Ulundi in accordance with my instructions.'[69] In his journal Sir Garnet noted with satisfaction, 'Those papers will I think finally settle that report for ever.'[70] He appears to have been successful, at least so far as HM Govt were concerned; with Cetshwayo and the Zulu question still rumbling on in August, the Prime Minister (writing in the third person) told the Queen that Chelmsford's retreat after Ulundi was 'his last and crowning mistake, and the allegation, that he was instructed to do so by Sir G. Wolseley, has been investigated by Lord Beaconsfield, and found to be without foundation.'[71]

Wednesday 9 July was a day of mixed feelings for the two generals: Wolseley wrote again to Chelmsford offering his congratulations, 'most heartily and sincerely', and wishing the 17th Lancers had captured the Zulu king, 'or had killed him in their brilliant charge'. His mind now made up, his lordship sent letters of resignation to both Sir Garnet and the Secretary-of-State for War, explaining to Wolseley in a clearly disgruntled manner:

> The inferior command accorded me in your G.O. of 28 June does not agree with the position which the Sec. Of State

> for War in his despatch last night states I was to occupy consequent upon your appointment. Looking therefore to the decisive nature of the battle of Ulundi … I feel that I can without loss of reputation retire at once from a very false position … and to leave by the earliest opportunity for P'M'burg en route to England. Do you wish to see me? What orders shall I give to my Head Quarters Staff? I shall await your reply at St Pauls.[72]

Put simply, Chelmsford's opinion was that he should have remained field commander after Wolseley's arrival, while his superior ought to have stayed distant (in the same way that Frere had done). Replying to his lordship Sir Garnet tried to pour oil on troubled waters, while at the same time re-stating his position: 'I have no wish to find fault. I did not come here to do so … and had the war lasted I am sure we would have got on very well together, but of course there could not have been two Commanders in the field.'[73]

The wet weather had stopped by 10 July and Wolseley enjoyed riding through the rich grassland 'very green after the rains', though he noticed the ground was dotted with ant-bear holes. In a letter to 'Loo' he told how he felt sorry for the way in which Chelmsford had 'suffered', but went on to say that the general had 'no genius for war & should never again be given any independent command in the field'. He declared that John North Crealock had been his 'evil genius' and was a man with 'no pretensions to be gentleman, either by birth, manners or appearance … this young fellow is a greater snob & swaggerer than the elder brother,' who, in turn, 'was so repulsive that I hate even speaking to him.'[74] Wolseley admitted to his wife that 'I should very much have liked to be present' at Ulundi. Brackenbury was proving 'as hard-working and useful and selfish as ever', while Fricke 'never grumbles' and Maurice 'is the greatest fun here; he is so earnest that he sometimes bores my life out, but I try to keep my temper for I know he means so well.' Sir Garnet and his officers were on a 'tea diet', much to the annoyance of Billy Russell, as the camp had run out of beer and spirits. The general explained: 'We have no wine and brandy, but twice a week a glass of rum is issued to everyone. So my mess expenses are not large.'[75]

By 12 July Wolseley's relationship with Chelmsford was starting to show cracks. 'I can understand his being very much put out by my arrival,' wrote Sir Garnet in his journal, 'but his contumacious disobedience of my orders to correspond only through my Chief of the Staff does not recommend him to me as a soldier.' The next day, in glorious sunshine, that long-awaited chief of staff, George Colley, along with Baker Russell and Archibald Forbes, managed to get over Port Durnford's heavy breakers after three unhappy days struggling to reach land. At one point Herbert had teased Russell with a heliograph message – 'A cavalry operation just starting. Why don't you come ashore. Are you afraid of the surf?' This brought back a classic Baker Russell response: 'Damn the surf! I am longing to get ashore.'[76]

The main camp was moved on 14 July to a drift on the Mfolozi ready for Wolseley's meeting with the coastal Zulu chiefs planned for 19 July. It was a lovely day and the general was escorted by the 57th Regiment, a native contingent, and 200 mounted colonials, 'very rum-looking fellows whose object seems to be to make themselves as much like bandits as possible'. In talks with his intelligence officers Wolseley was amused by how Maurice and Frederick Fynney, the Natal Government interpreter and political agent, always sided against John Dunn.

Next day near the ruined St Pauls mission, Wolseley and Chelmsford finally met. 'I cannot say that my meeting … was a pleasant one,' wrote Sir Garnet in his journal. In an undated letter to Louisa clearly written about this time Wolseley was at his most vehement – and anger always made him exaggerate things – saying how Chelmsford

> behaved very badly to me ... He tried to make out that I had only come out to supersede Frere & that I was not to command the Troops in South Africa ... I trust never again to have any official duties with so incapable a commander ... He won a victory on the 4th instant that was really a walkover, the enemy's attack only lasted seventeen minutes & the enemy never came on seriously. He hardly followed up his success at all and bolted back to his laager that same evening & then retired altogether from the position. The result is that I shall now have to send a column back to Ulundi & most probably go there myself to finish his half-done work. He is a poor creature & I believe would never have done what he did if he had not had Wood & Buller to carry him on. Both of them are sick & tired of him, liking him personally, useless as a commander ...[77]

Showers were drifting across the Mfolozi when Sir Garnet inspected Wood's flying column on the morning of 16 July. With great pride – and a subtle jibe – he described in a letter to the Duke of Cambridge how the occasion was 'remarkably done. I never hope to command better soldiers than those comprising the three regiments of that column, the 1/13th L.I., the 80th Regt. and the 90th L.I. The last named is the youngest corps as regards men's ages, but General Wood tells me he has every reason to be perfectly satisfied with their behaviour in action as well as in camp. The 80th is a splendid body of men.'[78] After the march past Wolseley turned on the charm, praised Wood, said he hoped that he would soon be confirmed as a general, and asked him to go to the Transvaal and subdue the Bapedi under Sekhukhune. Evelyn Wood had guessed this request would be coming and now pointed out that he, along with Redvers Buller, was exhausted by seven months campaigning and needed badly to rest. Even Wolseley could see that his old comrade was 'pretty well worn out', so he wisely let the matter drop.

All the troops were on parade and generals Wood, Chelmsford and Wolseley stiffly saluted as they rode down the lines. In the centre Sir Garnet moved out a few paces and commanded Major John Chard R.E. to step out and receive his Victoria Cross medal. This was pinned by the general on Chard's breast as Colley read out the warrant. *The Graphic* reported how 'Sir Garnet Wolseley shook hands and congratulated the gallant major and the ceremony terminated with a march past of all the troops,' omitting the flogging parade that followed, 'to teach three of Wood's Swazis that they must not now murder Zulus' wrote Captain Molyneux sardonically.[79]

Sir Garnet's personal remarks on Chard have been oft-quoted by historians: the general wrote that 'a more uninteresting or more stupid-looking fellow I never saw'. To be fair to Wolseley these remarks were never intended for publication and they were his spontaneous impressions of the man. He went on: 'Wood tells me he is a most useless officer, fit for nothing. I hear in this camp also that the man who worked hardest in defence of Rorke's Drift Post was the Commissariat officer who has not been rewarded at all ... Bromhead of the 24th Regt. who was the 2nd in command of the post is a very stupid fellow also.'[80] Invariably omitted by everyone quoting these remarks is another sentence: 'The only one who behaved badly was the Doctor & reports say that he is a coward.' This gossip seems a dreadful slur on Surgeon-Major Reynolds whose Victoria Cross had already been gazetted on 7 June 1879. Returning to Chard, while Wolseley's opinions seem cruel, he was certainly not alone in being dismissive. Lieutenant Curling who had escaped from Isandlwana, described the Rorke's Drift officers: 'Chard is a most insignificant man in appearance and only 5 feet 2 or 3 in height. Bromhead is a stupid old fellow, as deaf as a post. Is it not curious how some men are forced into notoriety.' Major Clery, one of Chelmsford's staff officers, thought both men were typical of 'the very dull class' of officers who figured in all regiments. Bromhead was 'reported confidentially as hopeless', while Chard 'is a very good fellow – but useless'. Chard's company commander after the battle was angered by his indifference to fame or promotion, bemoaning the way 'he smokes placidly on his pipe and does nothing. Few men get such opportunities.'[81]

These criticisms of Chard do not make him any less a hero. He was the officer commanding Rorke's Drift and had every right to share in the glory of its defenders. He might well have been dull, even unimaginative, and possibly not the man who came up with the post's main plan of defence, but when forced to fight or die, showed hidden depths of courage and resilience. 'I never met a nicer humbler fellow than Chard,' wrote Captain Watson, 1st Dragoon Guards, who dined with him in May 1879. Later writers have also pointed out that he might have been displaying post-battle stress and fatigue when he met Wolseley. A new view has come to light in the letters of Captain Elliot, who was present at the awards ceremony. He wrote: 'He [Chard] is a rum 'un to look at, and most unprepossessing. It is generally understood that the V.C. is a most unsuitable reward and it would have been better to have given something else. Chard was the senior officer at Rorke's Drift and got the chief kudos, whereas Bromhead was in point of fact in charge of the fighting element. The man to whom the chief credit for the defence of the post is given is a commissariat officer ...'[82]

The rains returned with a vengeance and Sir Garnet was not happy to hear from John Dunn that Chelmsford's departure from the oNdini area 'has had a very bad effect on the country'. There were rumours of 3–4,000 warriors supporting the king in hiding. In his journal Wolseley wrote: 'I feel there is nothing else for it but to return with a force to Ulundi and dictate terms to everyone from thence. Cetewayo must be either killed or taken prisoner or driven from Zululand before the war is considered over ...'[83] In a letter on 18 July to Colonel Stanley he reiterated his determination to dictate 'terms of settlement of the Country at the King's Kraal itself [as] a visible sign of our power'. He explained how Buller, Chelmsford, the Crealocks and Wood were returning home: the 1st Division was being broken up while General Hugh Rowlands would command a portion of them on the Lower Tugela; Mansfield Clarke's brigade, some Royal Artillery and colonial detachments would move towards Ulundi; Baker Russell was to command a flying column composed of 2nd Division men and operate north and west of Ulundi; General Newdigate was 'useless in the field', but he would be retained for a short time and command the remainder of the 2nd Division; General Clifford remained to oversee embarkations and the 1/13th, 1/24th, two batteries of Royal Artillery, a battalion of Marines and a cavalry regiment would leave South Africa without delay; finally, an uncertain host of Swazis, bitter foes of the Zulus, were to mass near the frontier as a threat if Cetshwayo tried to prolong the war. In his journal Sir Garnet noted of the Zulu king, 'I wish some amiable assassin would kill him.'

Wearing their best regalia with plumes of feathers and carrying ceremonial knobkerries, some 250 coastal chiefs waited outside Wolseley's tent on 19 July. The historian of Zululand's fall, Jeff Guy, has written that the cessation of hostilities was due more to this meeting than the battle on the oNdini plain because Sir Garnet made clear that if the Zulus 'laid down their arms, they would remain in possession of their means of production'.[84] The general's talents as a public relations man were never on better display; he told the chiefs that the British 'bore them no ill-will whatever for having fought against us ... We did not want their territory or their property & those who submitted now had nothing to dread from us.' Wolseley thought the Zulus were 'highly pleased' with his speech, though Fynney, suspicious as ever of them, thought the chiefs wanted to hoodwink the British. Always gloomy, Fynney argued that Cetshwayo 'does not yet consider himself beaten' and that his younger warriors wished to prolong the fight.

Over the next few days Sir Garnet made his way to Durban to say his farewells to a man who had nothing to say to him. It was a triumphal journey south for Chelmsford with cheering crowds wherever he went. Wolseley tried his best to be polite and attended a lavish farewell dinner given by the Mayor and Corporation of Durban. He had come to the conclusion that his rival was 'a gentleman and a nice fellow, but the Lord forbid that he should ever again have command of troops in the field'.[85] Just before Chelmsford was due to sail Sir Garnet went to his hotel, but the general was out so a final, perhaps embarrassing, farewell was avoided. That night Wolseley dined with Bulwer; next day Sir Henry told his brother that Chelmsford had advanced prematurely on Ulundi: 'Everyone says he did it because of Sir G's coming out and I fancy they are right.' Bulwer also thought there was 'rather a rush to the conclusion that the success at Ulundi has ended the war' and time 'has thus been lost'.[86]

Finally, with Chelmsford and most of the other generals departing from Natal, Sir Garnet could at last start to act according to his own plans. Cetshwayo had to be found before he became a rallying symbol for any Zulus who might want to fan the flames of rebellion. The situation was still tense. Zulus had fired at Border Police from the Hot Springs down to Mpisi Drift on the Tugela. While the king remained at large, Chief Manqondo continued to be bellicose and on 25 July hundreds of armed young warriors gathered, sang their war-songs, shouted defiance, and fired volleys at a patrol of the Ixopo Native Contingent. Natives living on the Natal side of the Middle Drift were refusing to sleep near the river. They complained of having to live in caves and wished to rebuild their burnt homes, 'which they cannot do until something is done to place the border in a secure position.'[87]

4

CATCHING CETSHWAYO

He was the finest Zulu I have ever seen.

Captain Fitzroy Hart

Chelmsford gone, Wolseley was at last free to settle Zulu affairs in his own manner and this he wished to do swiftly. Cetshwayo was free, a rallying-point for any remaining discontented warriors and a major stumbling block that had to be removed before a new settlement of the country could be presented to the Zulu people. During August, as the king refused to surrender, the search for him would get increasingly frantic and brutal as the British commander watched the days slipping away, while storm clouds gathered on the horizon in the direction of the Transvaal and its discontented Boers.

The embarkations were well under way. Clifford and his team worked tirelessly to tie up the loose transport and commissariat aspects of the war. Many a British soldier was grateful to be leaving South Africa having never met a Zulu on the battlefield. Those that had were left with a new respect for a remarkable race and could bid adieu to the heat, dust, disease and dangers of Zululand in the certain knowledge they could dine off their adventures for many months to come.

Despite his pushy reputation, Sir Garnet always preferred diplomacy, with the use of military force used only as a last resort. His policy was initiated on 26 July in a minute issued by Colley for 'all officers commanding Posts and of all political officers having dealings with the Zulu people'. This policy document advised that the Zulus needed to be encouraged peaceably to return to their homes before a final settlement could be made with the chiefs. Guns and the king's cattle were to be seized, but during all of this the chiefs, their people and property were not to be molested by the British soldiers. While the people were expected to hand over their guns, 'it is not advisable to be too exacting on this part'. In a big public relations exercise the Zulus were to be told clearly that 'we bear them no ill-will whatever ... they fought against us very bravely', but now the land needed to be restored to 'peace and quiet'. Queen Victoria, they must be told, wanted the Zulus to 'prosper and grow rich as the natives in Natal have done'. The Zulu military system of Cetshwayo's 'cruel and bloody rule' was ended, the men could now marry and come and go as they liked, the war was with the Zulu king 'and not with the Zulu people, with whom we have no quarrel ...'[1] The new British General Commanding would ride to Ulundi and meet with all the chiefs of Zululand to give the names of the men who would in future rule the country. The fly in the grand plan's ointment, as Sir Henry Bulwer pointed out to Wolseley in a letter on 27 July, was Cetshwayo whose 'influence is still a visible and tangible thing.'

The willingness of the Zulus to meet the British in major pitched battles might have been extinguished at Ulundi, but while their king roamed the land it was far from clear at the start of August 1879 that the war was truly over. Indeed, in north-west Zululand, as well as in parts of the south, especially along the Middle Thukela, districts were unsettled.

Heading towards the oNdini area with instructions to re-occupy the place and send out patrols in search of the king was a column from the disbanded 1st Division under the command of Lieutenant-Colonel Charles Mansfield Clarke. One of his officers at this time described Clarke thus: 'Never was there a stricter or more exacting C.O., never was there a better soldier to serve under.'[2] In his twenties Mansfield Clarke had taken part in the Maori Wars and on one occasion narrowly missed the fate of his commanding officer, whose head was cut off, boiled and shrunk! During Chelmsford's 2nd Invasion, in command of the 57th Regiment, Clarke had ably led his men in defence of the right face of the British square at Gingindlovu (2 April 1879). Then he had gone down, like so many men, with a bad attack of fever. Fully recovered he was now once more in the saddle. His column consisted of the equivalent of three battalions of British troops, a detachment of British cavalry and a squadron of mounted infantry, three troops of mercenaries, a Gatling gun section and a small detachment of Royal Engineers. The native troops included the 4th Battalion, Jantze's Horse and the Mafunzi Corps – in all, including non-combatants, about 3,500.

Baker Russell had been given command of a separate column tasked with pacifying north-western Zululand while also searching for Cetshwayo. In mid-July the normally affable Russell had got into an argument with Wolseley because he was 'disappointed ... in a war in which both Evelyn Wood & Buller have done so much and brought themselves so prominently before the public'.[3] Sir Garnet confessed annoyance in a letter to his wife that Russell seemed so little to appreciate how he had done all he could to further the career of 'Master Baker'. Now at last Russell was free to prove his abilities. His force comprised units drawn from the 2nd Division and Wood's flying column. Information coming in from spies led the political officers to think that the royalist abaQulusi of the north-west were still in a mood to fight. There was also a proud *inkosi* (chief) in the Ntombe Valley, Manyonyoba kaMaqondo of the Khubeka, who was still armed and in the field. Wolseley ordered Russell to advance on 26 July from St Paul's, via the White Mfolozi, towards the vicinity of the Black Mfolozi. Here he was to build a small outpost, to be called Fort George, and commence operations. With Russell were 537 mounted men, Harness's battery of six guns and six companies of the 94th Regiment. The general apologised to Russell in a letter on 3 August for the modest number of infantry, but told him 'they would be of no use to you; for I want you to operate solely with cavalry reconnoitring parties in all directions ...' If Cetshwayo was captured he was to be treated 'as well as you possibly can'. Sir Garnet urged Russell to make special use of the Natal Mounted Police detachment as scouts, 'a very superior body of men'.[4]

The north-westerly sweep from the south was to be supported by a simultaneous advance down from the north across the Phongolo by Swazi forces and British troops from the Transvaal operating in concert via Luneberg, 'both of whom would clear Baker Russell's front'. The Transvaal soldiers were to be commanded by Lt-Colonel the Hon. George Villiers ('the arch adulterer' Wolseley called him) and were to consist of mounted Boers and friendly Zulus led by Prince Hamu kaNzibe (one of Cetshwayo's brothers who had defected to Evelyn Wood in March).

Such was the general's north-western strategy, but it was to encounter serious problems in execution. A major difficulty, very worrying to Sir Garnet, was the attitude of the Boers. They were to refuse to join Villiers' little army and were, in fact, in regular and friendly communication with the Zulus. The British victory at Ulundi had kept the Boer danger in check, but as late as 4 August the Zulus warned one Afrikaner farmer to 'shift over' as an impi was coming to kill blacks friendly to the British and, as a result, Boer farmers north of the Phongolo trekked into laager until the threat was past.

Elsewhere, things also looked ominous. Along the Buffalo River frontier with Zululand, in northern Natal, John Sutcliffe Robson, the bearded giant who commanded the Buffalo Border Guard, reported in early August that he had twice sent out patrols into Zululand to see if the warriors had returned to their homesteads (*imizi*), but his men reported after two days scouting that they had not seen a single Zulu, all the imizi were empty and crops stood waiting to be cut in the fields. Robson reported that when the Zulus did return he expected further troubles as they would try and cross into Natal to steal cattle to replenish the ones they had been forced to hand over to the authorities. Near the Middle Drift section of the Thukela it was reported that Godide kaNdbela, seventy-year-old chief of the Ntuli clan, had moved his cattle into the Nkandla forest, a clear signal that he intended to resist. Dealing evasively with the authorities and stopping short of the conditions imposed by Wolseley were other chiefs in the same area, including Manqondo and his son, Qethuka of the Magwaza, and the blind Sokufa and his son, Singnanda of the Cube. Zulus were also arguing among Zulus; John Laband has noted how 'the married men seemed content to accept the British terms, the younger warriors resented having to give up their arms, and were prepared to carry on the struggle'.[5]

Before Sir Garnet could head upcountry, see Cetshwayo captured or killed and put in place the plans now forming in his mind for the settlement of Zululand, there were other matters to be taken care of. One of these was the curious business of Private John Snook, a soldier in Wood's column, who had caused a storm of controversy back home by sending a letter to the manager of the Royal Oak, Tiverton, who duly passed it on to the *North Devon Herald*. According to Snook, on 30 March 'about eight miles from Camp [Kambula] we found about 500 wounded, most of them mortally, and begging us for mercy's sake not to kill them; but they got no chance after what they had done to our comrades at Isandula.'[6] Questions were asked in Parliament about 'whether operations in South Africa are being conducted by the British troops according to the usages of civilization'.[7] The Aborigines Protection Society then complained to the War Office. Sir Garnet was requested by the Secretary-of-State to provide an official explanation. He duly demanded one from Wood who replied 'there is not a shadow of truth' in Private Snook's report. He added:

> The whole of the infantry were employed all day on the 30th, except when at divine service, in burying the dead Zulus lying close to camp. No infantry were outside our pickets. The horses being exhausted by six days hard work, only a patrol of 12 men was out. They saw no Zulus, and I, passing over the ground covered by patrol two days later, did not see a body. I believe no Zulus have been killed by white men except in action ...[8]

By the time of the furore Private Snook had retired to the Royal Oak tavern, which was his address. The whole matter can be dismissed as a flash in the pan, but the smoke lingered elsewhere, such as in a letter from Lieutenant Alfred Blaine, another soldier who served at Kambula, who wrote, 'As soon as the kafirs retreated, we cheered tremendously. Buller led us out to shoot them down as they retreated ... and I can assure you that we did, and had our revenge. We shot two or three hundred ...'[9] The exact truth will never be known of massacres by the British, or even war crimes, but letters by people like Snook, implying an unjust war forced on the Zulus, were to be like manna-from-heaven to the opponents of the Tory party during the 1880 general election.

Sunday 27 July saw Wolseley enjoying a busy day at Pietermaritzburg of receptions, news reports and letters from correspondents. There was early morning divine service in the drill shed, the kind of service the general liked – short, sharp and delivered by a military chaplain. There was sunny weather to enjoy and later in the day a farewell dinner for General Marshall, Chelmsford's cavalry commander, 'a very nice fellow', wrote Wolseley, 'but … even Chelmsford told me he was of no use.'[10] A report from Clarke arrived saying that Cetshwayo had sent a messenger with the news that he wished to surrender but feared for his life. The Zulu king was also asking John Dunn to help him. Sir Garnet wrote back that the messenger was not to meet with Dunn, and to tell the king 'that if he surrendered he would be well treated', though the general privately hoped Cetshwayo might be 'either killed in a skirmish or assassinated by some of his own people'.[11] News came that day that the Swazis were on the march towards the Zulu frontier. In a letter to Colonel Stanley the general launched into a blistering attack on the record of Commissary-General Edward Strickland who, to Wolseley's disgust, had just been given a KCB. Frequently referred to by Sir Garnet in his journal and letters as 'a blathering ass', Strickland had gone on the sick list and wished to go home, but Wolseley told the Secretary-of-State that 'he should finish off what he has begun. I am afraid he has much to answer for …'

Relations with Sir Bartle Frere continued to deteriorate. He had written on 20 July to complain 'of an inconvenience I am sure you did not intend to impose on us here', namely 'that you have strictly forbidden anyone to correspond with me on official matters. Consequently I am entirely in the dark as to what is doing or going on to be done North of Lat. 28° or East of Long. 29°.' Trying to soft-soap Wolseley, Frere said it was 'a great relief' to him personally knowing affairs were in the general's 'good hands', but it was 'awkward to be asked by the Ministers here, especially when the Parliament is sitting, for news …' Sir Bartle claimed that he had to rely on newspapers and war correspondents, such as Archibald Forbes, who had written to him direct from Ulundi, yet Wolseley did not send his report of the battle until three days later. Details of killed and wounded had only arrived that day (20 July) in a printed funeral order from Sir Garnet's headquarters and Frere complained that up until then he had been forced to rely on a 'mutilated' list in one of the newspapers. In the coming months Wolseley's attempts to cold-shoulder Frere, actions that many saw as arrogant, would breed bitterness and revenge from the old pro-consul and his supporters.

On 29 July the general and Bulwer went to see an amateur show at the theatre. It was here, just before dinner, that a wit brought the house down with laughter by shouting out, 'Have you heard the news? They've found Crealock!' It may have been at this event that Sir Garnet also first heard a riddle that amused him: 'Why is it that the men in Lord Chemsford's Column could not be regarded as Christians?' Answer: 'Because they made an idol of Wood and did not believe in the Lord!' He included this joke in a letter to 'Loo' on 31 July and added, 'Very neat as well as true.'[13]

About 10.45 a.m. the next day Wolseley and his staff set off again for Zululand. The first leg of the trip – forty-four miles from Pietermaritzburg to Greytown – was done at a gallop, the general travelling in a four-horsed open carriage. On arrival he went off to inspect the laager and was far from happy with the state of the local field hospital, whose tents were pitched in a filthy area and the sick men left lying on the ground; Sir Garnet, to his credit, was always concerned about the conditions of his private soldiers and he immediately ordered the hospital be moved to better ground and the men provided with bedsteads and an improved diet. A final touch of excitement came at sunset when the post cart arrived at camp, hit a bump and turned over, throwing out its occupants. One of these was Frederick Fynney, the lugubrious Natal border agent, who sprained his wrist; another was Fricke, who 'just escaped being badly hurt, but he was much shaken'.

Next morning, after a night of howling winds, Sir Garnet set off on horseback accompanied by Brackenbury and Braithwaite. So fast and hard did they ride that they missed completely the country inn where breakfast had been arranged and so had to feast on strips of tough oxen while the rest of the party, travelling behind, stopped at the right spot for a decent meal. Fynney's wrist was so painful that Wolseley had to write to Bulwer and request John Wesley Shepstone to take his place and hurry to meet them at Rorke's Drift. That evening Sir Garnet wrote to Captain MacLeod, who was leading the Swazis, urging that he get them across the Phongolo River 'as quickly as possible'. Cetshwayo was in the Ngome forest vicinity, wrote the general, and 'I am in great hopes that he may soon be deserted by his friends and disposed of in a Dingane War, or killed in one of the Swazi skirmishes. His death would be a much better solution to the question and to our difficulty than his capture; but dead or alive we must strain every nerve to get hold of his corpulent body.' Nervous of letters falling into the wrong hands, Sir Garnet advised MacLeod to write 'in French, or in the Greek character, and send concealed in a hollow stick, in a kafir snuffbox, or under the string fastening on the head of an assegai'.[14]

Two more days' travel saw Wolseley and his staff encamped at Rorke's Drift near the river. His biggest irritations on 1 and 2 August were meddling priests; a missionary called Dalziel had dared to suggest that he wanted to set up missions all across Zululand, a remark that led the general to sarcastically reply that it would be 'far better' to first convert the '30,000 heathen in Natal'. Then a note arrived from Bishop Hans Schreuder, the hardy old Norwegian missionary who had been living and working among the Zulus for thirty-five years. He offered to try and encourage Cetshwayo to surrender, while at the same time reassuring the monarch that he would not be sent into exile across the sea as Chief Langalibalele, the amaHlubi rebel chieftain, had been in 1874. Wolseley was incensed by this kind of well-intentioned interference in military affairs and wrote quickly to Schreuder: 'In communicating with Cetewayo, please give him *no* guarantee except that his life will be spared ... and that he will be kindly treated. I can promise him *nothing more* ... one should *not say anything* to him about Langalibalele, or about being sent over the sea.'[15]

Among Wolseley's letters at Hove are a small collection written on campaign to his seven-year-old daughter, Frances. The earliest of these is dated 1 August and they reveal another side of this extraordinary man. Addressed to 'My Dear Miss Puss Cat', he tried to sketch his journey in words for the youngster: 'We ride all day over a lovely country where you can gallop in every direction. This would be delightful country to play hide and seek in ... The only drawback is that there are a great many holes in the ground made by ant-bears, which holes are so covered with grass that it is very difficult to see them as horses occasionally tumble into them in consequence.'[16]

At 11 a.m. on 3 August the two companies of the 2/24th left at Rorke's Drift were drawn up on parade as Sir Garnet, attended by Colley, Brackenbury and Braithwaite, Colonel Degacher of the 24th and several other officers, pinned the Victoria Cross on the breast of Private Henry Hook, one of the heroes of the famous battle. Trying to steady a restless horse made the general think his little speech was not well-delivered, but he told his listeners that the pleasure of bestowing the decoration was doubled as it was presented on the spot where it was earned. After being shown around the main scenes of the defence, Sir Garnet rode over in the early evening to Fugitives' Drift to see the graves of Coghill and Melvill, who had died trying to escape from Isandlwana with the Queen's Colour of 1/24th. Throughout his life Wolseley had reservations about officers who did not stick with their men in a fight (his own body bore the scars of several such desperate encounters), and he recorded in his journal: 'I am sorry that both of those officers were not killed with their men at Isandlwana instead of where they were. I don't like the idea of officers escaping on horseback when their men on foot are killed.'[17]

Sir Garnet's guide on this excursion, Captain Herbert Stewart, General Marshall's brigade-major, led the horses gingerly along a path described by the general as 'about the worst I have ever ridden over owing to the boulders and large loose stones'.[18] It was the first time Wolseley had a chance to assess properly this young officer who was so disenchanted with soldiering that he was thinking of resigning his commission; within five years, and three campaigns later, Stewart would be Sir Garnet's favourite rising star and a leading member of his inner circle of friends.

The news trickling by despatch riders into Wolseley's camp was not encouraging from Macleod; he had held the Swazis back from crossing the Phongolo because he feared they might do more harm than good by laying waste all in their path. Sir Garnet was in a funk; he knew that, as he wrote in his journal, 'if the Swazies are allowed to invade Zululand, they will murder all the Zulus they meet whether they have or have not surrendered to us,' yet at the same time he was tempted to punish the northern Zulu clans 'as a warning to all others in South Africa as to what they may expect should they ever be fools enough to make war upon the English.'[19] Some of the general's critics have used his remarks as proof of an innate brutality in Wolseley, and he had indeed written, 'Perhaps I am brutal, but ... our leniency ... may possibly be mistaken for fear.' Yet it is typical of the man that having vented his puff of anger in his journal, he calmed down and reconsidered. Sir Garnet told Macleod to halt his Swazis for a further eleven days in order that the Zulus along the borders should have more time to submit.

From the south came more bad news: Bulwer was expecting another Zulu battle – 'I don't,' commented Wolseley, 'but I shall act with caution'); there had been telegrams from the northern Cape reporting fighting in Pondoland; and to top it all, Frere was complaining of the general's troop reductions because he wanted more British bayonets to be sent to quell possible outbreaks all of a sudden in Griqualand East and West, Pondoland and the Transvaal. Wolseley bluntly told Sir Bartle, by cipher telegram, that his mission was to end the Zulu War and settle matters in the

Transvaal using persuasion, moderation and conciliation. No new wars would be started without clear instructions from London. Frere was permitted to land the 1/24th when the battalion reached Cape Town, if it seemed desirable that they form a local garrison force, but only so that colonial units, such as the Cape Mounted Rifles, might be deployed to deal with any tribal or frontier disputes. Sir Garnet predicted this letter would make Frere furious. It did.

Despite vexations Wolseley was able to smile at the eccentricities of his hard-working intelligence chief, John Maurice. In a letter to Louisa he wrote at length of how Maurice had arrived in camp on 4 August having lost his horse, helmet, sword and pistol:

> So he appeared in the early morning mounted on a mule in a pair of breeches, with a pair of elastic-sided boots, and a waterproof coat over all, the cape of which was fastened down over his head and round his neck with a strap. This morning he came to my tent in a night-cap, the same elastic-sided boots & a military overcoat, one of the buttons at the back of which he had dragged round in some mysterious manner & fastened to a buttonhole in the front. He never sees that there is anything peculiar or grotesque in all this, but if you refer to it, he is always prepared to argue with you that his dress is admirably devised for what it is intended. When I laughed at him this morning, he at once opened his coat & said you see what my plan is. Around his waist was fastened a blanket like a kilt with a leathern strap: it protected his loins he said. His tent, I am told, is a picture of confusion: everything lying about as if his bags were turned upside-down and their contents shaken out 'anyhow'. He can never find anything. I employ him as an 'Intelligence Officer', that is, to collect information of the enemy's doings. I cannot say he has ever given us a scrap of information worth having, but he works

> away hard at his duty & he is such an honest fellow and so very clever withall, that I feel bound to employ him, and in his present occupation, neither order or regularity or neatness is of any consequence ... Yet he is brim full of courage, pluck, ability and energy ... He is such a loyal, honest, earnest friend that I always hate myself for laughing at him, but to refrain from laughing is simply impossible.[20]

Next morning before daybreak the camp was struck and Wolseley's party set off across the drift in the direction of Fort Marshall. The route took them over the battlefield of Isandlwana. 'Although most of these white men had been covered with earth & stones & although piles of debris had been burned,' wrote Wolseley, 'still the ground where the camp stood was littered with books, letters, papers, bits of clothing, equipment, tents & all the paraphernalia that belongs to camp life.'[21] He thought it all 'a sad sight' and told Louisa in a letter, 'Brackenbury picked up a most affectionate love letter written by some Dutch girl at the Cape of Good Hope to her lover in the 24th, winding up by the assurance that if anything should happen to him she would never forget him.'[22] This melancholy keepsake of the battle was in contrast to Hugh McCalmont's groom, who looted forty Zulu skulls as ghoulish souvenirs to sell back in England.

Fricke, Sir Garnet's manservant, now went everywhere carrying a loaded revolver. 'I believe he longs for a chance to shoot a Zulu,' the general told his wife, 'I now call him – behind his back of course – 'Captain' Fricke.'[23] Brackenbury continued to grow fat despite all the marching, while Arthur Creagh was doing 'very well' helping the recently arrived Lord Gifford V.C., another Ring member from Ashanti days, who was charged with keeping the convoy in order, 'which with our train of waggons is no easy matter.' 'By Jove, its nearly as hot as Cyprus,' one of the staff told Wolseley. The weather was delicious. Hugh McCalmont, disappointed not to be off leading a pursuit of Cetshwayo, asked the general several times, 'Do you think, sir, Cetewayo will fight again?' Sir Garnet's opinion was that he would not, though he dearly wished him killed or captured quickly.

It was after dark and getting very cold when Wolseley reached Fort Marshall. This little earthwork was clean and well-built but its commanding officer, Lieutenant-Colonel Collingwood of the 2/21st Regiment, was a loud and vulgar Irishman described by the general as a 'cunning fool' in his journal. In a letter to 'Loo' Sir Garnet wrote how Collingwood was 'without any one redeeming trait. He gave Colley and me some dinner, but the moment the last bit was down my throat I bolted, for I could not stand *mine host* no longer. He is neither a soldier nor a gentleman.'[24]

Next day the convoy reached Fort Evelyn, an irregular oblong earthwork built on the edge of a steep escarpment. Numerous oxen and horses lay dead all around the place, the sad remains of Chelmsford's 2nd Division transport column, while flocks of vultures continued to gorge on what was left of the smelly entrails. Steep hills on 7 August led to a camping ground, soon to be named Fort Victoria, lying at the foot of the Mthonjaneni Heights. Here envoys from Cetshwayo were waiting to deliver another letter in which the Zulu monarch made apologies for the war and hoped he might be left alone to rule Zululand. Via John Wesley Shepstone the indunas were told to return to their king and simply say that 'if he surrendered his life will be spared & he shall be well treated'. Messengers had also come to see John Dunn and they told him that Cetshwayo simply wanted to be given a kraal and live quietly among his people. Dunn and Wolseley were in agreement that Cetshwayo would intrigue to re-establish his power if he was permitted to stay in the country.

In the afternoon Mansfield Clarke's column arrived to swell Wolseley's numbers. The day had been sunny but at dusk a fine mist and drizzle soon developed into a downpour with very high winds. In the darkness before dinner Brackenbury's tent crashed down, soon followed by many others including those of Maurice and Herbert, all of whom would be made homeless that night. Shortly after the meal the general's own tent was blown over. Hard-working Fricke and a fatigue party rushed out in the blowing rain to set it up again. Around 10 p.m. Maurice took refuge in Sir Garnet's tent where he stayed the night. Wolseley, who had an amazing ability to sleep in the toughest of circumstances, 'slept soundly' under two layers of coats and a sleeping bag, but dawn saw the rain 'still pouring in bucketfuls'. As soon as it was fully daylight Colley left his dripping tent and saw that 'about two-thirds of the camp was blown down, the people scrambling among the ruins for their kits. I went to Sir Garnet's tent and found him, jolly as ever, holding on to his tent-pole with might and main, and laughing heartily.'[25] Maurice, 'enveloped in a great coat much too long for him', and with a ripped trouser leg, departed the general's tent with 'a crumpled and dirty air' and the interior 'an awful sense of disorder'[26]. Other soldiers had also faced a rough night and a miserable dawn; Henry Harford, now serving as one of Clarke's staff officers, called it 'the worst night I ever spent in my life ... Many of the tents had been blown to ribbons, and some carried off for miles.'[27] Captain Fitzroy Hart, also a staff officer, shivered in wet blankets throughout the gale, but wrote of 9 August, 'the sun rose upon a perfectly blue sky ... The day was beautiful, but what a scene of death lay around. Four hundred and fifty two of our oxen lay dead in the camp, killed by that storm!'[28]

Spirits rose in the bright sunshine over luncheon; Wolseley noted how 'Brackenbury's appetite is now as good as Herbert's. Those two would eat Fortnum & Mason up in a short time. Brack's figure is now like a barrel & his face is bloated with fat.' There was nothing for it but to remain stationary for a day or two; the ground all about was a morass of mud and dead oxen while animals not killed by the great storm needed to be rounded up and counted. In a letter to Louisa that day the general expressed his fears over Frere's policies causing 'disturbances in every province' and 'chaos everywhere'. Outwardly jolly and serene, inwardly deeply insecure, Wolseley feared that Frere might suddenly resign and HM Govt would expect him to fill his place. He told his wife that he was hoping that the post of C-in-C, India, when it next became vacant, might fall to him because the healthy rise in salary would 'enable you & me to live comfortably in our waning years'. Sir Garnet romantically told his beloved 'snipe', 'You will never be old, or look old, but I am, and look & feel old already ...'[29]

On Sunday 10 August the column finally reached Ulundi. This gave Wolseley much satisfaction but in truth the situation throughout the country was still unstable. No clear end seemed in sight. At Government House, Natal, Sir Henry Bulwer wrote to his brother, Edward:

> I saw General Newdigate last evening ... He is on his way home – disappointed, I fancy, with his share in the war ... I think Sir G. is perhaps a little too hurried in getting rid of so large a portion of his forces ... His object is to reduce the war expenses as fast as he can ... But I fear the difficulties of the situation are by no means disposed of: Cetewayo is at large; half the Zulu country has practically been untouched; and, besides the tribes living there, I have reason to think many of the young men from different parts of the country have rallied there, being by no means as willing to give in their submission as the stay-at-home elders have done. And even in this nearest part of Zululand there are many chiefs who have not given in and are in communication with Cetewayo. The great mistake or misfortune was that our Ulundi success was not followed up and another mistake was jumping to the conclusion that the war was over. I told Sir G. that I hoped he would not be too sanguine. I fear another misfortune is that Sir G. made up

> his mind to depend very much on the Swazis to finish what there was to finish. The Zulus have now had time to muster sufficiently to make the Swazis doubtful as to venturing in without a backing of Europeans. And altogether I see many difficulties in the way of ending this business satisfactorily. [30]

The camp at oNdini was fixed in the centre of Cetshwayo's great burnt-out kraal but next day was moved to less dirty ground nearer Clarke's troops. Sir Garnet and his staff looked over the battlefield but could find few dead Zulus or any souvenirs of the fight. Brackenbury came across fifteen dead bodies in one small space, which was acclaimed a record. 'There is nothing so dead and harmless as a skeleton,' wrote Fitzroy Hart, 'yet when you contemplate them in solitude they appear to possess a life of their own, especially when there are many together. Some look angry, some threatening, some foolish, some astonished, and those that are on their faces seem asleep.'[31] Henry Harford picked up a few shields and assegais lying in the grass, Wolseley was presented with the carved wooden block that was supposedly Cetshwayo's pillow, while the war correspondent, Charles Norris-Newman, a 'real bumptious snob' in the general's opinion, was instrumental in unearthing portraits of Queen Victoria and the Prince of Wales buried near the Zulu king's European-style bungalow in his kraal. Hugh McCalmont accompanied a patrol led by Major Percy Barrow that discovered the two 7-pounder guns of Major Harness's battery lost at Isandlwana. Quickly mounted on their carriages, they were returned in triumph to Ulundi and placed 'on either side of the flagstaff, just in front of the General's tent, at Head-Quarters camp, with the Union Jack once more floating over them'.[32]

Things began looking up for Wolseley from 10 August when a young Dutch trader, Cornelius Vijn, arrived at camp in threadbare clothes but with a message from Cetshwayo. He claimed to have left the king at a kraal five miles beyond the Black Mfolozi the day before.

In his letter Cetshwayo said that 'he had no more army, and was employed in collecting his cattle to hand over to the whites'.[33] The general offered Vijn a secret bribe of £200 (about £16,000 by today's standards) if he would lead a party of cavalry to the kraal. If the assignment could be completed in less than two days Vijn would receive a further £50. Sir Garnet thought the young man had told him several lies (and the fact that he had watched the Battle of Ulundi in the company of Zulus raised the general's hackles), but Vijn in one respect was bluntly honest; he told Wolseley that Cetshwayo would never surrender unless he was caught. Vijn's visit to the camp and his mission were kept secret; John Dunn was apparently in the know, and also Colley, but Wolseley did not inform Maurice, John Wesley Shepstone or any of his other advisors. He explained in a letter to Louisa that Dunn 'has continually far better means of obtaining information on all points than others, especially Maurice, who does not understand a word of the language'.[34]

Vijn went off alone, found Cetshwayo, but he still refused to surrender; he told the Dutchman that he thought the British would 'play crafty tricks' and shoot him if he gave himself up. He simply wanted them to 'leave him in peace with his people, to dig the land and get food'.[35] Cetshwayo was nervous and with good reason; he had been on the run for six weeks. The first month had been spent at a homestead on the Black Mfolozi but as the British net closed in he had moved by stages to the mountainous country of the Ngome forest. Messengers came regularly to the king and he digested all the news. Prince Dabulamanzi, who had led the attack on Rorke's Drift, had surrendered on 15 July to General Crealock, yet he still got word to the king that he suspected the British meant to kill him. Such threats Cetshwayo took very seriously indeed.

Late on the morning of 13 July the Dutchman returned to oNdini. The general rode out to meet him, had a brief conversation and advised Vijn to get some food and be ready to leave by 3 p.m. with Barrow and a mounted contingent of over 300 men. Only

Colley was told of this plan and in a letter home that same day he wrote: 'I wish Baker Russell was here for I should have much greater confidence in his determination and endless pluck than I have in Barrow. I am afraid Barrow is over-cautious. I wish I was going to command myself. What a lucky man Barrow is to have such a chance.'[36]

'Barrow was in a fever of impatience, but made slow progress,' wrote Donald Morris. 'The men continually blundered off the trails in the dense brush of the broken hills and Vijn ... was vague about distances and landmarks ... by sunrise the force was in a foul temper, and the scarlet jackets of the dragoons were in shreds ... the Boer "mile" was worth four English ones and it was noon before Vijn led the sullen men up to the kraal where he had left Cetshwayo two days before.'[37] To everyone's annoyance they found the bird had flown. The kraal was empty (Vijn later blamed Barrow for everything). Cetshwayo, given good warning of his pursuers, had left in good time.

The failure of the Barrow expedition ushered in the great 'King Chase' as it became known. 'Catching Cetchywhale', as the Tommies called it, would amount to a virtual obsession for the next fortnight as everyone went searching for the king. During the evening of 13 August a report reached camp that at daybreak Baker Russell had started his own hunt. Now with parties under the command of both Barrow and Russell scouring the country, Sir Garnet thought 'it will be an interesting race between the two as to which is to have the honour of bagging the ex-king'.[38] Lieutenant Henry Curling R.A., one of the lucky officers to escape from Isandlwana but now serving with Russell's column, found his commanding officer to be 'a smart, go-ahead man' who was 'far more energetic than the commanders we have been under before'. Russell made his men sleep in their greatcoats with their saddles for pillows, to be up at dawn and ride hard until dark, 'taking nothing with us but some preserved meat and biscuit in our haversacks ...'[39]

Everyone wanted in on what all expected to be the last Act of the war. Captain Herbert Stewart managed to get permission from Clarke to lead his own patrol and Lieutenant Harford went with him as an interpreter. He wrote:

> We took no food of any sort with us, intending to live on what we could get or find at the Kaffir kraals, but Stewart carried a flask of brandy in case of accidents. Our transport consisted of a mule and my Helpmekaar pony ... First we headed towards St Lucia Bay, travelling over some beautiful country ... Being still at war, nearly all the kraals we visited in the hope of learning something of Cetewayo's whereabouts were denuded of men, none but the very old, and the women and children remained ... Travelling on now, we continued our search ... No trace, however, of the King could be found, but in several of the huts a good many guns and other weapons were stowed away, and these we ordered to be collected and taken at once to Headquarters at Ulundi ... By a curious coincidence, one morning ... three, if not four of the expeditionary parties that were out passed within sight of each other, only a few miles apart. But only Major Maurice R.A., accompanied by an orderly, came up to us, and this worthy, having pumped us with regard to our movements, put spurs to his horse and rode off, declining to give us any further information than that he got very reliable news as to Cetewayo's whereabouts. The execrations that followed him as he went off can be imagined. Stewart, who knew his character, could only say, 'That's Maurice all over!'[40]

Meantime, events generally across Zululand were moving Wolseley's way. On 14 August several Zulu dignitaries including two half-brothers of the king, the regent of the emGazini in the north, and the chief of the Mbatha in central Zululand, along with 150 lesser chiefs and headmen turned up at Wolseley's camp. Leading this large group were Cetshwayo's two senior generals, corpulent Mnyamana kaNgqengele Buthelazi and his great friend, Ntshingwayo kaMahole (who had directed the fateful attack at Isandlwana). All were clad only in animal skins and carrying sticks as signs of abasement. They brought 617 cattle as a peace offering on the king's behalf. 'We had gone simply to ask for his head, that he might live and not perish,' said Ntshingwayo.[41] Two days later Cetshwayo's favourite brother, Prince Ziwedu, came in and was also detained. Throughout central Zululand families were surrendering in greater numbers at Fort Evelyn, Fort Marshall and at kwaMagwaza in the south-east. In the north-west Prince Hamu complained of stomach pains and was unwilling to advance his friendly Zulus very far in support of the British, but the Swazis looting along the Phongolo had to be held in check by Norman MacLeod. During his scouting expeditions Baker Russell took submissions and encountered no outright hostility despite a general unfriendliness among the inhabitants. Only the Qulusi seemed to be preparing for war.

On the very day that Wolseley's patience finally snapped – 20 August – many of the Buffalo border chiefs formally surrendered at Rorke's Drift, though the number of guns and cattle given up were 'hardly satisfactory'. By mid-August the resident magistrate at Umvoti, William Wheelwright, had collected only ninety-nine guns out of an estimated 2,000 supposed to be in Zulu hands in his district. But the surrenders kept coming, even though the chiefs cunningly evaded the full terms of submission and were particularly reluctant to give up royal cattle. Hundreds of chiefs owned royal beasts presented to them in times past as tokens of loyalty to the king. Zulu society was such that there was little possibility of royal herds being handed over while Cetshwayo was still free and might be in a position one day to reclaim them. Special border agent Eustace Fannin, based near the Mpisi Drift of the Middle Thukela, was grateful, however, when old Chief Godile grudgingly made a token submission on 15 August and included, among a bunch of rusting flintlocks, a smart Swinburne-Henry carbine taken at the Battle of Hlobane.

As the days passed every officer except for Brackenbury and Colley seemed to have deserted the general and were out of camp hunting Cetshwayo. They included Barrow, whom Sir Garnet now thought 'not worth his salt', young Herbert, Maurice – who wrote 'most hopefully of being able to catch him' – McCalmont, Stewart and even Arthur Creagh who 'lost most of his breeches torn to shreds in the dense brush'.[42]

On 12 August, when about ten miles from camp, Cetshwayo's secret reserve of gunpowder was found in a cave on the side of a cliff. Sir Garnet and John Dunn led a party to examine and destroy it. In all, about 1,100 lbs of gunpowder had to be hoisted up the cliff. Finally a long train was lit, ammunition placed on top of the barrels and the whole lot exploded. A large mamba, over ten feet long and head erect, came spitting out of the cave as the last barrels were being lifted up. Dunn, who was an excellent shot, blew its head off (this being in contrast to Cetshwayo, who had merely been scotched).

By 20 August ten days of chasing Cetshwayo had produced no results. Always the elusive monarch managed to stay one step ahead of his pursuers. 'I had been a long time in Zululand,' wrote one of the guides tracking the king, 'I knew the people and their habits, and, although I believed they would be true to their King, I never expected such devotion. Nothing would move them. Neither the loss of their cattle, the fear of death, nor the offering of large bribes, would make them false to their King.'[43] Wolseley now decided to take a tougher approach. 'My forbearance must now cease,' he wrote in his journal, 'I have sent out orders to burn Kraals & carry off cattle where the King is known to be & to be concealed by the inhabitants ...'[44] In these last days of the war the British, according to the American historian Robert Edgerton, indulged in 'exceptional brutality ... Some Zulu men were beaten, and others tied up to tree limbs and flogged ... Several times Zulus were threatened with death and taken out into the bush to be shot.'[45] One of the perpetrators, Hugh McCalmont, explained it all rather differently: he admitted to looting 'one or two kraals' during two days' hard scouting over eighty miles of territory; in one place he got hold 'of a couple of prisoners, but found it quite impossible to elicit from them where the monarch was, although they evidently knew; so I burnt the hut of one of the fellows and threatened to shoot him. He promptly made a bolt for it, and we fired at him, but rather to my relief, I must confess – we missed him ...'[46]

All agreed that the most energetic – some would say ruthless – hunter of the king was Captain Lord Edric Gifford V.C., thirty-year-old son of the 2nd Baron Gifford. In 1874, when barely twenty-three years old, Gifford had been chosen by Wolseley as a special service officer in Ashanti. Here he won the Victoria Cross leading parties of scouts and capturing the town of Becquah. Sir Garnet vaunted young Gifford's prowess and described him as 'a trump; he works like a slave, and although a delicate man is always to the fore and ready for anything'.[47] Gifford remained close to Wolseley after the war and served on his staff in Cyprus. Now, having missed the action of the Zulu campaign, he was determined to prove himself the man who captured Cetshwayo, even if it meant flogging natives, burning homesteads, scaring blindfolded men into talking by firing revolvers in front of them and using torture; Chief Mbopha of the Hlabisa, an important elderly royal councillor, 'was kicked to the ground and burnt with firebrands in an unsuccessful attempt to make him reveal Cetshwayo's whereabouts'.[48]

The King Hunt started to produce its own side-effects. Wolseley noted in his journal on 24 August that 'all these parties sent out are most jealous of one another & don't like new men trespassing on their reserves.' McCalmont and Maurice had been quarrelling over their respective rights to lead search parties. This led to the general letting off steam in his journal at Maurice, a man he considered lion-hearted, energetic, loyal and self-confident, yet lacking in any knowledge of human nature or the importance of time, order or calmness. He concluded: 'His mind is like a cleverly devised instrument made to prove that perpetual emotion is a possibility.'[49]

That same day, back in an England suffering one of the wettest summers on record, the Prime Minister was trying to deal with another of the Queen's moans about him. Lord Beaconsfield wrote to her a subsequently oft quoted critique of his South African supremo: 'It is quite true that Wolseley is an egotist and a braggart. So was Nelson ... Men of action, when eminently successful in early life, are generally boastful and full of themselves.'[50]

In Zululand the weather at least stayed bright and warm. Sir Garnet's increasing insecurities and frustrations boiled over in a letter to his wife on 26 August. After a breakfast of real porridge and fresh milk, he wrote:

> It is now that I realize Chelmsford's stupidity in not staying here after the fight. Five weeks were lost by the course he followed ... I am so anxious to get to the Transvaal where my presence is urgently required & yet I cannot leave this until I see my way more clearly before me. I have never been more worried than I am at present, for although I am doing my best, I am afraid the Home Ministry will be disappointed that I have not already cleared out of Zululand altogether.[51]

Gifford and Barrow were both out leading scouting parties in the rugged Ngome Forest region when spies reported at oNdini on the night of 26 August of a special area worth exploring. The next morning under orders from Colley, via Mansfield Clarke, a force was assembled consisting of one squadron of the King's Dragoon Guards, a company of the 4th battalion, Natal Native Contingent, and an officer and ten mounted infantry with Lonsdale's Horse. Command of the expedition was given to forty-six-year-old Major Richard Marter, a handsome officer with thick wavy hair and a full curling moustache, who had served with his regiment since joining them as a cornet in 1851. He had taken part in the expedition to recover the Prince Imperial's body but missed the chance to fight at Ulundi.

There had been many false alarms before so hardly anyone in camp wished Marter and his men success as they moved off. He was not sanguine either about his chances of capturing Cetshwayo; talking with Zulus on earlier patrols, wrote Marter, 'some of the most friendly, who had surrendered their arms and submitted quietly, wishing for peace, had told me frankly that if they knew him to be close by at the time of speaking to me, they would not tell me; nor could I wonder at this, or blame them for it ...'[52] Local Zulus in the Ngome area were helpful – up to a point. 'I have heard the wind blows from this side today,' one told Marter, then pointed up a track towards the forest, 'but you should take that road.'

Around noon on 28 August, amid mountainous terrain, guides led Marter to the edge of a summit and pointed down. Looking through the trees he saw some 1,700–2,000 feet below a strongly fenced kraal, 'in an open space at the bottom of a basin, three sides of which were precipitous and clothed with dense forest'.[53] Unbeknown to Marter, the homestead had been spotted that same morning by Lord Gifford, but he decided to return to his camp and prepare for a night attack. Not so Marter, who told his N.N.C. to strip out of their clothes and carry only rifles and ammunition, while his cavalry disposed of kit, swords, scabbards and anything that might make a noise or impede progress. The descent was hair-raising, loose stones were everywhere underfoot and clinging creepers barred the path. Everyone went down in single file, two horses were badly injured and one man dislocated his elbow, but finally the ground floor of the forest was reached.

The men silently formed a large circle around the kraal to cut any line of escape. Finally Marter rode forward and his interpreter, Martin Oftebro, son of a Norwegian missionary, called out loudly that if any resistance was offered the British would shoot everyone and burn the huts. Marter dismounted and entered the enclosure. A retainer met him and pointed out the king's hut. For some minutes Cetshwayo refused to come outside, clearly nervous he would be shot, but eventually made his appearance, 'and throwing his mantle over his shoulder, stood confronting me, erect and quite "the King"'. He asked Marter how he had found him and on being told replied, 'I never thought troops could come down the mountain through the forest, or I should not have been taken.'[54]

By 3.45 p.m. Cetshwayo was on his way to Ulundi as a prisoner. Seven male attendants, a boy, five women and a girl accompanied him. Major Marter was struck by the fact that the Zulu king did not look, as he (and Wolseley) had been expecting, 'footsore and weary', but was in 'splendid condition', and 'a noble specimen of a man'. Next morning a none-too-pleased Gifford rode up and learned how Marter had pulled off his coup. There was nothing for it but for Gifford to hasten on towards Ulundi and deliver the news. It was actually to be one of the worst days in his lordship's life, as Wolseley had already heard of the capture as he came out of the mess tent after breakfast; Clarke's orderly officer and a couple of horsemen rode up and Colonel Cecil East, a special service officer who had acted as Chelmsford's D.A.Q.M.G. during the second invasion, yelled out, 'They've caught him, sir!'

Sir Garnet heard the words with what he later described as 'joy and satisfaction'. He wrote to Louisa: 'I cannot describe to you how my heart jumped within me ... All my plans for the pacification of the country hinged every day upon his capture ... As days went by, and he managed to slip through my patrols, I became very nervous ... Old Frere has promised to accept the charge of Cetewayo at Cape Town, and so ends his reign.' Wolseley telegraphed the good news to

London, adding, 'All the Troops will vacate Zululand forthwith, and I hope to leave this, on 5 September, en route for the Transvaal.'[55]

The good news kept coming. Arriving back in camp that same day was a large party of officers and men under Yeatman-Biggs' command who had started from Port Durnford on 17 August and traversed eastwards along the coast to St Lucia Bay, then struck inland to explore previously unvisited parts of Zululand. Everywhere they had found Zulus returning contentedly to their homes. The British were impressed with how relaxed and affable their former enemies now were. 'I have taken rather a fancy to the Zulus, they are always so thoroughly manly ...'[56] wrote one officer whose description is repeated in many letters. On patrol Henry Harford had got chatting with a warrior who had fought against him at Isandlwana:

> He caught hold of both of my hands and shook them firmly in a great state of delight, saying it was a splendid fight. 'You fought well, and we fought well,' he exclaimed, and then showed me eleven wounds that he had received, bounding off in the greatest ecstasy to show how it all happened. Rushing up towards me, he jumped, fell on his stomach, got up again, rolled over and over, crawled flat, bounded on again and so forth, until he came right up to me. His movements being applauded by the warriors squatting in the centre of the kraal with a loud 'Gee!' I now had a look at his wounds. One bullet had gone through his hand, three had gone through his shoulder, and had smashed his shoulder-blade, two had cut the skin and slightly into the flesh right down the chest and stomach, and one had gone clean through the fleshy part of the thigh. The others were mere scratches in comparison with these, but there he was, after eight months, as well as ever and ready for another set-to. Could anything more clearly show the splendid spirit in which the Zulus fought us? No animosity, no revengeful feeling, but just sheer love of a good

> fight in which the courage of both sides could be tested, and it was evident that the courage of our soldiers was as much appreciated as that of their own.[57]

Wolseley was also able to write that the health of the troops 'is curiously good. I never remember – except during the Red River Expedition – so few men in hospital.' Despite some pain that day from his bad eye (an occasional malady) Sir Garnet thought he and the staff were 'the picture of health and as fat as pigs'. The only officer unhappy in the whole force was Gifford, who was described by Wolseley as a man living 'in a state of chronic discontent'. He had returned to camp that evening with Creagh in tow, 'all their clothes torn to shreds by the thorny country they have been operating in'. To cheer up Gifford, the general decided to send him home with the campaign despatches – a signal honour that came with a gift of £300. 'I wish, poor devil, that he had caught the king,' wrote Sir Garnet, 'for he has worked hard to do so.'[58]

Cetshwayo, meantime, in his royal progress towards oNdini used some classic delaying tactics and got sulky when Major Marter, with firm politeness, refused to bend to his ways. In the end Marter found the best way to hurry along the king was by taking his sabre out of its scabbard, which seemed to make Cetshwayo quite nervous – 'So I made an arrangement with him that whenever he gave trouble I should guard him with the sword, but when he was good I should let him off with the revolver.'[59] On the evening of the second day three men and a woman tried to escape. Marter had given orders to his men to open fire if anyone tried to run away and in this incident two of the males were killed (the other man and the woman made good their escape into the bush).

Late morning on 31 August the king finally reached oNdini. Earlier he had seemed dejected when he saw the sight of his burnt capital from the hills. 'He stopped,' wrote Marter, 'and placing his hands upon the top of his long staff, rested his forehead upon them for about half a minute – then raising his head, he threw off all signs of depression, and marched onwards ...'[60] The entire British camp turned out to see him. He had to go through flanking parties of dragoons with drawn swords but the effect, though intended as a security measure, simply gave added stateliness to the king's natural dignity and gravitas. All who saw Cetshwayo were impressed: Captain Wyndham Murray, 61st Regiment, wrote, 'When Cetewayo was brought in as a prisoner to Ulundi he was travelling in a small mule-cart, but at the river ... he got out and crossed the shallow river looking like a real King. He was dressed in a tablecloth with a pattern of large roses and carried a long walking-staff with a knobbed head, like a knob-kerry.'[61] Henry Harford thought him 'a magnificent specimen of his race'. He noticed how Cetshwayo looked terrified when stepping down from the cart, yet strode in to the camp proud, dignified and graceful. In Harford's opinion the king was 'well over six feet, fat but not corpulent, with a stern, severe and cruel countenance, he looked what he was, a savage ruler'.[62] Fitzroy Hart wrote home in a letter that Cetshwayo was 'the finest Zulu I have ever seen, very tall; of herculean build ... and remarkably handsome!'[63] George Colley was quite shocked; the Zulu king was not 'the enormous bloated savage I had imagined, or like any portraits I had ever seen, but a singularly fine-looking man ...' He admitted, 'I feel very sorry for him.'[64]

Wolseley had no time for such sympathies, but he admitted that Cetshwayo had 'a very wise countenance and is quite the King in his bearing and deportment'.[65] The British commander refused to meet with his captive, who was treated simply as 'a mere fugitive from justice'. A very uncomfortable John Wesley Shepstone had to give the Zulu monarch the bad news that since he had broken his 'coronation pledges' he was now being deposed and his kingdom would be divided between several chiefs. Tears ran down Cetshwayo's cheeks when he was told that he must leave Zululand forever. He begged that John Dunn might come and talk with him, but the man who had been made a white chief among the Zulus refused to leave his tent with the pathetic excuse that he was sick. Around 2 p.m. Cetshwayo and his attendants started their journey southwards in an ambulance waggon heading towards Fort Victoria. Next day, as the king was taken towards the coast he murmured wistfully, 'I am no longer a king: let me go and live in Pietermaritzburg like any other poor Zulu.'[66] It was 1 September, ironically the sixth anniversary of his 'coronation' by Sir Theophilus Shepstone.

Sir Garnet had found the departure of the king a 'lovely' event, though he also received a startling letter from Alfred Aylward, an Irishman living in the Transvaal, saying that the Boers were preparing to revolt. Wolseley thought the sooner he could get upcountry the better. In a letter to Louisa he said that he was sending home a necklace of lion's claws that had belonged to the Zulu monarch and wished to have some of them individually mounted in gold, with an inscription, 'Cetewayo – 29 August 1879', as a 'charm' for his favourite ladies including Lady Cardwell. The Queen was sent Cetshwayo's assegais and the Duke of Cambridge a carved Zulu stool. Wolseley refused to give the Princess of Wales the Zulu king's pillow because she had not thanked him for some glass sent to her from Cyprus.

For several days chiefs had been arriving at the general's camp ready to hear news of his settlement, which was fixed for 1 September. Thankfully, in the nick of time, Cetshwayo had gone into exile and could no longer disrupt things. Sir Garnet had given a great deal of thought to his new arrangements for Zululand. It was time to reveal all to the Zulu people.

5

SETTLING THE ZULUS

I am restoring Zululand to the Zulus.

General Sir Garnet Wolseley

On the steamy afternoon of Monday 1 September 1879 between two and three hundred Zulu chiefs and headmen sat in a clustered semi-circle in the centre of the British camp at Ulundi. It was a muggy, hot day and the Union Jack hung limply at its flagpole. When Wolseley arrived the Zulus greeted him with loud and guttural hurrahs, the visitors being hemmed into a large square formation by a phalanx of British redcoats. The general spoke for three-quarters of an hour, stopping after each sentence for his words to be translated by John Wesley Shepstone. Sir Garnet found the heat oppressive and was irritated by the swarms of flies and stench of dead oxen that hung over the camp.

The Zulus listened impassively to the news that their monarchy and military system were now abolished. Henceforth the country would be ruled by thirteen chiefs appointed by the British. Those chiefs were to be guided in their endeavours by a single British Resident whose role would simply be an advisory one. The largest swathe of territory, about one-fifth of the country comprising most of southern Zululand, was awarded to the white chief, John Dunn.

Less than half of the chiefs were at the meeting. One of the appointees, *inkosi* Mnyamana kaNgqengele Buthelezi, Cetshwayo's most respected councillor, stood up and refused his chieftainship, possibly out of loyalty to the deposed king, and certainly out of concern that he was being given a new district, with many of his own kraals now placed under the turncoat, Prince Hamu kaNzibe, who had sided early on with the invaders. Mnyamana was a lone voice at the meeting; as their names were called out the appointed chiefs and two indunas approached the table, constructed directly beneath the British flag, where Shepstone helped each man to hold the tip of the pen and make his mark. Finally, the whole Zulu assembly stood up, shouting out '*inkosi*' in one voice, and departed.

Sir Garnet thought the signing had all gone off with 'general satisfaction' and that the Zulus had been impressed by the leniency of the British terms. This may have been so, but confusion reigned for a time. Eight weeks later John Wesley Shepstone admitted to Sir Henry Bulwer that some Zulus 'still have a misty perception of the settlement ... none of the headmen south of the Umhlatoosi River were at the Ulundi meetings; hence the ignorance of John Dunn's true position.' He concluded that the Zulus 'believe that an enemy is only subdued when complete spoliation of all he is possessed of takes place'.[1]

As the Zulus drifted away from the stench of Ulundi, a mighty stink was about to break around Wolseley's head. His settlement was damned then and right up to the present day. No matter that he wrote to Louisa that same evening, 'I have done my best to end the war quickly and satisfactorily & I could have done no more.'[2] Missionaries, churchmen, Natal colonists, the colonial Press, Frere and his influential friends across South Africa, Sir Theophilus Shepstone and his allies in England, all roundly condemned Wolseley's settlement.

Bishop Colenso, as one might expect, was furious that Cetshwayo's overthrow was 'the crowning act of infamy to this iniquitous war ... Sir G. W. has announced that he will *never*, under any circumstances, be allowed to return to his native land. What right has he to bind the English Nation under this permanent disgrace & to commit all future Governments to carry out his arrogant decree?'[3]

Missionaries, such as the Norwegians Hans Schreuder and Ossumund Oftebro, found the new settlement quite unsatisfactory since it appeared to restrict what they could do in Zululand. They were furious that John Dunn 'had got almost half of the country', a man 'who more than anyone else has caused this Zulu war by having armed the Zulus with guns in order to enrich himself', moreover a man who was antipathetic towards missionaries, an attitude that would make the Zulus think 'missionaries are objectionable as he, a white man, who ought to know all about it, does not allow them to settle in his territory, etc.'.[4]

Editorials and letter columns of the colonial Press thundered with denunciations of the new settlement. The *Natal Mercury* blasted Wolseley personally for leaving Zululand 'in all but one or two respects a more complete domain of barbarism than it was two years ago ... in fact, he has deposed and banished one big tyrant, but he has established 13 small ones', who would rule without 'an astute and tangible assurance of authority'.[5] On 16 September the *Cape Times* noted rather smugly that the 'so-called settlement of Zululand is regarded with anything but satisfaction in Natal ... such a peace, however, has no guarantee for continuance, but on the contrary, an inherent weakness, forbidding any hope of permanence'. There was 'not a single colonist in Natal', declared the newspaper, 'who had 'the smallest faith in John Dunn who armed the Zulu nation'. His appointment as a chief over a tract of Zululand was 'a shock to civilization'. Priggishly the newspaper summed up the settlement along the lines of the Natal Press as 'simply the appointment of a dozen Cetywayos with a white man to look after them, who is a Cetywayo in all but colour'.[6]

At Cape Town an incensed Frere complained to Sir Garnet on 15 September that he had still not received an official dispatch relating to the settlement terms (Lord Gifford failed to deliver it on his way home to England and it had to be sent back to the Cape), and all he could glean was via the newspapers. Sir Bartle now told Wolseley that a Resident who could only give advice to the Zulu chiefs, but exercise no real authority over them, would be 'of no use, unless backed by power of some sort – moral, intellectual or physical, and best of all by all three combined'. Excluding colonists and traders from Zululand, Frere went on to say, would only make the territory a refuge for 'the rogue or vagabond, the idler and outlaw', until the 'scum' became so 'noxious' that a 'law-sustaining force has to come to cleanse the foul den'.[7]

The most significant contemporary criticisms of the settlement came from Sir Garnet's old mentor, Sir Theophilus Shepstone. He was now retired and visiting England. He had not been consulted by the Government prior to the settlement, but they now asked his opinions on Wolseley's plans. Privately, on 24 September, Shepstone wrote to one of his sons that the treaty 'should, in my opinion, have been based upon the principle of actual active control ... I think that to appoint a man like John Dunn as a chief over a section of the Zulu Country is a scandal to the Government and to civilization ...'[8] One month later, in a letter to the Colonial Office, Sir Theophilus described the settlement as 'too feeble'. What Zululand needed was 'effective control' by a white agent of the Natal government placed with each chief, all under a tough Chief Resident.

The sharpest pen to stab at Wolseley's settlement was that of the young man who had rung up the Union Jack at Pretoria, Shepstone's former assistant and disciple, Rider Haggard. He ridiculed the general's 'calm contempt' in creating a 'cruel settlement', though he thought this 'political monster' was 'dictated to him by authorities at home'. The thirteen chiefs, wrote Haggard, 'were so carelessly chosen that they have no authority whatsoever over the districts to which they were appointed',[9] while John Dunn's chieftainship was labelled as 'mischievous'. The only kind words Haggard had to say for the settlement were reserved for Melmoth Osborn (appointed as second Resident) who, it just so happened, was a close personal friend and another of Shepstone's old staff from the Transvaal.

Historians sitting in their ivory towers and with the great advantage of hindsight have laid the civil war that rocked Zululand in the 1880s, colonial partition and eventual annexation, all very much at Wolseley's door. 'No historian has ever praised the Ulundi settlement,' wrote Dunn's biographer, 'and those writers who do not castigate it have sought to attach a Machiavellian virtue to Wolseley's tactics in destroying Zulu unity without annexation.'[10] Eighty years ago the constitutional historian, C. W. De Kiewiet, called the treaty 'an act of scuttle ... It was folly to suppose that a Zululand ruled by thirteen weak nobodies, with as much cohesion as dry sand, could really remain independent or at peace.'[11] Thirty years later Donald Morris wrote of 'Wolseley's folly' in creating a 'patently disastrous' settlement, 'the thirteen kingdoms he had established were at one another's throats like so many Kilkenny cats. No one seemed to care a quarter of a million people were sliding towards anarchy.'[12] Brooks and Webb in their important history of Natal called the treaty 'completely unsuccessful'. More recently John Laband has referred to Wolseley's cynicism, his 'ragbag' of chiefs, and a 'railroaded settlement' which 'consigned the Zulu people to civil war and ruin'.[13]

A few historians have gone even further in denunciation. Leonard Thompson in the *Oxford History of South Africa* dwelt on the settlement's 'Machiavellian quality', describing it as 'an astute device' for 'setting Zulu against Zulu and thus consummating the military victory without further cost or responsibility'.[14] This line of argument was accepted by a recent writer who described Wolseley's 'draconian plan' as 'deliberately unreasonable'. The thirteen chiefs were appointed with 'the deliberate intention of creating political disharmony and rivalry'. The general's 'diktats', along with his 'hurried and hard-headed settlement', so this theory goes, were all part of a British government conspiracy to destroy the Zulus and acquire their territory by stealth. The principal historian of the war's aftermath, Jeff Guy, is wary of the Machiavellian argument because it 'credits Wolseley with an understanding of the Zulus he did not possess'. In Guy's opinion – and the present writer must concur – the general thought he had conceived a settlement that gave 'expression to real forces within the Zulu political structure'. Events would prove him wrong. Yet in the summer of 1879, 'Political expediency, cultural arrogance and ignorance played a far more important part in the planning of the settlement than did conscious political manipulation.'[15]

Sir Garnet's contemporary defenders were few; his secretary, St Leger Herbert, demonstrating a remarkable flair as a Victorian spin doctor, managed to insert anonymous articles called 'The Zulu Settlement' into the London *Times* in October and the *Cape Argus* in December. He described the settlement as 'the very best that could be devised for the country itself, and for our own peace and security'. Next came a swipe at Sir Bartle Frere, clearly with Wolseley's backing: 'Sir Bartle Frere would probably have annexed the country, would have harassed it with missionaries, and would have compelled the Zulu children to attend Sunday school ...'[16] The only historian I can find to defend the settlement is Joseph Lehmann, one of Wolseley's biographers, who described it as 'a well-conceived scheme of reconstruction, arranged with great skill', though he noted how 'the absence of a central control caused a break-down'.[17]

The indefensible cannot be defended. Later events demonstrated that the settlement was a disaster. But it is all too easy to be smug with hindsight. Was Wolseley's plan one of well-intentioned folly, or a crafty act of conquest-by-stealth? Are there clues among his letters? What were his expectations for the Zulus and their country? Before examining some of Sir Garnet's own personal and official correspondence in an effort to try and better understand his settlement and the intentions of its instigators, it is necessary to look first at the treaty itself, the terms offered to the Zulus and the men chosen to rule the country.

Sir Garnet had begun his 1 September speech by commenting on the curious coincidence that Cetshwayo, now a prisoner, had been proclaimed king exactly six years earlier. He had been deposed because of failing to live up to his coronation pledges. Wolseley went on to explain that the land would now be divided into thirteen districts under separate chiefs and resettled. The chiefs would sign a treaty of eleven clauses. The first clause required each of them to recognise British supremacy by agreeing to 'observe and respect whatever boundaries' were assigned to them. The second clause disbanded the Zulu military system and successive conditions forbade the import of firearms and ammunition; witchcraft was outlawed; lives could not be taken without an impartial trial; fugitives from British colonies must be surrendered when demanded by that colony's government; and the chiefs were ordered not to make war on any other chief without the sanction of the British government. One clause talked of chieftainship succession according to 'ancient laws and customs' (rather farcical, when applied to John Dunn). The *Natal Times* reported:

> The British Government were extremely anxious to prevent the settlement of white people in the country, and therefore no sale of land on any pretence whatever will be recognised or allowed by the Government. This Sir Garnet considered most important, as he told them that most of the quarrels and even wars have arisen through the sale and purchase of lands. If, therefore, missionaries came and they wanted them, enough land for the mission could be lent for any time, but not absolutely sold.[18]

Articles 8 and 9, which dealt with land, thus reinforced the authority of the chiefs and gave them the right to bar colonists and missionaries. The 10th clause required the chiefs to submit to the authority of the Resident in all cases where British citizens were involved. The final clause gave the chiefs a power of discretion in obscure matters, or anything not covered by the other articles. The powers of the British Resident were intended to be without administrative authority. Five days earlier Wolseley had written to Hicks Beach to explain his intention to 'disturb the existing conditions of life and government only where, as in the cases of the military system, and the barbarous practices of witchcraft, these conditions were irreconcilable with the safety of British subjects in South Africa, or the peace and prosperity of the country itself'.[19]

The man who accepted the poisoned chalice of first Resident of Zululand on a modest salary of £600 a year plus £100 expenses was William Douglas Wheelwright, formerly resident magistrate of Umvoti County. He was far from Sir Garnet's first choice – several others such as the political officer Captain Marshal Clarke R.A. had wisely turned down the offer (and Wheelwright himself would soon be forced to resign when he saw how tightly his hands were tied). Later Sir Garnet would make disparaging remarks about Wheelwright, remarks that seem to have been based on the snobbish belief that he was not what the general termed a 'gentleman'. The Resident was thirty-two years old and had been born in India, emigrating to South Africa at the age of twelve with his parents. During the Langalibalele Rebellion he had served as a volunteer and been wounded in action. He had obtained his first magistracy in 1875, and though he lacked experience and was considered impulsive by some officials, he was thought of generally as a modest and fairly intelligent person.

This, then, was Haggard's 'cruel settlement', though as one witness of the signing ceremony wrote afterwards, the Zulus 'at the end, appeared to be, with few exceptions, much relieved to have found things no worse'.[20] The weakest link in the treaty, of course, was its collection of chiefs and the way it upset traditional allegiances. The chiefs have been clumped together and labelled variously as 'infirm', 'elderly' and 'nonentities', images that are misleading. John Laband has suggested that Sir Theophilus Shepstone may have advised his brother in the selection. John Dunn may have discussed names, but the choice seems to have come largely from John Wesley Shepstone who clearly wanted to install safe, pro-British chiefs along strategic border territories. One of these was John Dunn and another was also an alien, Hlubi of the Tlokwa, whose Sotho-speaking men had served in the irregular colonial cavalry during the war, who was granted the land near the junction of the Thukela and Mzinyathi rivers. The pro-British Prince Hamu was rewarded with a large territory in the north-west where his status and hereditary authority could be relied upon to control events. Mnyamana, who turned down a chieftainship, was replaced by the elderly Ntshingwayo kaMahole, the commander of the army at Isandlwana. But he was reluctant to accept a district full of Buthelezi and Mdlalose people and the personal homestead of another of the thirteen, Chief Sekethwayo who, in turn, was expected to rule a district further west. Zibhebdu kaMaphitha, one of the best Zulu commanders in the war, retained a now enlarged territory in the north-east. In the interior of the country two of the new chiefs had been important men before the war, Mgitshwa kaMvundlana and the crippled Gawozi; a third man, Mfanawenendlela kaThanga of the Zungu, was an *isikulu* (tribal aristocrat), but a fourth, Faku kaZiningo, was a nonentity and one must surmise that John Wesley Shepstone owed him a favour. Two appointments seemed to mirror Sir Theophilus Shepstone's remarks on favouring pre-Shakan tribes, Mgojana of the Ndwandwe and Mdlanlela of the Mthetwa.

The map of Zululand was also withdrawn and the country lost territory in the north and west. Critics such as Donald Morris have declared this revision as 'a neat way to add to Crown lands'. Wolseley told Hicks Beach that the Zulus had been encroaching for years on Swazi territory to the north of the Phongolo River and he now declared this to be the northern boundary. The reality was that the Swazis had to be repaid for their active support as allies in the war. In remaking the western boundary with the Transvaal he was forced to admit that it ignored the 1878 boundary commission proposals, but that Sir Henry Bulwer agreed it to be more 'equitable', as if this somehow made it alright. The stark and very obvious truth was that by giving up Zulu territory to the Transvaal, the general was hoping to win Afrikaner support for British rule in the new province.

The greatest controversy – and Wolseley was well aware of the outcry he would create – was his appointment of John Dunn, a white man, to rule the vast area of southern Zululand between the Mhlatuse and Thukela rivers. When Sir Theophilus Shepstone called Dunn's chieftainship a 'misfortune' it was one of the milder epithets slung at this remarkable man. More typical was the denunciation of the Anglican Bishop of Cape Town, who looked upon the award as 'a scandal and a reproach, and as a grievous and most uncalled for attack upon the cause of civilization and Christianity',[21] especially since Dunn's trade in firearms was viewed by most colonists as one of the chief causes of the war. Not only was Dunn a villain for arming the Zulus, but the fellow had several black wives and had turned his back on white society.

Wolseley felt very differently about Dunn and his view of the man deserves some explanation. Dunn's antecedents and behaviour, for a start, fascinated the general. He had been born in 1834, either at the Cape or after his parents arrived in Natal. Dunn grew up in a tough settler environment and, after a rudimentary education, followed his father, a Scottish emigrant, into the bush on hunting expeditions, learned Zulu and several native tongues at the same time as he learned English, and at fourteen saw his father trampled to death by an elephant. For a while he attempted to make a living as a guide. In 1853 he became a transport rider. Cheated out of his wages – and money was one of Dunn's obsessions in life – he set off into Zululand and wandered for two years living among the tribes. He might have ended his days as a nomad except for a chance meeting with Joshua Walmsley, a retired army officer and newly appointed border agent. Joshua took a liking to the young man, tried to improve his education, offered him work and pay as an assistant and allowed the youth, who was growing into a tall, muscular and handsome young man, to augment his income by guiding hunting parties into Zululand.

Dunn's adventurous life now became even more dangerous; in 1856 a civil war between King Mpande's sons came to a head. According to his memoirs, Dunn volunteered to help some white traders trapped between two opposing Zulu armies, one of which was led by the future king, Cetshwayo. In the battle that followed, a whirl of confusion and killing, Dunn only escaped death by stripping off and swimming a river holding his gun aloft. The white traders had lost several thousand head of cattle and offered £250 (over £25,000 by today's standards) to anyone who would try and get back the beasts. Dunn accepted and courageously entered Zululand again. He had talks with King Mpande, who was sympathetic, but sent Dunn to see Prince Cetshwayo. This task required a cool head. Cetshwayo, luckily, did not want to antagonise the Natal authorities and he permitted Dunn to leave with 1,000 cattle – and he got his reward.

Perhaps impressed by the white man's courage and also his language skills, Cetshwayo subsequently invited Dunn to move into Zululand as his adviser on white affairs. He accepted the offer and built a farmhouse near the Lower Thukela drift, 'ideally placed to monitor all European movements, and trade, into the country'.[22] In 1853 Dunn had married Catherine Pierce, half-English, half-Cape Malay. Now he adopted more cross-cultural ways, marrying (over time) a total of no fewer than forty-nine Zulu wives and spawning a large offspring. With his tweed suits, Purdey shotguns and pedigree horses, Dunn aped the life of an English country gentleman. He was intelligent, modest, courageous and a kind paterfamilias to his huge gaggle of wives and children. These qualities must be set against his materialism, lack of integrity and sharp eye always for a lucrative and often shady deal.

Dunn made plenty of enemies; many Zulu councillors viewed him with suspicion. He acted as mediator between the Natal authorities and Cetshwayo after his coronation, but men such as Theophilus Shepstone were suspicious of everything about this renegade, they resented his power in Zululand, and they noted the way in which he imported firearms into the country, improving the Zulu army while he lined his own pockets.

During the tense months of 1877–78, with war ever closer, Dunn urged Cetshwayo to accede to British demands. In December 1878 Lord Chelmsford asked Dunn what his plans were. Neutrality was his reply. To this Chelmsford retorted, 'I cannot allow you to do that.' Believing he had no quarrel with the Zulus, Dunn and his people entered Natal between 31 December 1878 and 3 January 1879.

Rider Haggard quite rightly described Dunn as a 'prudent' man. Once the invasion of Zululand was under way the always practical Dunn realised that Cetshwayo had no hope of winning. 'Faced with the idea of voluntarily forfeiting all his material possessions, and his authority in Zululand, on the strength of a vague "feudal" bond with a Cetywayo whose own moods and loyalties had begun to vacillate, he did not have difficulty in making up his mind.'[23] Some writers have since labelled Dunn a 'traitor', but it should be recalled that he did not volunteer to help the British, but was pressed into service. It was not until March 1879, after the disasters at Isandlwana, Intombi Drift and Hlobane that Dunn supplied some of his men as scouts and messengers, finally agreeing to supervise Chelmsford's scouts himself on the march to relieve Eshowe. Captain William Molyneux at this time described him thus:

> John Dunn was a handsome powerful man of about forty years of age, a perfect rider and rifle-shot, rode an excellent *jagd paard* (shooting-horse) on all occasions, had the best of saddlery, breeches, boots, and other clothes (which he always got from England, though he had never been there), and for his large wideawake hat and tanned face might have been taken for an English country gentleman. Familiarity with the Zulus had not bred contempt in him. Almost the first thing he said to me on the 29th, when a bad drift had temporarily lengthened our column, was, 'We shall have to do better than this if we are to beat Cetewayo's impi.[24]

He turned out to be an excellent chief of scouts and at the Battle of Ginginhlovo stood on the top of a wagon calmly potting Zulus at 300 yards range.

The first mention we have of Dunn in any of Wolseley's journals is on 11 June 1875 when, after a visit from Bishop Schreuder, the general wrote: 'John Dunn, he says, hates missionaries & is a hard man ...' Six weeks later Sir Garnet met this notorious celebrity and was impressed. 'He is a fine looking fellow,' wrote Wolseley, 'very good-looking although somewhat stout. He has a very determined face ... He receives £300 a year from the Govt. as our representative with the king, and we also pay him for every man ... that comes through Zululand into Natal. He also does a large business in trade. He has numbers of native wives, and has in many ways adopted the Kaffir mode of life.'[25]

Barely six weeks after this meeting Wolseley left South Africa and did not see Dunn again until 9 July 1879 at Crealock's camp. In his journal Sir Garnet noted how Dunn looked very like 'dear Evelyn Wood', but added a significant remark – 'I am afraid that his honesty of purpose is not like Wood's.' He then referred to what he was turning over in his mind regarding the settlement:

> However, he is a power in Zululand and I intend making as much use of him as possible. My idea is to increase his powers by making him paramount Chief over the District of Zululand lying along the Tegula & Buffalo Rivers frontiers of Natal. I shall thus secure the civilizing influence of a White man over the district of Zululand nearest to us, and he and his people will be a buffer between us and the barbarous districts of Zululand beyond.[26]

Six days later Wolseley added another very interesting comment about Dunn:

> Maurice brings a very keen intellect to bear upon his duty, and although sometimes a little easily carried away by the news of the moment, generally comes to very just conclusions as to the position of the King and his doings. He is prejudiced very strongly against John Dunn, thinks him a blackguard of the deepest dye, and is carried away so much by this dislike that he cannot see how thoroughly Dunn's interests are wrapt up in ours. I myself see no reason why I should put any trust in Dunn, but I feel that he must for his own sake serve us well.[27]

Maurice was not alone in his dislike of Dunn – border agent F. B. Fynney also had several arguments with him. Reading between the lines of Wolseley's journal it seems, as the days passed into weeks, as if Dunn's abilities slowly won over Sir Garnet. 'I cannot see what J. Dunn has to gain by deceiving me …' he wrote on one occasion during the King Hunt, 'and I am sure he is more likely to know what is going on north of the Umvolusi river than any other white man in South Africa.'[28] The pair had much time for talks and mutual respect and fondness grew until, on 22 August, with the settlement meeting barely one week away, Sir Garnet wrote in his journal:

> I never met a man who was more of a puzzle to me than Dunn. He has never been in England & most of his life he has passed in Zululand without any English or civilized society, and yet in his manner he is in every way the Gentleman. He is quiet, self-possessed and respectful without any servility whatever, and his voice is soft and pleasant. He is much more of the English Gentleman than many of the self-opinionated & stuck up people who profess to be our 'leading citizens' in Natal ... He leads a curiously solitary life, but he says he enjoys it thoroughly, being in every way his own King ... He has as many wives & concubines as he wishes to keep & he has a clan about him who are all ready to obey his slightest nod. He pays periodical visits to Natal & has his books, letters & newspapers sent to him regularly. I wish I dared make him King of Zululand, for he would make an admirable ruler ... [29]

Wolseley clearly envied what he saw as Dunn's free and easy lifestyle, but by this date he was also much impressed by him.

It was about this time that the general offered a chieftainship to Dunn. In his own memoirs, Dunn says he accepted '*on condition that Cetywayo should never hold any position in the country again*' (underlined and in italics in the original text).[30] The emphasis by him on these words suggests that he was fearful how the monarch might react if he returned. Clearly he knew that Cetshwayo was hurt by his betrayal, as indeed he was, and that on return he might exact revenge. After the king's capture Dunn had suddenly got sick and refused Cetshwayo's requests to meet with him. This certainly demonstrated a weakness in his nature and Wolseley noticed it immediately and commented: 'John Dunn said he was sick yesterday, but I have an idea that his sickness was got up as an excuse for not seeing Cetewayo: he was naturally anxious to avoid an interview with his former benefactor.'[31]

Dunn's gun-running activities prior to the war (his biographer claims they ceased in 1877), his ostracism by Natal society, even his polygamy, all were brushed aside by Wolseley when he wrote to Hicks Beach on 3 September:

> The section in Natal who hate John Dunn, some because he has long since adopted the customs & habits of the natives, and lived as a Zulu Chief, and others because he has been a successful man, will join the cry of each and all ... I know that Sir Theophilus Shepstone dislikes Dunn very much ... His dislike ... is based upon the theory that he ought not to have trafficked in guns. I don't see either how he could or why he should have acted otherwise than he did in the matter. He was made a great man in Zululand by Ketchwayo in order that he, Dunn, should act as the king's agent and obtain the arms that he, the king, wished to purchase, and whilst it is a notorious fact that nearly every merchant in Durban broke the Natal law in dealing with the Zulus in guns, I can't understand in what just principle Dunn can be condemned for doing openly what our merchants did clandestinely. The former had constituted himself a Zulu Subject and broke no law by his action in this matter ... Dunn's actions were done openly and with the knowledge of the Natal Government ... [32]

Wolseley went on to say that John Wesley Shepstone might have been expected to share the prejudices of his brother towards Dunn but, on the contrary, 'he most fully and cordially endorsed my views: indeed he regards the position I have assigned to Mr Dunn as a most important feature of the settlement I have made.' Sir Garnet concluded by saying that he thought Dunn would be a force for justice and civilization in the region. He remained loyal to Dunn even in public; when the colonist Harry Struben sat next to the general at a banquet and was impertinent enough to criticize his choice of John Dunn as a chief, Sir Garnet 'got so annoyed with me that he wished us "good night", and went to his room.'[33]

For his part Dunn genuinely seemed to like Wolseley. 'The opinion that I formed of Sir Garnet,' he wrote in his memoirs, 'was that he was a good general, a thorough soldier, and, in fact, a man fit for any emergency ... we had many a pleasant ride together.'[34] No doubt they talked as they rode. In his memoirs Dunn confessed that he would have preferred outright annexation 'without sending Cetywayo away'. This remark seems somewhat at odds with what we know of Dunn's behaviour because this highly materialistic man must have realised that if the Zulu king had stayed in his place he might have punished Dunn for his 'treachery' and, indeed, the white chief did all he could to prevent Cetshwayo's return in 1883. In his memoirs Dunn also called the settlement 'the maddest piece of policy ever heard of' – hardly a ringing endorsement for a treaty he was connected with – but he implied that Wolseley had no alternative and noted the settlement would have 'worked well for some years if the Resident had been vested with greater authority'.[35]

Annexation, HM Govt had made clear, was not on the cards. Wolseley was tasked with settling Zululand quickly and with the minimum of fuss. He needed initiatives; strategic and military considerations were paramount. The historian Adrian Preston, who edited some of the general's journals, was also an expert on the defence of British India. He formulated a theory, constantly trotted out as gospel ever since, that after the Afghan War (then in progress), George Colley, Wolseley confidant and advisor to the Viceroy of India, had a scheme to break Afghan military power into several important principalities ruled by British Residents or agents and that this plan 'uncannily resembled' what Sir Garnet engineered for Zululand. He concluded that 'the settlement would appear to be Colley's rather than Wolseley's in inspiration'. No historian seems to have challenged this view, but there are grounds for believing it has gained an authority in the retelling which perhaps it does not deserve. I can find no reference in any of the general's correspondence – or Colley's – where either man refers to the latter's involvement in the settlement. Of course Colley, a man of great intellect and one of Wolseley's best friends, must have had talks with him about Zululand; there is no doubt the general would have listened to his advice, but then Sir Garnet also must have talked with the equally brilliant Henry Brackenbury and the intellectual John Maurice, and no one has ever suggested that they played a major role in his settlement decisions.

The general's advisers were in the main men with great local knowledge – Henry Bulwer, John Dunn and John Wesley Shepstone. It should also be remembered that Wolseley, shortly after the signing, asked the government to thank only two people for helping him with the settlement – Bulwer and John Shepstone. In the early stages he was also possibly influenced by Charles Brownlee, one-time Secretary for Native Affairs at the Cape, who in June 1879 made some suggestions to Chelmsford on possible peace terms to be offered to the Zulus. These included the banishment of Cetshwayo and the appointment of a single Resident with supreme authority under the High Commissioner or Governor of Natal.

Wolseley's early opinions on the settlement were shaped in talks he had with Bulwer. In a letter to his brother Bulwer explained what they had discussed and his general feelings:

> My proposition to Sir G. was to divide the country into four or five divisions only; with a political agent in each. By this means you would have established four or five independent chiefs each with a territory and a power that it would be worth his while to keep – against the Zulu family dynasty and against any comer. And as with each chief we should have had an agent: we should have had an ever-present working for good ... Sir G. altered the arrangement, made thirteen

> independent chiefs, and has appointed only one resident. The consequence is that you cannot maintain total influence over the chiefs which you would otherwise have done ... and our hold will, I fear, be very weak. I think the appointment of John Dunn also a mistake – but this is strictly between ourselves.[36]

It looked for a time as if Wolseley might have followed Bulwer's plan but, as he told the Foreign Secretary on 9 October:

> At first I had intended to divide Zululand into only about five or six territories, but Sir Theophilus Shepstone, remarking upon that, said it would be much better and safer for the country, which would be more manageable also, if these districts would be smaller and more numerous. To meet Shepstone's views on this point I finally decided to increase the number of chieftainships to thirteen.[37]

Thus it appears that the thirteen Kilkenny cats were Sir Theophilus's offspring. Wolseley also later said that he 'partly followed' Shepstone's advice in creating some chieftains from the lineal descendants of pre-Shakan rulers. Where the general and Sir Theophilus parted company was on the powers of the Resident, which Shepstone assumed would be all-encompassing.

As the weeks passed and while on the move up-country the influence of Dunn grew, but Wolseley gave even more attention to the *éminence grise* behind the settlement – John Wesley Shepstone. The fifty-two-year-old Secretary for Native Affairs in Natal had for years been acting, as Ian Knight so neatly puts it, as his elder brother's 'enforcer'. Where Sir Theophilus was austere, John was hot-headed, where the elder brother spoke slowly and with an awesome finality, the younger man rasped loudly and arrogantly. Subtlety was unknown to him; time and again he chose bluster and violent language over diplomacy and moderation. With his huge walrus moustache and heavy-set eyebrows, 'Misjan', as the Zulus called him, looked uncommonly like a fierce wart-hog minus the tusks. Many Zulus disliked him and some had good reason to fear him.

A true South African, John Wesley was born at Grahamstown, the fourth child of the family. He was working for his brother as a deputy agent when barely sixteen years old and followed him to Natal in 1846. As an officer in the Native Police Corps, responsible for dealing with problems ranging from squatters' rights to native raids, John Wesley also got a reputation as a tough tax collector. One incident in 1857 gave him lasting notoriety. He tried to arrest an important *inkosi,* Matshana kaMondise, promising he would be unarmed, but at a critical moment produced a gun. In the ensuing fight Matshana managed to escape but several others were killed. Almost two decades later the matter was dredged up by Bishop Colenso during the trial of the rebel chief, Langalibalele, and George Colley, then serving in Natal as one of Wolseley's bright young team of administrators, questioned George Wesley under oath. Shepstone not only perjured himself, but was largely damned in a subsequent report. His reputation took a huge knock and with deep feelings of humiliation he never forgave the Colenso family.

Over the years John Wesley came to the belief that Christianity tended to demoralise the native peoples. One year after the Zulu War he was referred to in a sketch by the *Natal Witness* as 'a dark, beetle-browed individual with a melancholy, pre-occupied sort of air ... a silent man – modest, retiring – a disappointed man who has worked his way up under the influence of his brother ...'[38] Wolseley on one occasion referred to Shepstone as 'stupid', while the Zulus, never forgetting the Matshana affair, considered him deceitful. Yet, as Jeff Guy has also drawn attention to in *The Destruction Of The Zulu Kingdom,* 'it was he who suggested the names of most of the appointed chiefs and who, in his discussions with Wolseley on Zulu customs and history, gave him the rationale with which he judged the settlement'.[39]

A close study of the hundreds of letters that Wolseley wrote during his first six months in South Africa puts to rest several myths connected with the settlement, including the hoary old chestnut that he completely ignored the 1878 boundary commission report. Even Jeff Guy castigated Sir Garnet for this, yet in a previously unpublished letter, sent to the Secretary of State for War on 18 July, the general had this to say:

> The general idea I have in my head is, however, as follows: to split the kingdom into three or four provinces *recognising as the boundary of Zululand that fixed upon by our own Commissioners at the beginning of the year, or rather at the end of 1878 and which was communicated to Ketchwayo when we sent him the Ultimatum* [my italics]. One of these three or four provinces to be continuous with the entire extent of the Natal frontier along the Tugela and Buffalo rivers. My present idea is to make John Dunn the chief of this district ... with the proviso that when he dies his successor to be appointed by the Natal Government. Mr John Dunn is, and has long been, the most powerful chief in Zululand, and I believe his nomination to this position would give general satisfaction ... We should incur no responsibility on his account recognising him only as a Zulu Chief. I have not asked him if he would accept the position or not, but I know he intends living all his life in Zululand, where he owns an immense tract of country. I have therefore no doubt as to his accepting the offer in the event of my finally determining to make it ...[40]

Eight days earlier Wolseley had written to Herbert at the Colonial Office along much the same lines. John Dunn and Prince Hamu were already in his mind as chiefs: 'I have not yet fixed upon the others but I have a good list to select from.' Dunn was instrumental to his plans because 'he knows our real strength & that when we are in earnest we can always crush any resistance to our wishes. He will therefore always be our ally …'[41] Sir Garnet also told Herbert that if the Zulus opposed his plans at the great meeting he would abandon the whole project and rethink the matter.

Sir Garnet was under no illusions that his plans would be controversial. In a private letter to a friend in England, written on 15 August, he declared that the colonists 'will turn out to curse me as I leave these shores for England as I am restoring Zululand to the Zulus. The colonists write a black man has no rights that should be respected, are eager for acquisition of his country, although there are millions of acres … never yet been cultivated in the province … under our flag.' The stresses Wolseley was working under are apparent in the next sentence: 'The Zulu has no idea of time & it is not easy to make him understand that I am in a hurry and want him to move quickly in settling the country and in helping to restore it to peace.'[42]

Five days later a change is apparent in Wolseley's thinking. He now told Colonel Stanley at the War Office that he was planning to divide Zululand 'into about seven districts', with the Resident being 'the eyes and ears of the English government'. It is thus apparent that Wolseley almost doubled the number of proposed chiefs during the last ten days before the Ulundi meeting. Possibly he thought more about what Sir Theophilus Shepstone had said to him earlier, or maybe John Wesley Shepstone was of the same view as his brother.

In two important letters on 3 September, the treaty having been signed less than two days earlier, Wolseley wrote candidly to his imperial masters. First he told Hicks Beach, 'I believe the Settlement to be a most satisfactory one that will bear the test of time.' He added that John Wesley Shepstone 'is thoroughly satisfied with it and believes in its permanency.' The general continued:

> I am well aware that it will not please the colonists nor possibly Sir Bartle Frere, all of whom were bent on annexation. The missionary class will cry out loudly against it, as I have not handed

> the country over to their tender mercies, and have prohibited the sale or transfer of land in Zululand to them, or any white traders or settlers. The Colenso party – to whom native complications gave notoriety – will denounce the banishment of Cetewayo as a crime worse than the imprisonment of Napoleon ... The Transvaal Boers will complain bitterly that I have not given them the position they conceived themselves entitled to ...

Sir Garnet went on to say that if he had attempted to reconstitute a Zulu kingdom 'in any way whatsoever' he would have 'sown the seed of certain trouble for us in the future'. He had thus tried to follow a 'middle course', well aware that in doing so, 'I shall be howled at by the various factions in South Africa ...'[43]

Wolseley's next letter was penned to the War Office. He told Stanley that unless Her Majesty's representatives 'be carried away by mad folly or by lust of conquest, we should never again have serious trouble in Zululand', a statement that shows his good intentions, arrogance and naivety. The chiefs would be compliant and never combine against the British precisely because 'their jealousy of one another is so great'. Newspapers would attack the settlement, noted the general, Frere and the colonists wanted annexation 'pure and simple', the missionaries wanted Zululand handed over to them, and Bishop Colenso was angry that his 'pet king' had been exiled.

Letters to public officials are one thing but perhaps the general's real feelings are best expressed in a hitherto unpublished letter to his mother written one week after the treaty signing. He told her:

> I shall be abused by every newspaper in the country because I have not annexed Zululand to the British Empire and in other words handed it and its people over to the mercies of the Colonists. However, I don't in the least care for local abuse provided the ministers at home approve of the arrangements I have made. I believe myself that what I have done will secure

> peace for generations to come unless the plan I have laid down is departed from. All the missionaries will be up in arms to abuse me for not having given Zululand over to their rapacious clutches. But I had gone steadily at the work I had before me uninfluenced by any feeling except to carry out my instructions in the most effective manner possible. When I say my 'instructions' I really had none, for I was trusted by the ministry so fully that they left almost everything to me. I knew their views however generally and I have endeavoured to the best of my ability to carry them out. I believe I have been most successful and I only pray God that I really succeed as well now as in the new job before me.[44]

With the storm breaking about his head during the second week of September, the general told the Colonial Secretary that he expected the Resident to communicate with him via the Governor of Natal as 'the safest person to direct his conduct'. He added that Frere might try and upset the settlement: 'He has cast in his lot unreservedly with the party in South Africa that denies that the Black Man has any rights at all.' This 'anti-black party', declared Wolseley, was 'brimful of goody-goody clap-trap sentiment' about civilizing their 'heathen brethren', which got them sympathy at home with the Aborigines Protection Society and others. Civilization in the minds of such men, he argued, was bound up with making the black man 'the settler's servant'. Frere and his cronies would launch South Africa on a 'sea of troubles', he warned, troubles such as agitation in Pondoland 'fomented by zealous magistrates', especially if they felt they had the support of a man like Frere. In future Sir Bartle should have 'no voice or part whatever' in dealings with the Zulus. The man had 'zeal' and 'ability', admitted Sir Garnet, but he was 'reckless'.

Missionaries were dismissed by Wolseley in the same letter as 'little more than traders in sacred garb'. He had never heard of a Zulu who was a Christian apart from a few converts hanging around the mission stations. If white men were allowed into

Zululand they would cause land disputes, questions of trespass, title and boundary problems, all 'fruitful sources of tension between the black and white races'.[45]

His letters reveal Wolseley to be clearly antipathetic towards colonists, churchmen and missionaries. These prejudices were with him throughout his career and stemmed back to his India days. With his usual arrogance he could respect the views of a colonial governor – and fellow Englishman – like Bulwer, but for South African politicians he only felt disdain. They were, he told his wife in a letter in 1875, 'as ill-conditioned a lot as I have met with'. Ordinary Natal colonists were described by him variously as 'sly', 'ill-dressed', 'ugly' and 'dull', among a host of other disparaging epithets.

Bishop Colenso and Wolseley had not hit if off from their first meeting in 1875. The general's immediate impression of the prelate was of a 'tall and commanding' man with 'a remarkably fine head', but a 'dishonest' expression – 'I would not trust him in anything'. At a dinner five days later Colenso lectured Wolseley – always a dangerous thing to do –and the general admitted this 'riled' him. A disastrous meeting at the bishop's home confirmed Wolseley in his prejudices; the whole Colenso family had attacked Natal government native policy, the bishop had lost his temper and started shouting, his wife was 'a drivelling idiot', and 'all the lot have Kaffir on the brain & to be really mad on the subject ...'[46] Feelings were mutual: Bishop Colenso had decided Sir Garnet was 'a sort of high-minded military prig', while the 'drivelling idiot' – in reality Sarah Colenso was a very astute lady – had taken a measure of the general and summed him up wittily as 'this little featherhead of a fighting man ...' Things were no better in 1879; in his journal on 8 August Sir Garnet had railed how 'that pestilent Bishop is at the bottom of every native trouble here ... He has long been in conversation with Cetewayo since the war began. He is a busybody and a meddler in affairs of which he has no concern.'[47]

Both John Dunn and John Shepstone had their own personal reasons for hating the Colenso family. Dunn, of course, was also anathema to the missionaries. One of Wolseley's core beliefs was that missionaries were a subversive force within the empire. No doubt Dunn had a similar view, but he had also seen them at work in Zululand and not been much impressed by their evangelism which, in his opinion, did 'more injury than good' to the natives. 'Let them say what they like in their reports to the societies,' wrote Dunn in 1877, 'they make no converts to their faith, besides the pretended ones or vagabonds, who imagine that by being clothed and under the garb of Christianity they will be exempt from all king's service and laws of the country, and be allowed to roam about and do as they please.'[48] During his advance across Zululand the general had utilised the local knowledge of the aged Hans Schreuder of the Norwegian Missionary Society, a pioneer of Natal's early days, who arrived to deliver the gospel among the Zulus in 1844. Dining with Wolseley and his staff left Schreuder with a jaundiced view:

> On 11 August I ate dinner with Sir G.W. From the conversations he and his staff had, one could conclude that missions could not expect anything good from them. Among other things Sir G.W. said, 'If I were Cetshwayo, I would not have allowed missionaries to work in the country, because he could not see anything good coming from their work …' Sir G.W also hinted that he did not think much of Christianity amongst the so-called 'believing Kaffirs', and finally he asked me rather intrusively exactly how many people in our native congregation were serious and converted Christians. I replied that … there was still a limited number … He asked how it could be that when native girls went to the mission stations they became whores … I am certain that these whores and loose men in the area of the Umvoti station do not belong to the mission congregation or have access to the Lord's Supper.[49]

As the hunt for Cetshwayo went on and on, Schreuder realised that he was losing favour with Wolseley, who wrote in his own journal that he 'was of no use and I distrusted his judgment'.

One missionary described Dunn very nastily as 'worse than a kaffir'. He was aware of all this hatred and did all he could to frustrate their work. Within days of the settlement Dunn refused to let veteran missionary Ossumund Oftebro return to his Eshowe mission (he later relented), while he kicked an Anglican missionary, Alfred Adams, out of Zululand in October on the grounds he was neither a missionary nor teacher, 'but a working man and a trader' (indeed he was – operating a busy store near the Lower Drift).

The settlement question rumbled on throughout Wolseley's remaining months in South Africa. It was not until the New Year that he got replies from London on the settlement. On 1 October he sent a forceful letter to Frere pointing out that Zululand would be maintained 'for the use and enjoyment of its present inhabitants without any interference whatever from the Cape and Natal Colonies'.[50] Frere, one assumes, got the picture. When the question of paying for the Zulu War cropped up in early October, Wolseley fired off a letter to Hicks Beach arguing that any attempt to extort a subsidy or tribute from the Zulus would be unwise. Sir Theophilus Shepstone was proposing just such a tax. But the general asked what would happen if the Zulus were taxed and refused to pay? Matters could escalate into conflict and he reminded the Colonial Secretary that his settlement had been aimed at avoiding war. Sir Garnet declared that he had tried to choose between two courses – either complete annexation of Zululand or a settlement that regarded it as a foreign country in its internal administration. He had followed 'the only sensible course that was open to us'.

It seems clear from his letters that Wolseley wanted a just peace for the Zulus and security, a chance to rebuild their lives free of interference from white men. He held no romantic notions of Cetshwayo's dynasty and would have pointed out that it had been

1. Major-General Sir Garnet Joseph Wolseley (a photograph from the early 1880s).

2. Lady Louisa Wolseley about 1879, her husband's soul-mate and 'rumpterfoozle'.

3. Looking every inch a proconsul of Empire, Sir Henry B. E. Frere, architect of the Zulu War.

4. Lieutenant-General Lord Chelmsford showing the strain of Zulu campaigning circa the summer of 1879.

5. A last stand at Isandlwana – the scale of the disaster horrified the British public and Disraeli's government.

6. *The Graphic* newspaper's idea of the morning after the battle (the reality was far worse).

7. The 17th Lancers charge at Ulundi.

8. The royal kraal in flames after the battle.

9. 'Like a wild boar' – Wolseley's friend and fighting general at Tsate, Brigadier Sir Baker C. Russell.

10. Wolseley's none-too-bright but courageous aide, Major Hugh McCalmont.

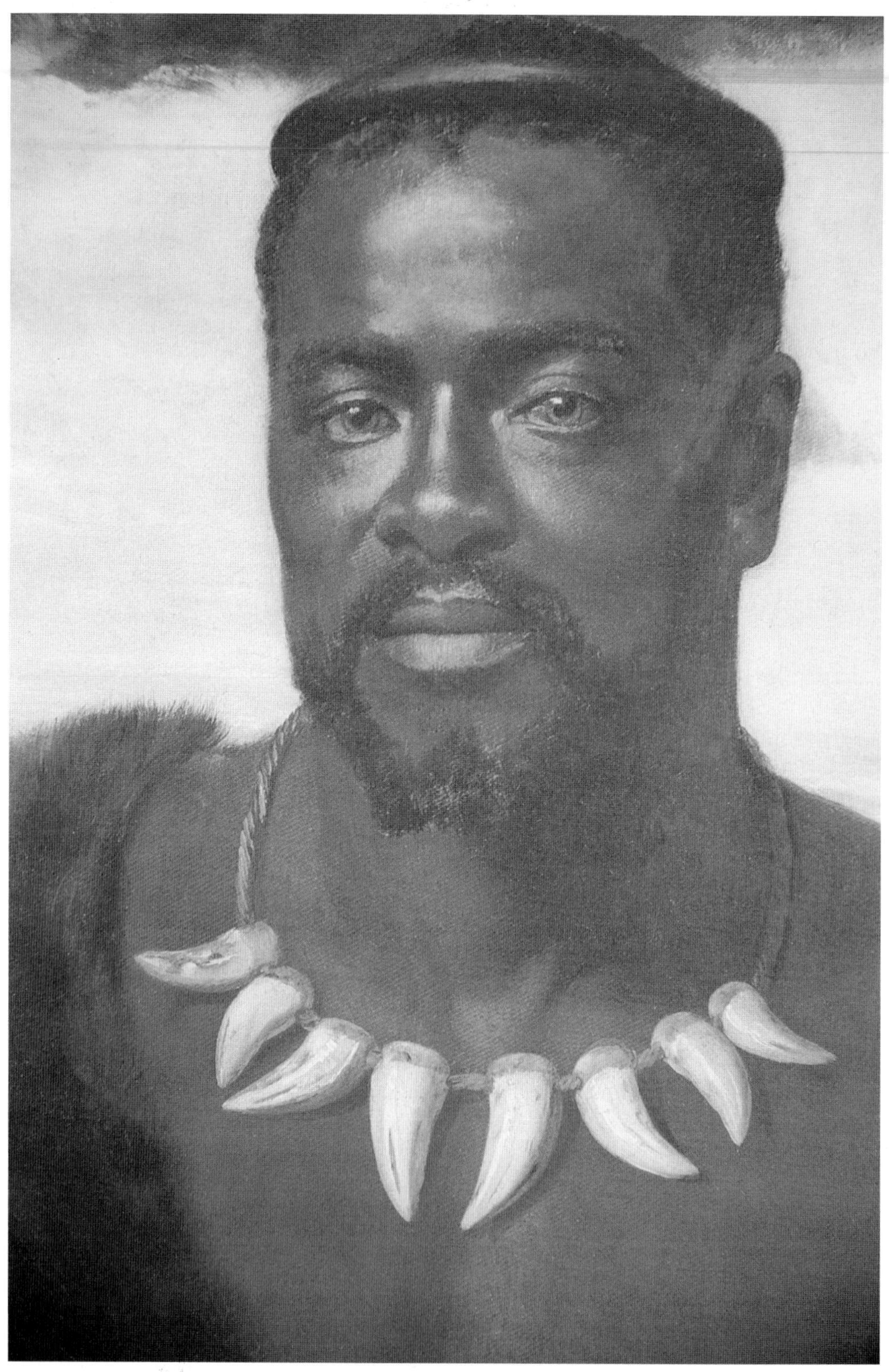

11. Every inch a king – Cetshwayo painted by Carl Sohn, a portrait commissioned by Queen Victoria in 1882.

12. The inscrutable apostle of South African confederation, Sir Theophilus Shepstone.

13. Prime Minister Disraeli and Lord Chelmsford as lampooned in *Fun Magazine*, 19 March 1879.

14. 'The Double Perambulator and the Nurse for all our South African Babies' – Wolseley takes care of Generals Chelsmford and Crealock, *Fun Magazine*, 11 June 1879.

15. Wolseley on horseback, a bearded Chelsmford on his left, presents Lieutenant Chard with his Rorke's Drift V.C.

16. The King Hunt – a guide listens for sounds of the enemy.

17. The man whose row with Chelmsford led partly to Wolseley's appointment as South African supremo, Major-General the Hon. Henry H. Clifford V.C.

18. The man who finally caught the Zulu King – Major Richard J. C. Marter.

19. John Dunn, the white chief of Zululand, hated by many colonists but supported by Wolseley.

20. Gruff, uncompromising Wesley Shepstone, younger brother of Sir Theophilus, a man feared by many Zulus and Wolseley's chief adviser on the Zulu Settlement.

21. The King Hunt – Lancers returning from burning kraals.

22. An armed Pedi warrior – note his battle axe design, horn and head dress.

23. Dupe of the British or Boer patriot – President Francois Burgers of the Transvaal.

24. Burgers' bitter enemy, the old-style Afrikaner Paul Kruger.

Above: 25. Seated and surrounded by his family, Sekhukhune (wearing a kaross) was extremely nervous when this photograph was taken upon his arrival at Pretoria.

Right: 26. The Storming of the Fighting Kopje – the artist has caught the actual perspective quite well and the real event probably looked similar.

27. Colonel Sir W. Owen Lanyon, who was treated as a puppet while Wolseley was in the Transvaal; later this sour man became the scapegoat when the Boers finally won their independence in 1881.

28. 'One-Armed Clarke', who had the delicate task of trying to prevent the Bapedi from going to war.

29. Captain Norman Macleod, son of the clan chief, tasked with forming and controlling a Swazi army sent first to attack the Zulus and then the Bapedi.

30. Major Fred Carrington, who commanded the colonial mounted troops in the 1879 Anglo-Bapedi War.

31. Sir Garnet shown cheering on the Swazis in the final assault on Ntswaneng.

32. A sketch made by McCalmont of the tense stand-off at Sekhukhune's cave hideout after the battle.

33. Henry Nourse in later life.

34. The courageous but sometimes brutal colonial commander, Colonel Ignatius Ferreira.

Right: 35. Private Francis Fitzpatrick V.C.

Below left: 36. Private Thomas Flawn V.C.

Below right: 37. Captain Walter G. Lawrell, killed in action at Tsate.

38. Lieutenant-Colonel Philip Anstruther, who led his men bravely against Zulus and Pedi warriors in 1879 before being mortally wounded by Boers at Bronkhurstspruit, the first battle of the Transvaal War.

39. Lieutenant Cecil P. M. Weatherley, supposedly the first British soldier to reach the summit of the Fighting Kopje at Tsate.

40. A typical road in the Lulu (Leolu) Mountains; it looks flat but the perspective is misleading and it is steep, perfect country for an ambush.

41. Sekhukhune's name is everywhere today in his native country – from roadside cafés to social centres.

Above: 42. The main road leading from Lydenburg towards the Pedi country and the route taken by Bushman's column.

Below left: 43. A modern carving of Chief Sekhukhune outside his kraal at Tsate.

Below right: 44. The memorial to the British dead at Tsate.

45. A good idea of Ntswaneng's scale from ground level – note the warrior above and the cave, one of many used by the Pedi during the fierce fighting.

46. Ntswaneng or 'the fighting kopje' taken from roughly Wolseley's own position. The hill of rocks continues to slope backwards but rises to a summit.

47. Sekhukhune surveys his valley – in 1879 the foreground would have been filled by hundreds of burning huts on the afternoon of the battle.

48. Some things hardly change as in this pastoral scene of transport in the valley.

49. The Swazi army attacked along the crest of this ridge.

50. The magnificently beautiful low veldt, which is home to the tsetse fly and dangerous for humans and horses. Over the hills to the right lies the gold country of streams, crags and old goldfield ghost towns.

51. A Zulu chief teaches John Bull a lesson in a contemporary *Punch* cartoon by John Tenniel, published 1 March 1897.

52. A caricature of Sir Garnet, the very model of a modern major-general.

founded by a bloody tyrant barely fifty years previously (the Ashantis, his enemies on the Gold Coast in 1873–74, by comparison, had been a great power for over 300 years). The Zulu War had cost the British people millions of pounds and well over one thousand lives. The fact that the Zulus had suffered even more in manpower and now forfeited much of what they knew and held dear in their society was not one of his major concerns; restoring peace, preventing more bloodshed, establishing some control without annexation – and getting it all done quickly – these were things that mattered.

Other voices than Wolseley's can be allowed the final word on the settlement. In February 1880 the normally astute Sir Henry Bulwer, one of the treaty's architects, after admitting that there were one or two things he would have done differently, had this to say in a long letter to the general:

> But the general character of the settlement, its general features, and the principles upon which it is based are, I believe, such that it would difficult to find any which would be at once more satisfactory to the justice of the case and better calculated under the circumstances to secure the peace and good order of the Zulu country and the adjoining British communities. There were, in fact, so far as I can see, only five possible courses or modes of settlement open to your Excellency – a) One was to make peace with the Zulu King, and after exacting certain conditions from him ... leave him otherwise undisturbed ... b) Another was to leave him with reduced powers by a reduction of his territorial limits, and by hedging him in with chiefs independent of him ... c) A third was to depose the King and place in his stead another member of his family ... d) A fourth was to annex the Zulu country ... whilst the fifth was the complete deposition both of the King and of his dynasty, the abolition of the Zulu monarchy, and the breaking up of the Zulu kingdom ... To have left the

> King at the head of the Zulu nation would, after the events of the war, whatever the conditions imposed on him, have been a course ominous of future trouble ... The Zulu power would have been bent, but it would not have been broken; and the Zulu King would have lost no time in setting to work to re-establish that power ... The last of the five named alternative courses was the one taken by your Excellency ... it has avoided a policy of aggression ... it has taken securities for the future peace of this part of South Africa ... In the division of the Zulu kingdom into separate districts under chiefs independent in themselves and of one another, a guarantee is provided against the country and the collective power and resources of the country ever falling into the hands of one man ... a greater respect for life will grow and a greater encouragement will be given to peaceable occupations ... [51]

No matter if Wolseley, Bulwer, Shepstone, Dunn, Colley, Brownlee and all of them had got it wrong. What did HM Govt think of their efforts? One of the reasons Disraeli always liked Wolseley was because he realised that he was a good public servant. No matter that the general might have his own views, misgivings or grumbles, if he was tasked by the state to do a job, he always tried to do it to the best of his ability. Sir Garnet had been told to end the war, settle Zululand swiftly and without further loss of life, do it without annexation – and do it all quickly. Little wonder then that the Prime Minister told a fellow politician on 28 September, 'All he has promised and proposed he has fulfilled.' How Wolseley's turkey-cock little breast would have stiffened with delight if he had heard Disraeli say: 'I entirely approve of everything he has done and look upon him as a first-rate man.'[52]

PART TWO

THE BAPEDI

6

TROUBLE IN THE TRANSVAAL

I say the land belongs to us …

Chief Johannes Dinkwanyane

'The Zulu War is ended,' wrote a jubilant Wolseley to the Duke of Cambridge on 2 September 1879. The day was going to turn into a hot one as the spring sun rose quickly in the sky, and after breakfast Sir Garnet held a review of his troops before breaking up the units. Mansfield Clarke's column commenced its journey back to Natal, the 80th Regiment was sent north towards Utrecht and the general and his staff prepared to make their way to Pretoria, capital of the Transvaal, via Evelyn Wood's old camp on the Blood River. That night a 'highly pleased' John Dunn dined one last time with his mentor before turning homeward.

On the next morning Wolseley attended to his despatches, planning to set off on the 4th, but the heat in the tents was 'very unpleasant', while the flies in their thousands were 'maddening', drawn by the carcasses of many unburied bullocks and general camp detritus. Fed up with the sickening smells and keen to get going, Sir Garnet gave the order to start the march that night at 10 p.m. under 'a very good bright moon'.

In fact, Zulu campaigning was not quite over; Manyonyoba, an *inkosi* of the Khubeka people in the Ntombe Valley, had still not surrendered, though he sent word that at sunset on 4 September he was prepared to lay down his weapons. The Zulu War, which might have ended without further loss of life, was now destined for a last blood-letting; on the morning of the 4th Baker Russell received orders from Wolseley to 'clear Manyonyoba out'. Sceptical of his opponent's intentions, Russell duly ordered Major Wilsone Black, a peppery Glaswegian from 2/24th, to take a force consisting of Teteluku's Mounted Natives and some mounted infantry and march on the chief's stronghold near the banks of the Ntombe. Force was to be used only as a last resort and seven Zulus found hiding in a cave were allowed to surrender with the promise that their lives would be spared. Climbing up a steep hillside where other Zulu men, women and children, along with their livestock, were all sheltering in other caves, Black's force was fired upon by one of Manyonyoba's people. This lone shot by a nervous warrior was enough for Teteluku's men, whose white officers were absent, to assegai the unarmed prisoners and butcher them all. Manyonyoba's Zulus, naturally enough, got wind of this killing and refused to leave the caves shouting out that they no longer believed the words of the white men. Teteluku's warriors, much to Black's fury, were completely unrepentant and marched to their bivouac singing victory songs.

Next day, 5 September, Russell sent a large patrol to take Manyonyoba's main cave on the left bank of the Ntombe. The events were described by Captain W. E. Montague:

> It was a stiff climb, pretty enough to watch – the red coats dodging in and out, half hidden by the undergrowth ... The trees had been fired by the Zulus as we came up, and the place was in a blaze ... Knots of soldiers watched the holes

> and natives searched the crevices. Above all, the fire crackled, covering up the earth with ashes. The spaces between the boulders had got filled up with black powder, the debris of the burning rubbish, and it required the greatest care to prevent stepping on it and getting smothered. Just then we hear a shot, followed by a shout, and a native falls wounded with an assegai through his thigh; a Zulu had plugged him unseen from a hole. The place was like a rabbit-warren in which the enemy are unseen, while we stand out plain and distinct. Nothing could be done by ordinary means, so the wood, mats, mealies and other combustibles were piled up in the principal entrances, and set on fire in the hope that we should smoke the people out. The fire blazing in the trees all round grew hotter; the smoke was stifling, and there was no wind to drive it away; a drink of water would have been priceless; on every height near, the men were perched with their rifles ready. But all for nothing – no one bolted ...[1]

The Royal Engineers then tried 'with little success' to blow in the caves on the next day, though Manyonyoba's brother and a few followers were captured.

After a day of rest on Sunday 7 September an irritated Baker Russell began a determined effort to end Zulu resistance early on the next morning. He lead the 94th Regiment, Lonsdale's Horse, some Natal Police and Teteluku's Africans back to the caves, while Colonel E. W. Bray (an officer Wolseley thought was 'an ass'), took men of the 2/4th from Luneberg and headed across the Ntombe to the mountain of Prince Mbilini, a renegade Swazi who had fought the British and been killed in April, though his people were still belligerent. Despite all Russell's efforts his soldiers found just 'four poor stranded old women who crawled out of a cave'.[2] The British troops then dynamited all the cave entrances on the assumption that no more Zulus were inside. On Mbilini's mountain, however, a final act of war took place. Two British NCOs, Sgt-Major Smith and Corporal Pomfret of the 4th Regiment (later the King's Own Royal Lancaster Regiment), approached too close to some caves and were shot and killed. The Zulus were then told to lay down their arms or be dynamited. They replied with a stream of abuse. Royal Engineers then blew in the caves killing, it was believed, thirty or more Zulus trapped inside. Their deaths, and those of the two unfortunate British soldiers, thus concluded the Zulu War's butcher's bill. It was an ugly end to the campaign and, as one of the officers involved wrote to his wife, 'very stupid'. To make matters worse, Manyonyoba managed to escape and irregular cavalry patrols searched for him in vain. When Wolseley got news of the affair he wrote of Colonel Bray: 'I wish he had blown himself up.'

Sir Garnet had declared the war was over and he was not going to be diverted from hastening to the Transvaal because of one petty chieftain. Villiers' 'riff-raff' were sent home and on 10 September the general ordered Russell, 'looking so well, but burnt as black as a Zulu', to proceed immediately to Lydenburg. Manyonyoba remained free and dangerous until 22 September when the fear of starvation caused him, with his wives and principal induna, to surrender. The chief was well treated and allowed in October to build a new homestead with his followers in the Batshe Valley. Further south, as Charles Mansfield Clarke led his column towards Natal, Zulu chiefs who had not made full submission to the authorities were heavily fined, cattle were collected and firearms broken up; 450 guns were collected by patrols in 'a sullen atmosphere of passive resistance that stopped just short of violence'.[3]

Life throughout Zululand began returning to normal. One British officer complained in a letter home that the Zulus 'are becoming too friendly', as they strode into his camp asking for food and snuff (more popular than tobacco). He shot two oxen for some of them and they had 'a good feast with which they were highly delighted'. The general consensus among the British was expressed by the Honourable Fitzwilliam Elliot, 93rd Foot, who wrote: 'I have taken rather a fancy to the Zulus, they are always so thoroughly manly ...'[4]

By this time Wolseley had left Zululand and was well on his way to Pretoria. In his letter to the Duke of Cambridge on 2 September the general had pointed out how Boer agitators had planned a pro-independence rally for the 24th of the month. He did not expect war, but added ominously, 'an accidental spark might possibly blow up the magazine at any moment.'[5] He was taking to the Transvaal a battery of Royal Artillery, the 1/21st Fusiliers, 58th and 94th Regiments, while positioning the 80th Regiment and some cavalry near the Zululand-Transvaal border so that they could be moved to any place where their services were required.

The Boers were not Wolseley's only problem. Ever since the annexation 'a desultory sort of war' had been taking place against Sekhukhune, paramount chief (*kgosikgolo*) of the Bapedi tribe. This wily character had defeated the Boers twice, including a major expedition led in person by the ZAR president back in 1876, and Pedi warriors had left settlers and soldiers more than a little jittery ever since. A British expedition in 1878 had been no more successful. Almost uniquely, the Bapedi could exult in the fact that they had beaten white invading armies three times. Frere and Shepstone feared that the Bapedi victories and their black-over-white connotations could destabilise southern Africa with more native revolts. Colonial pressure was thus being exerted on Wolseley to crush the Bapedi but the general was not keen to risk British lives in another war. 'I confess that I do not share their eagerness for fighting,' he said of Frere and his supporters, 'and I have every hope to settle the troubles in that part of the country without any loss to our troops ... if the worst comes to the worst, I shall hire a Swazi army to go and wipe up Sikukuni, paying our allies by letting them keep the cattle they take.'[6] The general's own opinion was that the king would sue for peace once he heard of Cetshwayo's overthrow.

To better understand the Transvaal situation facing Wolseley we need to look at the historical connections between the Boers, the British, the Bapedi – and even the Zulus. The Boer republics had been established after the Great Trek in the 1830s. This event used to be seen by Afrikaner historians as an epic pioneering movement that gave the people (*volk*) a unique identity. The idea in English history books that it was simply a flight from British policies and modernization has also been challenged by scholars. The current notion, in the words of Bridget Theron-Bushell, is that the *trekboers* 'were drawn into the interior to seek opportunities to accumulate resources, notably land, and that by setting up simple state structures, they hoped to legitimize their standing as a settler elite'.[7] The Boers were, of course, vastly outnumbered and surrounded by African societies – the Zulus, Swazis, Bapedi, Sotho and others – who were well-organized and more powerful militarily. The independent spirit of Afrikaner society, with its strong emphasis on farm and family, combined with a strong distrust of organized civic institutions (save only the Church), left the fledgling republics in a fragile state. As the years rolled by the Orange Free State began to settle down to a degree of peace with its neighbours and internal prosperity, helped by having an intelligent and fair-minded president, Sir Johannes Henricus Brand, who was in office for twenty-four years (1864–1888).

Not so the Transvaal (ZAR). A common danger could unite the citizens (*burghers*), but they generally ignored tax-collectors, disobeyed magistrates – in fact generally resented control of any kind – and barely acknowledged their 'government'. Though fiercely religious they spent as much time bickering over that subject as they did politics; the different sects all had a low opinion of one another. During its early years the ZAR saw frequent disorders and a comic opera civil war before 1864 when, to the relief of many, Marthinus Wessel Pretorius, son of one of the most famous *voortrekkers*, was recognised as President, with granite-faced Paul Kruger as his Commandant-General.

The catalyst for change was the discovery of vast mineral resources in that corner of Africa where Cape Colony, the Orange Free State and the Transvaal all met. The first spectacular diamond was picked up in 1866; soon hundreds of prospectors were flooding into the region, and in 1870 astonishing diamond deposits were found in the region of Kimberley. A commission under Robert Keate, lieutenant-governor of Natal, was set up to arbitrate as to which republic owned the diamond fields. Using his casting vote, Keate finally declared that the best land lay within an area called Griqualand West, home to the Thlaping people. It just so happened that the local chief, Nicholaas Waterboer, had canvassed for the possibility of British protection. He now renewed this request and his territory was 'temporarily annexed' to the Crown. Maps were redrawn and Kimberley found itself detached from the Orange Free State and made capital of Griqualand West. The ZAR Boers, though disappointed, could hardly complain since they had asked for the boundary hearings in the first place.

Then, in 1873, gold started to be found all over the eastern Transvaal. Quickly, a stream of diggers turned into a torrent, a vast reservoir of human flotsam – adventurers, rogues, heroes, saints and sinners. They journeyed on horseback or on foot, alone and in companies. For many the back-breaking mining work would only end in disappointment or tragedy, for a few untold riches, but they all began with a boundless optimism. The streams and creeks of the rocky low veldt country along the Blyde River soon saw the shanty-towns of a gold boom rising almost overnight. Mac-Mac, Zeerust, Sabie and especially Pilgrim's Rest were as boisterous as any towns in the American Wild West. The inhabitants of these places came from all over the globe, but the largest grouping were Englishmen, or English speakers, such as a contingent of Australian miners. They had a healthy disrespect for authority and there was plenty of drunkenness and fights, though not too much real criminality. A Gold Commissioner, with the authority of a sheriff, collected the government tax of five shillings a claim each month, and the miners organised their own committee to judge disputes with a code of conduct towards one another devised and strictly enforced. There were duels and duckings, crazy characters like 'Charlie the Reefer' and Big 'Mac' Macpherson, who once demolished a hotel in a fight over a lady. Real villains did not last long in the goldfields and usually came up against the law. Particularly amusing because it says a lot about the state of the ZAR at this time is the yarn about a desperado called Matthew Smith who was thrown into the gaol at Potchefstroom in 1873. Smith found a novel way to escape – he simply leaned against one wall of his cell with a couple of other prisoners and the whole building keeled over into the dust!

Some of the gold finds were impressive: in May 1875 a nugget weighing 123 ounces was found. Two months later this discovery was surpassed by a 213-ounce monster named the 'Reward Nugget'. During that one year alone the two banks in Pilgrim's Rest exported £106,000 worth of gold while a further £100,000 was carried away by the miners (a sum approaching £20 million today).

In 1872 the ZAR needed a new president. For a time it looked as if President Brand of the OVR might take the job but he preferred to champion a man of liberal and progressive views, Thomas Francois Burgers. Reactionaries in the ZAR, and there were plenty of them, had a shock, for, as Joseph Lehmann wrote, Burgers was 'a most implausible Boer'. He was a Cape Dutchman and minister of the Reformed Church, thirty-eight years old, who had been educated in Holland, a persuasive speaker in Dutch and English, smart in his attire, with a red beard and striking eyes. His beautiful and gifted wife, Mary, was of Scots descent and the couple, who turned Boer society on its head with their dinner parties and receptions, also had four charming daughters. Such a man put at the head of an introverted people like the Transvaalers was bound to make enemies quickly; some sniped at the fact he was born outside the republic, or that he had been educated overseas. The leader of the extreme Dopper sect, Paul Kruger, who became Burgers' chief critic in the *Volksraad* (parliament), was also appalled that a 'godless instrument' in the shape of a piano had been spotted in Burgers' home. Historians too have not all been kind to Burgers; one of the most critical, C. J. Uys, called him 'a Cicero instead of a Caesar ... the Transvaal badly needed a shrewd and resourceful statesman, it received a loquacious ex-minister of religion.'[8] This is unfair. Burgers was egotistical, too optimistic and politically naive yet his heart was in the right place. Other historians have viewed him as a man ahead of his time and thus out of limbo in the Transvaal of the 1870s. He wanted desperately, perhaps too desperately, to make his country a modern, financially sound and independent republic. One man who served under him, C. J. Read, later wrote of Burgers' overweening ambition, but summed him up as 'a true patriot'.

The start of Burgers' presidency looked fruitful enough: the land was fertile, the treasury was rising thanks to the gold rush, other mineral wealth such as copper and diamonds were waiting to be exploited. Within a few weeks Burgers had managed to raise a loan of £66,000 from a Cape bank to redeem the liability of ZAR banknotes, then only worth about one quarter of their nominal value. He won over the gold prospectors on a visit. They appreciated his cheery plain speaking. Yet the less progressive Boers – and there were plenty of those – disliked the way Burgers gave two seats in the Volksraad to the miners, or designed a new flag for the republic or, worst of all, had new gold ZAR sovereigns struck with his own graven image displayed on them. The president roared on defiantly and ignored the rumpus. His dream was to give the ZAR its own railway to the sea so that the republic would no longer have to depend on Cape Colony for its supplies.

To drum up finance for his proposed railway Burgers set off on a lengthy fourteen-month tour of Europe. Not all Boers were in favour of such an expensive project because they thought it might offend the Almighty. They were also displeased with Burgers' imposition of a railway tax to pay for the line. In Europe the president, for all his dinners and speeches, met with only modest success; less than one-third of the money he hoped to raise was forthcoming and it came at a high rate of interest. When he returned to the ZAR he discovered to his dismay that the burghers had not dug into their pockets to pay his new tax and the sum gathered would not even pay the first half-year's interest on the loan. Worse still, there was not a penny to pay the construction costs. A humiliated Burgers then discovered that railway materials purchased with his precious ZAR gold sovereigns had been seized as freight on arrival by the Portuguese at Lourenco Marques and left to rust on the dock.

During the president's absence Paul Kruger and other reactionary Boers had been active poisoning the minds of their pious and backward-thinking brethren. Perhaps worst of all, the eastern Transvaal was in ferment over various depredations carried out by the Bapedi. Farms had been burned, cattle stolen, isolated homesteaders murdered and the road to the goldfields made unsafe. The Volksraad wanted the tribe punished severely once and for all. The Bapedi territory lay to the north of Burgers' proposed railway line but Lydenburg, one of the oldest towns in the ZAR (and formerly the heart of an earlier voortrekker republic), was under constant threat. Burgers had wanted to avoid conflict, but told a friend, 'the die is cast ... unless we now shut up Secoecoene we may as well drop the whole district of Lydenburg, and more.'[9]

The Bapedi, naturally enough, had a different view of the situation. They called their land Bopedi and tribal elders spoke of how they had once held sway over a vast expanse of territory stretching from Pretoria to the Swazi frontier. Those days had long past by 1876, if they had even ever existed, and the Bapedi occupied that triangle formed by the Olifants (Lepelle) River, its tributary the Steelpoort (Tubatse) and the Lulu (Leolu) Mountains which run diagonally across Bopedi. The mountains are unique for their conical peaks, steep gorges and numerous cave systems. John Laband has described the terrain thus:

> Characterized by the rivers deeply incised into the rocky terrain, much of Bopedi falls under the rain shadow of the encompassing mountains. As a consequence, the summer rainfall is grudging, except during the violent thunderstorms that turn the sluggish streams into wildly raging torrents. Arable, well-watered land is scarce and highly prized ... In the western parts of Bopedi the featureless, treeless, highveld of the country's interior gives way to the undulating bushveld. Distinctive, rocky hills, or koppies, thrust out of the red soil with its dense cover of bush and low trees. On Bopedi's eastern marches the land falls away to the lowveld with its subtropical vegetation. This deceptively green profusion is infested by deadly malarial mosquitoes and by tsetse flies whose vicious bites inject the fatal trypanosome parasite into humans, horses and cattle.[10]

It appears that sometime in the mid-eighteenth century the Bapedi had splintered from the Tswana-speaking Bahurutshe people, then living to the north of modern-day Pretoria, and eventually settled in the valley of the Steelpoort River. A royal house was formed from the Maroteng, the senior Pedi lineage, and under a vigorous *kgosikgolo*, Thulare woaMorwamotse, the tribe soon held sway over their neighbours and controlled trade routes as far as the Indian Ocean. Very importantly, especially in view of what would happen in the 1870s, the Bapedi state was not strongly centralized but operated as a federation. In practice this meant that while chiefs accepted the king's paramountcy they still retained most local powers for themselves. Early in the nineteenth century southern Africa suffered a major period of tribal upheaval known as the 'Mfecane'. It was an era when complex forces led to bloody unrest and it saw the rise to power of two remarkable generals – Shaka, who forged his Zulu nation and Mzilikazi, heading northwards with his 'Matabele' or 'marauders'.

Thulare ruled until about 1820 and his death was followed by a power struggle between his sons. The 'Mfecane' also dislodged and splintered the tribe so that it was not until about 1828 that Sekwati, one of the king's sons, was able to take his Bapedi back to the Steelpoort area and re-establish a tribal power base. Sekwati seems to have been a remarkable man, and he created a capital on a hilltop and called it 'Phiring'. Here he withstood attacks by Swazi and Zulu armies. Realising that the Zulus were much stronger militarily than his own people, Sekwati sent them presents every year, and tried to stay on peaceful terms. It was for this reason that Cetshwayo referred to the Bapedi as his 'dogs'. The Swazi kings also considered the Bapedi to be vassals but their overlordship was rejected. The result was a blood feud between the two tribes.

At first relations between the voortrekkers and Bapedi had gone well but in 1852 a dispute over joint hunting expeditions led to a Boer *commando* (army) attacking Phiring and laying siege to the place. After twenty-four days, by which time the defenders were reduced to sucking the liquid from the stomachs of cattle that had died, the Boers finally departed in failure. An uneasy peace followed as the Bapedi rustled livestock from Boer farms which they considered encroached on their land. Finally, in 1857, the Boers of Lydenburg, who had their own small republic (1856–60), sent a boundary commission to Sekwati. He agreed to accept the Steelpoort and Olifants Rivers as the edges of his domain. It was a coup for the king, since the Afrikaners accepted that he no longer needed to send them a yearly tribute of any kind – a clear indication of Bapedi independence.

Sekwati breathed his last on 20 September 1861. Before he died he had moved his stronghold to another fortress, which he called 'Thaba Mosego', on the eastern slopes of the Lulu Mountains in a valley called Tsate. Here, with good soil and adequate rainfall, the old, half-blind, Maroteng paramount chief felt safe with his wives and large family. Thaba Mosego could only be approached after a stiff climb up narrow, winding paths where stone walls and hidden caves made perfect spots from which his warriors could ambush any invader.

Just before he died Sekwati declared that he was to be succeeded by a favourite son called Mampuru and not by his eldest male heir, Sekhukhune. There was no love lost between the two contenders: Mampuru had always stayed close to his father and also become friendly with missionaries led by Dr Alexander Merensky and Albert Nachtigal of the Berlin Missionary Society. They had been permitted into the country by Sekwati, who valued their advice in his dealings with other white people; Sekhukhune had spent much of the time in the south-west of Bopedi living with an aunt and creating a following from refugees escaping conflicts in Swaziland. At Sekwati's funeral a startled Mampuru was brushed aside by Sekhukhune, who demanded, as eldest son, that he should conduct the last rites. Once the old *kgosikgolo* was wrapped in the skin of a black bull and buried in the great cattle kraal Mampuru took the hint and fled, eventually finding refuge among the Swazis, although several of his followers were killed on the orders of Sekhukhune.

The new Bapedi paramount chief was a little under fifty years of age and a tough warrior. The skinny and tragic old man who stares out with frightened eyes from photographs after his capture in 1879 cannot be compared with the chief who was to play such an important part in southern African affairs for the next eighteen years. Modern historians have been kinder about Sekhukhune than his white contemporaries: Laband calls him 'energetic and resourceful', Greaves says he was 'an able and determined ruler'. He was all these things, yet he also managed to display a remarkable cunning in dealing with his Boer and British adversaries – both diplomatically and militarily – and this ingenuity or, as his opponents viewed it, his 'craftiness', made the entire white community very wary of him. To soldiers such as Wolseley, politicians like Frere, and settlers such as Aylward, Sekhukhune was a robber baron whose tribe, safe in the fastnesses of their Lulu Mountains, were not dissimilar from the kind of rogues in a Victorian melodrama set in Sicily or the Balkans. Typical are the remarks of one settler who called Sekhukhune 'a menace to the state ... insolent and insulting'. C. J. Uys described the chief as 'tall, well-shaped ... and ruthless', but Sekhukhune seems to have no more blood-thirsty than many African rulers and a lot less tyrannical than the majority. During the Zulu and Boer attacks at Phiring the young prince had fought bravely and led a sortie that encouraged the Boers to give up and go home.

The historian Peter Delius, who has written the seminal work on this period, says Sekhukhune was 'profoundly suspicious of Boer motives and intentions', but the king was clearly distrustful of everything done by white people and labelled both the Afrikaners and the British as 'liars'. He was a traditionalist who wanted to be left alone within his borders to rule over his *baditsaba* (community of traditionalists) as he pleased, without interference from the whites. His hope was that white society would stay far away in their *makgoweng* (urban areas). Sekhukhune was especially wary of the missionaries and suspected that their strange rituals might in some way threaten his people or his own rule. In December 1865 he closed the mission stations and tried to get their converts to apostatize. Merensky opened a new station at Botshabelo to the south-west, creating his own stronghold, called Fort Wilhelm, on a hill above the village. Sekhukhune naturally saw this as a direct challenge to Thaba Mosego. To make matters worse, the king's half-brother, Kgalema Dinkwanyane, converted and became a Christian (*majakane*). He was baptised as 'Johannes', took refuge at Botshabelo and soon had a following of Pedi Christians.

In September 1869 the Swazis attacked again, probably aided by supporters of Mampuru, but their impi got lost in the Lulu Mountains and were soon easy prey for the Bapedi. 'Kill the locusts' was the war cry. The Swazis afterwards claimed that the Bapedi had bewitched them with strange sounds. As the invaders stumbled out of the mountains and onto the plain they were cut down in their hundreds. Sekhukhune had won for his people a great victory. Feeling safer than ever, he now moved his capital down to the valley floor near a vast pile of boulders that became his last redoubt, his 'Fighting Kopje'. The Bapedi named their capital Tsate and the Boers called it Sekhukhune's 'Stadt' (town).

Matters rumbled on as the Boers watched Sekhukhune's power begin to rise, with many Africans moving into Pedi territory and resisting Afrikaner demands for their labour and taxes. In 1873 Johannes Dinkwanyane along with 300 followers left Botshabelo and built his own stronghold around a large church at Mafolofolo on land still disputed by the Boers as their territory. The missionaries took exception to this move since Dinkwanyane started to drain converts away from them. Merensky described Mafolofolo as 'obnoxious and threatening'. Sekhukhune, who seems to have been generally of a forgiving nature in relationships with his family (he had even extended an olive branch to Mampuru), patched up his quarrel with Dinkwanyane. He despised his *majakane* religion but was willing to treat him as a tributary chief, a wise move since his half-brother's people could act as a buffer on his Lydenburg flank. Johannes, who started to feel more confident of his position under the protection of Sekhukhune, was outspoken to the Boers and told them:

> You men who know God; do you think there is a God who will punish lying, theft and deceit? I ask you now for the truth ... I say, the land belongs to us, this is my truth, and even if you become angry I will nonetheless stand by it ...

> Your cleverness has turned to theft ... you came to this country, you knew God's word but ate everything up ... and said nothing to anybody, only flogged. Your theft has now come into the open.[11]

A contemporary view of the war is provided by the mercurial Alfred Aylward, an Irish character in the gold district who was rumoured to be an ex-Fenian terrorist (C. J. Uys did some investigating and scotched this myth), but who certainly had worked as a journalist in America: he blamed the war partly on Johannes, whose actions encouraged other Bapedi to become aggressive, and partly on the missionaries, who accused the tribe wrongly of various depredations. In March 1876 some of Dinkwanyane's Bapedi removed boundary beacons on the land of a farmer called Jancowitz east of the Steelpoort River. They also threw timber off his waggon. This trivial affair was the *casus belli* for war declared by Burgers on 16 May. It is hardly surprising that Sekhukhune was later to declare that he did 'not know the cause of the war between the Boers and me ...'[12] It was, as C.W. de Kiewiet has pointed out, to be a 'war for the land'.

The ZAR had no formal army. Its commando system was based on a militia and was very egalitarian in its notions; every able-bodied male Boer between the ages of sixteen and sixty years was required in theory to serve without pay in time of war. The men wore their normal clothes and provided their own weapons. Many non-Afrikaners also served in what was to be called 'the Great Commando', the largest force the Boers had ever assembled up to that date. Some were volunteers including men from the goldfields. There was a smattering of professional soldiers, among them George Denison, who served in the Rustenberg Rifles, and the giant, elderly Lt-Colonel Frederick Weatherley (who was to die bravely at the Battle of Hlobane fighting Zulus in 1879), accompanied by his wife (the only white woman permitted on the expedition), along with their sons, Cecil and Rupert. Other non-Boers were commandeered to act as substitutes for burghers who, for personal reasons, could or would not accept the call to arms. An English youth who was thus commandeered, C. J. Read, has left us a vivid (and hitherto unpublished) account of the war. He marched with sixty men from Potchefstroom on 3 June; they were all 'fully armed', he noted, 'but badly equipped having 30-odd horses, ten waggons and a blacksmith's forge on wheels'.[13] On the march to Pretoria contingents from other towns such as Standerton and Heidleberg joined them and they reached the capital 800 strong (three-quarters of them mounted).

Burgers had decided to accompany his army. He was counselled by friends, including the half-Dutch colonist, Harry Struben, that if the Boer forces met with a reverse he would get the full blame. Many thought the expedition needed an expert in native warfare such as the Commandant-General, Paul Kruger, but he was sick with enteric fever and, anyhow, refused the offer of command because of Burgers' participation, 'for, with your merry evenings in laager and your Sunday dances, the enemy will even shoot me behind the wall: for God's blessing will not rest on our expedition.'[14] The president was not bothered. In his typical fashion he told Struben that his 'star was in the ascendant' and that he would come back safely.

After a rousing speech from Burgers, the Great Commando set off. Total numbers are uncertain: historian Laband says there were about 2,000 Boers and 600 native auxiliaries, but participant Denison put the figures as 2,500 and 1,300 respectively, while Read, another participant, went as high as 4,000 men and, including the Swazi allies, some 1,400 natives along with 500 African waggon drivers. The army soon divided into two commandos – a western one headed towards the stronghold of Chief Mathebi who accepted Maroteng overlordship while an eastern one cleared the Magnet Heights on the east bank of the Steelpoort.

C. J. Read travelled with the eastern commando which was reinforced at Middelburg by mounted troops under a dashing commander called Ignatius Ferreira. Progress was slow with the waggons barely managing ten miles a day. The first white casualty was a young man named Keith who, unlike most of the convoy dressed in corduroys, wore instead a conspicuous fawn-coloured suit and high boots. When the commando ran into its first ambush Keith galloped forward shouting, 'Hurrah, I have just shot the first nigger!' but his opponent, who was only wounded, waited until the rider approached and then shot him dead, 'the bullet entering poor Keith's mouth and passing out at the back of his head'.[15]

Once within the hilly district known as the Magnet Heights the Bapedi ambushes began in earnest. A region of rocks with magnetic properties, now traversed by hundreds of iron-clad waggon wheels, led to some incredible sights, much to the surprise of the commando. 'The whole countryside seemed suddenly to be endowed with life,' wrote Read, 'every loose stone over a distance of 30 yards on both sides of the waggons rose up like living things.'[16] Even sand and pebbles were heavily magnetised and hung 'in long cobweb chains' from the wheels, while knives suddenly had the power to jump a distance and adhere to the rock.

A few days later the column led by Marthinus Pretorius was attacked by a Bapedi army estimated by Read to be about 4,000 in number. He thought they looked 'imposing ... one surging mass of heads below a sea of muskets and assegais. Their large plume-tipped ornamented shields and fantastic headdresses adding not a little to their general ferocious appearance, while their cries and war-horns blown at full blast caused a veritable pandemonium ...'[17] The Bapedi rushed forward en masse 'with considerable pluck', fired a single volley, then a flight of assegais, before turning tail. One young chief tried to rally the warriors but was then riddled with fourteen bullets. Several Boer horses and men were injured though none severely. Next day, along the line of march, wounded Bapedi were gleefully despatched by the commando's African allies, including some 2,400 Swazis led by a warrior called Matafini.

The two commandos were reunited near the Olifants River. Read estimated the number of Boer horsemen as 1,200 with a train of 430 waggons protected on each flank by infantry. The eastern commando under Commandant Smit, and accompanied by President Burgers, had been bloodied in a two-day fight at Mathebe's Kop. Three whites had been killed and several injured in this attack on what Burgers termed 'another Gibraltar'. After the battle he was forced to write to Pretoria: 'We have no more lead, no gun caps and no cartridges. Do what you possibly can and immediately forward lead and other ammunition.' Now he had more respect for the Bapedi, who had proved tough fighters and very ably prevented the Boers from getting most of their cattle. 'The kaffirs are exceptionally well equipped and hold impregnable positions,' noted Burgers. 'War was not declared too soon; within one year we could not have withstood them in this country.' A fear was also growing in the president's mind: 'I pray that Ketzwayo is quiet now, otherwise we will have a rough time of it.'[18] The ZAR citizen-soldiers were now starting to become unruly. 'Every man considered himself as good as his officer,' wrote Read. 'Grumbling became daily louder.'

On 13 July the western commando attacked Dinkwanyane's stronghold at Mafolofolo near the Spekboom River. Shortly after dawn the Boers began firing but were too far away to effectively defeat the Bapedi. Then Commandant Coetzee's two small Krupp cannon began knocking holes in the mission church, but did little real damage. They had dragged along a rocket-gun and now decided to use this unusual weapon. With a roar the first rocket exploded as it left the tube 'and almost blinded everybody', while the second shot out for about fifty yards before turning around 'like a boomerang' and headed straight for the commando, 'causing no little stir among the men and horses'. Thus ended the artillery barrage for the day. A conference was held by the attackers and at noon Matafini's Swazi broke into storming parties and headed for the kraal. Johannes was sick in bed but the Swazis stabbed him to death along with forty-seven other men and twenty-two women and children. The Boers provided covering fire for the attack but held back on a hillock on the other side of the river some 2,500 yards away. The amaSwazi *embutfo* (army) were disgusted by what they considered to be white cowardice. Refusing to be cannon fodder for the Boers, they rounded up all the cattle they could find and set off homewards, angrily plundering Lydenburg as they passed by.

Most of the Boers, as Denison later recalled, 'were homesick and had no heart to fight'. Burgers urged them on to attack Sekhukhune's capital at Tsate. The plan of attack was simple: the eastern commando of 300 white men and 800 native allies under Jan Joubert was to advance over the mountains behind Tsate while Smit's western commando made a frontal attack across the valley floor. The president would remain with Smit's army but was not to be allowed to take part in the attack.

Things went awry almost from the beginning. C. J. Read noted how after just three miles the eastern commando was spotted by Bapedi scouts who lit signal fires on the hills. Suddenly they were met by a wall of rifle fire on all sides. The commando pressed on in darkness, stumbling over mossy boulders, clambering up the loose rocks, sweating and cursing. At last they reached the summit of the hills and their enemies vanished in the darkness. The Boers were exhausted and wet through with perspiration that soon turned to a clammy cold. Some of the men settled down in the rocks to build small sangars of stones to use as protection for themselves or as props for their rifles, ready for a Bapedi attack which was expected at dawn. Next morning, just as the enemy did begin firing, the men heard the roar of a cannon in the distance. It was the western commando starting their assault. While Denison and a few others urged the men forwards the Boers refused to go very far without the support of an army of African auxiliaries. The Bapedi hit them with a concentrated and well-aimed fire that pinned them down for several hours. They almost captured a big gun but Denison's men somehow rallied to save it by a whisker. Eventually it was decided that the army must withdraw. Watching from above, the men of the eastern commando could not believe their eyes as they saw this retreat. There was nothing for it but to somehow clamber down the rocks again while the Bapedi 'swarmed like ants', noted Read, over the vacated ground.

Once all the men had regrouped President Burgers urged them not to retreat any further since an evacuation would mean 'political annihilation' for the republic. England, he warned, would assume the Afrikaners could not govern themselves if they let a native race humiliate them. He preferred that the men should shoot him rather than desert him. Did they want the British to seize their country? 'The sooner the better,' shouted several disgruntled men. 'The President's last trump was played and lost,' noted an observer. Several officers tried in vain to rally the men but the vast majority had had enough; they were tired, hungry and dispirited, while rumours were flying about that the Zulus might be marching to ravage the land and settle old scores. 'The burghers sorely disappointed me,' wrote the president. He then added with his usual optimism, 'Our cause is, however, not so bad as reported and can still be retrieved if the burghers will only come forward as men.'[19] But it was not to be. The commandos broke up. By the time they reached Pretoria the men were, as Read wrote later, 'a dispirited and broken rabble ...' The Boer treasury was empty, and many conservative Boers now considered their President to be the Anti-Christ. Only Sekhukhune, in Read's opinion, 'remained master of the situation'.

During their march out of the country the Boers constructed two forts – Fort Burgers at the meeting point of the Steelpoort and Spekboom Rivers, below Morone Mountain, and Fort Weeber on the wide plain to the west of the Lulu Mountains. C. J. Read, who helped build Fort Weeber, described it as triangular in shape, with walls ten feet high made from wood and grass sods. The top was protected by a layer of *haak*, a thorny bush with terrible curved nails. This covering projected over the edges and was staked fast. Fort Burgers was a 'bleak, hexagonal, mud-walled enclosure surrounded by a ditch and possessing for its protection a parapet and a drawbridge. Two long curtain walls enclosed a cattle kraal on the eastern side. The whole affair lay baking in the heat, with the great 4,645-foot triple summit of Morone Mountain glowering down on it from the west.'[20] Any undergrowth in the vicinity of the forts was also removed to create a clear line of fire. The president created his own little foreign legion to man the forts – the Lydenburg Volunteers. Aylward went to Kimberley to look for men and returned with a strange bunch of characters from at least ten countries with little in common, 'save a love of strong drink'. From Fort Burgers a 'dashing but dubious' Prussian ex-officer reputed to hold the Iron Cross, Captain Conrad von Schlickmann, led cavalry patrols to rustle cattle and, so it was rumoured, shoot down unarmed women and children (the Bapedi caught up with Schlickmann and killed him in an ambush on 17 November 1876). Similar sorties were led from Fort Weeber by Commandant Ferreira and his 100 men of the Middelburg Volunteers. In one such raid it is recorded Ferreira killed 318 Bapedi, a figure that implies a massacre of some kind. The Bapedi were, however, often well-armed and even had a few elephant guns, which they loaded with nails, pebbles and other odds and ends. It is recorded that occasionally a leg from one of the giant cooking pots would come sailing through the air 'like a miniature cannon-ball'. On 29 September the Bapedi launched an attack on Fort Burgers. It failed miserably. Drought was also affecting their cattle herds and the tribe needed a respite to plant crops. The whole situation was summed up neatly by a British observer who wrote that the conflict had 'degenerated into a series of petty marauding expeditions, conducted with daily increasing animosity and barbarity on both sides, and tending to lead to no conclusive results'.[21]

The two sides finally agreed to meet at the Botshabelo mission station. Their agreed terms were taken to Tsate on 15 February 1877 by Ferreira to be signed by Sekhukhune. What happened that day is shrouded in ambiguity. Ferreira was not the most diplomatic of men and it seems that the king was forced to sign a document that he did not fully understand. There was a cattle tribute, which he tried to wriggle out of paying, and Bopedi lost a lot of land, but the main problem was caused by the ZAR maintaining that Sekhukhune was thereafter its subject. The king ever after steadfastly maintained that he had never agreed to such a thing.

One of the reasons Burgers was keen to tie up the war was that he was expecting a visit from Sir Theophilus Shepstone who, as outlined in this book's Prologue, had Transvaal annexation on his mind. Shepstone was intent on implementing the giant scheme for South African confederation that was the obsession of the British Colonial Secretary, Lord Carnarvon. In September 'Twitters' Carnarvon had told the Queen 'there was a very real prospect of bringing back the Transvaal under Your Majesty's rule' and that 'when the Transvaal republic becomes British, the Orange Free State cannot long retain its independence'. Force was to be used only as a last resort because, as Carnarvon told the Queen's secretary, 'the game we are playing is a delicate one ...'[22] To justify annexation the Colonial Secretary harped on about the panic caused by Bapedi attacks, the exhausted ZAR treasury at the end of the war, the instability along the eastern frontier.

Shepstone arrived in Pretoria on 22 January 1877. The road was strewn with flowers and the British community turned out to sing 'God Save The Queen'. It was an open secret that the British were planning to annex the republic and yet, curiously, the Boers seemed hardly to care, 'all busy hating one another'. Much of the time was spent on arguing over the disasters of the recent war including court-martialling figures such as Commandant Coetzee. Burgers tried his best to rally the Volksraad to save the country but its members listened apathetically – and then returned to their cows. A weary Burgers wrote a sad letter to his daughter Adeline in Holland: 'Now the game is played out. Our poor young state is gone. In their folly the Volksraad refused to pass my programme today and so the state is lost. I shall, however, secure our honour and our creditors. Ere this reaches you the English flag will most likely fly over this beautiful country. I have done all I could to save it, but the people are so much swayed by rascally traitors, that there is no chance for us.'[23]

The British plenipotentiary did not hide his intentions; Shepstone told the chairman of the Volksraad that 'if the republic could not guarantee a proper and strong government in the country, as well as a peaceful relationship with the natives, he would appropriate the country, voluntarily if possible, otherwise he would adopt other measures'.[24] Even this statement shook few burghers out of their apathy. There was no resistance when the annexation proclamation was promulgated on 12 April 1877. Sir Theophilus, who either had a strange perception of things or was an outright liar, sent a message to Carnarvon: 'Great majority of Boers welcome change.'

One month later a broken-hearted Burgers packed his bags and left the country. People gossiped that he had accepted money from the British. In the final Record of Minutes the State Secretary jotted, 'God bless you and go and never come back.' Burgers knew he would be the scapegoat of the annexation. The gold prospector, Harry Struben, wrote a fitting epitaph:

> President Burgers was accused by the Boers of having sold the country to Shepstone; of using his protest as a blind; of leaving for the Cape Colony with much money and promise of a pension from the British Government. I knew him intimately and I am certain that *not one* of these accusations was true. He was sentimental and impulsive, and committed grave errors of judgment; but that he was guilty of intentional

treachery or wrongdoing is untrue, and he lived and died in Cape Colony a poor and disappointed man.[25]

Shepstone went on tour and was given a boisterous reception in the goldfields. The annexation was generally welcomed there as well as by the business community. The Afrikaners eyed their new ruler suspiciously and grumbled over their taxes. Two Boer deputations, one in 1877 and another in 1878, set off for London to argue for independence. Both were listened to politely and returned home empty-handed. In the eastern Transvaal the situation was still tense. Shepstone, for all his smart talk, failed miserably to turn the Transvaal economy around and get the burghers and Africans alike to accept their tax liabilities. In August 1878 Sir Michael Hicks Beach, the new Colonial Secretary, told Shepstone to return to London for talks. He was to be replaced as administrator of the Transvaal by Owen Lanyon, the coldly autocratic official who had proved an efficient tax collector in Griqualand West since 1875. Shepstone and Hicks Beach both knew what was on the cards and that this leave of absence was a recall and a demotion. The new man, Lanyon, arrived on 4 March 1879.

On the eastern Transvaal frontier the situation was slipping downhill fast. Shepstone, either through fear or genuine belief, had got it into his head that Cetshwayo was aiding Sekhukhune in fomenting trouble. The evidence for this is scanty although the two rulers certainly communicated with one another but, as Richard Cope points out in his study of the Zulu War's origins, 'all black rulers in South Africa were in communication with each other, as well as with white governments ...' This obsession of Shepstone's with a Zulu-Bapedi alliance, his references to the likelihood that Cetshwayo might send his impis to aid Sekhukhune and that 'these two acting in concert' could challenge white rule was, as Cope says, 'of great importance, as it influenced perceptions of, and responses to their actions'.[26] Even if messages from the Zulu king did urge 'mischief', as Shepstone seems to have believed, it hardly mattered if Sekhukhune refused to act on the advice. Nachtigal told Shepstone that Bapedi tribal elders at a *pitso* (tribal council) had reminded Sekhukhune that Cetshwayo had not helped them in the past and should 'now see to arrange his own affairs'. In other words, mind his own business.

Native affairs on the British side were now to be the province of a new player in our story who would take a leading role in events. This was Captain Marshal Clarke R.A., a proud Irishman from County Tipperary. He was born on 24 October 1841, son of a local rector, privately schooled in Dublin and then at Trinity College. From there he went to Woolwich and passed out in 1863. An encounter in India with a tiger, apparently while only armed with a carving knife, gave him his army nickname – 'One-Arm Clarke'. He moved to South Africa and was present at the 'crowning' of Cetshwayo as one of Shepstone's staff in 1873, then served in the operations against Langalibalele that year. In 1874 he had switched from military to civil duties as resident magistrate at Pietermaritzburg. Sometimes a figure of controversy, Clarke had only a short time before been court-martialled after the death of an African rebel prisoner under his care. He was acquitted after a five-day trial. When Shepstone set off for the Transvaal he had taken Clarke with him as an aide. Fellow soldiers like George Denison found him to be 'rough in manners but of a friendly disposition'. He was brave and was destined to see a lot of action under fire in the next two years. Some Africans disliked him but most thought he was willing to listen to their grievances. There are reasons for thinking that Clarke's chief weakness was a tendency to ignore good advice on occasions and trust to the bad. Harry Struben, who had grown up in the bush and seen Africa change much since the 1850s, did not like Clarke at all and thought his handling of Bapedi affairs lead the British 'into difficulties'. It seems that Struben rubbed against those rough manners.

Clarke had been made special commissioner for the Lydenburg district and arrived to find it, as he wrote, 'in a ticklish state'. In June 1877 he had overseen the disbanding of the riotous Lydenburg Volunteers. In February 1878, however, just before instructions arrived from Shepstone, Clarke sent twenty-five volunteers, called the Provisional Armed and Mounted Police (PAMP) to reoccupy Fort Weeber, then arranged for a further 107 Zulus from Natal, popularly called the 'Zulu Police' to reinforce them (local Afrikaners were horrified and made even more nervous when Zulus arrived as their protectors). Fort Weeber was close to the district of Lekoglane, Sekhukhune's sister, strongly entrenched on a rocky kopje at Masermule, who was accused by some of causing trouble as her warriors clashed with those of her brother-in-law. She was informed by Clarke that he was deposing her for allying herself with Sekhukhune. She was ordered to pay a cattle fine and go into exile.

The Bapedi paramount chief was now placed, as Laband says, 'in an impossible situation'. The Masermule chiefdom, west of the Lulu Mountains, had split between supporters of Lekoglane, who was regent for her young son, and Phokwane, the deceased chief's younger brother. Sekhukhune could not sit idly by while his sister, whom he had appointed as regent, clashed with Phokwane. For the king there was a real fear that other chiefs might be encouraged to oppose Maroteng supremacy. The king sent a message to Clarke saying that he was 'going to punish these people who were once my children' and 'fight them on my own ground'. He made it clear that he did 'not want to fight the white people' and they should 'remain quiet'. Sekhukhune made clear that he was 'paramount', a 'man' and 'not a child'. Captain Clarke, in classic imperial fashion, tried to point out that Sekhukhune would be in breach of his treaty obligations if he attacked Bapedi 'on this side of the country'. The king defiantly replied that 'the English Government had gone the wrong way to work with him; that he would return to the Boers; that we were afraid to fight ... that the country was his ... that he was quite ready for war.' Clarke realised that the situation was deteriorating. 'I have no native allies I can trust,' he wrote gloomily, and would have to 'act as circumstances suggest', but 'a collision cannot now be avoided'.[27]

On 6 March 1878 some 500 Bapedi arrived at Fort Burgers and made a show of force before departing. The commandant, George Eckersley, convinced that the Africans intended to attack the fort, slipped away at night 'in great haste'. Sure enough, two days later, the Bapedi returned and pillaged the fort. Bapedi began roaming the countryside, burning farmhouses, stealing cattle, attacking lonely white travellers on the roads. The citizenry of Middelburg and Lydenburg, at opposite ends of the Lulu Mountains, went into panic mode. When Clarke abandoned Fort Weeber and the Bapedi burnt it down the townspeople began constructing laagers to defend themselves. Americans working in the goldfields (and there were two in the Lydenburg Volunteers) were reminded of the Apaches on the Arizona frontier.

The major Bapedi offensive predicted by Clarke and Shepstone did not materialize. Clarke seems to have listened rather too closely to the missionaries but they were his main and most persuasive advisors. Both he and Shepstone accepted what the Reverend Nachtigal called 'the root of all evil' as being the Zulus and their king, Cetshwayo.

Sekhukhune was less powerful than Cetshwayo, his resources were smaller and his territory tiny compared to Zululand, but he could make up Bapedi weaknesses by his remarkable cunning. The king was clever enough to detect conflicts between the Boers and the British and to try and exploit these fractures in white society to his own advantage. He made friends with a shifty character called Abel Erasmus, a Boer farmer with several influential Afrikaner friends in the district, who disliked the British. Money, in turn, seems to have motivated Erasmus, who tried at one point to procure a cannon for

Sekhukhune from the Portuguese, was given Bapedi to work on his land, and may well have murdered a man thought to be a British spy. Erasmus began to be Sekhukhune's eyes and ears in settler society and for his own reasons encouraged Bapedi resistance.

In early April Clarke decided to take the offensive with a motley crew consisting of the Zulu Police, fifty white mounted volunteers from Pretoria under Captain Gerit van Deventer, along with some 750 Africans supplied by Phokwane and other chiefs. This little army attacked Masermule but ran into disaster: the Africans kept under cover at the base of the hill and refused to attack this rocky fortress, which had been cleverly constructed by the Bapedi with scarped wooden platforms, a stockade and prickly pear hedge flanked by rifle pits. Finally they withdrew completely after rustling some cattle. Lieutenant Lloyd and drill instructor Sergeant Mulligan, leading the Zulus, were both wounded, while Deventer died later of 'inflammation of the brain'. Reporting on the attack the *Transvaal Gazette* had to admit that it was a 'feeble' show. Shepstone and Clarke realized as a result of this dire affair that their best response, in view of the country's lack of money, was to build more forts at strategic points within the Pedi domain. These would be manned by volunteers 'under instruction to carry out regular patrols with the objective of disrupting production on the land and ultimately of starving the Pedi into submission'.[28] In the west, Fort Mamalube, a brick and sod construction surrounded by a ditch, was built close to Fort Weeber to control the passes into the Steelpoort Valley. Fort Faught-A-Ballagh ('clear the way' in Gaelic) was raised near the Magnet Heights. Built of stone, Faught-A-Ballagh was about forty feet square with five-foot-high walls.

For Captain Clarke, who seemed to be fighting his own little war, it was a time of successes and reverses. Men from the 13th Regiment were now garrisoning Middelburg and Lydenburg, much to the joy of the citizens, the Zulu Police were out daily harassing the Bapedi, and in June 103 officers and men of the Diamond Fields Horse, a colonial unit that had fought Africans in Griqualand West, galloped in from Kimberley. Then, in April, the chieftainess, Lekoglane, gave up the fight and fled to her brother's side at Tsate. Her followers were broken up and redistributed among the pro-British chiefs. At 5 a.m. on 22 June 1878 Captain Ferreira led an attack on the Magnet Heights, burning many kraals and proceeding upwards to the main one where he was able to destroy large quantities of grain. The Bapedi retreated into a honeycomb of caves and kept up a galling fire. Clarke realised that the stronghold could not be secured without a large loss of life and so the retreat was sounded. The fight was generally considered a disaster for the British with six killed on their side and nine wounded.

There was no serious fighting in July 1878. British patrols were active burning kraals on the east side of the Lulu Mountains. By the end of the month Clarke was convinced that Sekhukhune was tired of fighting. He got a shock on 7 August when 2,000 Bapedi ambushed eighty-three men of the Diamond Fields Horse at the Dwars River, stampeding most of their animals. 'Several had mounted horses and were driving them hard,' wrote the unfortunate officer in charge, Captain Ramsay Steuart. 'Their plans were very well arranged, nothing was seen or heard of them in the previous night, or in the morning until the attack was made ...'[29] This fiasco led the corps to break up and decide to return home. It was about this time that the Zulu Police mutinied and had to be disbanded.

Fresh from his successful conclusion to the Xhosa War, Lieutenant-General Thesiger (soon to become Lord Chelmsford) toured the Transvaal and decided that the Bapedi boil needed to be lanced properly before he could turn his whole attention to the Zulus. He had no faith in colonial volunteers and irregular mounted units. It was time, thought Thesiger, to employ imperial troops. October would mean the start of the dangerous horse sickness season in the low veldt, but he hoped that Sekhukhune could be finished off by then if a decisive blow could be delivered;

on 13 August he therefore placed all troops in the Transvaal under the command of Colonel Hugh Rowlands V.C. This unemployed special service officer had accompanied the general to South Africa. Fifty years of age, with a droopy moustache, Rowlands was a Welshman from Anglesey who had saved the life of his colonel at the Battle of Inkerman. His reward had been immediate promotion to brevet-major and the coveted gallantry medal. Twenty-four years of peacetime soldiering had followed Rowlands's Crimean War triumph and he was excited to see his career moving forward again after years of stagnation. He got off to a good start by touring the Transvaal outposts. Clarke was impressed and 'liked what I saw of Rowlands very much'. Shepstone judged him 'very reliable ... an able and well-qualified officer'.

The summer horse sickness season was fast approaching. Rowlands preferred to delay operations however until reinforcements arrived in the shape of the 80th Regiment and 200 tough riders of the Frontier Light Horse, commanded by a no-nonsense major, Redvers Buller, one of Wolseley's chums. Tasked with raising colonial troops for the coming campaign was brevet-Major Frederick Carrington, 2/24th Regiment, who had fought bravely at Centane against the Xhosa and was gaining a reputation as a leader of irregular horse. It was Carrington who had first raised the Frontier Light Horse and he now created two more mounted corps – the Transvaal Mounted Horse (TMH) and the Transvaal Mounted Infantry (TMI), soon to be renamed as the 1st squadron, Imperial Mounted Infantry (IMI). The force was enlarged still further by 500 Swazis sent by their somewhat reluctant king. Before campaigning began Rowlands constructed another fort, called Olifants, near the banks of the sluggish Olifants River. It was built by a company of the 1/13th Regiment under Captain Waddy and Rowlands intended to use it as a base for his attack on Tsate, but changed his mind in view of the distance and extended lines of communication. One more fort, also built by the 13th Regiment near the confluence of the Watervaal and Spekboom Rivers, some sixteen miles from Fort Burgers, was named after a town in Afghanistan that was then in the news – Jalalabad.

Rowlands had finally assembled a small army of 1,216 infantry and 611 mounted troops. He next reduced them in numbers by sending some units to reinforce the various forts. Gradually he concentrated his troops near Fort Burgers and finally set off for Tsate on 3 October 1878 with 130 men of the 1/13th Regiment, 338 men from the FLH and mounted infantry corps and two Krupp guns pulled by a mule battery. The summer had started early, the creeks already sandy beds and the tsetse fly breeding rapidly. From the start of the expedition things went badly; the Bapedi launched sniping attacks barely four miles out from the fort, water was in short supply and horse sickness had actually begun so that the army made just eight miles that day. On the next night, after more attacks, the Bapedi came on in their hundreds, running down from the hills yelling and blowing their war horns, a concentrated attack from three sides. The British drove them back after thirty minutes but the noise had caused many animals to stampede and a number of oxen were lost. Thankfully, only one soldier had been wounded. Next day Buller and his cavalry found some water, but barely enough for the troops to slake their thirst and none at all for two-thirds of the horses. At sunset that evening Rowlands called Clarke and the other officers together and it was decided due to the shortage of water and grass for the animals that they must return to Fort Burgers. Private Edward McToy, 13th Regiment, wrote, 'A forced march was necessary and for eleven hours that march was done with a vengeance. Half-pint of water issued to each man out of a water-butt ... the men were so exhausted with thirst, aggravated by the excessive heat, that they were merely toddling along the dry and sandy roads. The cattle could scarcely be got along. Many died of sheer exhaustion ...'[30]

A very depressed Rowlands told Shepstone that he was ready to resign. To restore some prestige to British arms the colonel decided to make one last sortie in overwhelming force: using three 7-pounder guns, 140 mounted troops, 340 British infantry and 250 African levies Rowlands stormed a Pedi stronghold called Tolyana Stadt, only five miles from Fort Burgers. Aided by the Swazis, the 'battle' was nothing short of a massacre. The defenders valiantly held off the British for more than one and a half hours before 600 of them were killed and wounded, while the attackers had eleven wounded, one of whom, Colour-Sgt John Pegg, died the next day (the first British soldier to be killed on active service in the Transvaal). One British soldier wrote that it was as if 'the gates of Hell were let loose and that demons were fighting'.[31] In a despatch Thesiger told HM Govt that only sixteen of the enemy had been killed, but this seems a very low assessment for such a big fight. Corporal McToy, who had been present, gives the vastly higher figure and, even if his numbers are inflated, it must be accepted that there is a huge discrepancy between sixteen and 600. The Swazis had a great predilection, unless well restrained by officers, for thrusting an assegai into any wounded Bapedi they found, so it seems probable that, as McToy says, there was considerable killing.

Thus ended what some termed the 1st Anglo-Pedi War, though contemporary apologists called it merely a 'strong reconnaissance'. The scarcity of water along with sickness and Pedi attacks had ended a second major white attempt to destroy Sekhukhune's power. It had cost HM Govt £54,592 and severely dented Rowlands' reputation. A lone voice in his defence was Captain C. L. Harvey, second-in-command, who called him 'a soldier all over, a practical man eager to do his duty ...' Redvers Buller felt very differently after Tolyana Stadt and told his friend, Evelyn Wood:

> You must allow me just once to say – Damn that Rowlands – There, I am better now, a little better, fancy. Here I have been for a month, what have I done, 'nothing'. What has anybody done, 'nothing' ... Between you and me my dear and please,

> keep it dark, Rowlands is quite useless. He cannot make up his mind to anything, sitting on his behind in this position and Harvey, unfortunately is worse, much more than useless for he possesses the same faults as Rowlands ... a charming man he is too, so nice, but I would rather be cursed by someone who would do something ... [32]

Another officer wrote home that Rowlands 'made an awful mess of his business. He failed utterly and completely and worse still, rather humiliatingly for our name and fame. He not only did not take Sekhukhune's place, but he did not even try to take it.'[33] Finally the coup de grace came from Chelmsford who told Shepstone that 'Colonel Rowlands does not possess the requisite qualifications of an independent commander of troops in the field ... and has produced failure where I had every expectation of success.' His lordship, who had spoken with Buller, had no time for a man who, he thought, 'sits in his tent and writes all day ...' He told the unlucky colonel to abandon any further campaigning against Sekhukhune 'and consider yourself at my disposal'.[34]

Sir Theophilus Shepstone seems to have been remarkably unruffled by Rowlands' failure. He wrote to him: 'The fact is that Sikukuni's power to resist or defend himself were underrated from the beginning; we had to act upon the information of those who said they knew; we knew nothing ourselves ... By the time you took over the command I come to the conclusion that to subdue Sikukuni was a more difficult task than to subdue Cetywayo.'[35] Before returning to England Shepstone found excuses to hang on in Pretoria until Owen Lanyon arrived to supersede him. The new administrator found the sixty-six-year-old Shepstone to be 'a charming old gentleman'. The pair had several talks and Lanyon concluded, 'Everything is pretty well chaos here ... I have no doubt all will come right, but the Transvaal will be an anxious work for some time.'[36]

If the Boers wished for a less draconian rule they were to be sorely disappointed. Lanyon at once embarked on what he termed a 'simple dictatorship'. He was singularly unimpressed by the burghers whom he called 'semi-civilized wind-bags' and 'that unwashed party who have things pretty much their own way'.[37] First and foremost a soldier, Lanyon, who saw Boer plots everywhere, quickly instituted a system of spies and formed a defence guard for Pretoria out of 500 British loyalists. In April 1879 Sir Bartle Frere paid him a visit and managed to head off growing Boer discontent by a superb display of his pro-consular skills. Kruger, Pretorius and the other Boer leaders were over-awed by the polished Frere who oozed confidence from every pore and was a smooth orator (cheekily called 'Sir Bottle Beer' by Wolseley, behind Frere's back, the great proconsul would have been equally mortified to know that the Boers nicknamed him 'Bottle Ferreira'). He agreed to forward a petition on their behalf to London and agreed to send a letter of his own to accompany the document. This letter was, in fairness to Frere, remarkably non-judgmental in tone and did much to calm the Boer leaders into feeling that Sir Bartle would ensure they got a fair hearing.

Settlement of the land issue in the eastern Transvaal meant sorting out the Bapedi problem. Unlike the Boers, who objected to black ownership of land, Lanyon had no problem accepting this provided all land disputes were resolved and taxes collected. In May he decided that the defences should be improved along the Transvaal's south-eastern and north-eastern borders. He was hoping that Evelyn Wood' troops based at Utrecht could assist him, but Chelmsford told Lanyon that he could spare no regular soldiers from the ongoing Zulu War. Understanding that he did not have enough men to attack Tsate, Lanyon decided instead to send out patrols to harass the Bapedi and prevent other chiefs from reinforcing Sekhukhune. This strategy had a good effect. Carrington led the operations. His cavalry were reinforced by a contingent of

1,000 men from the Knobnose tribe, requested by Lanyon, and raised by Henrique Shepstone, another of Sir Theophilus's sons, who was Transvaal Secretary for Native Affairs.

During a patrol in early July Captain George Denison's men of the Border Horse captured 161 head of cattle from the Bapedi. A few weeks earlier Denison had convinced Carrington that Sekhukhune wanted to discuss peace. The major thought it was a ruse but agreed to permit Denison to ride to Tsate with some Bapedi and one other officer, Captain Aubrey Wools-Sampson of Ferrreira's Horse, who volunteered to go. Arriving safely at Tsate the two men were given a hut for the night and told Sekhukhune would see them the next day. Around midnight an aged counsellor entered the hut and said in Afrikaans, 'Myn Heers, Ferraira is killing our people on the Olifants River and the chief now wants to kill you both.' Presently a friendly African told the pair that a *pitso* was in progress to decide their fate. 'Some, 'twas said, wished to burn us alive,' wrote Denison. 'Others to skin and torture us with ants or hot ashes or tied to a post as a target for a youth to be shot at. Alternatively, handed over to the women, who had lost their husbands, to dispose of as they thought fit.'[38] After a long day for the two men, one of Sekhukhune's sons thrust his head into the rondavel and said they could leave. It was fast approaching dusk. The pair set off but discovered they were being tracked by Bapedi. According to Wools-Sampson they were to be captured and offered a poisoned breakfast. The last part of the journey was done at a gallop and, according to Wools-Sampson's brother, they escaped a Bapedi escort who were 'firing and hurling assegais after them'.

It was with great irritation that Lanyon received a telegram from Wolseley, after the general's arrival in Natal, saying quite bluntly, 'I do not approve of your weekly expenditure ... do not embark on any new plans entailing large outlay of public money ... In future you will please take orders only from me.'[39] Sir Garnet explained his reasons for writing this way to Lanyon in a letter to Hicks Beach:

> Not only is the expenditure in the Transvaal apparently growing beyond bounds, but I consider it would be unwise to attempt operations against Sikukuni unless with a force sufficient to ensure the certainty of success. Colonel Lanyon has not such a force, and the result of another check from Sikukuni, who can already boast of his successes against the Boers, and the failure of Colonel Rowlands operations against him, might be disastrous, and tend to raise other tribes against us. When Ketchewayo is defeated I hope to be able to arrange matters with Sikukuni amicably without sending a military expedition against him. If I fail to so arrange I shall, at least have amply sufficient troops at my command to deal with him by force of arms.[40]

Lanyon was furious. He thought Wolseley knew nothing of the real situation in the Transvaal and wanted to keep the glory of defeating Sekhukhune for himself. While the general was certainly egotistical it is fair to say that he normally preferred diplomacy over armed intervention, and while he may have wished to keep the honour of bringing the Bapedi king to heel, he also genuinely wanted to do it without fighting. On 11 July 1879 Lanyon wrote to his father that Wolseley was 'throwing stones all round since he came out without the least knowing where they would fall or having cause for them being hurled ...' A few days later he wrote that 'the excellent and experienced' Chelmsford and Frere had been replaced by 'one who knows nothing of the position, and who further was wholly untried as a politician', a rather unfair remark in view of Wolseley's Natal diplomatic success in 1875. Frere, in particular, was 'one of the most able and conscientious men I have ever met'. Lanyon was scathing in his comparisons:

'He has more statesmanship and ability in his little finger than his successor has in his whole body, and I think I can set up as judge having served under both.'[41]

Officially, of course, Lanyon had to be polite to his new chief. He was not, however, prepared to take Wolseley's rebuff without some kind of fight, especially since the colonel was the kind of man who hardly ever admitted to public mistakes. He defended his operations against the Bapedi by pointing out that they had been 'endorsed' by Frere. Colonel Rowlands 'very prudently' had not attacked with his force weakened by sickness, but Sekhukhune merely saw this as a 'sign of weakness' and maintained an 'aggressive attitude'. Peace, which Lanyon was aiming to achieve, could bring 'a very large revenue from native taxes'. With all eyes on events in Zululand he had feared that Sekhukhune might have been encouraged to attack and thus it was necessary 'to take early steps' to prevent 'open rebellion'. In retrospect it is just possible that Lanyon's policy might have worked; Carrington wrote to say that the patrols were 'harming the Bapedi in a very real way' and that if they had been allowed to continue Sekhukhune 'would very soon have sued for peace'.

It was just dawning on Lanyon that while Wolseley was around he would merely be, as Theron-Bushell has termed it, 'an imperial puppet on a string'. The general had, in fact, put his own plan in motion at Ulundi about 10 August by instructing Colley to order forty-two-year-old brevet-Colonel Richard Harrison R.E. 'to proceed to Sekukuni's stronghold with orders to reconnoitre there and report on the position, and take command of the troops in the Transvaal'.[42] Harrison had served with Wolseley at Lucknow in 1857 and again in China three years later. The pair had also known one another in Canada; during the American Civil War Harrison had tried to tour the battlefields and almost got shot as a spy. Serving at Chelmsford's headquarters as A.Q.M.G. he was blamed for sending an 'insufficient escort' with the Prince Imperial and for a time it looked as if he might end up as the scapegoat for the young man's death. Knowing Harrison very well it is to Wolseley's credit that he rubbished any notions on the part of the Duke of Cambridge and others that his old colleague was to blame. One must suspect that it was with some relief that Harrison realised he had Wolseley's support and the chance to get away from all the horrors of the Zulu War. He reached Lydenburg on 24 August where he was met by Carrington and the local artillery commander, Captain William Knox R.A. The goldfields were about 100 miles from Tsate but on a tour up to Pilgrim's Rest through the mountains Harrison later wrote that 'all along the route the farms were deserted, the houses having been burned by Sekukuni's people'.[43] He saw the same scene near the partly ruined Fort Burgers, noted that Fort Weeber was 'in good order' and was most impressed by Fort Olifants where Denison was in command with his Border Horse.

By 7 September Harrison was in Pretoria after an exhausting ride from the eastern Transvaal. He dined with Lanyon and sat up late to write a report for the general. His opinion was that the citizens of the Lydenburg district lived in 'daily fear' and a large British force was needed to 'compel Sekukuni to submit'. Harrison estimated that such a force would require 1,000 British infantry, 4 guns, 400 good volunteer cavalry and a detachment of Royal Engineers besides a levy of 2,000 Africans. This report, sent to Colley on 9 September, detailed Harrison's reconnaissance of Bapedi country and the approach to Tsate from the north, a memorandum on the state of affairs in Lydenburg and, thirdly, a scheme of attack if active operations were deemed necessary.

It was not until 26 September that Harrison got to see Wolseley. He rode out some fifteen miles from Pretoria to meet the general, whose journey north had taken several weeks. The pair chatted near a small copse of trees, 'a relief to the eye' thought Wolseley after the bleakness of the high veldt. According to the general,

Harrison blamed the unsettled state of the eastern district partly on Marshal Clarke. This observation suggests that Clarke's little war against the Bapedi running all around the Lulu Mountains, with loss of life on both sides and much stress for all parties, had many critics. 'He and Lanyon have caught the war fever from old Frere,' noted the general in his journal.

Wolseley's progress towards Pretoria had been slow due to 'an infernally bad road ... which played the devil with our waggons'.[44] 'Sankey' Herbert was suffering from fever and confined to the ambulance cart. The general was convinced that Herbert did not have long to live, but thankfully he rallied. In an even worse state was the general's young orderly officer, Lieutenant Henry John Hardy (a nephew of Gathorne Hardy, Lord Cranbrook, Secretary of State for India 1878–79), whom Sir Garnet described as looking 'very seedy'. This 'nice young fellow in every way and an excellent officer' was destined to die at Landman's Drift of dysentery on 4 October. 'We are now in the Transvaal & out of Zulu territory,' Sir Garnet noted in journal on 7 September. His line of march was over the sparse undulating low veldt. Perhaps it was the monotony of the view combined with the slowness of the journey, but Wolseley got into an irritable mood so that his journal at this period is peppered with sharp remarks: Maurice was 'simply useless ... slovenly ... erratic & excitable'; Prince Hamu, who met with the general to sign the settlement, was 'a baboon ... I never saw such an unwieldy and disgustingly obese mortal before ... I hear he drinks two bottles of bad Hollands gin every day. I was glad to see the last of him'; Frere was sending 'silly despatches' and behaving like 'an injured old maid'.[45]

While at Utrecht on 11 September Sir Garnet presented Victoria Crosses to two of the heroes of Rorke's Drift – Lieutenant Gonville Bromhead and Private Robert Jones, both of the 2/24th Foot. In his journal Wolseley wrote, 'I have now given away these decorations to both the officers who took part in the defence of

Rorke's Drift, and two duller, more stupid, more uninteresting even or less like Gentlemen it has not been my luck to meet for a long time.'[46] Several modern historians have tried to dent Wolseley's appraisal of Bromhead who, it appears, suffered recurring deafness that caused him embarrassment and made him shy, as well as pointing out that besides his courage he was a good boxer, wrestler and top-scoring regimental cricketer. Sir Garnet's opinion was, of course, just a quick-fire assessment of the man, but it was not without validation elsewhere; the gossipy Major Cornelius Clery wrote that Bromhead was 'a capital fellow at everything except soldiering' and that his commanding officer deemed him 'hopeless' through 'unconquerable indolence'. Clery spent a month with Bromhead after Isandlwana and found him to be 'immobile' for hours and excessively modest. It is interesting to note that one spectator at the Victoria Cross ceremony was Sister Janet Wells, a nurse who had done much to ease the suffering of the sick at Rorke's Drift; she tried to engage Bomhead in conversation but found him unresponsive and 'a rather dull fellow'.

Two days later, huffing and puffing, Billy Russell of *The Daily Telegraph* finally caught up with Wolseley's party. The aging war correspondent had not been having much fun since leaving Pietermaritzburg. Once he had been considered the greatest journalist in the world, the man whose brilliant articles from the Crimea changed the perception of war for the man in the street forever. Now Russell was almost sixty, fat, tired, his face and body bloated from years of cigars and fine dining. His adventures in the Crimean War, Indian Mutiny, American Civil War and other places had given him a fund of anecdotes and tales, but those years, and many a long night at the banquet table, had taken its toll. In Zululand he had found it hard to rough it sleeping under a blanket on the cold ground. 'My bones ache all over,' he told a friend in a letter. 'I have no kit for all my things were left behind ... Our fare is coarse and bad, my stomach can't manage rations very well after my long sickness.'[47] On the way north he shared a tent with Maurice, but was most impressed by Colley, of whom he wrote, 'One of the most intelligent, solid men I know. He has reflection and calm, unprejudiced judgment. He inspires confidence and is full of shrewdness.'[48] Wolseley, Russell noted, seemed cool towards him, 'save ordinary civility'. Sir Garnet was, in fact, giving him a deliberate cold shoulder, offended by the way in which Billy 'tries to sponge off everybody', asking for blankets, a tent and food. The general's ill-humour now turned to Russell in his journal: he recalled how Billy had attacked in print his old comrade, General Airey, during the Crimean War; he was now a toady to the Royals and 'a Marlborough House jester' for the Wales's. Wolseley admitted, 'One cannot help being amused by him at times,' but was inclined 'to tell him to go to the devil.' Sir Garnet concluded: 'I have tried to get him on the Staff mess as an honorary member & hope I may succeed. He does not like a tea diet, so if we fall short of liquor he may possibly leave us.'[49]

During the next fortnight, passing through various small and lonely communities, Wolseley 'addressed gatherings which seemed to hang back at first awed by his august presence ...'[50] Sternly the general told them that the sun would cease to shine and the Vaal flow backwards before the British flag would be hauled down in their land. This little speech became Sir Garnet's core statement on Transvaal affairs. He repeated it often and asked both Lanyon and Frere to include the same words in their speeches. He told Hicks Beach 'not to falter in making it known that nothing would affect the permanency of the British occupation'.[51]

On 19 September the general met for the first time the dashing Captain Ignatius Ferreira. Years of dealing with the Bapedi had not clouded Ferreira's judgment. 'He says he believes Sikukuni will fight,' noted Sir Garnet in his journal. 'This is a great bore to me but Baker Russell will rejoice over the news.' The general did not know what to make of Ferreira, a man of Portuguese and Afrikaner ancestry. Lanyon, distrusting all Boers, had told Wolseley that the ex-ZAR soldier was dishonest and had pro-Boer sympathies. In a letter the general warned Baker Russell to be watchful of Ferreira who, he had concluded, was 'a first rate and gallant leader', but 'one whose views and opinions are not to be followed always …'

That same afternoon Wolseley met and lunched with the Boer leader, Piet Joubert, and told him frankly that annexation was 'irrevocable', but that he wished to hear Boer views and would do all that he could for the welfare and betterment of the people. Joubert refused to listen and kept trying to broach the annexation question. Sir Garnet was unwavering. Despite his dislike of colonials in general and Boers in particular, Wolseley was somewhat impressed by Joubert, noting in his journal that 'we parted good friends as far as a man who hates the sight of an Englishman could be a friend to an English Govenour [*sic*]'.[52]

While Wolseley was not the kind of general who had an easy manner with his troops, he was always nonetheless deeply concerned for their welfare; on 23 September he sent a letter to the Secretary of State for War suggesting that all soldiers who had served in the Zulu campaign ought to be given an additional three months' pay because clothing had been 'torn to pieces by thorns and destroyed by bivouacking on wet ground'.[53] In defence of his idea Sir Garnet pointed out that after his Ashanti expedition in 1874 the troops had been given one month's extra pay even though many of them had been employed for less than two months on the Gold Coast.

At Heidleberg on 24 September the general wrote to his 'dear little spider', Louisa Wolseley, to say that he had breakfasted on a rare treat – 'fresh eggs and butter'. For the first time in his private correspondence Sir Garnet mentioned Sekhukhune and told his wife that the Bapedi paramount chief might fight, though 'I don't think he will do so.' He went on to say that Baker Russell, taking Ferreira's line, thought the tribe would make a show of resistance.

The general explained how 'I receive addresses & make speeches at every little town I come to, which is very wearying, but I have to do it, and if I can only smooth down the ruffled dignity of these stupid and illiterate Boers by talking & without having to resort to force, I shall not grudge the bother.'[54]

It was while working on his despatches late that night that George Colley burst in to say, 'I am sorry, I have very bad news from India.' This was the shocking revelation that Sir Louis Cavagnari and his British mission to Kabul had all been massacred by the Afghans. A whole new round of fighting with the Afghans was on the cards and the Viceroy needed Colley as his right-hand man. Only a few days earlier Colley had written to his wife that he thought 'common sense' would win over the Boers, despite 'a certain number of obstinate, almost fanatical old Dutchmen, whom one cannot help rather admiring ...'[55] Now Colley would need to leave on the first available steamship and Wolseley would lose his favourite soldier, 'when I particularly wanted him'. Had he stayed on Colley might have changed Wolseley's attitude to the Boers. The general wrote to the Colonial Secretary on 25 September to say that 'they have all the bad qualities of the Zulu without his noble traits. It is much easier to deal with a clever knave than an illiterate Boer.'[56]

Dark skies and threatening rain clouds greeted the general at dawn on Saturday 27 September 1879. While breakfasting at a farm he was joined by Lanyon and a special escort for the ride into the capital – the Pretoria Horse (another volunteer corps) and a troop of the King's Dragoon Guards. At Conference Hill, two miles before the town, a large crowd of loyalists had gathered and Wolseley repeated his 'as long as the sun shines' speech. Outside Government House there was a 'splendid' guard of honour formed by men of the 80th Regiment looking immaculate in their red uniforms. During luncheon with all the civic worthies the band played, much to the general's enjoyment, and he found a huge pile of post waiting for him with three letters from 'his little sandpiper'.

Five days later at noon Sir Garnet was sworn in as Governor of the Transvaal, much to Lanyon's chagrin who now became merely the province's 'administrator'. It was 'a very dull ceremony', according to Wolseley, held in the old Volksraad meeting house followed by a garden party at Government House. 'A good show of petticoats' noted the general in his journal, though he had not enjoyed the French Roman Catholic bishop, 'a good little man' but with bad breath, pushing up against him. At a meeting on 28 September it was agreed to send Clarke to Sekhukhune and try and bring 'the robber chief to terms'. If possible, Clarke was to confer personally with the chief and tell him that the Great White Queen would 'forgive him the past and to regard him as a friend' if he agreed to pay his annual taxes, maintain the peace, hand over any Bapedi who robbed or injured farmers or friendly natives in his district – and settle immediately a fine of 2,500 cattle. Finally, he had to accept a military or police post in his district. Sir Garnet told his wife that it would be 'a sad blow' to Baker Russell if there was no fighting since the old warhorse was hoping for 'a despatch all to himself'. Young Arthur Creagh was being permitted to accompany Clarke so that he could gain some experience in dealing with native rulers. 'Every paper in South Africa is now weekly engaged in abusing me for my settlement in Zululand,' he told Louisa, 'This is just as I expected. I could not possibly please the Colonists and at the same time do my duty to the English nation.'[57]

In his opinion Wolseley still thought that he would be home for Christmas. So far all had gone well in his first few days at Pretoria. There seemed a good chance that the Boers might see sense and accept British sovereignty. Lanyon needed controlling but he could be brought into line. Sir Garnet had heard that Lanyon had been 'sore' about his Bapedi activities being curtailed. Well, he would just have to forget all that nonsense and grow up a little. Wars were always best avoided and Lanyon's weakness was to have been 'severely bitten' by old Frere's fondness for starting them. Anyway, with any luck, Sekhukhune would sue for peace.

In those first few days at Pretoria there had even been time for some high cockalorum; that naughty jester, Hugh McCalmont had played a capital practical joke on Billy Russell. Delighted at last in seeing a real bed and soft pillows, the old war correspondent blew out his candle and leapt between the sheets – only to find a large ape curled up in them! Russell almost suffered a heart attack and all hell broke loose. The baboon, according to Sir Garnet, 'remained perched on the head of his bed, whence he escaped from between the sheets & stood there jabbering in a fierce manner at all who approached him'.[58]

7

INTO THE LULU MOUNTAINS

> As far as work for the Royal Engineers goes the Zulu War was a joke to this one ...
>
> Lieutenant Charles Commeline

Sunday 5 October 1879, was one of those balmy late Spring days unique to southern Africa. Now settled in Pretoria, the new Transvaal governor was fast falling for the charms of his pretty little capital. Founded in the 1850s close to where Mzilikazi had once had his kraals, Pretoria nestled in a valley near the banks of the Apies River and only a short distance from its source at Fountains. Back then the land had teemed with wildebeest and springbok. In 1857 a church raised by a trio of British builders was consecrated and three years later Pretoria became the seat of Afrikaner government. The South African historian, T. V. Bulpin, waxed lyrical over a place 'Arcadian in its simplicity'. He noted:

> A magnificent supply of crystal-clear water ran down the sides of each road. Each house had a garden bulging with fruit trees and flowers; in the nights the antelope and hares would slip as silently as the shadows into the vegetable patches for a nibble at someone's lettuces ... Life was easy-going and

tranquil. There were few entertainments. There was only one bar in the place, the so-called 'Hole In The Wall', a combined store and canteen with a bog outside into which drunks could be thrown to cool off ... The quarterly nachtmals filled the town and brought a rush of business ... a deadly struggle raged between the rival gangs of small boys: *dorpies* (townies) versus *japies* (yokels) ... The hefty country boys would belt their town cousins. In return the town boys would cut tent ropes at night; and once nearly a hundred of them banded together and by prodigious efforts deviated all the water furrows of the town into Church Square. By 3 a.m. the place had become a shallow lake one foot deep ...[1]

Wolseley on that 'lovely' Sabbath had attended a 'very nice' divine service handled the way he liked it – 'plenty of music & singing & a very good sermon of seven and a half minutes.'[2] A profusion of roses now arrived daily to add their sweet perfume and colourful lustre to the rooms at Government House. That evening, accompanied by Lanyon, Sir Garnet took a stroll up the path leading towards the aqueduct that supplied the town with water. 'The more I see of this village the prettier I think it is,' he confided to his journal, 'every street in it like a grassy English lane boarded on each side by hedges of roses that are now masses of flowers.'[3]

The path Lanyon and Wolseley followed was called 'the Lovers Walk', a name which in relation to the two men didn't much reflect the reality. There is nothing in Sir Garnet's writings – letters or journal – that suggest a dislike of the younger man; he saw Lanyon as a conscientious soldier-administrator and an admirable tax-collector, pleasant though ordinary. In private the general had told his staff that 'Billy' Lanyon could be left to run the Transvaal while they concentrated their energies on the dual threats raised by the Bapedi and Boer militants. Lanyon's biographer has written that 'the root of Wolseley's rather patronising disdain of Lanyon was the administrator's esteem for Frere'.[4] By October 1879 the general viewed Sir Bartle as a personal enemy and a source of possible discontent in South Africa. 'I am afraid that Lanyon is severely bitten with Frere's madness for wars,' he noted in his journal on 20 September, 'He is always referring to various disturbances on his frontiers in a manner that makes me feel he would like to march a military force to the locality to put it down.'[5]

Owen Lanyon had not taken lightly the way in which his planned May–June 1879 expedition against the Bapedi had been nipped in the bud by the general. It fostered in his mind a nasty canker; but then Lanyon was the kind of man who stored bitterness in his soul. The terms 'stuffed shirt' and 'sourpuss' might have been coined with him in mind. Historian Joseph Lehman concluded that Lanyon was 'the worst possible choice' to govern the Transvaal. His frosty manner was not helped by his appearance – an intense stare, a monocle, a bushy moustache and thinning hair slicked down over a domed head. It is impossible to find any historian who can say anything in his defence (though Bridget Theron-Bushell makes a gallant stab here and there), while contemporaries either disliked the man or were modest in their praise; Sir Charles Warren, who worked with him in Griqualand West, thought him 'able, conscientious and painstaking', but admitted that he and Lanyon held differing views on just about every subject.

William Owen Lanyon had been born in Belfast on 21 July 1842, third son of a famous Anglo-Irish architect and civil engineer. As a boy his parents and six brothers and sisters had called him 'Willie' but by his teens Lanyon made it clear that he wished to be known as 'Owen'. Educated in England, he had wanted since childhood to become a soldier and so just after his eighteenth birthday he joined the 6th Royal Warwickshire Regiment. The corps soon departed for Jamaica. The tropics were considered the white man's grave and dreaded by many soldiers, but one must assume that Lanyon liked his time there (or he had calculated the odds of death, disease and advancement) because in 1866 he purchased a lieutenancy in the 2nd West India Regiment. Steps up the promotion ladder soon followed, first as an aide to the Commanding Officer of the West Indies and then, from 1868–73, as ADC to the Governor of Jamaica who declared his services to be 'invaluable'. In September 1873 Lanyon's regiment was sent to the Gold Coast to help quell the warlike Ashantis and on Wolseley's arrival he was made an ADC. The general thought him 'a very good fellow' and Lanyon, with his great experience of tropical climes, went to great lengths to get Wolseley a first-class hammock, among other things. After short breaks in England and Ireland at war's end, Lanyon returned to the Gold Coast for a few months as acting colonial secretary.

In March 1875, now clearly a rising star in Colonial Office circles, Lanyon agreed to a new appointment as administrator of Griqualand West, the troubled Crown Colony where the discovery of rich diamond deposits was creating tensions between Africans and settlers relating to land. Griqualand did not excite Lanyon: 'A more uninteresting country could not be found,' he told his father. In equal measure and with lofty disdain he despised most of the white residents as money-grabbing rough miners, while local Africans were 'uncivilized savages'. The colony needed firm control in his opinion and he ruled it, as Cecil Rhodes wittily reported, 'on the lines of a second-rate regiment'. Popular with Lord Carnarvon and determined to repay this patronage by implementing 'Twitters'' scheme to deliver Griqualand West 'into the none-too-welcoming hands of the Cape Colony' (an event that finally came in 1880 after Lanyon's departure and by which time the grand confederation scheme was in tatters), the new administrator set to work with some zeal.

By May 1879, after six months hard work, Lanyon had reduced the colony's costs by one-eighth. The saving had partly been achieved by doubling the police force and using them as tax collectors. Labour regulations for native Africans were overhauled and after one year he had doubled the state income from labour registration fees.

Balancing the books went hand-in-glove with Lanyon's plans to give whites more access to land but he soon met fierce resistance from both the Griqua (who had been declared the legal owners of the land at the start of the 1870s) and the Thlaping, who were the largest tribe among the southern Tswana people in the area. A fall in the price of diamonds in 1876 combined with labour problems in the mining industry to give Lanyon headaches. Increased police action against African workers caused extra tension and 'did not point to a higher crime rate, but rather to the increased efficiency and zeal of the police'.[6] Lanyon was convinced that the African communities needed to be rigidly controlled and resettled into locations where they could be used as cheap labour reservoirs for the mining industry.

Nervous of failure, a workaholic with little or no interest in leisure pursuits, a recluse who disliked people generally (apart from his distant family), lonely, introspective, yet also very sensitive to criticism, Lanyon was by now calling Griqualand West 'the most hideous and disgusting place it has ever been my misfortune to enter ... It is utterly dreadful living in a place where one is so utterly out of the world.'[7] His efforts though were appreciated at home and he corresponded with Carnarvon, in 1876 sending to London secret intelligence reports from the Transvaal. Though he may have had more than one spy sending information, only Colonel Frederick Weatherley, who had fought the Bapedi in 1876 and was to die at Hlobane in 1879, has been clearly identified; the reports had one theme: 'The Govt. is simply a mockery ... there are many Boers in favour of British rule ...'[8] Spurred on by these reports, the situation deemed urgent, led Carnarvon to hurry on Shepstone's annexation mission.

Unrest with the various Griqualand West tribes finally broke out into rebellion at the start of 1878. Delighted to get out of his office and back into the saddle, Lanyon, who always thought of himself as first and last a soldier, spent much of the year quelling these flare-ups. Like a series of bubbles rising in hot springs and bursting on the surface, Lanyon waged his own campaigns in various parts of the colony. He was assisted by Lt-Colonel Charles Warren as his chief of staff. Lanyon claimed that in April alone 'they had 700 volunteers riding to fight ten engagements as news of aggression, of cruel murder, and of wholesale plunder came pouring in from all sides'.[9] The whole business ended in November. With the rebellion quashed and an amnesty proclaimed, Lanyon's reward that Christmastide was to find himself made a Companion of the Bath and a full brevet-colonel.

On his departure from Griqualand West for the Transvaal, only the men of the Diamond Fields Horse bade him a fond farewell. By now Lanyon was loathed heartily by settlers and Africans alike. The Kimberley community watched his departure with indifference and complete silence, noted a local newspaper, 'because nobody there did wish to see him some day'.

Unlike Lanyon, who despised colonists and made no efforts to hide his scorn, Sir Garnet was always willing to try some champagne and sherry diplomacy to win over his opponents. On the afternoon of 6 October he held a levee at Government House. This was followed by a reception for the ladies of Pretoria 'and an uglier-headed lot I never met'. Hugh McCalmont was amused how Fricke, the general's manservant and acting butler, 'thought himself a much bigger swell than the guests'. His complaint that Fricke was being tight-fisted in serving the champagne drew forth from the snooty butler the remark 'anythink was good enough for the likes of 'em as drinks it'. With his usual high spirits McCalmont got young 'Sankey' Herbert to join him in organising an excursion to the Fountains where a picnic was arranged for all the unmarried ladies of Pretoria (plus a few older women as chaperones). The band of the 80th Regiment played waltzes and light airs and, as Hugh wrote later, 'We larked about till darkness came on, and then all the servants were drunk and no one knew where the horses were.'[10]

One of Wolseley's chief concerns in early October was the delay and problems experienced by Baker Russell's column. On the 7th he heard they were stuck at Luneberg after some transport teams had 'bolted'; next day he was told the troops had set off at last towards Derby, but they were a long way from Bapedi country. One of those marching up with Russell was Major Philip Anstruther of the 2nd Battalion, 94th Regiment (Connaught Rangers). For some weeks he and his men had been encamped by the banks of the Ntombe River, somewhat bored, though the fishing had been good. A hero of Ulundi and a supporter of Chelmsford, he told his wife in a letter, 'It is rather amusing to see the way the mutual admiration society i.e. Sir Garnet's collection, run down on Ulundi and anything that has been done up to the present. You see Ulundi finished the war and they were not in it – and they hate that. He has one or two great duffers on his staff and they are always so pleased with themselves.'[11] Anstruther did not think Sekhukhune would fight once he heard how Cetshwayo 'had been licked'. On 4 October orders came to move direct towards Fort Weeber but the first day saw the 94th and some seventy waggons move just five miles. 'The rain had made all the streams almost impassable and the ground very soft and at each ford and soft place the wagons stuck,' wrote Anstruther, 'It was no laughing matter.' The next two days saw the column managing just eleven miles before needing to stop a full day to cut wood before marching on to the treeless high veldt. A new commissariat officer turned up with some bottles of champagne. Anstruther was not impressed. He would have preferred a cup of tea, and champagne, he told his wife, 'does not taste well out of iron cups'.[12]

Derby, when it was reached, turned out to be a lonely outpost consisting of just one house, a farm belonging to the local magistrate. Moving into the Transvaal the soldiers stopped at Boer farms to try and buy food. Anstruther was happy with the results:

> This morning for early breakfast we had cold turkey at 5 a.m. and at 9.30 we had pork chops and eggs and tonight we had the legs of a turkey grilled and a leg of mutton, so you see

> we are doing well ... We have reveille at 4.30 every morning; march at 6; outspan about 9.30, breakfast and go on again at 12 for two hours so we are always in camp about 2pm and the men get their dinners about 4 ... This is lovely country ... not a single tree, just a vast expanse of undulating downs with occasionally a stony bare hill cropping out and a marshy stream running across the road. The whole place is covered with flowers, principally bulbs and they really are beautiful ... [13]

Besides the 94th Baker Russell led 200 men of Ferreira's Horse, a troop of mounted infantry (from the 94th) under Lieutenant John de Courcy O'Grady, and 20th Royal Engineers. Personally Anstruther doubted if there would be any fighting, which he ridiculed as a 'tuppenny ha'penny business'. He told his wife: 'We go (6 companies) to Fort Weeber and hope to finish Sekukuni in a week after we get there if we have any decent weather and he will fight, but I doubt the event coming off.'[14]

One of the two officers working hard to improve the roads washed away by heavy rains was twenty-three-year-old Lieutenant Charles Commeline, son of a Gloucestershire squire and a friend of John Chard V.C. In many respects his opinions at this time mirrored those of thirty-nine-year-old Anstruther. In July Commeline told his father in a letter that 'Secocoeni will probably cave in and save the Government the expense of sending an expedition ...' The thought of a campaign against the Bapedi did not excite him at all because he had heard their 'country is exceedingly unhealthy and difficult and the business would probably be merely hunting niggers through the bush or driving them out of caves'. He also was not impressed how Sir Garnet's 'crowd of Ashantee heros [*sic*] ... make fools of themselves at our expense'. Commeline thought the 94th Regiment 'all very good fellows'. Unlike Anstruther he found asking for milk and eggs at Boer farms was difficult since the Afrikaners were 'intensely ignorant' and spoke no English.

'We none of us know anything of Sir Garnet's plans or how matters stand,' he wrote home, 'The country is ... fatal to horses and the stronghold of the chief, Secocoeni, is very difficult to approach and surrounded by mountains ...'[15]

At this time Wolseley still thought he could settle matters in the Transvaal by mid-December, 'to reach England on the 7th or 14th January'. Things were soon to change but the general had plenty on his plate besides Bapedi affairs. Bishop Schreuder wrote a grumbling letter about the return of missionaries to Zululand and Sir Garnet replied, rather hypocritically, 'Though I for one should always be opposed to forcing upon any natives the gospel of Christ, the "Man of Peace", no one would rejoice more than I should to see Christianity making rapid progress beyond the Tugela frontier of Natal.' He hoped that Schroeder would appoint missionaries who were 'really Godly men' and not those interested in 'the profits of trading operations'.[16]

Next came a shock: a private letter from Hicks Beach suggesting that the Zulus might be taxed to repay the costs of the Resident. 'All this looks as if Hicks Beach contemplated and expected me to annex Zululand in some open or disguised form,'[17] noted Wolseley in his journal. Succumbing to his periodic paranoia, the general deduced that the Colonial Secretary had been 'got at' by Shepstone. Henceforth Sir Garnet came to dislike his Whitehall master less and less, referring to him in letters to Louisa as 'Hicks-Bitch'. He replied to London asking what would happen if the Zulus declined to pay a new tax? If troops were then required to force payment where might matters end? 'To avoid war was what I arrived at,' wrote Wolseley in his journal, and if HM Govt did not wish for outright annexation then his policy had been 'the only other sensible course that was open to us', because there was no safe middle course to follow.

Further stresses for the general about this time included his servant, Fricke, catching a bad fever, while Captain Braithwaite tried manfully to fulfil his duties as an aide but was rapidly falling victim to Bright's Disease and 'much worse than he imagines'. Then news came of a disturbance at Middelburg where around fifty armed Boers had ridden into town to stop the trial of a man called Jacobs, accused of torturing his African servant by stringing him up from the wrists. This news had been brought speedily to Pretoria by Captain Pieter Raaff, a thirty-year-old soldier who had raised a force of Transvaal Rangers in the Zulu War. This corps had fought bravely at Hlobane, Khambula and Ulundi before being disbanded in September. Raaff had galloped the ninety miles from Middelburg on one horse in eleven hours. Wolseley wanted Jacobs 'severely punished' for his act of cruelty and sent Lanyon off to oversee the trial along with a troop of King's Dragoon Guards moved up from Heidleberg.

Thursday 14 October was a day of decisions. Wolseley decided that he would move on the 18th towards Middelburg, assess the Boer threat, then march on to Fort Weeber and remain there until the Sekhukhune business was settled, either peacefully or otherwise. He also decided to send home poor Braithwaite 'who has not long to live'. (On his return to England he rallied, went on to fight alongside Sir Garnet at Tel-el-Kebir in 1882 and even served with the Imperial Yeomanry during the South African War two decades later.) Writing that same day to his brother Dick the general said, 'The Zulu is in every way the Boer 's superior ... The Boers can barely read & write. In their houses a great family Bible is their only book. In it they believe most implicitly, even accepting the old quaint pictures in it as sound authority ...' Wolseley, a product of his times, believed firmly in the superiority of the British race yet he had no sympathies with Boer attitudes towards Africans. He told his brother how the Boers 'look upon the black man as they regard their cattle. God, they think, designed him to be their slave & that he was never intended to have any rights or property ... they are cruel at times to the natives,' acts which he deplored.[18]

During the afternoon of the next day, a fine one, a band was playing outside Jellalabad Villas – two houses rented as government offices – when a five-day-old letter arrived from Captain Clarke; messengers had not been well received at Tsate, but a delegation from Sekhukhune, who professed peace and wanted to know the British terms, had visited him and were due to head back to the Bapedi capital on the 12th. Rather ominously Clarke wrote that an assault on Tsate would mean 'many lives lost'. Wolseley now accepted what seemed to be an inevitable conflict, 'so I must prepare for fighting'. Always fearful of the butcher's bill he wrote, 'I hate to think of our men shot down in such a ridiculous contest which can bring no honour or glory even to the survivors & the operations will cost money.' Explaining to his wife what might happen after he reached Fort Weeber he informed Louisa that he expected to take up a position on the mountain above Tsate, 'if I can get there by a night march. I am afraid we shall lose nearly all our horses as that district of the country at this time of the year is most unhealthy ... I hope, however, the brute may give in without fighting. If he does not it may possibly delay my return by a week or two.'[19]

Next day a scurrilous rumour was reported to Wolseley that Clarke had been killed or taken prisoner by the Bapedi. This kind of news did nothing to lighten the general's mood and he bluntly told Stanley at the War Office that Sekhukhune could field 7,000 warriors and an attack on Tsate would be 'no child's play'. He emphasized that while the Zulus were generally poor marksmen with a rifle the Bapedi had a reputation as first-rate shots. The general repeated his idea for a night attack moving 'a force of a few companies of infantry by some foot path up the mountains'. On 16 October he wrote to Captain Clarke agreeing with his assessment of Sekhukhune. 'To give him the thrashing he deserves will cost us a number of valuable lives,' Sir Garnet reiterated, and he still hoped to avoid fighting.[20] He told Clarke to tell the chief that the Swazis would be sent against him and the Knobnoses given all the Bapedi cattle. Sekhukhune was to be guaranteed his life and free possession of his lands provided he agreed to pay his taxes. Gold instead of cattle could be accepted as payment. In his letter Clarke had suggested that the chief wanted to submit, but feared for his life or thought the British might make him a prisoner. Wolseley replied that Sekhukhune must be disabused of this idea; the missionary, Alexander Merensky, was to be offered up to £300 if he could get the chief to come to terms. Failure to do so meant war. Clarke was told to impress on Sekhukhune that the British never gave up a fight and he would be destroyed as Cetshwayo had been destroyed.

Around the same time that Sir Garnet was penning this letter a great *pitso* was being held at Tsate with the *kgosikgolo* (paramount chief), his *magosi* (chiefs) and indunas. Sekhukhune's ten elderly messengers had returned to the capital and it was understood by the tribe that non-acceptance of the terms meant war. The *kgosikgolo* was for peace. He confessed to being tired of fighting and advised 'every person who could do it to bring two or three head of cattle so that they might pay the fine demanded'. One minor *kgosi* (chief) called Puttakle retorted, 'You are a coward. Let the white people fight for the cattle if they want them. We have no cattle to give.' These words were met with so much applause that Sekhukhune then slyly suggested that he had merely been sounding out the mood of the *pitso*. 'You are wrong to call me a coward,' he replied, 'Your words are my words, but I wished to hear what you thought.' The general mood of the meeting was that the Bapedi, in the words of one warrior, 'will never be subject to the English, who compel their subjects to build forts and work for them; that the English are liars; that rather than be in the position of the subject tribes they will fight; that that won't pay taxes before they had a good fight for it.'[21]

The irony was that the old chief, Sekhukhune, like his adversary, Wolseley, had been forced to accept the inevitable – a war neither man really wanted. It seems that the Bapedi ruler would have preferred peace but, as Peter Delius has observed, 'popular feeling remained on the side of continued resistance until the end ...'[22] The Bapedi, it transpired, were not totally convinced that the Zulus had been defeated. They wondered 'how was it that cattle were not to be seen in the towns for sale, and how was it that prisoners were not sent to work on the roads?'[23] After the war Sekhukhune told Henrique Shepstone that it was not until November that he became convinced of the fall of Cetshwayo and his impis.

With all the wagons loaded by 7 a.m. and sent off under Maurice the general prepared to depart Pretoria on 18 October. Lanyon was back from Middelburg, the Jacobs affair was not settled and Sir Garnet thought the administrator was 'impregnated by the funk' at that place. A letter arrived from William Russell, the war correspondent, also at Middelburg, and in Wolseley's eyes 'inoculated with funk ... The tall talk of the Boers has frightened him. I confess it has no effect whatever on me ... I believe the Transvaal Boer to be a coward pure & simple.' To calm himself down mentally Sir Garnet then let fly 500 words in his journal on how 'the Transvaal Boers are the only white race I know of that have been steadily going back towards barbarism ... I regard them as the lowest in the scale of men & to be also the most uninteresting people I have ever known or studied.'[24] Lanyon was furious at what he perceived to be further humiliations; six days after Wolseley left Pretoria, he wrote to tell his father how the general 'has incurred ten times the expense for which he wigged me. He is beginning to see that it would have been better had he been a trifle more careful in his orders and less precipitate in his jumping at a conclusion about matters of which he was totally ignorant.'[25]

A three-day march brought Wolseley to Middelburg where he could see matters for himself. It was, he found, a pretty little place of about twenty-five stores and attached cottages, mostly owned by English proprietors. That afternoon Baker Russell's column finally arrived and around 9 p.m. more British soldiers turned up. These were the weary men of the 2/21st Fusiliers who had lost their way on the previous night and done an extra nine miles. That night the general wrote to Hicks Beach, 'The Boers won't fight unless we manage our affairs very badly.' He was still hopeful that Sekhukhune would accept his terms, but went on to say, 'This is a war that was begun by the Boers in injustice ... but we have inherited it and cannot draw back now ...'[26] One day earlier Wolseley had written to Louisa outlining his latest thoughts:

> If Sikukuni fights, I intend giving Russell command of the operations against him; of course I shall be there to see that everything is properly done, but I want if possible to give poor Baker a chance of writing a despatch announcing a success. This fellow Sikukuni occupies a mountain up which there are few paths, so he may give us a great deal of trouble, and the attack upon him may cost us some valuable lives. I hate the idea of expending our men in these filthy little wars, so I am doing all I can to induce this savage to submit without fighting: he has however an overweening opinion of his own strength because he beat the Boers when they attacked his mountain in 1876 and an expedition of ours under a Colonel Rowlands that marched against him last year returned without effecting anything: in fact, Rowlands made a very inglorious retreat.[27]

While staying at Middelburg the general met several times with the Reverend Alexander Merensky, whose Botshabelo station was close by. The missionary, who loathed Sekhukhune, did all he could to fill Wolseley's head with low opinions of the chief. Sir Garnet was impressed by Merensky's no-nonsense manner and told him of how Padre George Smith during the battle at Rorke's Drift 'had not fired on the Zulu himself, but had gone round our men serving out ammunition and telling them to fire low'. When Merensky replied that he would have picked up a rifle and fought, Sir Garnet declared him, 'quite the fighting missionary'. A choir of Bapedi children sang 'God Save The Queen' for Wolseley at Botshabelo where, for the first time, he saw some Bapedi tribesmen and decided that they were 'a very inferior race to the Zulu'.[28]

Before leaving Middelburg Sir Garnet decided to meet any Boer threats in the district by leaving the Frontier Light Horse to guard the town, along with one company of the 94th Foot and a troop of the King's Dragoon Guards. More cavalry were ordered up from Wakkerstroom with extra ammunition. Baker Russell led out his force towards the Bapedi country on 24 October. Wolseley and his staff struck camp at 6 a.m. the next morning. Marching with Sir Garnet were eighty volunteers from Merensky's mission, a mixture of African races, many of whom knew the Bapedi country intimately. The general decided that they would make excellent hospital bearers.

On Saturday 25 October 1879, a note dated 23 October arrived from Clarke saying that Sekhukhune had written to say that he was too poor to pay the fine, but hoped that the officer might see him to settle matters. Whether this was a delaying tactic or a genuine olive branch from the chief will never be known since Clarke replied that no compromise was possible. There was no going back. In his journal Wolseley wrote, 'Negotiation is now, I feel, at an end: I shall have to fight and I am very sorry for it. However, God's will be done. I know that everything is for the best.'[29]

Fort Weeber was reached on 28 October. The march, according to Major Anstruther, was 'detestable'. On the night of 26/27 it rained so hard that 'the valley became a swamp'. Next day the troops managed just four miles, which took them ten hours because the 'wheels of the wagons continually went out of sight and we had to put on double spars, get the men to haul with drag ropes; dig out the wheels, put branches of trees & rushes down and, at last, we managed it.'[30] Hailstones rained down the size of hens' eggs. Wolseley was furious with the transport arrangements and blamed both Maurice and Brackenbury, his new chief of staff, 'who does not care a farthing for anyone in this world as long as he gets under cover & has his dinner'.[31]

Despite the rigours of the journey the army was now at last on the fringes of Bapedi country. The track from the high veldt had dropped 1,200 feet, the lonely, undulating and treeless plain giving way to a land filled with hills on all sides, of rugged canyons in which giant boulders of reddish granite towered like bygone sentinels. All the farms, noted Anstruther, seemed deserted owing to fears of Bapedi attacks, while the rich orchards of plums, pears, apricots and other fruit hung heavy and lush on the boughs, though so far unripened. Among the bushes wild jasmine gave off its rich scent, and even Sir Garnet was impressed by the profusion of colourful flowers – lobelias, sweet peas, daisies and others – growing wild by the wayside.

With Wolseley at Fort Weeber we will now examine his campaign plan. This had been taking shape in his mind ever since the Zulu Settlement had been promulgated. Into the mix of ideas he also threw the opinions of Brackenbury, Harrison, Clarke and other advisers. Originally, Sir Garnet thought Sekhukhune would accept his terms. He would have responded by garrisoning two companies of the 94th Regiment at a new fort to be built in the mountains overshadowing Tsate. Even if the chief rejected his terms the general thought at first that a British post on a mountain top would be sufficient to overawe the Bapedi and prevent them from raising crops or grazing cattle. Sir Garnet was unsure to what extent horse sickness might affect British operations. It was also unclear if the new fort should be garrisoned entirely by infantry, mounted troops or some combination of both, but on 2 October he gave instructions for the Transvaal Mounted Rifles, Border Horse, Ferreira's Horse and Lydenburg Rifles all to be increased. In general terms his plans at this stage were similar to the operations conducted by Carrington, with Lanyon's approval, a few months earlier. Yet harassing the Bapedi had distinct disadvantages: it might take months to bring them to terms; horse sickness could decimate the cavalry; logistical problems would be huge and expenses mount quickly.

About the middle of October the general reached a decision that Tsate would have to be attacked by an army. Brackenbury, writing twenty years later, explained how growing Boer discontent in the Transvaal was a major factor in changing Wolseley's mind and 'considered that nothing would have a greater effect upon the Boers than that we were both able and willing to destroy Sekukuni's power, against which they had themselves unsuccessfully contended'.[32] Sir Garnet told Stanley at the War Office that it was necessary to destroy the 'prestige' attaching to Tsate, 'and to break up its traditional importance ...' He reminded HM Govt: 'All the chiefs in the Transvaal and on the borders are watching Sekukuni. Until he is beaten no taxes can be collected, and the native difficulty is constantly growing in strength. It is absolutely essential for the safety and peace of the country – its internal as well as its external peace – that this chief, who is the leader of native rebellion, should be compelled to acknowledge the complete supremacy of the British Crown.'[33]

Wolseley had decided to raise native levies to help him in his assault. He knew that Tsate would prove 'a hard nut to crack' and realised that officers such as Clarke and Denison, who had seen the famously formidable 'Fighting Kopje', or *Ntswaneng* as the Bapedi called it, held the place in 'superstitious awe'. Some writers have suggested that the general wanted to use Africans as cannon fodder to preserve his white troops. The simple truth is that he wished to overwhelm the Bapedi by sheer numbers and this knockout blow could only succeed if he had a sufficiently large army to throw into a coordinated and two-pronged attack. From Fort Weeber the operational base would be moved to Mphahlele's Drift, the nearest point on the Olifants River to the northern entrance to the valley leading to Tsate, which lay about twenty-one miles away. Before the main attack a feature called the 'Water Kopje' or Koppie would be seized and supplies and tents moved up to it. This would bring the troops just two and a half miles from their objective. Meantime a second force of native allies would move from Lydenburg to Fort Burgers on the other side of the Lulu Mountains, form up at a hill called Morakaneng, then attack Tsate from the heights east of the Bapedi capital. Morakaneng was only four or five miles from the Water Kopje so the two armies could be in communication.

The chief native allies in this enterprise were to be the Swazi, long-time bitter foes of the Bapedi. Despite attempts to get the Swazi energised during the Zulu War, their king, Mbandzeni, had other ideas. Historian Philip Bonner has written of this wily monarch that 'there are no circumstances whatsoever in which he would have participated in a full-scale invasion of Zululand'. The British political agent with the Swazis, Captain Norman MacLeod, was not entirely truthful with the information he sent Wolseley during the search for Cetshwayo, suggesting that 5,000 Swazis were just waiting to launch themselves into Zululand, whereas Mbandzeni just fancied a little looting along the Phongolo River frontier. He also told MacLeod that it was impossible to collect an army together during the period of a waning moon. Bonner describes the Swazi performance during the whole Zulu War as 'a truly masterful display of fence-sitting. Without actually doing anything they had managed to project an image of loyalty, which won them tributes from all sides once the fighting ceased.'[34]

The Swazis viewed the Bapedi differently; they were blood enemies and there were old scores to settle dating back to the days of Sekwati. On 21 October Sir Garnet asked MacLeod to raise a Swazi army of 2,000 warriors. Knowing that the Swazis were difficult to restrain in battle, the general pointed out that 'they must not make war upon women and children'. MacLeod replied that the Swazis agreed to fight as allies, 'but think it hard that they must not carry away the girls'.[35] Wolseley wrote back reiterating that 'they must neither kill nor carry away women and children'. Sir Garnet also hoped that he could raise about 1,000 Knobnoses and a further 2,000 other native auxiliaries. He noted: 'In these rugged mountains the natives can hop from rock to rock much more quickly than our men can, and they also know exactly where to look for the enemy.'[36]

Sir Garnet was of the opinion that it would take until 25 November to assemble all his Africans. He expected to lose a good many horses by that date from sickness. The state of supplies also alarmed him and he blamed difficulties on the commissariat at Pretoria, writing acidly in his journal, 'It is a fatality apparently in our army that to rely upon a commissariat officer is to be destroyed ...' Deputy Commissary Walter Dunne has, however, left a different picture in his memoirs and outlined some of the difficulties:

> It was decided to form two depots, the more important one, established at Mapahlella's Drift on the Oliphant River, 25 miles from Sekukuni's Town, being destined to provide 20 days' supplies for the whole force. While this was being done a pack ammunition train was organised. For this purpose donkeys were bought, for they were not liable to suffer from 'horse sickness', but only a limited number could be obtained from a considerable distance, and some of them were found to be unequal to what was required of them; for when two boxes of ammunition, weighing about 80 lbs each, were placed on their backs they sank to the ground under the load. Others, after the manner of their kind, put down their heads, kicked up their heels, scattered the loads and galloped off into the jungle in search of their cherished freedom. Some pack oxen were also tried, but were found to be badly trained.[37]

Richard Harrison, in charge of the Transvaal garrison, wrote in his autobiography that the operations were undertaken at a distance of 500 miles from the sea base at Durban, the nearest occupied farm was about 50 miles away, and 'no supplies could be purchased within 100 miles'. Pretoria and Wakkerstroom, both supply depots, were 150 and 230 miles distant 'and fifty more had to be covered to reach Mapashlela's Drift'. Due to the scares of a Boer insurrection the lines of communication also needed to be guarded by troops. Wolseley was not alone, however, in his irritations with the commissariat arrangements; Major Anstruther grumbled in a letter home of 'being hustled to get here with no object ...' He decided that it was 'the old story. Sir Garnet is no better than Lord C. It was supposed that we would find lots of provisions at Fort Weeber but, on arrival, it was found not to be the case and now we have to wait here while all the wagons go back to Pretoria, 170 miles and fetch them. Is not it stupid?'[38] (Actually fifty waggons went to Pretoria while a new train of eighty set out from Wakkerstroom with fresh supplies.)

On 28 October the general wrote a long letter to Hicks Beach about the growing Boer discontent. Sir Garnet was clearly under some psychological pressure and confessed that he was troubled by nightmares, a rare occurrence for a man who could sleep soundly through a hailstorm. He did not mince his words – and we will examine this document in a later chapter. Two days later he got some upbeat news from Lanyon which was 'refreshing' after 'all the croaking and funk I had listened to & experienced at Middelburg'.[39]

With rain dripping into his tent, Sir Garnet wrote letters until 3 a.m. on the 29th, then snatched two hours sleep before being roused at 5 a.m. for a dawn reconnaissance of Tsate and the Fighting Kopje. He rode as far as Fort Mamalube with Major Carrington and Captain Clarke, where the trio dismounted and crept through the hills to scout the enemy position. Next morning he was off at 6 a.m. to reconnoitre the Magnet Heights. The Bapedi lit signal fires on the peaks, fired a few harmless shots and blew their war horns. By now Wolseley was convinced that his main assault must be up the valley towards Tsate, just as Burgers had done in 1876. This plan reduced the risk of losses in fighting the Bapedi in the mountains, where, he acknowledged, they were 'very nasty customers'.

Lieutenant Charles Commeline R.E. was fairly content at Fort Weeber until he moved to Fort Olifants about 11 November. Fort Weeber consisted of little, thatched round huts for a barracks while the main officers room had a fireplace – 'everything looked very clean and comfortable compared to canvas.' Working on a road to Olifants he found the terrain of immense boulders and bushes fresh from the nightly rains was a visual contrast in reds and greens. Along the way he encamped near the village of a friendly chief – a compound of thatched rondavels surrounded by a thick reed palisade – which seemed 'a very awkward place to attack'. From his base at Fort Olifants near the river Commeline used as many as 500 African labourers to improve ten miles of road towards the enemy. He reconnoitred as far as the start of the valley leading towards Tsate and saw no Bapedi, though we can be confident that they saw him.

A batch of British newspapers arrived on 30 October along with two letters from Louisa Wolseley. Her husband was appalled at the *Army & Navy Gazette* making a defence of Captain Carey, who had left the Prince Imperial to his fate in Zululand. The man was, thought Wolseley, 'an arch-coward'. In his opinion, 'no man, private or officer, will ever associate with him'.

On the morning of 1 November the general met with Njabel, chief of Mapoch, who promised to send 2,000 warriors, though he requested two weeks so that the men could be 'doctored'. Wolseley was impressed by these people who claimed Zulu descent. Njabel had, in his opinion, 'a nasty debauched face, but when he laughs it brightens up'. He reviewed Russell's troops in the presence of the Africans, who murmured with delight at the bayonet exercise. After an early dinner Sir Garnet and McCalmont, guided by 'Lankyboy', Clarke's tall servant, rode off to the top of a mountain and the native track that led down to the low veldt and Lydenburg, base of the second column. The ride was one of the most scary and exhausting of Wolseley's life, made worse by the fact that he had ignored Clarke's good advice not to attempt a mountain descent in darkness. Sir Garnet thought he could do this by the light of the full moon but dark clouds rolled in and completely obscured it; violent thunder and lightning followed and the rain came down in torrents. 'We were in total darkness,' wrote the general in his journal, 'We had to lead our horses & I do not think I ever took part in an operation more dangerous.' After a time an old leg wound started throbbing, '& at last I began to stagger about as if I was drunk.'[40] Once at the bottom of the mountain a winded Wolseley threw himself down on the wet grass and regardless of the rain drops fell fast asleep. Two hours later he was up, had some cocoa with McCalmont, 'Lankyboy' and his escort of Africans (who had ridden ahead earlier but been overtaken), then rode on with rest stops every three hours or so. McCalmont wrote: 'I made some soup, which we agreed was the greatest filth we had tasted under that name. I had brought some hard-boiled eggs, but the result of putting them in a saddle-bag was that when we came to eat them we could find no eggs, the only trace of them was a sort of yellow pipe-clay which enveloped the clothes and everything else in the bag.'[41]

Finally Lydenburg was reached at 6 p.m. on 2 November, a ride of eighty-seven miles in twenty-six hours. Major Bushman, who was in temporary command, rode out to meet the chief. After a good sleep the general awoke on the 3rd to inspect Lydenburg and declared it 'a pretty little village' lying in its plain between the Lulu Mountains on the one hand and the gold-reefed hills leading towards Pilgrim's Rest on the other. The place was well-stocked with provisions, though supplies of gunpowder and ammunition seemed weakly guarded and Wolseley replaced Bushman, whom he thought not fit for an independent command, with Major Charles Creagh, 80th Regiment, an officer who had seen active service in the Crimea, New Zealand and Perak.

Despite ordering his escort to be locked in the guardhouse on the night of the 4th so that they might be sober for the return journey, the men of the Bastard Corps were still worse for booze next morning. Wolseley thought them 'excellent fellows as long as you keep them away from a town or store where you can buy liquor'.[42] They had to be reprimanded for bringing a bottle of brandy with them for the ride into the mountains. For a time the guide got lost and McCalmont was a little unnerved by the war cries and signals from the Bapedi hilltops.

All seemed well at headquarters and the weather much improved. During the thunderstorms on 1 November two men of the 94th had been killed when their tent was struck by lightning. Now the days were warm and breezy with showers only at night. Irritated that he had to wait for his native levies to assemble, Sir Garnet confessed to a sense of boredom. There was little he could do but ride around with Baker Russell, inspect troops, write letters and grumble. He let his frustrations fall on two civilians, that 'sneaking sponge', Billy Russell of *The Daily Telegraph*, and an annoying Treasury official called Gurdon (one of a group tasked by HM Govt with examining Zulu War accounts). 'If only I could have him shot when I attack Sekukuni's town,' mused Wolseley in his journal.[43]

For Billy Russell his run of luck since the ape incident had not gotten any better. He complained to Maurice that he was not properly informed of what was happening, his horses grew sick, his servant was taken ill and then, as if to cap it all, while crossing a fast-flowing stream, his horse stumbled, an open-mouthed Russell's head was jolted – and his false teeth fell out and were washed away! Several officers including McCalmont thought the episode was hilarious, though they agreed that it did nothing to improve Russell's temper.

By 20 November Sir Garnet was so bored that he spent much of the day reading a novel, a rare event as he hardly ever looked at fiction. It was Bulwer Lytton's *Last of the Barons*, which he concluded was entertaining nonsense. In a letter written during this period to one of his friends, Wolseley explained how he had offered Sekhukhune 'very easy terms, so easy indeed that I know the Colonists would howl at them when they heard what they were', but the chief had rejected his offer, 'so on his head now be all the consequences'. He fixed a date for the final battle saying, 'I hope to take my afternoon tea' in Sekhukhune's house 'by the 1st December.' His task was made harder because the chief refused to fight as Cetshwayo had done, 'like a gentleman'. Instead the Bapedi king 'has fortified one naturally very strong position and he is wise enough to keep to it'.[44]

Gradually things started to gain momentum: the Swazis, over 7,000 of them, 'were playing the devil along the road with the farmers', but were definitely on their way; 1,400 Knobnoses had also set out, but 1,000 of them bolted in one night, soon followed by the remainder; a new fort was being constructed ten miles on from Fort Olifants, to be called Fort Albert Edward, at the closest point of the river to the entrance to Sekhukhune's valley; Baker Russell's patrols were frequently fired on; and a spy reported that the Bapedi were 'quite ready to fight us, the Swazies and all comers'. Most serious of all, some 2,000 to 5,000 Bapedi warriors had attacked Fort Burgers on 12 November in a deliberate attempt to rustle livestock, and got away with 123 cattle, leaving Wolseley worried how to feed the Swazis, who were 'such devils to eat beef ...' The cattle had been grazing some 400 yards from the fort. The small garrison only had six horses and were powerless to stop the Bapedi, with fierce firing on both sides for almost an hour.

Luckily only one African, a man in Eckersley's Contingent, had been wounded on the British side and the six mounted men had sallied forth and recaptured twenty-four cattle.

The soldiers realised that a day of battle was fast approaching. Major Anstruther, comfortably settled for a time in a thatched hut at Fort Olifants, was 'as fit as a fiddle' and expected the war to finish 'by the end of next week'. Lieutenant Commeline, along with senior sapper, Lieutenant J. C. Macgregor, had laboured to construct Fort Albert Edward, a turf affair consisting of two redoubts surrounded by a four-foot-deep trench. The fort's walls were six feet wide at the bottom though tapered near the top. The fort was completed after two days' exhausting work on 18 November, 'large numbers of men having been also employed in making the drifts practicable for the convoys of wagons bringing up supplies from the rear', explained Commeline. 'The scenery round the fort was very fine but the weather was intensely hot. The heat inside a bell-tent at midday is unbearable,' he declared. 'As far as work for the R.E. goes the Zulu War was a joke to this one ...'[45]

Wherever Wolseley went he tried to inspire his officers and men. The officers in particular found him 'chatty and amusing' with no signs of stress. One officer wrote that Sir Garnet rendered 'the most dry of official details interesting by his remarks'.

Tsate would not be Wolseley's largest set-piece battle but, as historian Kenneth Smith has written, he 'had planned his attack very carefully'. It had been arranged that on 23 November the troops being used in the valley assault would assemble at Fort Albert Edward, while on the same day the troops from the other side of the mountains would collect at Fort Burgers. Thus Baker Russell led a column out of the headquarters camp on the 20th and Sir Garnet followed on the next day. When the general arrived at Fort Albert Edward on the morning of 23 November he found there six companies of the 21st Fusiliers along with four companies of the 94th Regiment supported by colonial corps – the

Border Horse, Transvaal Mounted Rifles, Transvaal Artillery with four guns and part of the Rustenberg Contingent of Africans. Baker Russell was encamped seven miles nearer Tsate at a place known simply as Seven Mile Post. His advanced column consisted of two companies of the 94th, Ferreira's Horse, 1,150 Africans of the Zoutspanberg Contingent and a further 350 natives of the Rustenberg Contingent.

The next four days were to be critical. Wolseley wished he had more ammunition for his native troops but was pleased to hear that on the other side of the Lulu Mountains his second little army was on the march. 'Everything now goes well,' he wrote in his journal, '& promises well thank God; if we can merely keep our horses alive for another fortnight it will indeed be a merciful blessing ...'[46] He had decided to launch his 'great fight' at 3 a.m. on 28 November. First his troops had to get within easy striking distance of Tsate. It was time for action.

8

BLOOD ON THE FIGHTING KOPJE

I don't know how I am alive. We were nearly all killed.

Masschow, a Bapedi warrior

It was the strangest sound. A rhythmic thumping that could be heard coming from somewhere over the horizon. Like a train. Getting closer. A score or more of gold-diggers who visited sleepy little Lydenburg to whet their thirst on that day, 18 November 1879, 'stepped out into the dusty street from the little hotel, leaving their unfinished glasses on the bar counter',[1] all nervously wanting to see the cause of the increasing din, now likened to a 'muffled roar'. More and more townspeople stopped what they were doing to congregate on the sidewalk. When the cause of all the commotion was made known to them they stood transfixed in a mixture of awe, excitement, fear and surprise.

The noise came from 16,000 feet slapping against the sun-baked dry earth and 'the ceaseless swish of the long, sweet-scented grass as it rose and fell before the onrush of the quick-moving warriors'.[2] Eight thousand Swazi, assegais and shields glinting in the sun, their plumed and feathered headdresses making an extravagant sight, were on the march. Leading this Swazi army (*emabutfo*) on a white horse was Captain Norman MacLeod, 74th Highlanders, a very proud man; within sixteen days of getting Wolseley's request for Swazi troops he had negotiated with King Mbandzeni, collected together some 8,000 warriors (four times the number Sir Garnet originally expected), and marched this *emabutfo* 180 miles from the royal kraal, keeping them in good order, and even teaching some drill along the way. Sir Garnet told his wife that MacLeod, a son of the clan chief, was 'a gentleman, but a man without much brains or judgment', a man with 'a nasty duty to perform' who seemed to have 'no influence over the Swazis'. MacLeod would have been very hurt if he had known this assessment, though he had few illusions. 'No one believed I would get an impi at all,' he wrote home, 'and I think nobody but myself could for from twelve months' experience they have learnt to place confidence in me and believe what I say. I have had a very hard time, what with the hills and ravines, rivers and swamps, rough Kafir paths, rain every day and scarcely anything to eat.' He knew a tough battle lay ahead. 'From all accounts it will be very nasty work,' he wrote, 'and we shall lose a good many men.'[3]

Two days later Major Creagh left Lydenburg with the imperial and colonial troops. He had with him two companies of the 80th Regiment, two companies of the 94th, the hundred or so men of the Lydenburg Rifles and Eckersley's Contingent of Africans. Joining up with the Swazis the whole column reached Fort Burgers on 23 November. From there the 400 white men and 400-strong native contingent, along with the large Swazi *emajaba* set forth towards Tsate under Major Bushman because Creagh had fallen ill with fever and had to be left behind at the fort. One of the Lydenburg Rifles, E. V. Corrie, never forgot the moment the Swazis left Fort Burgers and years later described how each man was 'the perfection of a black warrior' with a war dress even finer than the Zulu. He wrote:

> Our crowd of 8,000 were magnificently attired in beautifully-dressed leopard skins, and thick head-dresses of black ostrich

> feathers. When on the march the dusky companies sweep along at a great rate, each warrior on his left arm carries a shield, black, white or striped, according to his regiment; from his waist hangs a kilt of leopard tails, or twisted strips of fur, and in his right hand is held the short stabbing assegai – a few of the 8,000 had rifles slung across their backs, but in the fighting that ensued most of the Swazies depended on the assegai.[4]

In command of this colourful and ferocious little army was Major Henry Augustus Burnham, the officer whose ability as an independent commander had so worried Wolseley on his visit to Lydenburg. A cavalry officer down to his spurs, the thirty-eight-year-old Bushman was now to prove himself worthy of respect. He had joined the exclusive 9th Lancers as a cornet in 1858 but never seen any active service. When offered a chance by his friend, Baker Russell, to go out to Zululand with the general he jumped at it. The Duke of Cambridge advised him not to go as he was due for promotion if he stayed at home, but Henry's colonel gave him permission for two months leave (this soon had to be extended to six). He met Wolseley in London on 31 May. A natural joker, it was Bushman who had disguised himself as the general on the train journey from the capital; on board ship he participated in a minstrel show. Now looking splendid in his uniform of deep blue with scarlet lapels, kneeboats, long white gloves and 9th Lancers helmet surmounted with its plume of black and white cock's tail feathers he looked almost as impressive as the Swazis.

On his side of the mountains Wolseley had been having problems with his native contingents. The Knobnoses had all fled due to rumours that Chief Mahate, an ally of Sekhukhune's, might attack their homes while they were gone, so they had returned to protect their families. Commandant Meyer and Captain Dahl had managed to raise 1,150 Africans from the Zoutpansberg district, but Captain Clarke failed miserably to get the promised warriors from Chief Njabel. The chief pleaded the somewhat lame excuse that the Boers had 'threatened to steal all his cattle and burn his outlying kraals if he disobeyed them'.[5] Clarke, who must have felt very humiliated, turned up at Fort Albert Edward with just 230 Africans from Mapoch's district supplemented by about 420 other men offered by nearby chiefs.

Around 10.30 a.m. on the 23rd Sir Garnet got a message at Fort Albert Edward saying that Commandant Ferreira and his men were about to lead an assault from Seven Mile Post on Umkwane's Kraal, which lay on a mountainside almost opposite and was a vital position since it commanded the road to Tsate. The kraal was surrounded by smaller ones and 'built on steep rocky kopjes and on projecting ledges of rock, the only accessible means of access being narrow paths'.[6] Ferreira personally conducted a reconnaissance and was told by Baker Russell to take the position if he felt that it was possible to do so. Ignatius Ferreira never missed a good fight and at 11 a.m. Russell got a heliograph signal saying an attack was under way. The firing was heavy. Soon smoke could be seen rising and extending across the valley. Wolseley arrived at the kraal while sporadic firing was still going on; as he looked up, Ferreira's men were searching the rocks above the kraal, while Zoutpansberg Africans burnt the huts, 'firing away in every direction, quite as much to the danger of friends as foes', as they made off with all the goats and cattle.[7]

Sir Garnet was a little miffed when Dahl, an old hand at fighting the Bapedi, suggested that the young warriors had not been present, just older men. 'I doubt this,' sniffed the general, 'as I cannot think Umguana would allow his fighting men to join Sikukuni's until our troops had passed his place.'[8] The women and children were taken prisoner and the kraal totally destroyed. Sir Garnet thought Ferreira had managed the attack very well and 'no injury was done to the women and children'. The women later told interpreters that

Umkwane had been caught unawares. The Bapedi had lost about 100 killed and wounded out of some 300 or so defenders. British losses had been six wounded and four killed, one of whom was Regimental Sergeant-Major Caufield of Ferrerira's Horse. Wolseley thought the capture of Umkwane's Kraal would awe the Bapedi while imparting 'pluck and confidence' in his own African troops.

Back at camp Charles Commeline had a 'very good view' of the attack watching its progress 'by the smoke rising from the various kraals set on fire, which approached gradually the topmost kraal'. About the time Wolseley returned to Fort Albert Edward the lieutenant was ordered to take some guncotton up to the caves above Umkwane's Kraal 'for the purposes of destroying them, some men having been killed by the firing from them'. When he got closer to the stronghold he thought it 'an awful place to assault ... and I was astonished at it having been taken with so little loss ...' The huge boulders, 'heaped one on another and forming any number of caves', made him decide that if the Bapedi 'were good shots and had better weapons it would have been impossible to advance against them'. Commeline helped in the work of blowing in some caves, despite a dropping fire, 'but we returned to camp without further casualties, meeting the native contingent returning to occupy the place for the night, driving before them a great herd of cattle and goats which they had captured.'[9]

That evening, after a scouting expedition, Carrington returned to camp with the news that the old Boer track down the valley towards the Bapedi capital was so overgrown by thick bushes that waggons would never be able to use it. Immediately on hearing this news, Baker Russell ordered his staff officer, Captain Stewart, along with his orderly officer, Captain E. Fraser, to proceed to Umkwane's Kraal and use the Zoutpansberg Contingent to try and clear the bush back to Seven Mile Post, while troops from Fort Albert Edward would be used to clear the track nearer to Tsate, about seventeen miles further down the gradually narrowing valley. On 24 and 25 November Fort Albert Edward was denuded of men as most troops marched to Seven Mile Post. Lieutenant Commeline was one of ten Royal Engineers and thirty infantry ordered to go forward with the help of Ferreira's Horse and the native contingent and prepare the road for the advanced guard.

Heat like a furnace made the very air seem oppressive. Brackenbury was 'seedy', but Maurice, Herbert and even the Treasury official, Mr Gurdon, all set off for Seven Mile Post on the 24th (Gurdon only made it as far as the field hospital complaining of 'stomach pains'; Wolseley recommended him a little 'jumping powder'). The *Daily Telegraph* correspondent, William Russell, hung back. Perhaps forgetting some of the scenes the old reporter had witnessed in the Crimea and Indian Mutiny, the general wrote spitefully in his journal: 'I very much doubt if he was ever under fire in his life ...' Sir Garnet inspected the men Clarke brought from the chiefs and labelled them 'a bloodthirsty looking lot'. They were given red puggaries to distinguish them from Bapedi hostiles, issued with ammunition, and sent to hold Umkwane's Kraal with the Rustenberg Contingent.

That evening Wolseley wrote to the Duke of Cambridge with an account of the action that day. He could not help pointing out that his soldiers 'had attacked and acted on the defensive' all along the way. Taking a swipe at the Commander-in-Chief's reactionary clique he added: 'I will be curious to see how the much abused young British soldiers will do when attacking a strong position under a heavy fire. I myself have every confidence in them if are well led by their officers.'[10]

After a day of unbearable heat 25 November was 'deliciously cool' and Sir Garnet was grateful. Fifty-five badly needed remount horses arrived led by Captain W. G. Lawrell, 4th Hussars, a friend of Baker Russell, with two officers of the King's Dragoon Guards.

The Water Kopje, with its supply of good water, was seized that morning by 130 infantry and twenty Royal Engineers conveyed on mule wagons followed by 240 soldiers on foot escorted by 300 mounted volunteers. They had travelled through the night, a difficult journey as the wagons bumped and rocked over the rutted track, the men sitting and wondering if at any minute they might hear the war cries and mournful battle horns of a Bapedi onslaught. All went well and the Kopje was seized at dawn on the 25th. There was minimal opposition and only a few shots were fired. According to Lieutenant Commeline the troops had set off expecting to meet heavy Bapedi opposition. All that happened was some yelling from the hills and a few harmless shots fired. Old colonial hands, puzzled by the ease of taking the Water Kopje, concluded that the Bapedi were either low on ammunition or saving all they had for the big fight. Crossing a nek of land they saw through their field glasses 'Secocuni's Town' for the first time. Once at the Water Kopje the men could see Tsate quite clearly. They hastily fortified their position and named it Fort Alexandra. Sir Garnet now had an abundant source of water for his army and an advanced post just three miles from the Bapedi capital. Two chaplains, the Reverend Mr Law and Father Walsh, arrived to give succour to the Anglican and Roman Catholic soldiers.

Exactly at the same time that Russell's troops were seizing the Water Kopje, the Lydenburg Column under Bushman climbed Morakaneng Hill and made a base there called Fort George. They were now about five miles from Tsate. Herbert Stewart went out scouting that day from Wolseley's side of the mountains and managed to meet a Lydenburg patrol. Thus Sir Garnet's 'careful preparations and planning had been rewarded,' writes Kenneth Smith, 'and the two columns were in communication with one another.'[11] Stewart reported back to the general that everything looked so quiet at Tsate that he feared there would be no fighting. Sir Garnet disagreed. He expected a stiff fight. When he heard that the Swazis had only about 500 rifles among them he thought, 'So much the better; the assegai must now do its work.' He sent a message to Bushman that the warriors must be given 'plenty of beef' to keep them satisfied.

The general dined at 3 p.m. on the 26th, tents were struck at 4 p.m., and he left Fort Albert Edward with the main body of his troops thirty minutes later. Rain had started earlier and it now came on in torrents, 'almost a sheet of water', but eventually the storm died away leaving the track a muddy morass. Sir Garnet had to travel about twenty-five miles that night to Fort Alexandra. In dim light from a cloudy sky and waning moon, it was a miserable night for the troops as waggons constantly got stuck in the mud or jammed into trees and bushes. The soldiers cursed in the darkness which also made it impossible to throw out flankers or cover the advance. Wolseley finally reached the advance post sometime between 6.30–7 a.m. Fort Alexandra lay on the right bank of a stream flowing from the mountains to the south. A small entrenchment had been made for extra protection on the left bank.

Despite feeling 'very tired' there was little rest for the 46-year-old general. He resaddled and with an escort of Ferreira's Horse set off to reconnoitre the place he called 'Sikukuni's Town'. He got within 800 to 1,000 yards without a shot being fired. The place seemed so quiet that some troopers thought the enemy had bolted. The general sent orders to Russell to move his guns two miles nearer to a position north-east of the Fighting Kopje. An advanced post was to be set up there. Obtaining a fresh horse from Carrington, Sir Garnet next rode over to Bushman's Camp on Morakaneng Hill. The Swazis seemed boisterous and MacLeod, in Wolseley's opinion, had little control over them. 'I am afraid he is a round man in a square hole,' noted the general in his journal. Via an interpreter Sir Garnet told the Swazi general what he wanted done, explained how the Swazis had to ascend the mountain behind Tsate in two columns and his plans for the actual assault. He returned to Fort Alexandra having been in the saddle for the better part of thirty-six hours. Baker Russell's main army of what was now called the Transvaal Field Force were marching into camp. The men were exhausted and Wolseley wanted them to get some rest before the big fight next day. Before turning in himself for a few hours' sleep he made sure that the horses and cattle were laagered in case some false alarm might lose him his vital animals.

To his everlasting embarrassment, George Denison, who 'could wake up about any time', had overslept that morning of the 27th and opened his eyes 'to find the Scots Fusiliers marching past me scarcely six feet away. My trumpeter lay asleep near my feet and I raised him with my foot.'[12] Denison hastily found his way to Carrington and they led their troopers quickly past Major Hazelrigg and his men. At first the colonials were cursed by stumbling soldiers who had to make way for them, but as the path lay through thick bush of prickly pear and black hook thorn, which was tearing at the men's already patchy uniforms and bloodily scratching their hands and faces, cheers rang out as horses and riders beat a path. The Border Horse spent much of the day helping to convey infantry and waggons and Denison spent a pleasant hour or two chatting with Herbert Stewart, Russell's affable staff officer.

It was 11 p.m. before Lieutenant Charles Commeline lay down for a brief nap. He had spent the evening with Lieutenant Macgregor, the other Royal Engineers officer, preparing guncotton to be used in the assault. From his bivouac he could see Tsate and its immense number of thatched huts. 'There were also several other towns or stadts perched about the neighbouring hills,' wrote Commeline, 'their positions always being chosen with a view to defence.' On the 26th his sappers had been hard at work making a road across an awkward stream. The Bapedi that day 'made a great deal of noise on the hills, blowing horns and chafing our fellows on the koppie, but still not firing and, of course, keeping themselves under cover of the rocks'.[13] Commeline had moved up to the forward position on the 27th and gradually the whole column came closer to Tsate. The troops included Major Anstruther and his men of the 94th Regiment. He described the valley as 'two and a half miles long between entrances. It is awfully strong and with Europeans defending it would be impregnable.'[14]

That evening of the 27th orders for the morrow were read out to the men of the different corps before they grabbed a little shut-eye. Wandering through his lines Denison popped his head into the Commissariat tent of the Border Horse where Mr Longlands, his Quartermaster, and Quartermaster-Sergeant McLeod were doing their ablutions. 'May I use your razor, Mr Longlands, when you have finished?' asked McLeod. The quartermaster replied that the young man would have plenty of time next day for a shave. 'You promised me I should go out next time,' replied McLeod. 'Oh did I?' retorted Longlands, 'Well, if so, then of course you must go ...'[15]

Old colonials who had fought the Bapedi before knew that the coming battle would be a hard one. In the darkness of the night, when soldiers' fears are at their worst, some reflected no doubt on the fact that their enemies had seen off Swazi, Zulu, Boer and British invaders in the past, were formidable rock rabbits who knew every cave and crevice of their hillsides, were crack shots and would put up a desperate defence of Tsate and their ultimate stronghold, the Fighting Kopje.

The Bapedi warrior did not look like the Swazi or the Zulu, whose images were fixed in Victorian minds as the perfectly masculine 'noble savage'. On his head and trailing down his back he wore a cap of animal fur. His chest and loins were covered by the main skin of the animal which was tied behind his neck, from which hung the *luveve*, a wind instrument reputedly made from human shinbone (or so said the Swazis), which, when blown, made a sorrowful and freakish sound that many British said resembled a fog-horn. Unless he carried a firearm the warrior would be armed with two or three assegais and either a battle axe, straight-pointed or with a flanged tip, or a heavy and vicious knobkerrie used to smash out an opponent's brains with one blow. Some Bapedi carried plume-tipped shields, and chiefs often had elaborate feathered headdresses like most southern African tribes. Warriors shaved their hair in a special manner before battle and decorated their top-knots.

In the days of Sekwati the Bapedi had fought with these ancient weapons, but ever since the discovery of mineral wealth at Griqualand West things had changed; it was Sekhukhune's menfolk who formed a large percentage of the African workforce in the mines and they returned to Bopedi having purchased guns and powder. Sekhukhune seems to have cunningly encouraged this activity. 'At knock off time our Kaffirs used to pass down streets of tented shops owned by white traders and presided over by yelling black salesmen whirling guns over their heads,' recalled one Kimberley miner, 'These they discharged in the air, crying "Reka, reka, mona mtskeka" ("Buy, buy, buy a gun").'[16] Traders sold thousands of these guns. When terms of employment at Kimberley were over, the Bapedi in large groups would begin the trek home carrying various articles – woollen goods and utensils – on their backs and the cherished guns across their shoulders. 'A pair of boots of which they were genuinely proud always formed part of their possessions,' wrote Read, 'but were carried, not worn', to impress friends in their villages. The most common and basic gun in the early 1870s was an inferior muzzle loader known as a 'gas pipe' gun. These dated from the end of the Napoleonic Wars and had their origin, as C. V. Read explained, in the disbandment of corps when 'the old muskets were stored for a while, and subsequently sold off to one of the first coal gas companies formed in London. The back of the barrels were cut off and turned with stock and die, the one to fit with the other ...'[17] The most popular gun was the Tower musket – a Brown Bess converted to a percussion lock. It sold for £4 – three months wages for a Bapedi digger – and was twice the price it cost in Cape Town, but the workers bought them up. Occasionally, Storey records, a miner might save the colossal sum of £25 and buy a breechloader. Delagoa Bay in Mozambique was another source for guns. It was estimated that in the years 1875–77 alone local traders sold the Zulu, Sotho and Pedi tribes an average of 20,000 guns with percussion caps and 10,000 barrels of gunpowder. One eighth of the traders were Bapedi and 'strong demand has arisen for breech loading rifles' reported the Portuguese Consul.

Huge elephant guns that fired a mass of metal projectiles, usually tin pots and pans, were known to be in Sekhukhune's arsenal. These guns had panicked the Boers in 1876. There was even talk that he might own a cannon and have the means to use it. This idea was not as crazy as it sounded since on at least two occasions Sekhukhune had tried to obtain such a weapon and offered a reward. One man who took up this offer was Herbert Rhodes, elder brother of Cecil; in September 1875 he bought a small brass cannon and tried to smuggle it into the Transvaal via Mozambique. When his crafty plan was rumbled Rhodes threw the cannon overboard his boat with a marker buoy attached to it. Portuguese authorities subsequently found the gun on a mud bank at low tide, but Rhodes had by then slipped quietly out of the country.

Bapedi warriors were formed into regiments but these, unlike their Zulu and Swazi equivalents, were more closely related to the various chiefdoms than to the monarch. This arrangement is best explained by Peter Delius, who writes,

> Regiments were formed consisting of men or women of the same age group. At intervals of from four to eight years boys and girls at, or over, the age of puberty attended separate initiation lodges and were constituted into regiments under the leadership of high-ranking youths, usually the sons and

> daughters of the incumbent chief … Regiments were also a principal prop to chiefly power.[18]

The youths attended a circumcision school and were forced to go through various rites of adulthood involving acts of courage and torture (such as repeatedly picking up hot coals). Whipped daily to show their subordination to their elders, beaten and sometimes killed if they flinched or failed, at last these young people would see the white chalk of childhood washed off their bodies and replaced by the red ochre of an adult. In time of war each Pedi fighting unit sent by an individual chief remained, as John Laband has explained, 'a separate unit in the army under its regional commander, and fought under its own distinct standard fashioned primarily from ostrich feathers'.[19]

An extraordinary account of events from the Bapedi perspective survives in the words of Masschow, a warrior of Chief Nkoane, a Bapedi sub-chief. A married man with a wife and child, Masschow responded to his chief's summons to join the main army at Tsate when the war bugle sounded a day or so before the battle. He and his friends rushed for their assegais and shields. Cleverly they avoided the British and made it safely to the town. The king, his counsellors, witch-doctors and generals were there along with thousands of warriors. Prince Moroamotshe, Sekhukhune's son and heir, had been ordered for his own safety into the hills across the Olifants River. On the night of 27 November he returned much to Sekhukhune's anger. The young royal answered his father's rebukes with the brave words, 'I am flesh of your flesh, bone of your bones and I will not act like an old woman and keep out of the fight.' Sekhukhune, known as 'the man who creeps by night', told the Bapedi, in the words of Masschow,

> We must not be afraid. He would beat the English. Hadn't he driven the Boers back two years before? He said he had some

> hives of bees. These he would release amongst the soldiers & they would chase them away. We were then inoculated so that the bullets would not harm us, and we were painted white with ashes so that we were not taken for the Swazi (the damned Kal Kaffirs) who were going to help the English. The women & children were sent up to the kraantzes & each regiment with its general leading went & took up positions.[20]

In his tent that night Sir Garnet was under no illusions that he had a 'hard nut to crack'. He was naturally confident of success, yet always dreaded what he termed 'the butcher's bill'. He did not expect the Bapedi to demonstrate the fighting qualities of the Zulus, though he knew they had a reputation as good marksmen, but his biggest fear, as general of an attacking force, was just how difficult the natural obstacles of a dawn attack on Sekhukhune's Town, Tsate, and the surrounding kraals in the hills might prove to be. Once achieved, he knew he must push on in broad daylight to assault the awesome fortress that was Ntswaneng – the Fighting Kopje.

Sir Garnet and his soldiers were camped in a flat valley a little over a mile wide. Facing the British in an angle made by the eastern range of the Lulu Mountains as they curved to partially close the valley to the south was Tsate, a town of some 3,000 round thatched huts (*rondavels*), built partly on the valley floor, partly on the slopes of the wooded hills. Each kraal was surrounded by a fence of prickly pear or thorny wood. In front of Tsate were a series of rifle pits. Stone walls, like Afghan sangars, along with more thorn hedges, ascended in terraces in front of the British and on the slopes to the sides. Covered bulwarks or sconces were built at regular intervals along the terraces. The town itself could only be entered by two steep and narrow paths, which were heavily defended. Sekhukhune for weeks before had put a large thorn fence across the valley in front of the town. It stretched from hill to hill, was fifteen feet high and fifteen feet wide. The Bapedi thought 'nothing can penetrate it'.

A little distance away near the chief's own kraal was the tribe's final defence, the Fighting Kopje. It was – and remains to this day – a most remarkable natural wonder. One writer once wrote that the place looks as if God had lifted a vast pile of igneous rock in the air and let the boulders fall in a colossal jumble. Geologists assert that Ntswaneng is, in reality, 'a norite extrusion from the level plain of the Bushveld Igneous Complex'. To the Bapedi it had a more spiritual significance. Ntswaneng is 300 feet long, 200 feet wide and about 150 feet high, honeycombed with caverns caused by splits in the boulders or gaps between them. The Bapedi knew this natural fortification intimately and had laid in supplies of ammunition and limited supplies of water. In places they had built up stone breastworks to frustrate any attackers. Close up and at ground level it is very difficult to judge the true dimensions and secrets of the Fighting Kopje. At a distance of a mile or so one can see that its summit is dwarfed by two much higher ones: Modimolle ('the place of the spirit') has a rounded summit and was a taboo mountain reserved for rain-makers and witch-doctors, while Thaba Mosego ('the mountain of cutting') is where Sekwati is buried. A saddle runs between the two summits. Old timers in Wolseley's army could ruminate on the words of Private Edward McToy, who wrote of the defences of Tolyana Stadt during Rowland's ill-fated expedition just eleven months previously: 'One thing the attack taught us – the uselessness of pouring lead into these strongholds of natural formation. Fortresses in themselves ... where boulder towers on top of boulder ... affording sufficient cover for hundreds of men.'[21]

Wolseley's plan called for the attack on Tsate to be timed to coincide with Bushman's column falling on the Bapedi from the heights to the east of the town. On their side of the hills Baker Russell and Wolseley had divided their army into three attacking columns, a right one, a left one and a centre column. The right or western column was to be led by Ferreira with his famous horsemen dismounted, Mapoch's Contingent and two companies of the Rustenberg Contingent. They would assault and take the kraal and heights to the south of the town. This right column had, as Joseph Lehmann wrote, 'the position of honour' commencing the assault. Its commander, already encountered in these pages several times, was the dashing Ignatius Philip Ferreira, one of the toughest colonial soldiers. He had been born at Grahamstown on 5 July 1840, descendant of a Portuguese nobleman shipwrecked at the Cape in 1691, who married a Huguenot girl. While in his early teens Ignatius enlisted in Currie's Border Police and fought as a mounted trooper against the Bastards and Hottentots in the Cape's north-west and the deserts of the Kalahari. When his corps was disbanded young Ferreira tried his hand at farming, even married a Cape Dutch girl, but his restless nature led him, like so many others, to the diamond fields of Kimberley. Ill-luck dogged his footsteps and he moved again, this time to the eastern Transvaal. In 1875 he was elected field cornet of the Olifants River ward and shortly afterwards took part in the disastrous Boer expedition against the Bapedi. He thought it a 'useless' one. Something about soldiering suited the dark-haired and bushy-bearded Ferreira, who stayed in the saddle gaining a reputation as a cool and efficient commander of mounted troops. The Boers called him 'Naas Ferreira' and the Africans nicknamed him *Umtakati* ('the warrior who cannot be killed').

Serving under Ferreira as his senior captain was twenty-five-year-old Henry Nourse, son of a farmer from Port Elizabeth. The pair had also been comrades in the Zulu War and years later Nourse wrote:

> In native warfare, Colonel Ferreira was by far the greatest soldier and strategist that this country has yet seen. He was a born leader of men, and inspired confidence wherever he went.

> During the second Sekukuni campaign, I noticed that Sir Garnet Wolseley ... used to hold daily consultations with Ferreira during the whole time we were in the danger zone. And this was also the case with all the British officers, for whenever they wanted any information or advice it was always: 'Let's ask Ferreira.'[22]

Wolseley suggests in his journal that Ferreira was ruthless. On 10 November he recorded after a talk with him that 'he recounted deeds that showed he did not regard killing a native as killing a human being: he is most anxious the town should not be burnt until it is well looted ...'[23] These remarks suggest that Ferreira was a cruel white supremacist; possibly he was, but no man ever doubted his bravery under fire, and in the months following the battle he would remain loyal to Wolseley and British policies in the Transvaal.

The left column, led by Major Frederick Carrington, 1/24th Regiment, was to move to a position 730 metres north of the Fighting Kopje and seize the defences to the north of the kraal. They would also detach a force to scan the hills to the west of the valley and make sure that no reinforcements reached Sekhukhune. With Carrington were the Border Horse, the mounted infantry, Transvaal Mounted Rifles and Zoutpansberg Contingent. Carrington is a soldier whose career, in hindsight, was not dissimilar to that of a more famous man – Redvers Buller. Both men were considered dashing heroes of irregular mounted troops in 1879, and both suffered military and political reverses in the South African War two decades later, by which time they had grown fat and fleshy. At the time of the Bapedi War 'Fred' Carrington, with his beagle face and splendidly long moustache, was popular with Wolseley. He had been considered a dunce at school whose only abilities were on the sports field. In 1864, shortly before his twentieth birthday, he bought himself a commission in the 24th Foot. Ten years later he sailed for the Cape with his regiment. There his skills as a horseman won him the job of forming various mounted corps during the Griqualand West troubles and the 9th Xhosa War.

Commanding the Border Horse was thirty-five-year-old George Denison. The regiment had suffered badly at Hlobane and Kambula and Denison had taken over command after the death of Colonel Weatherley in the former battle. Born at Cradock, Cape Colony, George was a first generation descendant of 1820 settlers. In 1865 he had taken part as a teenager in the storming of Thaba Bosego during the Basuto War, then shared the humiliation of Burgers' retreat with the Boer commando from Tsate in 1876. Now he was back in a second attempt to storm the place.

Facing the Bapedi in the centre was a third column under Lieutenant-Colonel John Murray, 94th Regiment. He had with him six companies of his regiment led by Major Anstruther, six companies of the 2/21st Royal Scots Fusiliers under Major Arthur Hazelrigg, a detachment from the 80th Regiment, the remainder of the Rustenberg Contingent and the Transvaal Artillery fielding two Krupp cannon and two 7-pounder guns. The column's task was to help keep down fire on Ferreira's and Carrington's men from the heights and reinforce if necessary. After Tsate was taken the centre column would then lead the assault on the Fighting Kopje.

Murray was Anstruther's 'pal' and tent-companion, an easy-going type, somewhat miffed that his return to England had been disrupted by the Bapedi war. Sir Garnet had a low opinion of Hazelrigg and thought him 'a dreadful bully with his men', often talking to them in a brutish manner. While the general lacked the common touch with soldiers that journalists later glorified in the career of his rival, Frederick Roberts, 'our Bobs', Wolseley could not abide officers such as Hazelrigg or Henry Hope Crealock who scorned their own men. Sir Garnet thought the 2/21st were not a very satisfactory battalion but he blamed this on bad leadership by its officers. William Knox, in charge of the four guns, had served since 1867 and seen quite a lot of action in Abyssinia in 1868, Ashanti in 1874, where he took charge of the rocket troughs at the Battle of Amoaful, volunteering in the Russo-Turkish War 1877 and recently serving in the first phase of the Afghan War.

Waiting five miles away in the mountains behind Tsate was Bushman accompanied by the ever-dependable Yeatman-Biggs as his staff officer along with 3 officers and 91 men of the 80th Regiment led by Captain Charles Roworth, a further 3 officers and 167 men of the 94th Regiment, the Lydenburg Rifles (a small corps of 4 officers and 40 men) under Commandant L. M. Owen with Edgar Corrie as his senior captain. The bulk of Bushman's force was his Swazi Contingent led by MacLeod and Campbell, with three other officers supported by a further 250 Africans known as Eckersley's Contingent and led by a colonial volunteer captain, George Eckersley, with Lieutenants Glinister and Rawlins. That night Baker Russell, who officially commanded the Transvaal Field Force, was putting in harm's way 79 officers, 1,204 imperial and 277 colonial troops supported by 1,650 native levies on his side of Sekhukhune's Town; 15 officers, 258 imperial and 40 colonial soldiers on Bushman's side supported by a further 8,250 natives – a grand total of 1,873 white officers and men and 9,900 Africans. Back at Wolseley's camp and not included in these figures were a further officer and 250 men. The numbers were almost double those of Chelmsford's army at Ulundi (5,170 men) where the British faced almost four times the number of enemy. However two vital differences were that Chelmsford had eight heavy guns and two machine-type Gatling guns and his men were not attacking a well-defended position behind which about half the enemy had firearms.

How many Bapedi faced Wolseley's troops? This is debatable; Laband quotes Delius's figure which in turn is based on Merensky, who thought that Tsate was less well-defended than in 1876 because minor chiefs may have held back some regiments to defend their kraals in case the Swazis went on the rampage. Years of internal upheaval among the Maroteng may have reduced the warriors at Tsate to a little under 4,000 defenders. Possibly the figure was higher; based on the number of firearms picked up after the battle, which was 2,041 guns, it seems reasonable to assume that at least half of Sekhukhune's warriors and maybe as many as three-fifths fought only with traditional weapons. A calculation of 55–60 per cent without guns and the remainder with them would give a figure of nearer 4,500 defenders.

Just like the red soldiers who had fought and died so bravely at Isandlwana ten months earlier, Her Majesty's troops at this last battle of 1879 were not yet wearing khaki and fought in their red serge uniforms. Yet those tunics no longer looked spick and span. The men of Wolseley's and Russell's Transvaal Field Force were possibly the most rag-tag British army that ever fought a Victorian battle. The men of the 80th, for example, had marched 1,000 miles across Africa and their uniforms bore 'rips and holes covered with patches of different colours on both trousers and tunic', writes Robert Hope, 'in turn discoloured by blood, sweat, tears, mud and grime'.[24] Writing six years after the war, Sergeant J. Clark, who served in the campaign as a private, recalled that in the 21st Fusiliers, 'Each man endeavoured as best he could to repair the rents and holes in his apparel, but the material obtainable was neither the colour nor texture of the garment itself.'[25] The men were forced to use patches of biscuit-bags, blankets and even waterproof sheets. The same situation existed in the 94th Regiment, as Anstruther explained in a letter to his wife:

> You would laugh if you saw the state of rags our men are in. Their coats are all in rags, having been patched like Irishmen with every conceivable colour & stuff and their braces are positively absent. Some few managed to buy corduroy trousers at Greytown and they simply are in rags & torn but the bulk

> of the regiment is wearing (and has been the whole time, having no other) the suit they embarked on board the 'China' in between 8 & 9 months ago and have never worn anything else day or night. Lots of the bayonet scabbards are lost and the men make rough coverings for the bayonets of the skin of beasts as they are killed. They are better off for boots than anything but bad is the best. I found 2 men riding on a wagon today and found their captains had put them there because they had no boots at all and the road was rather stony. It is a great shame because the men are entitled to 2 suits, their April & October issue, of everything. It is very laughable! The helmets too have been slept in and so often that there is no shape about them. I don't think there are 160 forage caps in the regiment and when the men lose their helmets they make skin caps out of the hides of beasts as they are killed.[26]

Not all the army wore red; officers of the Royal Artillery, Royal Engineers and staff officers wore blue patrol jackets. The tunics of each regiment had collar tabs coloured as per allocation. Yellow, for example, was the designated colour of the 80th. Black leather boots were worn by all ranks with black leather gaiters. Headgear in imperial regiments was usually a 'Glengarry' forage cap or a cork sun helmet known officially as 'the foreign service helmet'. Several officers of both the imperial and colonial forces wore on their headgear what was called 'Sekhukhune's button', a meerkat's tail fashioned into a button.

Colonial troops were often more casually dressed; officers might wear an infantry pattern patrol jacket, possibly with a forage cap, a soft velveteen hat or a sun helmet stained to various shades of brown with a puggaree of a different colour wrapped around as a head band. Most colonials wore corduroy breeches with brown riding boots. The 1879 manual, *Volunteer Forces Of The Transvaal And Instructions For Their Guidance*, lists the following collection issued to irregular corps raised in the Transvaal such as Ferreira's Horse: 'A coat, a pair of trousers, a hat and puggaree, two woollen shirts, a pair of boots, a greatcoat, two pairs of socks, a pair of leggings, a rifle sling, a bandolier (50 rounds), a haversack, a water bottle, a canteen or patrol tin, a plate, knife, fork and spoon, a saddle, a headstall with Pelham bit, two reins and a brush and curry comb.'[27]

What made Wolseley's army at Tsate so very different from any other was the huge African contingent, five times the number of the white troops. Two thousand, five hundred of these black warriors came from Transvaal tribes, wore their own battle regalia and looked, as Sir Garnet admitted, very 'bloodthirsty'. They were given coloured puggarees so as to be recognised as friendlies in the battle. Most vibrant of all were the Swazis in their ostrich plumes and leopard skins, each man carrying throwing spears, one of two kinds of a short-hafted stabbing assegai, along with a battle axe or knobkerrie.

The British infantry soldier was equipped with a formidable firearm, the Martini-Henry Mark II rifle. Introduced into the British Army in 1875, the Martini-Henry was a single shot breech-loading rifle that fired a 0.45 bullet rolled brass Boxer Henry cartridge with a 480 grains slug. The impact of the weapon was vicious, the slug flattening when it hit a victim, splintering bone lengthways. Soldiers complained that the rifle jammed, especially if grit got in the mechanism, and was difficult to keep clean. Its least popular characteristic was a kicking recoil that left soldiers with sore shoulders. Rapid firing also made the barrel too hot to touch and there was no safety catch. Rankers were issued with a socket bayonet, sergeants got a sword bayonet. By the time of the Sekhukhune campaign the troops knew that the damned bayonets had a tendency to bend double.

Officers usually carried a .45 Adams or Webley revolver along with a sword. Colonial mounted troops such as Border Horse and Ferreira's Horse, were equipped with Martini-Henry, Snider or

Swinburne-Henry carbines. The aim of a carbine was to reduce the recoil when fired from the saddle. Colonial officers usually carried a revolver and the 1822 light cavalry sword.

There is no record of what Wolseley wore himself on 28 November 1879 but most likely it was his loose-fitting patrol jacket with sword and revolver. Almost certainly in his pocket was his famous repeater-watch since he was a careful timekeeper on such important occasions. Baker Russell could have worn the elaborate uniform of his beloved 13th Hussars, all gold braid on blue, with a plume-tipped busby and white busby-bag, but it is believed that he wore something almost as exotic – a special 'fighting coat' of Canadian beaver skin.

Quietly in the darkness, without a bugle call so as not to rouse the Bapedi, the Transvaal Field Force began its preparations at 2 a.m. All the troops in the valley were under arms by one hour later and the volunteers left camp for their respective posts. It was a cool, cloudy night and, rather ominously, all was quiet on the opposite hills, while in Sekhukhune's town the fires that had been numerous on the previous evening had now all been extinguished. Denison recorded that at 2 a.m. Carrington's column had moved out of camp and crossed over a stream. Around them masses of infantry were assembling. The Border Horse galloped on their horses for about a mile, then dismounted, the animals being sent to the rear. On the western side of the British front it seems likely that Ferreira was also getting his troops into position. 'A grim reminder of what the day would bring,' writes Kenneth Smith, 'was given by the movement of the ambulance wagons and medical corps to a point about a quarter of a mile from the main attack.'[28] Surgeon-Major Kerr had five officers and fifty-eight men under him of the Army Hospital Corps with a bearer company of fifty men and seventy-four Africans under Surgeon-Major Hector.

Sir Garnet and his staff moved to a level area about 400 yards from the Fighting Kopje and slightly closer the town. Always remarkably calm once a battle commenced, Wolseley slipped out of the saddle and for some time rested under a great tree. His day had started badly: at 2.15 am he had received a note from Bushman saying that his force was at the bottom of the mountain behind Tsate, but that the Swazis 'positively refused to go up it in the dark …' The general found this news 'somewhat took the starch out of me', but too much was at stake just to depend on the Swazis. He hoped that when they heard the sounds of the British in action on his side of the hill they would regain their courage. Baker Russell was told not to 'rush' the business so that the Swazis had ample time to cooperate.

Dawn was just breaking about 4–4.15 a.m., throwing a glimmer of light across the horizon (Brackenbury and Smith say the earlier time, Commeline and Wolseley plump for the latter and the general would have checked it against his watch), when a shell was fired into the Fighting Kopje. Immediately and like a hive of angry hornets the Bapedi responded with war cries and melancholy blasts from their war horns. Simultaneously, on right and left sides Ferreira and Carrington led their columns into the attack.

Yelling 'Forward!' Ferreira set off at a pace, dodging from rock to rock, followed by his men. From the cover of boulders they fired their carbines until the barrels grew hot. Within minutes the Bapedi had spotted their hated old enemy and shouts rang out – 'It is Umtaki, kill him!' The commandant's supposedly charmed existence certainly seemed to hold true that morning as he dodged from boulder to boulder supported by about 100 men under his two captains, Henry Nourse and Aubrey Wools-Sampson. The Bapedi kept up a withering fire as the troopers spread out in distended order, 'keeping as low as possible and creeping slowly forward under cover of whatever rocks, bushes and tiny dongas they could find'.[29] Here and there several troopers staggered and fell, hit by bullets or hurled assegais. The 800 or so Ndzundza Ndebele of the Mapoch and Rustenberg Contingents hung back and eventually slunk off to go further up the valley cattle raiding, 'since this was a far safer and more profitable pursuit'.

The Bapedi fire grew even more intense as step by step Ferreira and his men climbed up the hill to a kraantz from whose plateau they could look down on Sekhukhune's kraal. It also commanded another rocky summit from which the Bapedi were firing down on Carrington's column as they attacked the eastern side of Tsate. Soon the defenders pressed them down the other side of the kraantz where the white troopers were hemmed in around the chief's head kraal and finally penned in their own stockade. All around were the shrieks and screams of death and battle, the fresh dawn air made thick and cloudy with gunpowder. The right column could go no further and, as Macdonald has written, it was 'here that the fiercest of the fighting took place ...' Watching how the right attack seemed to have stalled, Russell gave Murray permission to reinforce Ferreira with one company of the 94th. Just as Captain Nourse emerged from the burning stockade a despatch rider, sent by Ferreira, handed him a message from Wolseley ordering that he take command of the Transvaal Mounted Rifles, who were fighting desperately on the other side of Tsate. Their commandant, J. E. Macaulay, had been killed.

Carrington's column on the left was having an even stickier time than Ferreira's on the right side. The original plan called for Meyer and Dahl's 600 or so Zoutpansberg Africans to break down the Bapedi thorn fence, but a well-directed fire from the Tsate defenders made the levy flatly refuse to advance. Carrington had a famously short temper. An argument broke out between officers of the various corps, and not wishing to waste time he ordered the Border Horse and Transvaal Mounted Rifles to charge on foot, while the three officers and thirty-four men of the mounted infantry covered the attack. It was now daylight. The Transvaal Mounted Rifles were off first and hit by a stiff fire from the Bapedi cunningly concealed in trenches in front of the town. Macaulay's troopers broke through the fence to the shouts and jeers of the Bapedi and reached the first line of huts. Here it looked as if the attack might falter or even be repulsed. 'Forward the Border Horse for all you are worth,' yelled Carrington as the dismounted men charged into action with the mounted infantry, also on foot, close behind. The Transvaal Mounted Rifles now rallied and charged on their left. The Bapedi were forced backwards, out of their rifle pits and slowly up the mountain side, barricade by barricade. George Denison recalled,

> The enemy remained in their *schanse* [barricades] to our front until we got within about seventy-five yards of them. They were firing, but all high, and would not risk their head above the breastworks. We were getting close when they rose and bolted further into their barricades higher up. Some fell, and as the last of them leapt the walls my men were up on them. Poor young McLeod was among the first and as he reached the wall a kaffir placed his gun against the lad's chest and fired. He fell instantly and his men lifted him up, and carried him to one side under the rocks.[30]

'Write to my mother,' said McLeod before dying.

The Bapedi warrior Masschow has left us a good account of this phase of the battle from his perspective as a defender. In old age he recalled,

> We sat & watched the troops coming along & when they reached the fence we laughed to ourselves & shouted. In a few minutes we saw the fence going up in smoke and flames. 'Yo', 'Yo', 'Yo', 'Yo' we shouted, telling them to come on. And they did. Shortly bullets were whistling over our heads. Yes, the guns were strong. Some of our men were shot. The women in the hills were shouting and egging us on & we were doing

> well ... The boys from Kimberley spoke a little English & they shouted to the soldiers to hurry up ... [31]

The left column climbed up to the first spur of the mountain after having taken one terrace of barricades. Commandant Macaulay sat down to have a smoke and chat with Carrington. A shot rang out and Macaulay fell back dead as his brains splattered over the rocks. Despite this calamity the higher kraantzes were gradually reached, where Bapedi marksmen lay concealed like eagles in an eyrie. Denison had been leading the advance at this point but was recalled by Carrington. His men naturally followed downhill to the jeers of the Bapedi who retook some of their old positions. The problem lay down in the valley where the Bapedi had made a determined rush on the Zoutpansberg Africans and looked as if they might overwhelm them.

The time was about 6 a.m. Bullets were whizzing all over the place and one struck Baker Russell's horse in the rump. He was forced to dismount and obtain another horse (the bullet was subsequently cut out and the animal recovered). 'A few inches higher & it would have hit Baker Russell's posterior instead of the horse's' noted an amused Wolseley.[32] The eyes of the headquarters staff and all those standing near the guns were now focused on Denison's left attack. He led a charge that scattered the Bapedi and seemed to instil life into the Zoutpansbergers, who now followed the men of the Border Horse across the mealie fields and back into the fray. A first rush was repulsed, but a second was successful and soon smoke was rising from burning huts on the left side of the town.

Ever since the start of the battle Captain Knox's four guns had been peppering the enemy. The general, who was watching from nearby, was not impressed and noted in his journal that 'the practice was very bad at first & indifferent all day though the range was only 450 yards'.[33] Standing next to the gunners was Lieutenant Commeline R.E. who was employed making guncotton charges in sandbags. He wrote that 'a pretty brisk fire opened up on us from the koppies though only two or three men were hit ...' Gradually the Bapedi fire slackened and their men seemed weary or were possibly running low on ammunition. The guns pounded away at the stone sangars, but Commeline thought 'their calibre was rather too light for the work, though they did a good deal of damage. Some of the shells landed right inside the caves and such was the hollowness of the hills, smoke was seen to rise from holes on the far side of it.'[34]

The attacking forces gradually worked their way above the town but the Bapedi were good marksmen – had they been equipped with state-of-the-art breechloaders like the Martini-Henry, instead of their old Tower muskets, then British losses would have been much higher. Lieutenant O'Grady leading the mounted infantry was wounded. So too was Captain Maurice R.A., the general's long-time friend and acting camp commandant; he asked to take part in the attack and got shot in the shoulder near the entrance of a cave. The wound was quite a nasty one but, as irrepressible as ever, he insisted on personally reporting back to Wolseley that victory was assured. An amused Sir Garnet exclaimed, 'Now I know the value of Maurice – to lead forlorn hopes!'[35]

The Bapedi were fighting doggedly. Clearly the taking of Tsate was going to be as tough, if not tougher, than the British had feared. Tables were finally turned, however, around 6.20 a.m. when silhouettes on the skyline of the mountain turned out to be the long-awaited Swazi host. Wolseley was elated. The delay had been caused by bad memories of the way the white men had turned tail in 1876 leaving 500 Swazis (and fifty Europeans), stranded at the base of the Fighting Kopje. Witch doctors had warned that the British would leave all the fighting to the Swazis. So despite entreaties by MacLeod, Bushman and others, the *emabutfo*, had decided to wait until there was enough light for them to receive covering fire from the British. With whoops and yells the warriors now rushed down from the summit and fierce hand-to-hand fights broke out all over the place. In their towering headdresses of black ostrich plumes the Swazis looked magnificent. Edgar Corrie of the Lydenburg Rifles, who followed them over the summit and into the melee, wrote, 'I cannot describe the wild effect produced by the great host of sable warriors ...'[36] Assistant-Commissary Walter Dunne thought they looked 'somewhat grotesque. Immense bunches of feathers and horsehair covered their heads; skins and tails of various animals hung from the shoulders, waist and knees; the whole dress giving them a rather cumbrous appearance; and as their wrists and ankles were loaded with wire bangles, one could not help wondering how they could fight in a hot climate under such a weight.'[37] Hundreds on both sides – Swazis versus Bapedi – died on the narrow ledges in dozens of fights. Masschow suggests that some of the Bapedi women's regiments fought because he remembered how 'some of our women were brave & they killed some of the Swazi & then it was hell'. Wearing his leopard-skin regalia Prince Moroamotshe and his regiment fought their blood enemies until he and all his men fell killed or wounded. 'The screaming was terrible,' recalled Masschow, 'I don't know how I am alive. We were nearly all killed.'[38]

The Swazis fighting downwards, and the British colonial troops pushing upwards, met somewhere on the middle of the kopje. An induna asked Denison to lead them into the caves but Carrington was having none of it. 'Tell him no, Denison ... I don't want my men mixed up with them, for these fellows will kill friend and foe when heated.' Regardless of these words, Corporal E. B. Mitchell rushed forward but was shot dead at a cave entrance. Their blood now hot, the Swazis entered the cave and 'left nothing there alive, not even a cat or dog'. Denison was not impressed by his native allies despite their fame as warriors. 'We would have been far better without them,'[39] was his opinion. A British flag was seen flying on a topmost summit and the figure of Captain Alastair Campbell R.N. was spied through a telescope. Shortly after he vanished and was never seen again. It was rumoured that he had tried to enter a cave and was killed. Masschow stated that the witch doctors had cut him up and some of the body parts had been eaten 'as he was a brave man'. (Wolseley later ordered a big search but no remains were ever found.)

It was while colonial troops, Swazis, Bapedi and native levies were all engaged on the kopje, much of Tsate below in flames, thick columns of smoke rising in the sky, that the only two Victoria Crosses of the campaign were won. Lieutenant C. J. Dewar, 1st King's Dragoon Guards, attached to the mounted infantry of the 94th, was severely shot in the groin. Two privates, Francis Fitzpatrick and Thomas Flawn, along with six of the native contingent, were the only persons near Dewar when he fell. The officer was unable to move so Fitzpatrick, as Irish as his name and the senior of the two Tommies, got the natives to carry Dewar. It was a steep climb down. 'Oy, you there,' he motioned to the natives, 'Carry him, will ye. Gently, now, gently. It's not a sack of potatoes ye're handling.' Twenty-one-year-old Flawn (sometimes referred to as an Irishman but, in fact, born at Irthlingborough in Northamptonshire, the son of a farm labourer), bet his comrade 'sixpence to a penny' that they might meet some Bapedi. Fitzpatrick accepted the bet. Sure enough, a short distance on they almost walked into about thirty of the enemy, the sight of which made the six African bearers drop Dewar and run for their lives. At ten yards distance Fitzpatrick and Flawn fired a round with their rifles, dropping a few of the enemy. 'We can't stay here forever,' said Fitzpatrick, 'You carry the boy and I'll cover them.' Quickly firing and reloading his Martini-Henry he led the way with Dewar carried over Flawn's shoulder. Later they reversed the roles with Flawn holding off and killing more Bapedi. The plight of the two privates was noticed at some point and a rescue party sent off to help them. Toasted later as heroes, it is said that Flawn told his mate, 'Before you get too swell-headed, what about that penny you owe me for our little bet?'[40]

During this period Lieutenant Commeline and five of his men accompanied two companies of the 94th sent to assist the right column. 'Here we lay down and kept up an attack on the caves for nearly an hour,' he wrote. 'The doctors were now very busy, but the hills behind the town were swept clear of the enemy, and the town was in flames all along the line, the Fighting Kopje alone holding out.'[41]

So far that morning the main body of Her Majesty's troops had done no fighting, but at 9 a.m. Russell began preparing for his assault on Ntswaneng. Where possible, colonial troops were pulled out of the firing line on the mountain for a short rest. The fighting walrus was now in his element. Wolseley had been observing Russell all morning and thought him 'splendid', but 'over-excited and a little too inclined to force the fighting'. Two rockets were fired at 9.45 a.m., the signal for a grand assault on all sides of the Fighting Kopje. Leading the attack on its northern face were three companies of the 2/21st Fusiliers, the headquarters escort of the 80th Regiment and a portion of the Swazi contingent; the Border Horse supported by more Swazis were to attack the east side; two companies of the 94th and the mounted infantry attacked from the south; while Ferreira's Horse and the remainder of the Swazis fought from the west. Normally the commander of an army keeps himself out of the firing line, but Wolseley gave special permission for Baker Russell to waive this rule so that the burly warrior, sword in hand, could lead the northern assault. The general's staff all wanted to participate and Sir Garnet was never happier than seeing his officers show courage, so Brackenbury, Herbert, McCalmont and lanky Herbert Stewart, Russell's staff officer, were all allowed to enter the fray. Young Stewart had never seen a battle before and he had a close scrape when a Bapedi threw an assegai at him from just fifteen yards. It scraped across Herbert's shoulder but luckily missed its target.

Officers and men had been up since 2 a.m. and the fighting had already lasted almost six hours. Perhaps this explains why Commeline wrote later than the assault began at 11 a.m. and Denison, who must have been physically exhausted, recalled the time many years later as having been four in the afternoon.

Loud hurrahs rent the air as the British went into the attack. The 21st Scots Fusiliers advanced with pipes playing. 'I never saw a prettier sight in my life,' thought Wolseley. Only the Swazis hung back again, seemingly fearful that they might be expected to bear the brunt of the attack. Impatiently Sir Garnet rode over to them, waving his hand in the direction of the Fighting Kopje and yelling, 'Come on, you fellows, come on. Is there no one to make them understand?' The Swazis, however, now saw what was happening and replied deafeningly with their battle cry. Striking their shields against their knees to make a characteristic 'whish' sound they charged after the British. Painting a fine word-picture, Joseph Lehmann wrote, 'Thousands of knees pounding in unison had the sound of roaring surf. It seemed in harmony with the fusillades, the screams and yells, the skirls of the pipers – the very breath of battle. The pipers stood at the foot of the hill beating the ground with their feet while playing with fiendish energy. The deep furrow that ran across Wolseley's cheek – a souvenir of the Crimea – grew purple.'[42]

Moving into battle with Ferreira's troopers was Hugh McCalmont, who had not expected to join in the attack and now thought it 'the best ten minutes possible'. He thought the Bapedi put up 'a most determined resistance'. McCalmont and his soldier servant, Trooper Barford, 9th Hussars, fought their way together up the hill. One Bapedi fired at McCalmont at close quarters. Somehow the bullet missed or its force was spent. Hugh fired his revolver and 'pinned' his assailant. The first man to reach the top of the Fighting Kopje was Lieutenant Paulett Weatherley, Border Horse, eldest son of the regiment's founder, who had died at Hlobane eight months previously. Commandant Denison met with Baker Russell on the summit. The colonel had found the climb a stiff one. Turning to Brackenbury on the way up he had said, 'My God, Brack, I am beat. I am too old for this kind of work!'[43]

The fighting was still far from over. Hidden in the honeycomb of caves were a large number of Bapedi including women, children and some livestock. 'In fact while standing on the top it was as if one was standing on an immense beehive,' wrote Denison, 'for a continual humming sound came from beneath.'[44]. The time was now about 10.30 a.m. The defenders were asked repeatedly to come and surrender. None did so. The caves were truly a last refuge for the Bapedi and getting close to them was dangerous. Many Swazis were killed in hand-to-hand fights near the cave entrances. Captain W. G. Lawrell, Russell's friend who had turned up with some remount horses and stayed for the battle as his orderly officer, gingerly approached a cave. A Bapedi shot him through the throat. Lawrell staggered back and spectacularly toppled down off a rock some twenty feet.

Gradually – very gradually – a few women and children started to come out of the caves, but their menfolk hung back. British soldiers fired down holes in the rocks 'and used their bayonets freely', wrote Commeline. It was turning into dirty work, the kind of work that some soldiers and officers did not like. Guncotton charges were thrust into the caves or pushed through holes. 'We afterwards found they did not kill very many of those below,' noted Commeline, 'yet wounded many and from the dust and smoke produced terrible thirst …' The Bapedi still managed to retaliate from odd places, 'and several men fell, and you may imagine that lighting fuses and dropping charges in such circumstances was not very pleasant or even glorious work.'[45] The Bapedi warrior, Masschow, was one of those trapped in the caves. He recalled the rock rabbits scampering over him in the darkness and urinating, presumably through fear. He confirmed Commeline's comment about the difficulty in dynamiting the caves since ex-Kimberley miners among the defenders knew enough about explosives to cut the fuses. Thirst was a problem, but during a rainstorm on the 28th 'we caught the water in our mouths as it trickled down the walls and we licked the water from the rocks'.[46]

A wall of flame stretched across the valley, crackling and roaring, smoke filling the sky, as Wolseley rode off that afternoon back to camp. He admitted to 'feeling tired' and did not remember until about 5 p.m. that he had not eaten a thing all day. Before he left Tsate, the general told Captain Clarke to try and get as many of the Bapedi to surrender as possible. Major Anstruther, put in charge of the Fighting Kopje that night, wrote, 'I had a very rough time of it … as the beggars kept trying to bolt out of the caves. In fact we were firing hard the whole night all round the koppie.'[47] A terrific rainstorm lashed the mountains and in the pitch darkness large groups of Bapedi left the caves willing to stab and shoot their way to freedom. One of the Transvaal mining pioneers, William Macdonald, wrote:

> In the fitful silence of the raging storm, the tense and anxious troopers heard a curious and ominous sound. It was the tinkling of scores of powder horns striking against the rocks and boulders, and a moment later a lurid flash revealed the 'Fighting Kopje' black with hundreds of Bapedi creeping stealthily down the mountain-side. At the foot of the kopje, as was afterwards learned, the Kafirs paused and rallied under their leaders into a loose and irregular impi. Then shrieking their wild war-cries, they swept like a restless wave through the worn-out but watchful cordon.

'Never in all my military experience have I seen anything like that furious night attack,' wrote Captain Nourse many years later. 'For a moment we seemed to be caught in the midst of a human cyclone, with masses of savages charging clean through us, assegaiing our men from all sides, and actually leaping over our heads in their wild efforts to escape from the imprisoned kopje.'[48] A 'gigantic plumed induna' paused to transfix Aubrey Wools-Sampson with his stabbing spear, but Nourse shot him just in the nick of time and 'he fell dead across my comrade'.

One of those trying to escape was Masschow. He crept out of a cave with a friend and in the darkness 'fell over a soldier who swore at us'. Rather than run down the hill Masschow and his companion worked their way upwards and into the mountains.

'We saw Sekhukhune sitting near a rock with two small girls. He did not look at us. He was finished.'[49]

Tsate continued to burn all the next day. Marshal Clarke worked hard to get more Bapedi to stop fighting and about 350 warriors, women and children left the caves. Major Anstruther described them surrendering 'in driblets … I got about 120 rifles. There were a lot of women and children. I sent them all to the camp where they had food given them.' On the night of the 29th, 'We had more firing keeping those in who did not surrender.'[50] The Bapedi put up a resistance all the next day and night too, though things had quietened down considerably. It was not until 1 December that the final defenders surrendered, having held off the attackers for four days.

Groups of Bapedi staggered into the British camp to surrender. The warriors were told to throw down their assegais and battle axes in a heap. Hands had to be placed on shoulders in a token of submission. One of the defeated was Masschow, who was near Wolseley when the general made a little speech saying, 'Men, you see the sun. Have a good look at it for it will be the last time.'[51] An induna asked Sir Garnet if he killed prisoners? 'Yes,' the general lied, but he promised to spare the Bapedi if they could help him locate Sekhukhune.

In talks with some of the captives Clarke learned that Sekhukhune had not been present during the battle but watched proceedings from a cave in the mountains. Wolseley knew that to end the war he had to find the chief quickly and capture him. After drinking plenty of champagne with Wolseley at dinner on 29 November the gallant and inebriated Ignatius Ferreira agreed to lead Sekhukhune's pursuit. Next day the commandant left with eighty-five mounted men to scour the Lulu Mountains. Using Bapedi prisoners to help him, including one of the chief's brothers, Ferreira's search took him high into the peaks. Eventually the trail led to a cave fifteen miles from Tsate and about nine miles from Fort Victoria, a place too inaccessible for the British to mount an effective attack. It was a famous retreat to the Bapedi known as *Mamatamageng*. As the British got closer a young girl ran out of the cave and said Sekhukhune intended to fight. This left Clarke and Ferreira with much to ponder and they decided at first to try some explosives. After this attempt failed it was decided to starve the chief out and cut off any water supply. Charles Commeline, who was one of the party, wrote that on the climb up to the cave, 'The scenery was beautiful, far finer than anything we had seen in S. Africa as from our great height we overlooked many miles of undulating country. We were where white man had never penetrated.' The actual cave was 'within an immense square-sided rock like the keep of an old castle'.[52] There were several possible entrances so men kneeling with rifles tried to cover all exits. All that night and next morning the Bapedi kept up a desultory fire from the cave but hit no one. Clarke at one point tried to start a bonfire near the entrance in an effort to smoke Sekhukhune out, but this failed also.

Several writers say that it was Ferreira who talked the Bapedi *kgosikgolo* into surrender on the morning of 2 December, after sending in a note with some women. William Macdonald, a friend of Ferreira's, wrote that the chief threw down his assegai and shield at the officer's feet after making a little speech saluting his opponent in the best traditions of Rider Haggard. This story is almost certainly an invention, a classic frontier tall tale. Commeline says Ferreira failed to get the chief to surrender and it was Clarke who managed to do the deed. Sekhukhune was carried out on a stretcher with some of his wives by his side. He then squatted with a dozen chiefs around him and 'shook hands with all the officers as we came up to see him', noted Commeline, 'and after a good strong tot of rum began to get quite chirpy having at first been rather nervous for his personal safety'.[53] Relaxing a little, the king called for his royal snuff-box bearer. Hugh McCalmont, another of those present, described the chief as 'an oldish man with a grey beard and very frightened eyes ... it cannot be said that in appearance, nor yet in demeanour, he compared favourably with Ketchwayo'.[54] Commeline felt quite sorry for Sekhukhune and said 'A more wretched old specimen I have seldom met'. The chief was wearing only a tattered kaross and unlike his followers had no ornaments of any kind. 'He is able to walk leaning on a stick,' wrote the Royal Engineers officer, 'and though not an old man seems quite broken down.'[55] Sekhukhune's demeanour was indeed tragic and perfectly understandable; he had lost no less than three of his brothers and eight of his children, all killed in the battle, including his much loved son and heir, Prince Moroamotshe. The *kgosikgolo* was grieving and probably suffering from shock.

While the hunt for Sekhukhune had been going on, the Swazi army had been permitted by Wolseley to go off for a few days' cattle rustling and spreading fear amongst the Bapedi kraals in the mountains. Sir Garnet bluntly hoped that this brief reign of terror would make the tribe realise that their power was a thing of the past. At Tsate, now a scorched ruin of burnt timbers, almost 2,000 bodies lay bloating under the African sun. Charles Commeline, along with Hugh McCalmont, George Denison and many other British soldiers, were appalled by the bloodlust of the Swazis who 'spared none but a few girls, seeming to delight in the mere taking of life. They even assegaiied the dogs and goats.'[56]

'I don't know how many we killed but ... it must have been a tremendous lot, more than at Ulundi,' wrote Major Anstruther.[57] Thinking of the dead and wounded – some fifty-six white officers and men, around 600 Swazis killed, about 200 wounded, losses of about 150 in the native levies and not less than 1,000 Bapedi dead and upwards of 300 wounded – Charles Commeline wrote on 29 November, 'As a battle Ulundi could not be compared to this one where we were the attackers, whereas in the former, the Zulus attacked our square and were beaten off in half an hour. Our casualties there also were not more than about half of yesterday.'[58] He was wrong regarding white troops – the British had lost thirteen officers and men killed at Ulundi and seventy wounded, compared to eighteen dead and forty-eight wounded at Tsate – but quite right when the whole British losses of Wolseley's battle (around 2,300) are counted.

Far and away the biggest British losses had been sustained by the men of the Royal Scots Fusiliers. No easy answers are forthcoming and the regimental history is mute on the subject. Yet the 21st lost three privates killed (Donohoe, McNally and Weston) and Captains Gordon and Willoughby, Surgeon Wallis along with Colour Sergeant Finch, Corporal Leedham and twelve men wounded. The 94th, in comparison, lost one officer killed and ten men wounded. The Transvaal Mounted Rifles had lost its commandant killed and five men wounded. Oddly enough, none of Ferreira's Horse were killed though eight men were wounded, seven of them severely so.

The Bapedi had lost between 25–30 per cent of their entire fighting strength in dead and wounded, a very high figure. The Zulus at Ulundi, in comparison, are reckoned by most experts to have sustained 15 per cent losses.

For the first time in 1879 the British had been the attacking force, and while winning a decisive victory it must be said that their opponents had fought magnificently; the Bapedi, outnumbered over three to one, had held the superior-armed British force at bay for seven hours, refused to surrender and gone on fighting in dribs and drabs literally to their last bullets, four days later.

With the Bapedi beaten, Wolseley spent 1 December in his tent writing letters. First in a long letter he told Louisa about the battle:

> My dearest little Sandpiper
> I have cracked the nut thank God and Sikuni's Town is a thing of the past, everything destroyed, his people killed, prisoners or dispersed as wanderers & his property falling into our hands daily. If we can only kill or catch the Chief himself the thing will be the most competent affair possible. He is hiding away in a cave somewhere and as the Leolu Mountains are a mass of caves and rocky crannies where fugitives can conceal themselves it will be no easy task matter catching the villain. I am very glad I came here with a large force; with a small one I should have failed, for the

> position occupied by the enemy was strong & easily defended. Baker Russell is a splendid fellow and I felt proud of him as a friend of mine as I saw him standing on the top of the 'Fighting Koppie'. His impetuous daring forced him on to the assault, in which as the Commanding Officer of the Troops engaged he was not expected according to custom to take any part. Maurice left here early this morning with such of the white wounded as could be safely moved. He has had a nasty wound in the shoulder, but he will be all right before he reaches England. He is as brave a fellow as ever walked in shoe leather: he is useless as an officer except to lead men in action; there he shines as a really brave fellow. I have just written to his wife to tell her about him. I think you might with grace also pen a line to say how glad you were to learn from me that he was not badly wounded & was going home ... Baker will leave within a week for India via London, so you will meet him there. How I wish I were able to go with him, but I cannot leave until I have done something here with the Boers.[59]

Bad news had arrived from Hicks Beach asking the general to stay on for some time to 'watch over my settlement of Zululand'. Angrily Wolseley told his wife that he had 'no intention' of staying unless they made him a peer. He admitted to being furious that the government 'has never written to me a civil line thanking me either for my Natal services in 1875, for Cyprus or my work in Zululand'.[60]

Tuesday 2 December dawned a nice cloudy morning and after some stuffy days the air was fresh and invigorating. At 9 a.m. Sir Garnet was just about to send off his post when McCalmont galloped in with the news of Sekhukhune's capture. An elated Wolseley now determined to get back to Pretoria without delay, break up the Transvaal Field Force at once and send the Swazis home. Captain Clarke was immediately told to finish the settlement of Sekhukhune's country and to give the Reverend Merensky a free hand in establishing mission stations. 'Thank God,' wrote the general in his journal. 'So ends the Sikukuni War.'

PART THREE

THE BOERS

9

A MULTITUDE OF GRUMBLES

> Some idiots go about saying that they are sure the Boers will break out but it is all rot, they won't.
>
> Major Philip Anstruther

The Boers, a subject people not known for showing much enthusiasm for British rule, did however turn out in large numbers to welcome the return of Sir Garnet Wolseley to Pretoria on 9 December. The reason for all their rejoicing, of course, was not to hail the conquering hero but to view his captive – the despised and feared Sekhukhune of the Bapedi. The old chief looked miserable, 'escorted by 100 dragoons, himself seated on a heap of skins in a mule wagon', wrote McCalmont, 'the mules of which were hardly able to crawl, surrounded by his wives and daughters – only three spouses left, out of, well, I don't know how many.'[1] Colonel Richard Harrison agreed with McCalmont that Sekhukhune 'had a wretched worn-out look' and housed him, two indunas, wives and children in the Pretoria gaol. The humiliation of being jeered at by thousands of people must have been an awful experience for the old ruler. He became absolutely terrified when Mr H. F. Gros, the town's photographer, started to take his photograph. It took several minutes to calm him down.

Two days later Pretoria was *en fete* again for a grand review of the troops; the 94th Foot and several other detachments were still scattered across the eastern Transvaal, but Wolseley was able to muster 1,625 officers and men, 392 horses and six cannon to parade through the rose-filled town. Sir Garnet made sure a lot of blank ammunition was fired to impress the Boers. He could truly pride himself on the fact that in exactly three months he had captured two of Africa's greatest potentates. Congratulations arrived from the Queen, Frere, Bulwer, Stanley, Hicks Beach and others. Sir Garnet was especially pleased to get a letter from John Dunn in Zululand hoping that his tent 'was pitched on the top of Sikukuni's stronghold' (it is the only Dunn letter in the Wolseley Collection at Hove).

Public euphoria aside, Sir Garnet hoped that the capture of Sekhukhune and a big show of British military power might impress moderate Boers while cowing the dissenters. The reality was rather different; with the Bapedi threat now eliminated, the inhabitants of the Transvaal could see no reason why the British should be invited to stay any longer.

Wolseley, it must be said in fairness, did not view the Boers through Lanyon's arrogantly complacent eyes or the rose-tinted spectacles of some other officers. Six weeks earlier he had written a long and remarkably frank appraisal of the Transvaal situation for Hicks Beach. Sooner or later 'the Boers meant to fight' and while expecting to be beaten would stand up for their independence. Sir Garnet had reached the conclusion that 'the great bulk of the Boer population is hostile to our rule ...' There were moderate Boers who did not want things to go back exactly to the ways of the old republic, but for sentimental reasons they, too, would support a war against the British. He told the Colonial Secretary that at meetings across the land he had genuinely tried to find out the wishes of the people. 'The only measure they want,' he wrote to Hicks Beach, 'is the annulment of the annexation.'

The situation, Sir Garnet accepted, was a tricky one since a British withdrawal would have an injurious effect on the local Africans, Zulu minds and rival European powers. 'At present the feeling against us is bitter in the extreme,' summed up the general. 'We are hated by nine-tenths of the Boers with an extreme hatred.' The one-time disciple of Shepstone and confederation now concluded that support in the Transvaal for British rule 'never could have been of sufficient strength to have justified the annexation and that consequently the annexation was a great political blunder ...'[2]

Tough words and yet, as events were to prove, remarkably perceptive ones. While the general's little army had been marching back to Pretoria some 3,000 Boer men (a vast number out of a total male population of 8,000), met at Wonderfontein on the high veldt to demand independence and talk of war. Before departing, after seven days of meetings and speeches, the assembly expressed an intention to convene a new Volksraad and agreed to meet again in April. Wolseley thought the malcontents were 'silly' but he accepted that fighting 'may in the end ... be upon us'.

In testimony before Henrique Shepstone, another of Sir Theophilus's brood, who was Commissioner for Native Affairs in the Transvaal, Sekhukhune blamed the war on the shifty Boer, Abel Erasmus, 'who counselled me and led me to resist'. At meetings Erasmus had told the chief not to pay his taxes. The Boers, he said, would rise up against the British and aid the Bapedi. A new ZAR would leave Sekhukhune alone to rule his land. Of the actual battle at Tsate the *kgosikgolo* told a sombre tale of hiding in a cave before the fight, then coming down after the Swazi attack to see things for himself:

> I saw my brothers Muriwani and Simpupuru dead, the first was shot and the other assegaied; the death of Untubatsi, another brother, was reported to me, he was shot on fighting Koppie. I saw my two sons, Moramutye or Moteshe and Matsibi lying

> dead, assegaied by the Swazis: I also saw six other children of mine dead, killed by the Swazis ... my people were beaten early in the morning. They never had a chance, they had no time to make a stand ... The English are not like the Boers, the Boers cannot fight; the English do not fear death ... I have heard it said that I have a lot of diamonds, but it is not true ... I had very little money, only 50 sovereigns which were in my hut ... As you have beaten me you have conquered everything. I was the only Chief in the country, there is no other black Chief who will raise an assegai against you now.[3]

Orders were at once issued for the arrest of Abel Erasmus on a charge of inciting rebellion. Meantime life in the eastern Transvaal was returning to normal. To the dismay of Ignatius Ferreira the words of Sekhukhune rang true and no diamonds or gold were found in the burnt-out embers of the king's kraal. Two huge elephant tusks were the most exciting find; one was presented by Wolseley to the Queen and the other was acquired by the 94th Regiment and duly mounted as a battle trophy. Soldiers picked up assegais and shields as souvenirs. Hugh McCalmont found a set of 'curiously sewn animal skins' in Sekhukhune's cave. 'No doubt they were his own,' he wrote. 'The one he had on was not nearly so good.'[4]

The Swazis were quickly rounded up and Captain MacLeod was ordered to march his bloodthirsty host back to their homes. He admitted to being 'nearly done up with the constant hard work ... The fighting has been very severe.' MacLeod felt that 'whatever may be said about employing the Swazies, I can assure you that it could not have been done without them.' In a later letter he referred to his warriors as 'tigers and to them belong the chief credit of the complete success ... I estimate the Swazie loss at between 500 and 600 killed, and about the same number wounded, but I cannot say for certain. They are wonderful fellows. Many with fearful wounds walked back the 200 miles as if nothing had happened.'[5]

It was reported by MacLeod that the Swazis marched back without doing any 'mischief' along the way. When news of the campaign reached England there was a howl of protest that the Swazis had killed or stolen some of the Bapedi women. Sir Garnet requested a report be made and Clarke, MacLeod, Herbert and Stewart all attested that there was no truth in these rumours. Yet Denison, Dunne, McCalmont and the Bapedi warrior, Masschow, all claimed that the Swazis did kill women and children. Possibly some of the Bapedi women's regiments fought in the battle? Wolseley later told the Colonial Secretary that it was 'impossible' to supervise all Swazi actions during the fighting: 'Individual instances of women and children being wounded by bullets doubtless occurred in the action, as they must in any action where women and children have the misfortune to be present under fire.' The general rather disingenuously played down the use of gun-cotton to blow in the caves and declared, 'Very few, if any, of the enemy were killed,' a very bold and incorrect statement. Sir Garnet had made it clear before the battle that the Swazis must not steal Bapedi women. It seems that this order was strictly followed.

Within days of the close of fighting Clarke sent word to the various Bapedi chiefs that they would not be punished for supporting Sekhukhune. The reign of the king was over. In future the land would be ruled by a resident magistrate. Taxes must be paid. Killing without trials must stop. Disputes would be settled by the magistrate. All firearms must be handed over along with any cattle belonging to the king. Within a month the British had collected almost 3,400 guns (1,349 surrendered, the rest found at Tsate).

Changes were made at the forts; a new fort was built on the Magnet Heights while Albert Edward, Olifants, Weeber and Jalalabad were abandoned. On 31 December the various colonial corps, including Ferreira's Horse, were also disbanded. Only Eckersley's Africans and the Transvaal Mounted Rifles, now to be called the Transvaal Mounted Police, were retained.

Tsate was abandoned. Many of the caves on the Fighting Kopje were sealed up or their mouths blown in. The place would be returned to the baboon and the goat, the cobra and the hawk. A new law forbade the Bapedi from building their villages within 1,000 yards of any hills. The famous mountain warriors would be rock rabbits no more.

With the coming of peace Sir Garnet hoped he could convince Marshal Clarke, 'the best man for the job', to take over from Wheelwright as Resident of Zululand. Clarke was understandably exhausted and wanted leave to get married. He left that same month. Major Creagh, now restored to good health, took over the jurisdiction of the eastern Transvaal. Eventually Melmoth Osborn, Shepstone's cool acolyte, agreed to administer Zululand on a salary hugely increased to £1,000 a year. Wolseley comforted himself that Osborn was perhaps 'the better man' as he spoke Zulu fluently.

Baker Russell left to go home on 13 December. 'How I wish I were going home too!!' wrote Sir Garnet in his journal, 'I have felt utterly pumped out today.'[6] Now that his little war was over he felt exhausted. He had stomach disorders and little energy, yet still had to deal with 'a lot of credulous idiots' trying to worry him with tales of possible revolt and massacre. Chief among the moaners was Sir Bartle Frere. The pro-consul admitted that the Sekhukhune campaign was 'more complete and brilliant even than I first supposed'. Wolseley, he thought, deserved 'great credit'. What infuriated Frere was that the general had permitted his secretary, St Leger Herbert, to pen an article in *The Times* as a 'special correspondent' that accused him of being antipathetic to Wolseley's administration of Transvaal affairs. To pour oil on Sir Bartle's hurt feelings, Sir Garnet replied to his complaints by saying it was not his concern if some of his staff acted as journalists and he had no wish to muzzle a free press. Wolseley slung back the insults: 'I think I should be quite as well justified in coupling your staff with the numerous articles in the colonial press that supports your policy, in which my settlement of Zululand is constantly denounced.'[7] Frere was not a fool; he realised that Wolseley had obviously known what St Leger Herbert was up to and acquiesced in it.

In late January 'Sir Bottle Beer' worried Wolseley further about events in Pondoland and Basutoland. Sir Garnet made it plain that he would not give Frere imperial troops for 'little cattle stealing rows such as that of Pondoland'. Frederick Carrington was permitted to lead the Cape Mounted Rifles against the Pondos, but the 80th Foot, marching south, were forbidden to engage in any military operations without strict instructions from Sir Garnet.

Christmas Day 1879 saw the general and his staff dining with Lanyon in the latter's home. Clearly in a seasonal mood, Sir Garnet noted in his journal, 'What a hospitable figure he is.' Back in England, if he had but known it, how Wolseley's chest would have puffed with pride if he had heard the Prime Minister tell a friend on Boxing Day: 'Sir Garnet Wolseley has not disappointed me. He is one of those men who not only succeed, but succeed quickly. Nothing can give you an idea of the jealousy, hatred, and all uncharitableness of the Horse Gds. against *our only soldier*' (my italics).[8]

As the days passed the general found himself doing less and less. The administration of the Transvaal he left entirely to Lanyon, whom he thought a 'slow-coach' and over-confident. From time to time Wolseley made suggestions: Lanyon was told to try and bribe Pretorius and, later on, Paul Kruger, but both attempts failed; then he recommended a bi-weekly pro-government newspaper in Afrikaans, but this public relations exercise came to naught; Lanyon, on Wolseley's insistence, pushed harder at tax-gathering, never easy, though the administrator thought 'it will come alright in the end'.

Shadows from the Zulu War cast patches across Wolseley's remaining time in South Africa. When the promotions for the campaign were announced in January he found them 'most amusing'. Carrington, 'never once in Zululand during the late war', was made a lieutenant-colonel while Stewart, a brigade-major of cavalry, was ignored (a mistake rectified in a later gazette). Reading the news in Lydenburg, Major Anstruther of the 94th agreed it was 'a most meagre gazette ... They have left out all sorts of men whose names ought to have been [in].'[9] 'Decorated dullness and promoted pusillanimity' was how William Butler summed up the awards.

Far more important was the debate on whether a clasp to the South Africa or Zulu War medal might be issued for 'Sekukuni's Town'. Sir Garnet fought long and hard to get the work of his soldiers officially recognised. He told Stanley at the War Office:

> In no action in the Zulu War had we on our side so many men engaged. Over 2,000 white men and about 10,000 natives. It is the only offensive action we have fought: it was the only action followed up by a pursuit of the enemy (which ended in four days by the capture of the chief Sekukuni) and we had a large number of killed & wounded on our side & I believe inflicted a larger loss upon the enemy than took place in any of our previous battles this year, the disaster of Isandlwana excepted. The killed and wounded on our side were 50 white men and about 500 natives. I hope, therefore, that it may not be ignored ... [10]

Three months later Wolseley wrote again when he heard the war medal was to be fixed on all operations up to 4 July only:

> If this be true the services of the Field Force which entered the Ulundi valley under my personal superintendence in the beginning of August and which really brought the war to an end by the capture of Cetewayo on the 28th of that month are altogether ignored ... I therefore naturally feel most keenly this attempt to deprive me of whatever little credit may be due to anyone for bringing the disastrous and miserable Zulu War to a satisfactory end.[11]

Complaining to the Duke of Cambridge, the general said there had been some sharp skirmishes after 4 July and he would feel 'deeply aggrieved' if his operations to capture Cetshwayo were 'entirely ignored'; Lord Chelmsford should not have 'the credit for ending the Zulu War.' To Wolseley's relief, on 14 April it was decided to fix the close of the Zulu operations to the end of August. Thus the hunt for the Zulu king would find its way into the official history but not the second biggest battle of 1879. Sir Garnet's hopes for a medal or even a clasp for the Bapedi War were to fall on deaf ears. This was one fight he did not win. In retrospect, and putting aside Wolseley's own thirst for glory, the relegation of his campaign into obscurity does seem unfair. Tsate or 'Sekhukhune's Town' was the only truly offensive battle fought by the British that year, a large-scale, bloody and lengthy affair, that saw the complete destruction of a major African tribe. Before long the campaign became confused with the Basuto Gun War in the minds of people who dimly remembered it. After all, Basutos or Bapedi, surely they were all much the same?

On a happier note, the general continued to pin Victoria Crosses on the breasts of some brave men. At a parade on 11 January he congratulated Captain Cecil D'Arcy of the Frontier Light Horse for trying to save the life of a dismounted trooper at a reconnaissance before the Battle of Ulundi. Privately Wolseley did not approve of the award as D'Arcy 'did not succeed in saving the life of the man he dismounted to assist'.[12] He was more comfortable giving the Victoria Cross on 3 February to Corporal Ferdinand Schiess, Natal Native Contingent, an injured soldier who nonetheless fought courageously at Rorke's Drift.

Cowardice, on the other hand, was something Wolseley loathed. Appalled at the outcome of the Carey court-martial following the death of the Prince Imperial, he set out to make a special case of Lieutenant Henry Harward, 80th Regiment, who galloped away from the battle at the Ntombe River on 7 March 1879 and left his men to fight or die under the command of their sergeant. Convening a court martial, Sir Garnet hoped 'the ruffian may be convicted'. That 'Harward galloped away to the rear [rode 'off at speed'] from his men when they were engaged with the enemy, he being the only officer present, is a fact which he does not dispute ...'[13] Sergeant Anthony Booth had formed a small square of those men not killed in the massacre and then led them in a masterly retreat, firing all the way, took two hours to reach safety.

To protect the regiment's honour a cover-up was organised. The incident came to light after three survivors wrote to Wolseley on 20 December 'to be of service' to Booth, now a colour-sergeant. The officer commanding the 80th, Major Charles Tucker, then nominated Booth for a Distinguished Conduct Medal. Wolseley was intrigued. He asked Tucker why he had delayed his colour-sergeant's recommendation. The major was forced to admit that not to have done so would have highlighted the 'far different conduct of Lieutenant Harward'. On 26 December in a 'most unusual ceremony' the general said farewell to the 80th who had fought so well at Sekhukhune's Town. It was in the 80th that Wolseley had seen his first fighting in Burma as a subaltern. Perhaps this is why he felt an attachment to it and why he wanted to do something for Colour-Sgt Booth. In front of the regiment he presented Booth with a revolver, a holster-belt and a knife, the gifts of settlers. That same day Sir Garnet wrote to the War Office personally recommending Booth for the Victoria Cross. The sergeant's gallantry, control of his men and use of personal initiative under fire were the kind of things that Wolseley thought exemplary. He also demanded a report be made on the incident. Out of this came his demand for Harward's court-martial.

To Wolseley's indignation the court found the lieutenant not guilty. He declined to confirm or approve the proceedings. 'It is monstrous that the two officers who proved themselves to be cowards & behaved in a most shameful manner before the enemy,

Carey & Harward, should both escape punishment,' roared the general, 'I should like to have hanged them both on the one gallows and I myself would have been a willing volunteer to act as hangman.'[14] For once the Duke of Cambridge and Wolseley were in complete agreement on a subject. Together they hatched a special humiliation for Harward: the officer might have escaped a public stripping of his honour, but a General Order criticizing his conduct was to read out on parade to every regiment in the British Army (Harward got the picture and resigned his commission on 11 May).

Giving the Victoria Cross to Melvill and Coghill, the two officers who tried to escape with the Queen's Colour of the 24th from Isandlwana, was something else that disturbed Wolseley, who coupled the incident with the Harward and Carey cases. He stood opposed to

> a monstrous theory – namely – that a regimental officer who is the only officer present with a party of soldiers actually and seriously engaged with the enemy, can under any pretext whatever be justified in deserting them, and by so doing, abandon them to their fate – The more hopeless the position in which an officer finds his men, the more it is his bounden duty to stay and share their fortune, whether for good or ill – It is because the British officer has always done so that he occupies the position in which he is held in the estimation of the world, and that he possesses the influence he does in the ranks of our Army.[15]

In retrospect Wolseley's condemnation seems fair. The reports of Harward and Tucker made later are clearly a whitewash. Sergeant Booth told his wife in a letter that Harward simply rode away as soon as the battle started. The ferocious Zulu attack came just before dawn and Harward must have thought he was in a second

Isandlwana massacre. He had in fact leapt onto his unsaddled pony with the words 'Fire away boys. I'll be ready in a minute', odd things to say as he did not 'ready' anything, but turned tail and rode away for all he was worth. Once he reached the 80th Regiment's main camp Harward had dashed up to Tucker's tent, shouting, 'Major, major, the camp is in the hands of the enemy, they are all slaughtered, and I have galloped in for my life!' He then collapsed on Tucker's bed in what was called a dead faint, but clearly demonstrated his nerves were shot to pieces.

January saw Wolseley have a dispute with his Zululand boundary commissioners. One of these was Major James Alleyne, a minor member of the general's circle, who had served on the Red River Expedition in Ashanti and Cyprus (and would go on to work under him in Egypt and the Sudan). Alleyne had dared to send in a report on the character of the various Zulu chiefs who now ruled the country – and it was far from complimentary. He wrote of the 13 rulers that those who 'were not cripples from age and bodily infirmities were idiots'. Wolseley saw red because he had not asked for this kind of reporting and Alleyne's views did 'not in any way compare with what I gathered of their character from men like Mr John Shepstone who was my chief adviser in such matters, from Bishop Schreuder and from John Dunn'.[16] He thought Alleyne and Lt-Colonel Villiers, another of the commissioners, had listened too much to the views of Wheelwright, the Resident, 'who is not a wise man' and a one-time 'trading peddlar' in Zululand. An incensed Wolseley had Alleyne's comments erased from his official report. In hindsight, the worries of the boundary commissioners can be seen as some of the first cracks in a settlement that was soon to crumble further.

Letters from the Colonial Secretary, described by Sir Garnet as a 'goose', repeated excuses for refusing to permit him to return home. The latest such reason was that he might be required to take over in Natal, as Bulwer's departure was imminent.

A long-awaited telegraph line from London to Pretoria finally began in late December. This technological marvel was to break down constantly. In his first use of it Wolseley told Hicks Beach that he had little to do unless he interfered with Bulwer in Natal or Lanyon in the Transvaal. Sir Garnet convinced himself that HM Govt wanted him to remain in case Frere attempted to start another costly native war. 'I fancy the Queen has been well manipulated by Old Mother Frere & does not like the idea of his being dismissed,' the general told his wife.[17]

In January Wolseley received news from an angry Duke of Cambridge that William Russell had written an article published in *The Daily Telegraph* on 21 November accusing the troops of bad behaviour in the Transvaal. What was the truth, asked Prince George? The general was furious and blamed Russell's acerbic pen on McCalmont's notorious jape with the monkey in his bed. He told Cambridge that the war correspondent was 'the victim of a hoax' and the article was full of 'gross exaggerations and untruths'. An investigation found that British soldiers had committed one housebreaking, three assaults, one disturbance and three thefts – nothing more. The men, wrote Sir Garnet, were 'neither better nor worse than comrades in other parts of the globe'. Their biggest weakness, after the long and arduous Zulu campaign, was a tendency 'to drink more than was good for them'.

Poor Russell's run of bad luck had continued after the fall of Tsate. He had been returning from the eastern Transvaal when his horse got frightened by a storm while crossing a stream. The animal reared up, throwing Russell off, then fell on top of him. Eventually the drenched reporter got free and hauled himself up the bank, but the accident exacerbated an old leg injury from the Indian Mutiny, and he had to rest up at a farm for a few days before proceeding to Pretoria. In his article he accused the soldiers of drunkenness, scares, stampedes and thefts. The storm burst over his head just as he embarked from Cape Town. To the proprietor of *The Daily Telegraph* he declared, 'Every word of my statement was true.' He went on to say, 'I hold the strongest notion that the annexation of the Transvaal was an incurable and criminal blunder.' He accused 'my friend, Sir Garnet', of being 'in direct opposition to the principles of liberty, justice and sound policy'.[18] Wolseley was thus damned as a dictator.

On his return to England Russell refused to back down, and since he owned the *Army & Navy Gazette* he had a lot of power. He accused British soldiers of sacking the small town of HeidlebErg and even looting the church clock. Such tales turned out to be, as Wolseley had predicted, 'grotesque absurdities'. The truth was that Russell, like many journalists before and since, had been the victim of tall stories and foolish jests. On one occasion he had tried to interview some Swazis. Alistair Campbell (who died on the Fighting Kopje) offered to act as interpreter. Russell asked questions. Campbell translated. Then, at a signal from Campbell the Swazis all began singing 'Do you know the Muffin Man, the Muffin Man, the Muffin Man'! The whole thing had been an elaborate practical joke. Campbell did not speak Swazi.

The Duke of Cambridge took the unprecedented step of writing publicly to defend his soldiers. General Newdigate did the same. Wolseley wrote to Russell in March accusing him of listening to 'malicious untruths'. Rather than blaming him directly, Sir Garnet said the journalist had relied too much on tales told him by that 'Fenian', Alfred Aylward, a Transvaal newspaper editor who was 'a bitter hater of the Army'. It was a classic Wolseley letter, full of 'sincere regret' and hopes that 'when we meet we may meet as old friends ...' Privately the general still thought, as he told Louisa, that Russell was an 'ass', a 'scoundrel' and a 'low snob'.

In late January the High Commissioner decided to escape dreary Pretoria and the infernal Boers and go south to Pietermaritzburg, where Henry Bulwer was very pleased to see him. The two men agreed that demands for Natal to pay £1,000 towards the cost of the

Zulu Residency along with £1 million towards Zulu War expenses were unjust. A depressed Bulwer complained how HM Govt 'have backed up Sir B. Frere in his interference with me and are still backing him up in what he did. They have accepted Chelmsford's lies against me, and they have treated me so badly and ungratefully that I want to wash my hands of them as soon as possible.' He admitted to his brother in a letter that 'if it were not for Sir G's friendliness and consideration life would be intolerable'.[19]

It was while in Natal that Sir Garnet got a long, gossipy letter from his wife in which she said how proud she was of the Sekhukhune victory. He replied: 'Believe me, that I value this little remark from you more than all the congratulations I received from others. This is the first time you have ever expressed an interest or pleasure in any public service I have successfully carried out.'[20] Writing of his manservant, Fricke, Sir Garnet told his 'little rumpterfoozle' that he 'has earned his wages ten times over' and deserved a special reward. Louisa was tasked with spending £10 (about £800 by modern standards) to buy Fricke a 'nice gold watch' as soon as he sent word that they were returning home.

Snatches of news reached the general's ears. It became plain that George Colley would be returning to South Africa to succeed him. The only question was – when?

Newspapers reported that the Empress Eugenie, mother of the Prince Imperial, intended to visit South Africa. Wolseley was aghast: 'I should dread any dealings with her whilst she is engaged in this pilgrimage to the spot where her poor son was killed,' he told Louisa, 'I don't understand women sufficiently well to enable me to get on with an Empress under such unusual conditions.' A few days later came a despatch from the Queen, who commanded Wolseley to help Eugenie in every possible way. 'Cannot you fancy my misery in having to attend on her and jabber away in my indifferent French,' he complained. 'What a nuisance the dear good lady will be to everyone here.'[21]

Not wanting to return to the Transvaal, Sir Garnet stayed over four weeks in Pietermaritzburg fretting much of the time over Frere, Colenso and Hicks Beach. On one occasion he wrote, 'I am restless & angry today: if only I had Hicks Beach within reach of my boots, I should enjoy making him feel the stiffness of the soles.'[22] There were occasional moments of pleasure: at a dinner party the general met the wife of Commandant Rupert Lonsdale, a Natal Native Contingent officer who had fought bravely in the Zulu War. She was, Wolseley told Louisa, 'the most beautiful woman I have ever seen in my life – you of course excepted'.[23] Mrs Lonsdale made such an impression on him that Sir Garnet talked of how he wished to have 'a picture of her hung up to look at as a joy for ever',[24] and later sent his wife a photograph of this 'simply lovely' creature. What Lady Wolseley, who was very much in love, thought of either Mrs Lonsdale or her husband's mild infatuation is not recorded, but we may very well guess!

Heavy rains had washed away many of the roads on Sir Garnet's return journey to Pretoria. He got back on 27 February 'black and blue' from the bumping of the post-cart. General Clifford had helped Lanyon during Wolseley's absence but his services had been rather 'obstructive'. Lanyon opened his new Transvaal Legislative Council on 10 March. This was in addition to an Executive Council already begun. Wolseley and Lanyon made much of a sham constitution framed in London on lines originally proposed by Frere but falling far short of his suggestions. It was, as one historian has written, 'hardly a safety valve for discontent'. One citizen, J. W. Matthews, wrote that the constitution was 'laughed and jeered at by nearly the entire country'. On 11 March the general had to telegraph his wife, 'at the cost of a small fortune', the 'sad blow' that his departure was dependant on Colley's arrival. Her Majesty's Government had written to him some 'humbug' that he was needed at least until the April meeting of the Boer malcontents. Disgruntled, the general wrote that 'Hicks-Bitch' was 'not a gracious man to serve under & I hope never again to have any official dealings with him …'[25] By now Wolseley had given up any hopes that he once held of succeeding Sir Frederick Haines as C-in-C, India. He had graciously accepted the post of Quartermaster-General on his return to London.

By mid-March the general was complaining regularly that he had 'nothing to do' and moaned how he was 'undergoing imprisonment with hard labour' in South Africa. He had to content himself with breakfast rides, lawn tennis and giving away prizes at sports days for his troops. Two bits of news did cheer him up: firstly, the large Boer meeting was cancelled; secondly, Colley looked as if he could get to South Africa sooner than originally expected.

Word reached Wolseley's ears that the Boers did not like Lanyon because they thought he was of mixed race. This racial slur was due to the administrator's skin, tanned darkly after many years living in the Caribbean and Africa. Sir Garnet thought Lanyon's chief defects were personal vindictiveness allied with a tendency to view everything from a personal standpoint. 'He will never be a good Govr. in my opinion,' summed up Wolseley, 'although he is a very good fellow & by no means wanting in brains.'[26]

Finally 1 April dawned bright and clear. In his journal Wolseley noted, 'Thank heavens the month of March is over & that next month will I hope find me on my voyage home.'[27] So keen was he to depart that next day he sent his servants and baggage towards Natal. He had a final dinner party with Clifford and Lanyon and set off south with Fricke, Herbert and McCalmont (Brackenbury, Maurice and Harrison had departed weeks earlier). Herbert Stewart brought up the rear and was acting military secretary. Before he left Pretoria Sir Garnet assured the Duke of Cambridge that everything was 'supremely quiet' in the Transvaal. This was true; Paul Kruger had decided not to risk a war with a general of Wolseley's reputation. His replacement might not be so clever – or so lucky. In Lydenburg, newly promoted Philip Anstruther, now a lieutenant-colonel on garrison duty, wrote in March, 'Some idiots go on about saying that they are sure the Boers will break out but it's all rot, they won't.'[28] He returned to the serious business of raising a salad garden and enjoying the 'delightful' country. He thought that if the Liberals won the forthcoming general election they would probably give up the Transvaal.

April saw the Conservatives thrown out of government by a large majority. The return of the Liberals under Gladstone was to have far-reaching consequences in the Transvaal, where many Boers like Kruger – once described by Lord Beaconsfield as 'an ugly customer' – realised that if push came to shove the new British government might accept Afrikaner independence. Wolseley was most unhappy since 'I detest Radicals, men of Mr Gladstone's stamp'. He was often upset, as he told Louisa, that the Queen thought him a Radical when he was, in fact, 'a Jingo of the Jingoes'. The new Liberal Government, he predicted, 'would not fight for the Isle of Man' in a war.

The first three days journey southwards saw Wolseley's party overtaken by a hailstorm, then heavy thunder and rain during which they lost their way, followed by a trek through long grass that emitted a phosphorescent glow. The general was appalled to discover that this eerie light on the horses' hooves and men's boots was a kind of frog spawn! Sir Garnet knew that he needed to be in Durban before the Empress Eugenie's expected arrival on 23 April. It was a rush but he got there just in time. Presented to the empress aboard ship, he found her 'charming & so lovely … her eyebrows are painted, but Her manner is perfect.'[29] The couple chatted in French and Sir Garnet noticed how the empress seemed obsessed with her son's death. The only thing he disliked was Eugenie's habit of 'making a very disgusting noise in her throat as if she were about to spit …'[30] After a couple of days he concluded that the Empress was an intelligent woman, and the pair dined together on 25 April before she set off for Zululand the next morning.

That day Wolseley too bade farewell to Natal. One of his last visitors before his ship sailed was John Dunn, who told him that all was peaceful in Zululand. Table Bay was reached on 2 May. Fifty-six hours later the general sailed on the *Conway Castle* for England. During his stopover at Cape Town he declined to meet with Cetshwayo, despite requests from the king, 'because he would overwhelm me with questions as to what I meant to do with him'.[31] One person he could not avoid seeing was Sir Bartle Frere, who was 'hospitality itself'. Wolseley thought Sir Bartle 'looked aged', but accepted the fact that 'doubtless he thought the same of my appearance.'

10

FAREWELLS

> Sir Garnet may return to England. And the sooner the better, I say.
>
> Major Hugh McCalmont

The dull skies of Tuesday 25 May 1880 could not dampen the joy in Sir Garnet's heart as he landed at Plymouth that lunchtime. Two hours later he was on a train bound for London and around 9 p.m. was reunited with his wife at Macmillan's Hotel in Mayfair. History does not record what they ate that night but months earlier he had fantasized over his perfect homecoming dinner. It would start with one dozen oysters each, clear turtle soup, fried sole, boiled turbot, 'any entree you like', perhaps some woodcock or snipe, and all washed down by dry sherry and very dry champagne. 'Delicious!'

With a new Liberal Government in power and an intelligent, reform-minded War Minister in Hugh Childers, with the Duke of Cambridge suffering from an attack of gout, and Wolseley, 'wild and dis-satisfied' in Prince George's opinion, talking balderdash about new ammunition boxes and advanced machine-guns, the stage was set for fireworks at Horse Guards. At least Wolseley's career was in the ascendant despite difficulties in the work place. One month earlier Gilbert and Sullivan's *The Pirates Of Penzance* had opened in London to rave reviews. Everyone loved the comic patter-song and everybody in Society noticed how George Grossmith's 'Modern Major-General' aped Wolseley's mannerisms, even down to the same slim, twirled moustache. Sir Garnet and Lady Louisa were cheered when they saw the show at the Savoy. At home he sang snatches of the song to his wife and daughter.

Two careers very much in the descendant after 1880 were those of Sir Bartle Frere and Lord Chelmsford. Queen Victoria remained loyal to both men but she was an exception. The Prime Minister had refused even to see Chelmsford on his return from the war. Not long after this his lordship had to squirm in his seat in the House of Lords during a debate on his 'military misconduct and incapacity', when Lord Strathnairn who (as Hugh Rose) had commanded the arduous Central India campaign in 1858–59 said,

> I desire to call attention to mistakes which occurred in the conduct of the Zulu campaign pertaining to Isandlwana in particular ... In the first instance, I maintain that the invading columns were too far apart to allow of mutual support and communication ... Had the dangerous ground been properly reconnoitred it was quite possible the calamity would never have occurred ... the camp should have been entrenched ... the warning that the Zulus had shown themselves in force was ignored.[1]

Skilfully Chelmsford tried to pass the blame on to others, especially conveniently dead officers. He was made a full general in 1888 but never held a service command again. He died at his London club after a game of billiards in 1905.

Sir Bartle Frere met with his Sovereign and wrote long memos to defend his actions, but the costly Zulu War was not forgiven or forgotten in the corridors of Whitehall. He died on 29 May 1884 having caught a sudden chill. His dying words were poignant:

'They would surely understand.' He seems to have gone to his grave unhappy and deeply concerned that his countrymen did not realise he had tried to do his duty as he saw it – destroy the power of the Zulus and continue the work of confederation.

History is full of little ironies and this chapter is full of them too; just 108 days earlier Cetshwayo, Frere's rival and nemesis, had died of heart failure (though no autopsy was conducted and he may have been poisoned). In August 1882 he had visited England looking regal and portly, delighted crowds of well-wishers and met the Queen at Osborne. This diplomatic overture met with only partial success. Cetshwayo returned to Zululand in January 1883 to rule over a small part of his former kingdom. Soon old hatreds and jealousies rose to the surface. Civil war broke out between the followers of the royal house and those of his former general, Zibhebdu kaMaphitha. Wounded in battle and forced to flee his new royal kraal, Cetshwayo was living on a small homestead when his sudden death occurred. After the 1879 war and subsequent changes in Zululand many local people – black as well as white – found the king's death to be somewhat convenient.

Sad, tired, old Sekhukhune was dead by an assassin's hand less than three years after he had witnessed the destruction of Tsate. He was held at Pretoria for almost two years, then allowed by the Boers to return to the land he knew as Bopedi. He settled on a small stadt on the western slopes of the Lulu Mountains. During his absence the British had allowed the king's scheming brother, Mampuru, to settle in the Pedi heartland. Naturally the two men jockeyed for influence, and on 13 August 1882 a group of warriors on Mampuru's orders stabbed Sekhukhune to death as he lay sleeping. The great chief who had bested Boers, British, Swazis and Zulus during his lifetime was laid low by a sibling. A Boer commando moved quickly to restore order; Mampuru was captured, tried for murder and after two trials subsequently hung on 22 November 1883.

In another of History's ironies the sly Boer, Abel Erasmus, who may well have encouraged Sekhukhune and other Bapedi to think they could beat the British, was released from gaol for lack of hard evidence. He was after a time duly appointed a native commissioner and became the most important government official in the eastern Transvaal for the next twenty years.

Several of the British officers in this story also met sudden deaths, though perhaps more glorious ones than the two African rulers they had fought. The likable cavalryman, Herbert Stewart, a renaissance figure who could talk about anything from army manoeuvres to architecture, was mortally wounded leading the Desert Column in the Sudan in 1885. By another twist of fate, young 'Sankey' Herbert died in the same battle; he had got himself a job as correspondent for the *Morning Post* but was shot through the head by a dervish bullet and died instantly. Arthur Yeatman-Biggs, the staff officer who impressed Wolseley by his quiet professionalism, rose to become a general but died on the Tirah campaign in 1898 'of exhaustion when his duty was ended' says his headstone at Peshawar, but the truth was enteric dysentery.

With Wolseley gone from the Transvaal, the groundswell of opinion against British rule and Owen Lanyon's tax-gathering methods grew until war broke out barely six months after Sir Garnet's departure. His replacement as military supremo, George Colley, the man Wolseley considered the brightest of all his ring of officers, led his troops into a disastrous engagement at Laing's Nek on 28 January 1881 when he tried to assault the pass over the Drakensberg Mountains. His frontal attack was repulsed with 197 casualties. Eleven days later at Ingogo he lost a further 150 men. On 16 February instructions were received from London to offer the Boers an armistice. Given some latitude as he saw fit, wishing to retrieve his honour and that of his country, Colley gambled on a final battle. He took a mixed force of 402 officers and men on an eight hour climb to the top of Majuba Hill on the Natal-Transvaal frontier. Here he waited and was duly rewarded by a Boer attack that saw him killed, stretched out on the summit like a medieval knight, while his troops ran for their lives (the British had 223 casualties, the Boers just six). An officer who served in the campaign wrote home that 'everybody was sorry about Colley, he was a most lovable person, but his death was a most fortunate thing for him, and as someone said, for the Natal Field Force also'.[2] It was all very tragic, especially so since Colley had told Wolseley eight months earlier that he hoped 'I may do my master credit'.

The Transvaal War saw the Boers regaining their independence. Sir Owen Lanyon was recalled home in disgrace. The war had been due in no small part, as his biographer notes, to Lanyon's 'unacceptable authoritarianism, his foolish complacency and his errors of judgment and strategy.'[3] The Colonial Office dropped him like a hot potato. Sir Garnet was more supportive of his old friend and gave him a sinecure as a base commander during the Egyptian War of 1882. Lanyon had married that same year to the daughter of one of the proprietors of *The Daily Telegraph*. He was genuinely happy but tragedy struck when his beloved Florence died suddenly a year later. Wolseley found a small role again for him in the Gordon Relief Expedition, but Lanyon's health was failing. He died of cancer on 6 April 1887. He was only forty-four years old.

The 'Garnet ring' of officers would reform in 1882 for the conquest of Egypt and then again 1884–85 in the expedition to save Gordon at Khartoum. Several of Wolseley's best friends – like their leader – all died within the two or three years leading up to the Great War. It is as if they were washed away on History's tide as their kind of warfare became obsolete in the face of a new and vastly mechanised killing machine. Baker Russell went to his Valhalla in 1911, Maurice in 1912 and Brackenbury in 1914. The latter two intellectuals worked hard in Wolseley's footsteps promoting army reform. Baker Russell, along with his chum, Hugh McCalmont, had some glorious moments commanding the cavalry brigade together in Egypt, leading the Household Cavalry in a glorious night charge at Kassassin and later quaffed champagne from a bucket as they rode into action at Tel-el-Kebir.

One of the last to leave South Africa, McCalmont, as Wolseley's aide had written in 1880 that as a 'last gasp' on leaving office Hicks Beach had telegraphed that 'Sir Garnet may return to England. And the sooner the better, I say.'[4] Hugh rushed off to Afghanistan but arrived too late for most of the fighting. He also missed the Sudan War 1884–85 but somehow managed to take part in a last Mahdist battle at Suakin in 1888. The old warhorse was placed on the retired list in 1906. At home in Ireland he painted, played music, enjoyed the company of his large family and finally died contentedly in 1924.

The Prime Minister, Lord Beaconsfield, already a sick man, passed away on 19 April 1881 at the ripe age of seventy-six years. Four weeks earlier a treaty had been signed giving the Boers back their independence and blowing to the winds any thoughts of British confederation across southern Africa. Sir Theophilus Shepstone, who had set the Transvaal ball in motion, also lasted seventy-six years though his death did not come until 1893. Wolseley's friend, the fair-minded and intelligent Sir Henry Bulwer, agreed to serve once more as governor of Natal until 1885. His career was not always a happy one and his last posting was as High Commissioner of Cyprus where, no doubt, he sometimes thought of Sir Garnet. He died in 1914. Bulwer was never raised to the peerage, an honour that Frere also missed, though one who did was Sir Michael Hicks Beach who remained a prominent Tory and was rewarded with the title of Viscount St Aldwyn in 1906, this honour later being made into an earldom. 'Black Michael', a canny Whitehall man if ever there was one, died in April 1916. Tragically his only son and heir had been mortally wounded in Egypt just one week earlier.

What of some of the ordinary people in our story? Masschow, the Bapedi warrior who has left us such vivid impressions of the Bapedi War, lived on and became a tribal medicine man, a *ngaka* or diviner. He recounted his adventures in 1935. By then Thomas Flawn V.C. had passed away; he died at his Plumstead, London, home in his sixty-eighth year. He shares a gravestone with his second wife in Plumstead churchyard. His memorial makes no mention of his Victoria Cross, which was finally disposed of by his family and in 1999 became the highpoint of Spink's first medal auction fetching a record £19,000. Today it is in a private collection. Flawn and Fitzpatrick were in action together again at Bronkhorst Spruit fighting the Boers. Here Francis Fitzpatrick was wounded and – horror of horrors – lost his V.C.! In due course he got two more – a replacement he had made and an official one. That latter medal is now in the National Army Museum, Chelsea. Fitzpatrick also volunteered for the South African War 1899–1902 (it could be argued he had a fair grudge against the Boers), this time joining the Argyll & Sutherland Highlanders. Later he worked in a post office and was buried in an unmarked grave in 1933. In July 2014, after a press campaign led by his descendants, the Lord Provost of Glasgow and Fitzpatrick's Irish relations unveiled a headstone to his memory in St Kentigern's Cemetery, Glasgow. Several newspapers, both local and national, carried the news. They all referred to the heroic action in the Basuto Gun War! A leading medals website still does the same. Wolseley must be turning in his grave!

The death of Colley came as a hard shock to Sir Garnet. Even worse perhaps, but another ring member, Evelyn Wood, signed the armistice with the Boers. Wolseley never really forgave him and gave Wood a minor role to play in his next and best-fought campaign, the invasion of Egypt in 1882. Most of the circle were there – Butler, Buller, Herbert, Maurice, McCalmont, Stewart, Yeatman-Biggs. Then Britain's 'only general' was sent to retrieve

Gordon from Khartoum in 1884. Gladstone and his cronies had left things to the last minute but Wolseley made matters worse by an over-elaborate plan involving Canadian boatmen, Australian troops and a mounted corps of camel riders led by Stewart. It was all too ambitious; on hearing of Gordon's death at the fall of Khartoum, he wrote in his pocket diary, 'May God have mercy on me, but this is enough to drive most men mad.'[5] After the death of Colley the general had been drawn closer and closer to Stewart. Many years later he wrote that 'the sun of my luck set when Stewart was wounded …' He rose in the Army, became a field marshal, tried to push through more reforms and modernise the institution he loved, yet his ego was mortally wounded and all his self-doubt and old insecurities took over.

On the retirement of the Duke of Cambridge as C-in-C in 1895 Sir Garnet assumed he would be the natural successor, but he had to fight off other contenders. One was Buller, whom he never fully forgave. By now he was suffering from the early signs of Alzheimer's Disease with short-term memory loss. So it was that when the great South African War broke out in 1899 Field Marshal Lord Wolseley, Commander-in-Chief of the British Army, was not at the height of his powers and knew it. South Africa had destroyed the reputations of many soldiers, and the Boers were to have a lasting revenge on Sir Garnet as their land was the anvil on which his career would be smashed. Redvers Buller was sent to crush the Boers but his generalship seemed to be a disaster. The war dragged on for three years, eventually costing Britain £200 million; there were 100,000 casualties on all sides, 22,000 of them were British and colonial lads who found a grave in Africa, many of them in the Transvaal. In Parliament and before a royal commission, Sir Garnet now became the scapegoat. The hammer to the anvil was the bright, ruthless, war minister, Lord Lansdowne, 'a little contemptible creature' in Wolseley's eyes, who publicly accused him in the House of Lords of being personally responsible for many of the army's failings. Refusing to hit back with the same personal, slurs Sir Garnet took it all on the chin. He admitted that mistakes had been made but was not responsible for most of them. It had not been all doom and gloom, the army that went to war in 1899 was the best the British had ever had. No one seemed to care. The field marshal resigned his command (it hardly mattered since he had not even been told when Lord Roberts had been sent out to correct Buller's mistakes). The next decade saw him slip into obscurity, surprisingly quickly forgotten by a public who lorded Roberts of Kandahar and Kitchener of Khartoum, the two new poster boys of the British Army. With almost total memory loss, estranged from his only child, Lady Frances, but still adored by his wife, Garnet Joseph Wolseley died in France on 26 March 1913. His body was brought back to London and the public remembered for one last time the master of the colonial 'small war' who had tried so hard to reform the army. He lies buried in St Paul's Cathedral.

Back in 1879 Sir Garnet had perceptively seen that the Boers would fight someday. That morning dawned on 20 December 1880 when Lt-Colonel Philip Anstruther, snobbish commentator on the Zulu and Bapedi wars, led his men of the 94th towards Pretoria. 'The Boers will turn tail at the first beat of the big drum,' he had once declared. By a little twinkling stream called Bronkhorst Spruit his cheery marching train of around 200 officers and men were stopped short, the bandsmen's tune of 'Kiss Me Mother, Kiss Your Darling' dying on the breeze as they ran into a large Boer commando. An unarmed messenger bearing a white stick told Anstruther that hostilities had broken out and that to advance beyond the spruit would be considered an act of war. The colonel replied that he did not want to fight, 'but had been ordered to Pretoria and to Pretoria I am going'.[6] Within minutes the Boers opened fire on the British soldiers, who looked like scarlet ducks in a shooting gallery. When the firing stopped the British had suffered

157 casualties. Dead drummer boys like 'lifeless red dolls' lay in pools of blood. Anstruther, wounded five times, lay by the bloody stream. He would die five days later when surgeons tried to cut off his leg.

The Boers had the last laugh on the colonel, Wolseley and the great British Empire. *Sic transit glora mundi.*

APPENDIX A

17TH LANCERS – DIARY OF THE ZULU EXPEDITION, SOUTH AFRICA, 1879

Buried in the Wolseley Collection at Hove is a slim volume titled as above. How it came to be among Lord Wolseley's papers is a mystery since he was not at Ulundi and had no personal connection with the regiment. Possibly Drury Drury-Lowe or Herbert Stewart presented it to him? The extract below covers the famous battle. So far as I know it has never been published.

4 July – Reveille about 4 o'clock the whole Column excepting sufficient to man the Laager which had been made more compact & strengthened the day before. Commenced to cross the river about 5 a.m. & moved in the direction of Ulundi. The kraals appeared to be deserted which we afterwards found was the case. Shortly after crossing the river we found we were surrounded by the enemy except in the direction of the river we had just crossed & it would have been a difficult job for us to have got back that way had we been so inclined but that was not our intention.

The Infantry, Artillery & Native Contingents moved on a little further & then formed a square, the Infantry four deep, two ranks kneeling & two standing. The 7 & 9 pounders & Gatling guns were able to command the enemy in all directions. The Native

Contingents were placed within the square. While the square was being formed Ours, Light Horse, Mounted Infantry & Basutoo scouted in every direction. The Light Horse, Mounted Infantry & Basutos exchanging shots with the advancing enemy, when they got pretty close we retired inside the square, dismounted & stood to our horses.

When the enemy advanced out to be about 20,000 strong got within firing distance firing was commenced on both sides, the Artillery firing grape shot & shells. This lasted about an hour when it sounded cease fire, we mounted & the Infantry opening out, we passed out of the square at a gallop. The bullets were whistling about our ears, on leaving the square, we wheeled to our right & charged the enemy in that direction & cut down & lanced I should estimate 5 or 6 hundred of them before they could retreat to the hills where it was impossible for us to follow them. However the Artillery dropped a few shells in among them there, which effectively scared them. After the enemy had retreated we fired their kraals, 9 of them altogether. Several of them were in a circle of about 2 miles in circumference, 8 & 9 huts deep.

Ketchwayo's hut in the Ulundi kraal was built square with a sloping roof out of which one of Buller's Light Horse brought a large looking-glass which had been left behind. Casualties in Ours – Captain Edgell shot through the head, Lieut. and Act. Adjutant Jenkins shot through the jaw, Farrier Taylor killed & 4 privates wounded. Trooper E. Jonas who was shot on the right side, while we were in the square died this evening. Arrives back in Camp about 5 p.m.

APPENDIX B

COMPOSITION OF THE TRANSVAAL FIELD FORCE, 28 NOVEMBER 1879

Major-General Sir Garnet J. Wolseley
Lieutenant-Colonel Baker C. Russell, commanding T.F.F.

Western Side of Mountains

TRANSVAAL ARTILLERY: 2 officers, 22 men, Her Majesty's troops; 2 officers, 22 men, colonial troops; 35 native levies; 57 horses; 2 Krupp guns & 2 7-pounder muzzle-loading guns; 2 men left in laager.

ROYAL ENGINEERS: 2 officers, 19 men, Her Majesty's troops; 2 horses; 1 man left in laager.

2ND BATTALION, 21ST REGIMENT: 18 officers, 444 men, Her Majesty's troops; 6 horses, 11 men left in laager.

80TH REGIMENT: 21 men, Her Majesty's troops.

94TH REGIMENT: 15 officers, 556 men, Her Majesty's troops; 5 horses; 11 men left in laager.

MOUNTED INFANTRY: 3 officers, 34 men, Her Majesty's troops; 37 horses.

FERREIRA'S HORSE: 6 officers, 103 men, colonial troops; 109 horses; 3 men left in laager.

BORDER HORSE: 6 officers, 68 men, colonial troops; 74 horses; 2 men left in laager.

TRANSVAAL MOUNTED RIFLES: 6 officers, 81 men, colonial troops; 87 horses; 2 men left in laager.
SMALL-ARMS AMMUNITION RESERVE: 1 officer, 5 men, Her Majesty's troops; 3 men, colonial troops; 60 men native levies; 3 horses.
ARMY HOSPITAL CORPS: 6 officers, 53 men, Her Majesty's troops; 6 horses.
BEARER COMPANY: 1 officer, 50 men, Her Majesty's troops; 74 men, native levies; 1 horse.
RUSTENBERG CONTINGENT: 6 officers, 219 men, native levies; 6 horses.
MAPOCH'S CONTINGENT: 1 officer, 651 men, native levies; 1 horse.
ZOUTPANSBERG CONTINGENT: 4 officers, 611 men, native levies; 8 horses; 200 men in laager.
ARMY SERVICE CORPS: 1 officer and 18 men left in laager.
51ST LIGHT INFANTRY: 1 man left in laager.

Total Western Side: 48 officers, 1,204 men, Her Majesty's troops; 20 officers, 277 men, colonial troops; 11 officers, 1,650 native levies; 402 horses; 1 officer and 250 men left in laager.

Eastern Side of Mountains
80TH REGIMENT: 3 officers, 91 men, Her Majesty's troops.
94TH REGIMENT: 9 officers, 167 men, Her Majesty's troops.
LYDENBURG RIFLES: 4 officers, 40 men, colonial troops; 44 horses.
ECKERSLEY'S CONTINGENT: 2 officers, 250 men, native levies; 2 horses.
SWAZI CONTINGENT: 3 officers, 8,000 men, native levies; 3 horses.

Total Eastern Side: 6 officers, 258 men, Her Majesty's troops; 4 officers, 40 men, colonial troops; 5 officers, 8,250 native levies; 49 horses.

Grand Total: 54 officers, 1,462 men, Her Majesty's troops; 24 officers, 317 men, colonial troops; 16 officers, 9,900 men, native levies; 451 horses; 1 officer and 250 men left in laager.

APPENDIX C

RECOLLECTIONS OF A BAPEDI WARRIOR

A version of the following memoir appeared in The Ranger Magazine *Vol. XI No. 51, November 1945. It was entitled 'The Defeat Of Chief Sekukuni' and written by the South African hunter W. G. Barnard. My version is longer and taken from what was possibly the original typescript, dated 'June 1935' which I found mis-filed with some loose papers relating to the Connaught Rangers in the National Army Museum.*

'The day had been terribly warm, 96 in the shade, and this was the beginning of winter. What it was in the summer of 1879 can be imagined & my thoughts went back to those days when British troops trudged with full packs over the long dusty roads from Middelburg, finally having to climb the mountain behind Sekukuni's stronghold at "Dsjate" – "Dsjate" meaning stronghold and Sekukuni, "the man who creeps by night".

I had been very busy from 5 a.m. & it was now 5 p.m. I had outspanned my horses and was making my camp ready for the night. Having picked my camping site at the foot of Mount Mosego, near the banks of the river where the troops in 1879 had bathed & obtained their water ... Baboons climbed the high rocks & crevices and did not appear to like my presence. I shot a *duiker* (antelope) for supper. Investigating the shot came old "Masschow", the local witch doctor. He greeted me "Damela N'kosi", carrying his knapsack of herbal concoctions, his old Boer War greatcoat, a necklace of wild cotton hung with charms, a small woven bag containing his "bones", a loin cloth, a dirty once-white shirt and a pair of sandals made from the forehead skin of an ox known as the "bsada".'

The two men drank some coffee together and Barnard asked the old Bapedi to relate his memories of the 1879 War:

'It is a long time ago. I was younger then, and I had a fine wife and one child. One morning we were at Pasha N'komo's Kraal. We heard the war bugle and we rushed for our assegais, battle axes, knobkerries & shields. Then a message came, telling us that the Red Coats were coming down the Olifants River. Chief Nkoane sent us to the point of the mountain to look around and we saw the soldiers with their wagons coming. We waited & when they passed us we ran from rock to rock ... Some of our men who had worked at Kimberley had guns and they fired at the soldiers, but our guns were weak and the bullets did not reach the soldiers. There were few soldiers but a lot of wagons & they were covered with tarpaulins. We decided to rush up & capture the wagons. When we came near the soldiers fired at us and at the same time the tarpaulins flew off & out jumped hundreds of soldiers. They shot & chased us, killing & wounding many of our men. We thought this was a dirty trick! They chased all who were not dead into the mountains but they were not so agile & we got away, followed by bullets from over our heads. The soldiers were very thirsty and they drank from bottles which they threw away ...

The soldiers continued along the road and foothills. We hurried on and came to Sekukuni's Kraal. The wagons & soldiers came on and camped just across the river (from where we were sitting). Chief Sekukuni & his generals, counsellors & witch doctors were there & thousands of our men. Sekukuni's son, Prince Moroamotshe, was not there with his regiment. He had been ordered to go & stay in the hills across the Olifants River, for, said Sekukuni, "If I am killed you will be able to carry on and rule the Bapedi tribe." But Moroamotshe was a brave man & when he saw the soldiers marching to his father's kraal, he decided also to take part & during the night he marched in. The soldiers allowed him & his men to pass in & when he arrived his father was very cross with him for disobeying his orders. The Prince replied, saying that he was flesh of his flesh, bone of his bone & could not act like an old woman & keep out of the fight.

Then Chief Sekukuni told us his plans. He said we must not be afraid. He would beat the English. Hadn't he driven the Boers back the year before? He said he had hives full of bees. These he would release amongst the soldiers & they would chase them away. We were then inoculated so that the bullets would not harm us and we were painted white with ashes so that we would not be taken for the Swazi (the damned Kal Kaffirs) who were going to help the English. The & children were sent up to the kraantzes & each regiment with its general leading went & took up positions. Early before it was daylight we heard the bugles blowing in the camp below & when it was light enough we saw the soldiers on foot & others on horses coming across the flats. Sekukuni for weeks before had had a large thorn fence built across the valley from hill to hill. It was 15 feet wide & 15 feet high and nothing could penetrate it. We sat & waited for the troops coming along & when they reached the fence we laughed to ourselves and shouted. In a few minutes we saw the fence going up in smoke and flames. "Yo", "Yo", "Yo", "Yo" we shouted, telling them to come on. And they did. Shortly bullets were whistling over our heads. Yes, their guns were strong. Some of our men were shot. The women in the hills were shouting and egging us on & we were doing well. The soldiers came on & we could hear them saying that they would get us. The boys from Kimberley spoke a little English & they shouted to the soldiers to hurry up. We danced & yelled, and then the women's shouts turned to screams. The damned Kal Kaffirs came over the hill amongst them. They killed a lot. Some of our women were brave & they killed some of the Swazi & then it was hell. The Swazi came & Prince Moroamotshe with a leopard skin on and his regiment were in the path of the Swazi. They fought & fought, hand to hand, until Moroamotshe (as is our custom) and all his regiment were killed. Fully 800 Swazi were killed. The screaming was terrible. I don't know how I am alive. We were nearly all killed.

We then crept down & into the caves. The rock rabbits scampered about, wetting & covering us with their wine but that was nothing as we could go in the morning to the spruit and wash. The soldiers came & put dynamite into the holes but the Kimberley boys were clever & cut the fuses. That night the soldiers slept & kept guard around the koppie & during the night it rained a little. We caught the water in our mouths, as it trickled down the walls & we licked the water from the rocks. Our mouths were parched & we were hungry. When it was very dark my mate & I crept out. We fell over a soldier who swore at us. We went into the mountain & up and up. We saw Sekukuni sitting near a rock with two small girls. He did not look up at us. He was finished. We then heard men calling us back. We returned & were told that the fight was over & we must go and "hands up". The soldiers were taking the things from the chiefs and then they burned the huts. When we arrived at the white man's camp we were told to leave our assegais & battle axes in a heap & place our hands on our shoulders. Some of our men had guns & they did not like to throw them down, but the bayonets soon made them obey.

The big chief (Sir G. W.) said, "Men, you see the sun. Have a good look at it for it will be the last time." One of our generals asked, "Do the white men kill prisoners?" He replied, "Yes", but he would let us off if we told him where Chief Sekukuni was. One of our general from Chief K said "Alright", he would show them where to find him. He then led the soldiers to the summit of the mountain to the caves at Namatamaking. When they arrived there the general spoke to Sekukuni telling him that his son, Moroamotshe, was killed & that it was all up with them, but he would not come out. A day later hunger drove him out. A mashibo was made and we carried him to the camp. He was sent to Pretoria. He remained 2 years there & on his return lived at Manogy where one night his brother, Mampuru, murdered him in his sleep.

We boys were then sent into the hills for 2 days looking for a white officer [Lt Alistair Campbell] but we did not find him. The witch doctors had cut him up for medicine for he was a brave man. The soldiers were good to us & gave us lots of food & clothes & many of us went with them to Lydenburg. The Kal Kaffirs [Swazi] took nearly all our dogs and a lot of our girls.'

APPENDIX D

TSATE & NTSWANENG TODAY

The road to Lydenburg woke me up with a jolt. I had driven several hours from Durban that morning, saying farewell to the lush Zulu landscape, passing through towns like Ladysmith that will be forever associated with the South African War, then up on to the sparse high veldt for endless miles.

A modern motorway – and South Africa has some excellent ones – rushes from Johannesburg to the sea. Taking the Lydenburg exit I swung my jeep around a bend and almost careered into an overturned lorry that had spread its cargo of vegetables across the road. It was late afternoon with the sun starting to drop fast the way it does in Africa. Soon I found myself in a landscape of low, forbidding hills and some lakes, the whole thing very reminiscent of parts of Ireland or the Scottish Highlands. Thin fingers of mist seemed to be streaking down on either side of the road as the sun set. It was all rather spooky and a bit Harry Potterish.

This was 2013. Perhaps things have since improved for the good burghers of Lydenburg, but the R36 road was quite awful. For what seemed like eternity through an empty landscape one drove dodging giant – I mean huge – potholes. Clearly Mpumalanga tourism (the old 'Transvaal' being no longer acceptable) did not rate Lydenburg as an important destination, or assumed everyone would drive there via Dullstroom, a quaint roadside village full of souvenir shops and Boer War memorials. I arrived in inky darkness, something which as a European was a little disconcerting. We spoiled Brits get used to street lights at night. There were or are none in Lydenburg save a few on the main street. Luckily I had a map and a torch in the car. My hotel, which turned out to be a cosy retreat once I could summon some staff, helped me unwind. I discovered that Lydenburg is limited on what might be termed 'fine dining'. The busiest place in town turned out to be a fish cafe packed with bulky Afrikaner farmers and noisy kids. It also seemed rather odd. I had been expecting some of the excellent restaurants serving game and steaks that are all over South Africa. The sea, THOUGH, is at least four hours away over the mountains.

Next morning a drizzly grey rain was falling despite being the height of summer. Lydenburg is no longer the rose-filled town of Wolseley's day. But it still has the feel of a small, sleepy, farming community town. I visited the Boer War graves in a corner of the local cemetery and photographed the oldest house in town, supposedly used by Wolseley in 1879. To find my way to Tsate, given the fact that nowhere could I seem to get a detailed map of Mpumalanga (though I had a large scale South Africa one), I decided to ask at the local museum. The director was most friendly when I told him the reasons for my visit. Yes – he had been there when the municipality had tidied up the place and put up some plaques several years ago. No – he could not exactly remember how he got there. But he offered to phone up the friend who had shared his journey. There then followed a phone call … a long phone call … in Afrikaans. Eventually he got off the phone to say, 'So sorry, but my friend can't remember exactly either. It's quite tricky you see …'

He had tried his best. I thanked him for his time. I had an idea in my head to try getting to Tsate via Jane Furse, as its now called, across the valley facing the Lulu Mountains. Everywhere one sees the name 'Sekhukhune' – health centres, cafes, banks. Clearly the Bapedi are immensely proud of their old king. This is striking when compared with the few times the name Cetshwayo appears in relation to modern-day Zululand. It was lunch time and the dirt roads were full of uniformed school children, many of them giving me a friendly wave. I decided to ask a local Pedi taxi driver for directions and showed him my map. He did not speak English but gestured for a pen and paper. Then he drew me a most elegant little map. It was the kind of simple, helpful deed for a lost stranger that leaves an impression.

The rain had by now stopped but the skies were dullish. About a mile or so up into the red rock mountains my uphill track seemed to split in two. Which way to go? It was late afternoon and I had visions of getting nicely lost. Suddenly I saw one of those incongruous happenings that belong to Africa. Marching sprightly down the track towards me came a little boy about ten years of age. He was immaculately dressed in clean shorts and a pressed white shirt. I asked him the way? He only knew a few words in English but implied that I might get more directions at the small township at the foot of the hills where he was heading. I offered him a lift and with immense pride he got inside the new (rented) jeep and enjoyed impressing his pals when we pulled up by a grocery store. Thanking me and indicating where I needed to go with a loose wave of his hand he was soon lost in a crowd.

I decided to return to Lydenburg, enjoy some more noisy fish and chips and to try my luck next day on the other side of the mountains. The country around Lydenburg is beautiful; the town sits in a wide valley with, on one side, a road rising with switchback bends to the old gold towns such as Pilgrim's Rest; and another straight road leading down into verdant low veldt bush country. A range of rocky cliffs and hills mark the start of what was once Sekhukhune's land. It's lonely, quite majestic country and not difficult for a car driver to imagine how it must have felt for lonely travellers on these roads 140 years ago. One recalls that in 1879 every farm here was burnt out, every place the haunt of marauding Bapedi bands. Even today baboons sit in the trees overhanging the roadside, the occasional leopard stalks through the bush. I saw several of the former, none of the latter – though I almost ran into a giant tortoise solemnly crossing the road (and was told later I was lucky to see one). Driving past Burgersfort and the site of the old Fort Weeber, I approached the Tsate valley as Wolseley's troops had done. I drove along the R37 and finally spotted a small sign by the side of the main road.

There is a line in Adrian Greaves' book *Forgotten Battles Of The Zulu War* in which, after a short description of the Tsate battle, he writes, 'Today the remote locations of Sekhukhuneland are rarely visited, except by mining companies keen to extract the unique minerals of the area.' This is absolutely correct, though he could have added, 'and they are hard to get to'. Tsate is about ten or eleven miles from the main road. The track gets smaller and smaller, asphalt quickly gives way to pounded dirt and then just the ruts made by cars, mules and goats. The fact that the valley is gradually narrowing is clear, the hills getting closer on each side. The approach is thus in the general direction taken by Wolseley's troops. Nothing remains of Tsate, and only a few modern dwellings dot the landscape.

Eventually, right by Ntswaneng – the Fighting Kopje – one is stopped by the sheer immensity of the boulders. The great rocks look as if they have been flung down like a pack of dominoes. The place remains impressive. A small fenced area encloses the great monument. There is a gloomy loo full of spidery horrors and lots of cobwebs. A couple of monuments speak of the great battle. Built into the rock face is a memorial to the fallen British dead. While standing there a tall young Bapedi male seemed to materialise out of nowhere and told me he looked after the place. He invited me to climb up the rocks of the fighting Kopje to a look-out point over the valley where a statue of Sekhukhune had been erected.

It is very easy from this place to imagine Wolseley's army attacking in the dawn light of 28 November 1879. No vast village now stretches across the valley floor. It is serenely majestic. I watched a donkey cart trundling along the track I had just driven. Turning to my guide I asked if we should climb higher. 'Not a good idea,' he said nodding his head. 'Ah yes,' I said, 'the rocks look dangerous, I'll probably only slip over and break my neck.' 'No,' he said, 'Thats not the problem ... it's snakes!' I looked rather uncomfortably about me. 'Er, snakes, do you have many here?' He looked grave. 'Too many.' 'Umm ... what kind of snakes exactly?' I asked. 'Oh, cobra, viper, black mamba, lots of mamba.' I looked nervously over the rocks. Everything seemed so peaceful in the sunshine. 'What about down there?' I indicated towards the grassy area surrounding the foot of the kopje. 'Especially down there,' he said. 'The snakes lately have been a big problem.'

I suggested with a false laugh that I'd follow him down and we retraced our steps off the Fighting Kopje with me staring intently at every rock I placed my foot on. He had been so helpful that I gave him a very healthy tip and drove away. The thought struck me then – and it has many times since – that somewhere Chief Sekhukhune's spirit and those of his brave warriors on Ntswaneng must be smiling in their ancestral halls. The British came with guns and cannon but could not enter those caves. Instead they tried to blow them in. Where once the British feared to tread the bones of the Bapedi are now protected by the cobra and the mamba, seemingly guardians for all time of this hallowed ground.

NOTES

Prologue

1. Cavendish, p. 160.
2. Ibid., p. 3.
3. Ibid., p. 10.
4. Lehmann, *All Sir Garnet*, p. 231.
5. Maurice & Arthur, p. 94.
6. HPL.
7. Scott-Stevenson, p. 34.
8. Callwell, p. 152.
9. Pollock, p. 42.
10. Magnus, p. 27.
11. Callwell, p. 151.
12. Kiewiet, p. 69.
13. Ibid., p. 67.
14. Martineau vol. ii, p. 163.
15. Williams, p. 141.
16. Fortescue-Brickdale, p. 95.
17. Hale, p. 103.
18. Laband, *Zulu Warriors*, p. 75.
19. Norris-Newman, *With The Boers In The Transvaal And Orange Free State In 1880–1*, p. 81.
20. Cope, p. 129.
21. Ibid., p. 130.
22. Laband, *Zulu Warriors*, p. 113.
23. O`Connor, p. 124–125.

24. H.S. – *The Kafir War* article.
25. NAM – Chelmsford Papers.
26. Kiewiet, p. 229.
27. Hicks Beach vol. i, p. 99–100.
28. Buckle vol. vi, p. 420.
29. NA CO 879/14.
30. Buckle, p. 421.
31. Guy, *Destruction Of The Zulu Kingdom*, p. 49.
32. Morris, p. 315.
33. Guy, *The Heretic*, p. 261.
34. Ibid., p. 265.
35. Ibid., p. 267.
36. Cope, p. 238.
37. GRO, Hicks Beach Papers.
38. David, p. 57.
39. Ibid., p. 57–58.
40. Laband, *Lord Chelmsford`s Zululand Campaign 1878–1879*, p. 5.
41. Ibid. xxxiii.
42. Based on the combined figures in Laband, *Zulu Warriors*, p. 206.
43. French, p. 43.
44. Greaves & Best, p. 83.
45. Emery, *Red Soldier*, p. 62–63.
46. Clarke, *Invasion Of Zululand*, p. 55.
47. REM – Main unpublished memoirs.
48. Wood vol. ii, p. 24.
49. Cavendish, p. 163.
50. Ibid., p. 164.

1 A Terrible Disaster

1.Vijn, p. 17.
2. Laband, *Zulu Warriors*, p. 225 quoting Nanzi of the uVe ibuto in *Natal Mercury*, 22 Jan. 1929.
3. Knight, *Zulu Rising*, p. 201.
4. Ibid., p. 216.
5. Ibid., p. 254.
6. Martineau vol. ii, p. 270.
7. Laband, *Zulu Warriors*, p. 230.
8. CC – Symons Papers.
9. Clarke, *Zululand At War*, p. 85.
10. Child, p. 34.

11. CC – Symons Papers.
12. Symons quoted Knight, *Zulu Rising*, p. 464.
13.Mainwaring letter to *Morning Post* c. 1921 – SWBM.
14. Symons quoted Knight, *Zulu Rising*, p. 465.
15. Child, p. 34.
16. Ibid., p. 34.
17. Parr, p. 230.
18. Knight, *Zulu Rising*, p. 466.
19. RAW.
20. Knight, *Zulu Rising*, p. 467–468.
21. Holt, p. 63.
22. Greaves & Knight, *Who's Who*, vol. ii, p. 96.
23. Lock & Quantrill, *Zulu Victory*, p. 228.
24. Hamilton-Browne, pp. 140–141.
25. Lock & Quantrill, *Zulu Victory*, p. 229.
26. Emery, *The Red Soldier*, p. 95.
27. Captain Symons' account, SWBM.
28. Norris-Newman, *In Zululand*, p. 63.
29. Knight, *Zulu Rising*, p. 553.
30. Laband, *Chelmsford,* p. 81.
31. Gordon, p. 280.
32. Greaves, *Isandlwana,* p. 155.
33. Fell typescript letters – Private Collection.
34. Lock & Quantrill, *Zulu Victory*, p. 255.
35. Clements, p. xi.
36. Blake, p. 670.
37. Buckle vol. vi, p. 424.
38. *Hansard,* 13 February 1879.
39. Blake, pp. 670 40.Worsfold, p. 223.
41. De Kiewiet, pp. 234–235.
42. Worsfold, p. 231.
43. Ibid., p. 228.
44. Clements, p. 108.
45. Morris, p. 503.
46. Clements, p. xv.
47. *Hansard,* 28 March 1879.
48. Blake, p. 671.
49.Roberts, p. 226.
50. Buckle vol. vi, pp. 428–429.
51. Ibid., p. 429.

52. Ibid., pp. 429–430.

2 *All Sir Garnet*

1. Clements, p. xiii.
2. *The Graphic* 1879, p. 522.
3. Wolseley vol. I, p. 70.
4. HPL.
5. Ibid.
6. Preston, *South African Diaries 1875*, p. 25.
7. Wolseley vol. I, p. 91.
8. Ibid., p. 90.
9. Spiers, *The Late Victorian Army*, p. 19.
10. St Aubyn, p. 131.
11. Wolseley vol. II, p. 233.
12. St Aubyn, p. 156.
13. Kochanski, p. 58
14. HPL.
15. Wright, *A Tidy Little War*, p. 124.
16. De Kiewiet, p. 43.
17. Preston, *Natal Diaries 1875*, p. 81.
18. Ibid., p. 221.
19. Forbes, pp. 170–171.
20. Butler, p. 197.
21. HPL.
22. Callwell, p. 152.
23. Maurice & Arthur, p. 152.
24. RAW.
25. LHCMH Archives, Sir John Maurice Papers.
26. HPL.
27. Callwell, p. 152.
28. HPL.
29. Preston, *1879 Journal*, p. 26.
30. Ibid.
31. HPL.
32. Ibid.
33. Preston, *1879 Journal*, p. 28.
34. Ibid., p. 29.
35. RAW.
36. Ibid.
37. Ibid.

38. Preston, *1879 Journal*, p. 31.
39. Lehmann, p. 245.
40. Preston, *1879 Journal*, p. 33.
41. RAW.
42. Buckle vol. vi, pp. 433–434.
43. Napier, p. 5.
44. HPL.
45. Preston, *1879 Journal*, p. 34.
46. Callwell, p. 158.
47. Ibid., p. 159.
48. Preston, *1879 Journal*, p. 34.
49. Wright, *A Tidy Little War, pp.* 123 quoting *Soldier`s Pocket-Book For Field Service* 1881 edition.
50. Butler, p. 173.
51. RAW.
52. HPL.
53. Ibid.

3 Generals in the Kitchen

1. Buckle vol. vi, p. 436.
2. Roberts, p. 227.
3. Lehmann, *All Sir Garnet*, p. 168.
4. Wright, *Warriors Of The Queen*, p. 31.
5. Gleichen, p. 176.
6. Wright, *Warriors Of The Queen*, p. 234.
7. Ibid., p. 180.
8. HPL.
9. Ibid.
10. Kochanski, p. 98.
11. Verner vol. ii, p. 159.
12. HPL.
13. Ibid.
14. Preston, *1879 Journal*, p. 41.
15. Elliot Letters.
16. Morris, p. 623.
17. HPL.
18. Preston, 1879 Journal, p. 44.
19. David, p. 338.
20. Clements, p. 109.
21. Greaves & Best, p. 121.

22. HPL.
23. Laband & Thompson, p. 72.
24. HPL.
25. Preston, *1879 Journal*, pp. 48–49.
26. Clarke, *Invasion of Zululand,* p. 225.
27. Butler, p. 199.
28. Beckett, *Victorians At War*, p. 127.
29. Preston, *1879 Journal*, p. 47.
30. Dawnay, p. 59.
31. CC.
32. Ibid.
33. HPL.
34. Ibid.
35. Lehmann, *All Sir Garnet*, p. 250.
36. Preston, *1879 Journal*, p. 51.
37. Montague, p. 255.
38. Molyneux, p. 179.
39. Ibid., p. 184.
40. Laband, *Zulu Warriors*, p. 256.
41. Emery, *The Red Soldier*, p. 229.
42. Ibid., p. 234.
43. David, p. 345.
44. Laband, *Kingdom In Crisis*, p. 214.
45. Laband, *Battle Of Ulundi,* p. 24.
46. Molyneux, p. 186.
47. Emery, *The Red Soldier*, p. 236.
48. Clarke, *Zululand At War*, p. 237.
49. Clarke, *Invasion Of Zululand*, p. 149.
50. Ibid., p. 195.
51. Dawnay, p. 67.
52. Grenfell, p. 66.
53. Prior, p. 118–119.
54. NAM.
55. Mossop, p. 94.
56. Dawnay, p. 68–69.
57. Clake, *Invasion Of Zululand*, p. 150.
58. Spiers, *Victorian Soldier In Africa*, p. 53.
59. Lock & Quantrill, *The Red Book*, p. 291.
60. Laband & Knight, pp. 143–144.
61. Preston, *1879 Journal*, p. 52.

62. Bennett, *Victorians At War*, p. 125.
63. Clarke, *Invasion Of Zululand*, p. 164.
64. Elliot Letters.
65. Lehmann, *All Sir Garnet*, p. 253.
66. Guy, *Destruction Of The Zulu Kingdom*, p. 58.
67. CC.
68. Preston, *1879 Journal*, pp. 53–54.
69. HPL.
70. Preston, *1879 Journal*, pp. 60–61.
71. Buckle vol. vi, p. 459.
72. French, p. 294.
73. Ibid., p. 298.
74. HPL.
75. Ibid.
76. Ibid.
77. Ibid.
78. Ibid.
79. Molyneux, p. 194.
80. Preston, *1879 Journal*, p. 57.
81. Greaves & Best, pp. 122–123.
82. Elliot Letters.
83. Preston, *1879 Journal*, p. 57.
84. Guy, *Destruction Of The Zulu Kingdom*, p. 59.
85. Preston, *1879 Journal*, p. 63.
86. Clarke, *Invasion Of Zululand*, p. 220.
87. PP cc2842.

4 *Catching Cetshwayo*

1. PP cc2482.
2. Child, p. 64.
3. HPL.
4. Ibid.
5. Laband, *Kingdom In Crisis*, p. 239.
6. CC.
7. Greaves, *Forgotten Battles*, p. 107.
8. CC.
9. Greaves, *Forgotten Battles*, p. 107.
10. Preston, *1879 Journal*, p. 64.
11. Ibid., p. 65.
12. HPL.

13. Ibid.
14. Ibid.
15. Ibid.
16. Ibid.
17. Preston, *1879 Journal*, p. 70.
18. Ibid.
19. Ibid., p. 71.
20. HPL.
21. Preston, *1879 Journal*, p. 72.
22. HPL.
23. Ibid.
24. Ibid.
25. Butler, *Life Of Colley*, pp. 235–236.
26. HPL.
27. Child, p. 65.
28. Hart, p. 163.
29. HPL.
30. Clarke, *Invasion Of Zululand*, p. 221.
31. Hart, p. 164.
32. Norris-Newman, *In Zululand*, p. 237.
33. Vijn, p. 88.
34. HPL.
35. Vijn, p. 61.
36. HPL.
37. Morris, p. 654.
38. Preston, *1879 Journal*, p. 87.
39. Greaves & Best, p. 140.
40. Child, pp. 67–75.
41. Laband, *Rope Of Sand*, p. 330.
42. HPL.
43. Vijn, p. 73.
44. Preston, *1879 Journal*, p. 92.
45. Edgerton, p. 159.
46. Callwell, p. 164.
47. Beckett, *Wolseley And Ashanti*, p. 199.
48. Guy, *Destruction Of The Zulu Kingdom*, p. 62.
49. Preston, *1879 Journal*, p. 96.
50. Buckle vol. vi, pp. 435–436.
51. HPL.
52. Marter, p. 4.

53. Ibid., p. 8.
54. Ibid., p. 13.
55. HPL.
56. Elliott Letters.
57. Child, pp. 72–73.
58. HPL.
59. Marter, p. 17.
60. Ibid., p. 18.
61. Murray, p. 70.
62. Child, p. 79.
63. Hart, p. 168.
64. Butler, *Life Of Colley*, p. 237.
65. Preston, *1879 Journal*, p. 103.
66. Laband, *Rope Of Sand*, p. 334.

5 Settling the Zulus

1. PP c.2482.
2. HPL.
3. Guy, *The Heretic*, p. 285.
4. PP c.2482.
5. *Natal Times* viewed CC.
6. PP c2482.
7. Martineau vol. ii, pp. 355–356.
8. Gordon, p. 286.
9. Haggard, pp. 41–42.
10. Duminy & Ballard, p. 121.
11. Kiewiet, p. 247.
12. Morris, p. 592.
13. Laband, *Zulu Warriors*, p. 261.
14. Wilson & Thompson, p. 264.
15. Guy, *The Destruction Of The Zulu Kingdom*, p. 76.
16. CC.
17. Lehmann, *All Sir Garnet*, p. 259.
18. *Natal Times* report in Lock & Quantrill, *The Red Book*, pp. 343–344.
19. Guy, *The Destruction Of The Zulu Kingdom*, p. 69.
20. Lock & Quantrill, *The Red Book*, p. 344.
21. Duminy & Ballard, p. 140.
22. Greaves & Knight vol. ii, p. 38.
23. Barber, p. 27.
24. Molyneux, pp. 125–126.

25. Preston, *1875 Diaries*, p. 226.
26. Preston, *1879 Journal*, p. 53.
27. Ibid., p. 56.
28. Ibid., p. 61.
29. Ibid., pp. 93–94.
30. Moodie vol. ii, p. 515.
31. Preston, *1879 Journal*, p. 104.
32. HPL.
33. Struben, p. 159.
34. Moodie vol. ii, p. 517.
35. Ibid., p. 516.
36. Clarke, *Invasion Of Zululand*, p. 223.
37. Brooks & Webb, p. 148.
38. Gordon, p. 316.
39. Guy, *The Destruction Of The Zulu Kingdom*, p. 71.
40. HPL.
41. Ibid.
42. CC.
43. HPL.
44. Ibid.
45. Ibid.
46. Preston, *1875 Diaries*, p. 176.
47. Preston, *1879 Journal*, pp. 78–79.
48. Ballard, p. 173.
49. Hale, pp. 118–119.
50. HPL.
51. PP cc2584.
52. Gathorne-Hardy, p. 122.

6 *Trouble in the Transvaal*

1. Montague, pp. 339–341.
2. Laband & Thompson, *Kingdom In Crisis*, p. 206.
3. Laband & Thompson, *War Comes To Umvoti*, p. 86.
4. Elliot Letters.
5. HPL.
6. Ibid.
7. Theron-Bushell, pp. 21–22.
8. Uys, pp. 148–149.
9. Delius, *The Land Belongs To Us*, p. 204.
10. Laband, *Zulu Warriors*, p. 33.

11. Delius, *The Land Belongs To Us*, p. 178.
12. PP cc2584.
13. CC Read Manuscript.
14. Bulpin, p. 165.
15. CC Read Manuscript.
16. Ibid.
17. Ibid.
18. NASAP.
19. Ibid.
20. Bulpin, p. 169.
21. PP cc1748.
22. Theron-Bushell, pp. 136–137.
23. Bulpin, p. 174.
24. Ibid., p. 175.
25. Stuben, p. 147.
26. Cope, p. 71.
27. PP cc2100.
28. Delius, *The Land Belongs To Us*, p. 239.
29. PP cc2220.
30. McToy, pp. 14–15.
31. Spiers, *Victorian Soldier In Africa*, p. 36.
32. Williams, p. 127.
33. Wright, *Soldiers Of The Queen*, p. 231.
34. Lock & Quantrill, *Zulu Vanquished*, p. 40.
35. Delius, *The Land Belongs To Us*, p. 240.
36. Lanyon Papers NASAP.
37. Ibid.
38. Lock & Quantrill, *Zulu Frontiersman*, p. 77.
39. Lanyon Papers, NASAP.
40. PP cc2482.
41. Lanyon Papers NASAP.
42. Harrison, p. 191.
43. Ibid., p. 201.
44. Preston, *1879 Journal*, p. 106.
45. Ibid., p. 110.
46. Ibid., p. 112.
47. Atkins vol. ii, p. 283.
48. Ibid., p. 284.
49. Preston, *1879 Journal*, p. 113.
50. Lehman, *All Sir Garnet*, p. 262.

51. De Kiewiet, p. 249.
52. Preston, *1879 Journal*, p. 113.
53. CC.
54. HPL.
55. Butler, *Life Of Colley*, p. 288.
56. HPL.
57. Ibid.
58. Ibid.

7 *Into the Lulu Mountains.*

1. Bulpin, pp. 131–132.
2. Preston, *1879 Journal*, p. 128.
3. Ibid., p. 129.
4. Theron-Bushell, p. 213.
5. Preston, *1879 Journal*, p. 118.
6. Theron-Bushell, p. 85.
7. Lanyon Letters NASAP.
8. Ibid.
9. PP cc2220.
10. McCalmont, p. 168.
11. Butterfield, p. 61.
12. Ibid., p. 62.
13. Ibid., p. 64.
14. Ibid., p. 66.
15. Commeline Letters, GRO.
16. HPL.
17. Preston, *1879 Journal*, p. 131.
18. HPL.
19. Ibid.
20. Ibid.
21. PP cc2482.
22. Delius, *The Land Belongs To Us*, p. 241.
23. PP cc2482.
24. Preston, *1879 Journal*, pp. 138–139.
25. GRO.
26. HPL.
27. Ibid.
28. Preston, *1879 Journal*, p. 146.
29. Ibid., p. 149.
30. Butterfield, p. 68.

31. Preston, *1879 Journal,* p. 149.
32. Brackenbury, *Blackwoods Magazine 1899.*
33. CC.
34. Bonner, pp. 153–154.
35. PP cc 2584.
36. Preston, *1879 Journal*, p. 151.
37. Bennett, p. 136.
38. Butterfield, p. 69.
39. HPL.
40. Preston, *1879 Journal,* p. 155.
41. McCalmont, p. 169.
42. Preston, *1879 Journal,* p. 159.
43. Ibid., p. 170.
44. CC. Letter to Lady Paget.
45. GRO.
46. Preston, *1879 Journal,* p. 171.

8 Blood on the Fighting Kopje

1. Macdonald, p. 172.
2. Ibid.
3. Moodie vol. ii, p. 558.
4. Kinsey.
5. Smith, p. 48.
6. Ibid.
7. Preston, *1879 Journal*, p. 173.
8. Ibid.
9. GRO.
10. HPL.
11. Smith, p. 49.
12. Lock & Quantrill, *Zulu Frontiersman*, p. 80.
13. GRO.
14. Butterfield, p. 75.
15. Lock & Quantrill, *Zulu Frontiersman*, pp. 81–82.
16. Turrell.
17. CC.
18. Delius, *The Land Belongs To Us*, p. 50.
19. Laband, *Zulu Warriors*, p. 42.
20. NAM.
21. McToy, p. 22.
22. Macdonald, pp. 169–170.

23. Preston, *1879 Journal*, pp. 162–163.
24. Hope, p. 136.
25. Clark, p. 80.
26. Butterfield, p. 67.
27. Castle, p. 41.
28. Smith, p. 51.
29. Macdonald, p. 176.
30. Lock & Quantrill, *Zulu Frontiersman*, p. 82.
31. NAM.
32. Preston, *1879 Journal*, p. 177.
33. Ibid.
34. GRO.
35. Grenfell, p. 194.
36. Kinsey.
37. Bennett, *Eyewitness*, pp. 138–139.
38. NAM.
39. Lock & Quantrill, *Zulu Frontiersman*, pp. 83–84.
40. NAM.
41. GRO.
42. Lehmann, *All Sir Garnet*, pp. 273–274.
43. Preston, *1879 Journal*, p. 178.
44. Lock & Quantrill, *Zulu Frontiersman*, p. 85.
45. GRO.
46. NAM.
47. Butterfield, p. 76.
48. Macdonald, pp. 180–181.
49. NAM.
50. Butterfield, p. 76.
51. NAM.
52. GRO.
53. Ibid.
54. Callwell, p. 175.
55. GRO.
56. Lock & Quantrill, *Zulu Frontiersman*, p. 84.
57. Butterfield, p. 79.
58. GRO.
59. HPL.
60. Ibid.

9 A Multitude of Grumbles

1. Callwell, p. 176.
2. HPL.
3. PP cc 2505.
4. Callwell, p. 178.
5. Moodie vol. ii, pp. 558–560.
6. Preston, *1879 Journal*, p. 189.
7. HPL.
8. Buckle vol. vi, pp. 473–474.
9. Butterfield, p. 89.
10. HPL.
11. Ibid.
12. Preston, *1879 Journal*, p. 189.
13. CC.
14. HPL.
15. CC.
16. HPL.
17. Ibid.
18. Atkins vol. ii, p. 295.
19. Clarke, *Invasion Of Zululand*, p. 229.
20. HPL.
21. Ibid.
22. Preston, *1879 Journal*, p. 236.
23. HPL.
24. Preston, *1879 Journal*, p. 230.
25. HPL.
26. Preston, *1879 Journal*, p. 265.
27. Ibid., p. 264.
28. Butterfield, p. 96.
29. HPL.
30. Preston, *1879 Journal*, p. 276.
31. Ibid., p. 284.

10 Farewells

1. Wright, *Warriors Of The Queen*, p. 59.
2. Marling, p. 55.
3. Theron-Bushell, p. 304.
4. Callwell, p. 178.
5. LPM.
6. Lehmann, *The First Boer War*, p. 116.

SELECT BIBLIOGRAPHY

Original Documents

Campbell Collections, Durban (CC)

Read (C.). 'The Campaign Against Sekokoeni In 1876' – unpublished typescript

Papers of Trooper Fred Symons, Natal Carbineers

Wolseley – Letterbook to the Secretary of State for War June 1879-April 1880

Letter to Lord Monck 15/8/79

Letter to Lady Paget 8/11/79

Gloucestershire Records Office, Gloucester (GRO)

Papers of Lieutenant Charles Commeline R.E.

Papers of Sir Michael Hicks Beach

kwaZulu Natal Archives, Pietermaritzburg

Papers of Shepstone Family

Liddell Hart Centre for Military Archives, London (LHCMH)

Papers of General Sir John Maurice

Low Parks Museum, Hamilton

Personal Diaries of Field Marshal Lord Wolseley 1877–1906

National Archives, London

C.O. 879/14 – Colonial Office files

W.O./7791 – Diary of the Transvaal Field Force, 22 October – 3 December, 1879
W.O./7794 – Chief of Staff's Journal of Military Operations, Transvaal, 1879
W.O. 98/4/59 – Correspondence Relating To V.C Awards Flawn & Fitzpatrick
W.O. 147 – Papers of Field-Marshal Viscount Wolseley (64 vols)

National Archives of South Africa, Pretoria (NASAP)
Papers of President Thomas Burgers
Papers of Sir Owen Lanyon

National Army Museum, London
9th Lancers – Diary of Major Henry Bushman
17th Lancers – Letters of Private George Turnham
58th Regiment – Letter of Private Tuck
94th Regiment – Letter of an Anonymous Soldier
Memoirs of Bapedi Warrior Masschow
Papers of General Lord Chelmsford
Canon George Lummis – Victoria Cross Files

Regimental Museum of the Royal Welsh, Brecon (SWBM)
24th Foot – letters of Captain Penn Symons

Royal Archives, Windsor
Papers of H.R.H. the Duke of Cambridge

Royal Engineers Museum, Gillingham
Papers of Lieutenant Thomas Main R.E.

The Wolseley Collection, Hove
Letters of Garnet Wolseley to his wife, 1878–1880
Letters of Garnet Wolseley to family members 1879–1880
Letters of Garnet Wolseley to friends & colleagues 1879–1880
Letters of Louisa Wolseley to her husband 1879–1880
South Africa 1879–1880 – Military Private Letter Book
South Africa 1879–1880 – Semi-Official Private Letter Book (Civilian)
17th Lancers – Diary Of The Zulu Expedition, South Africa 1879

Private Manuscripts

90th Regiment – Letters Of Lieutenant Robert Fell
93rd Regiment – Letters Of Captain The Hon. Fitzwilliam Elliot

Printed Works

Official Publications

Anon. *Narrative Of The Field Operations Connected With The Zulu War Of 1879*. His Majesty's Stationery Office. London 1907.
Hansard 1879.
Parliamentary Papers (PP) – Correspondence Respecting The Affairs Of South Africa – cc.1961, 2000, 2079, 2100, 2128, 2144, 2220, 2222, 2234, 2242, 2252, 2260, 2269, 2308, 2316, 2318, 2367, 2374, 2454, 2482, 2505, 2584, 2586, 2655 (24 vols).

Other Publications

Anglesey (Marquess of). *A History Of The British Cavalry 1872–1898*. Leo Cooper, London 1982.
Arthur (Sir G.) ed. *The Letters Of Lord And Lady Wolseley, 1870–1911*. William Heinemann. London 1923.
Ashe (Maj.) & Wyatt-Edgell (Capt. The Hon. E.V.). *The Story Of The Zulu Campaign*. Sampson, Low, Marston, Searle & Rivington. London 1880.
Atkins (J.B.). *The Life Of Sir William Howard Russell CVO, LLD The First Special Correspondent*. 2 vols. John Murray. London 1911.
Aylward (A.). *The Transvaal Of Today: War Witchcraft, Sport And Spoils In South Africa*. William Blackwood. Edinburgh 1881.
Ballard (C.). *John Dunn: The White Chief Of Zululand*. A.D.Donker. Craighall 1985.
Barker (D.). *Zulus At Bay*. Prvt pub. Pinetown 2005.
Bartlett (W.). *Zulu: Queen Victoria's Most Famous Little War*. History Press. Brimscombe Port 2010.
Beckett (I.). *The Victorians At War*. Hambledon. London 2003.
_______ ed. *Wolseley And Ashanti: The Asante War Journal And Correspondence Of Major-General Sir Garnet Wolseley 1873–1874*. History Press. Brimscombe Port 2009.
Bennett (I.) ed. *Eyewitness In Zululand: The Campaign Reminiscences Of Colonel W. A. Dunne, C.B. South Africa 1877–1881*. Greenhill. London 1989.

_______ *A Rain Of Lead: The Siege And Surrender Of The British At Potchefstroom 1880–1881*. Greenhill. London 2001.

Best (B.) & Greaves (A.) ed. *The Curling Letters Of The Zulu War*. Leo Cooper. London 2001.

Binns (C.). *The Last Zulu King: The Life And Death Of Cetshwayo*. Longmans Green. London 1963.

Blake (R.). *Disraeli*. Eyre & Spottiswoode. London 1966.

Blood (Gen. Sir B.). *Four Score Years And Ten*. George Bell. London 1933.

Bonner (P.). *Kings, Commoners And Concessionaires: The Evolution And Dissolution Of The Nineteenth Century Swazi State*. University Press. Cambridge 1982.

Brackenbury (Gen. The Hon. Sir H.). *Some Memories Of My Spare Time*. William Blackwood. Edinburgh 1909.

Brice (C.). *The Thinking Man's Soldier: The Life And Career Of General Sir Henry Brackenbury 1837–1914*. Helion. Solihull 2012.

Brooks (E. H.) & Webb (C.). *A History Of Natal*. University Of Natal Press. Pietermaritzburg 1965.

Bryant (M.). *Wars Of Empire In Cartoons*. Gould Street Publishing. London 2008.

Buckle (G.E.). *The Life Of Benjamin Disraeli Earl Of Beaconsfield Vol. VI*. John Murray. London 1920.

Bulpin (T.V.). *Lost Trails Of The Transvaal* Omnibus Edition. T.V. Bulpin. Cape Town 1974.

Butler (Lt-Gen. Sir W. F.). *The Life of Sir George Pomeroy-Colley 1835–1881*. John Murray. London 1899.

___________________ *Autobiography*. Constable. London 1911.

Butterfield (P. H.) ed. *War And Peace In South Africa 1879–1881: The Writings Of Philip Anstruther And Edward Essex*. Scripta Africana. Melville nd (c 1986).

Callwell (Maj-Gen. Sir C.) ed. *The Memoirs Of Major-General Sir Hugh McCalmont KCB; CVO*. Hutchinson. London 1924.

Castle (I.). *Zulu War – Volunteers, Irregulars & Auxiliaries*. Osprey. London 2003.

_______ & Knight (I.). *Fearful Hard Times: The Siege And Relief Of Eshowe 1879*. Greenhill. London 1994.

Child (D.) ed. *Zulu War Journal Of Colonel Henry Harford, CB*. Shuter & Shooter. Pietermaritzburg 1978.

Clark (Sgt. J.). *Historical Record And Regimental Memoir Of The Royal Scots Fusiliers Formerly Known As The 21st Royal North British Fusiliers.* Banks & Co. Edinburgh 1885.

Clarke (S.). *Invasion Of Zululand: Anglo-Zulu War Experiences Of Arthur Harness; John Jervis, 4th Viscount St Vincent; And Sir Henry Bulwer.* Brenthust Press. Johannesburg 1979.

_______ *Zululand At War 1879: The Conduct Of The Anglo-Zulu War.* Brenthurst Press, Johannesburg 1984.

Clements (W.). *The Glamour And Tragedy Of The Zulu War.* John Lane. London 1936.

Colenso (F. E.). *The Ruin Of Zululand: An Account Of British Doings Since The Invasion Of 1879.* 2 vols. William Ridgway. London 1884.

Cope (R.). *Ploughshare Of War: The Origins Of The Anglo-Zulu War Of 1879.* University Of Natal Press. Scottsville 1999.

Corrie (E.V.). *The Promised Land Or Nine Years Mining, Hunting And Volunteering In The Transvaal.* Blades, East & Blades. London 1884.

Corvi (S.) & Beckett (I.F.W.) ed. *Victoria's Generals.* Pen & Sword. Barnsley 2009.

Creagh (Sir O. M.) & Humphris (E. M.). *The Victoria Cross 1856–1920.* J. B. Hayward. Polstead 1985.

David (S.). *Zulu: The Heroism And Tragedy Of The Zulu War.* Viking. London 2004.

Dawnay (G.). *Campaigns: Zulu 1879, Egypt 1882, Suakim 1885.* Pvt pub. Spottiswoode. London 1886.

Delius (P.). *A Lion Amongst The Cattle: Reconstruction And Resistance In The Northern Transvaal.* James Currey. Oxford 1966.

_______ *The Land Belongs To Us: The Pedi Polity, The Boers And The British In The Nineteenth Century Transvaal.* Heinemann. London 1984.

Duminy (A.) & Ballard (C.) ed. *The Anglo-Zulu War: New Perspectives.* University of Natal Press, Pietermaritzburg 1981.

Dutton (R.). *Forgotten Heroes: Zulu & Basuto Wars.* Info Dial. Preston 2010.

Edgerton (R.). *Like Lions We Fought: The Zulu War And The Last Black Empire In South Africa.* Free Press. New York 1988.

Emery (F.). *The Red Soldier: Letters From The Zulu War, 1879.* Hodder & Stoughton. London 1977.

_______ *Marching Over Africa: Letters From Victorian Soldiers.* Hodder & Stoughton. London 1986.

Everett (Maj-Gen. Sir H.). *The History Of The Somerset Light Infantry (Prince Albert's) 1685–1914*. Methuen. London 1914.

Farwell (B.). *Queen Victoria's Little Wars*. Harper & Row. New York 1972.

_______ *For Queen And Country: A Social History Of The Victorian & Edwardian Army*. Allen Lane. London 1981.

_______ *Eminent Victorian Soldiers*. Viking. London 1985.

Fenn (T. E.). *How I Volunteered For The Cape And What I Did There*. Samuel Tinsley. London 1879.

Fisher (J.). *Paul Kruger: His Life And Times*. Secker & Warburg. London 1974.

Forbes (A.). *Service In Six Continents*. Methuen. London 1886.

Fortescue-Brickdale (Sir C.) ed. *Major-General Sir Henry Hallam Parr*. T. Fisher Unwin. London 1917.

French (Maj. G.). *Lord Chelmsford And The Zulu War*. John Lane. London 1939.

Gathorne-Hardy (R. E.). *Gathorne Hardy, First Earl Of Cranbrook. A Memoir With Extracts From His Diary And Correspondence*. Longmans Green. London 1910.

Gon (P.). *The Road To Isandlwana: The Years Of An Imperial Battalion*. A. D. Donker. Cape Town 1979.

_______ *Send Carrington: The Story Of An Imperial Frontiersman*. A. D. Donker. Craighall 1984.

Gordon (R.E.). *Shepstone: The Role Of The Family In The History Of South Africa 1820–1900*. A. A. Balkema. Cape Town 1968.

Greaves (A.). *Isandlwana*. Cassell. London 2001.

_______ *Rorke's Drift*. Cassell. London 2002.

_______ ed. *Redcoats And Zulus: Selected Essays From The Journal Of The Anglo-Zulu War Historical Society*. Pen & Sword. Barnsley 2004.

_______ *Crossing The Buffalo: The Zulu War Of 1879*. Weidenfeld & Nicolson. London 2005.

_______ *Forgotten Battles Of The Zulu War*. Pen & Sword. Barnsley 2012.

Greaves (Sir G.). *Memoirs*. John Murray. London 1924.

Grenfell (F.M. Lord). *Memoirs*. Hodder & Stoughton. London nd (c 1924).

Guy (J.). *The Destruction Of The Zulu Kingdom*. Longman. London 1979.

_______ *The Heretic: A Study Of The Life Of John William Colenso 1814–1883*. Ravan Press. Johannesburg 1983.

_______ *Theophilus Shepstone And The Forging Of Natal: African Autonomy And Settler Colonialism In The Making Of Traditional Authority*. University Of Kwazulu Natal Press. Scottsville 2013.

Haggard (H.R.). *Cetywayo And His White Neighbours*. New Edition. Kegan, Paul, Trench, Trubner. London 1900.

Hale (F.) ed. *Norwegian Missionaries In Natal And Zululand: Selected Correspondence 1844–1900*. Van Riebeeck Society. Cape Town 1997.

Hamilton-Browne (Col. G.). *A Lost Legionary In South Africa*. T. Werner Laurie. London nd (c 1912).

Harrison (Gen. Sir R.). *Recollections Of A Life In The British Army During The Latter Half Of The 19th Century*. John Murray. London 1908.

Hart-Synnot (B.M.) ed. *Letters Of Major-General Fitzroy Hart-Synnot CB; CMG*. Edward Arnold. London 1912.

Hattersley (A.F.) ed. *Later Annals Of Natal*. Longmans Green. London 1938.

Hicks Beach (V.). *The Life Of Sir Michael Hicks Beach (Earl St Aldwyn)*. 2 vols. Macmillan. London 1932.

Holt (H.P.). *The Mounted Police Of Natal*. John Murray. London 1913.

Hope (R.). *A Staffordshire Regiment In The Zulu & Sekukuni Campaigns 1878–1879, 80th Regiment Of Foot*. Churnet Valley. Leek 2007.

Jackson (F.W.D.). *The Hill Of The Sphinx: The Battle Of Isandlwana*. Westerners Publications. London 2002.

Johnson (B.C.). *Hook Of Rorke's Drift: The Life Of Henry Hook V.C. 1850–1905*. Bartlett's Press. Birmingham 2004.

Jones (H.). *The Boiling Cauldron: Utrecht District And The Anglo-Zulu War 1879*. Shermershill Press. Bisley 2006.

Jourdain (Lt-Col. H.F.N.). *The Connaught Rangers*. Royal United Service Institution. London 1926.

Kiewiet (C.). *The Imperial Factor In South Africa: A Study In Politics And Economics*. University Press. Cambridge 1937.

Knight (I.). *British Fortifications In Zululand 1879*. Osprey. London 2005.

_______ *A Companion To The Anglo-Zulu War*. Pen & Sword. Barnsley 2008.

_______ *Zulu Rising: The Epic Story Of Isandlwana And Rorke's Drift*. Macmillan. London 2010.

_______ & Castle (I.). *The Zulu War Then And Now*. Battle of Britain Prints International. London 1993.

_______ & Greaves (A.). *The Who's Who Of The Anglo-Zulu War*. 2 vols. Pen & Sword. Barnsley 2006–2007.

Kochanski (H.). *Sir Garnet Wolseley: Victorian Hero*. Hambledon Press. London 1999.

Laband (J.). *The Battle Of Ulundi*. Shuter & Shooter. Pietermaritzburg 1988.

_______ *Kingdom In Crisis: The Zulu Response To The British Invasion Of 1879*. University Press. Manchester 1992.

_______ ed. *Lord Chelmsford's Zululand Campaign 1878–1879*. Army Records Society. Far Thrupp 1994.

_______ *Rope Of Sand* Jonathan Ball. Jeppestown 1995.

_______ *The Transvaal Rebellion: The First Boer War 1880–1881*. Pearson. Harlow 2005.

_______ *Zulu Warriors: The Battle For The South African Frontier*. Yale University Press. New Haven 2014.

_______ & Knight (I.). *The Anglo-Zulu War: The War Correspondents*. Sutton. Thrupp 1996.

_______ & Thompson (P.). *War Comes To Umvoti: The Natal-Zululand Border 1878–79*. University Of Natal. Durban 1980.

_______ ed. *Kingdom And Colony At War: Sixteen Studies In The Anglo-Zulu War Of 1879*. University Of Natal Press. Pietermaritzburg 1990.

_______ & Henderson (S.). *The Buffalo Border 1879: The Anglo-Zulu War In Northern Natal*. University Of Natal. Durban 1983.

Lehmann (J.). *All Sir Garnet: A Life Of Field-Marshal Lord Wolseley*. Jonathan Cape. London 1964.

_______ *The First Boer War*. Jonathan Cape. London 1972.

Lock (R.) & Quantrill (P.). *Zulu Victory: The Epic Of Isandlwana And The Cover-Up*. Greenhill. London 2002.

_______ *Zulu Vanquished: The Destruction Of The Zulu Kingdom*. Greenhill. London 2005.

_______ ed. *The Red Book*. Nd. Np. Npp.

_______ ed. *Zulu Frontiersman: Major G. Denison, DSO*. Frontline. London 2008.

Low (C.R.). *General Lord Wolseley (Of Cairo)*. Richard Bentley. London 1883.

Macdonald (W.). *The Romance Of The Golden Rand: Being The Romantic Story Of The Life And Work Of The Pioneers Of The Witwatersrand – The World World's Greatest Goldfields*. Cassell. London 1933.

Mackinnon (J.P.) & Shadbolt (S.). *The South African Campaign, 1879*. Sampson Low, Marston, Searle & Rivington. London 1880.

Magnus (P.). *Kitchener: Portrait Of An Imperialist*. John Murray. London 1958.

Manning (S.). *Evelyn Wood V.C.: Pillar Of Empire*. Pen & Sword. Barnsley 2007.

Marling (Col. Sir P.). *Rifleman And Hussar*. John Murray. London 1931.

Martineau (J.). *The Life And Correspondence Of The Right Hon. Sir Bartle Frere, Bart, GCB; FRS; Etc.* 2 vols. John Murray. London 1885.

Marter (Maj R.). *The Capture Of Cetywayo: King Of The Zulus*. Army & Navy Cooperative Society. London nd (c 1880).

Maurice (Maj-Gen. Sir F.) & Arthur (Sir G.). *The Life Of Lord Wolseley*. William Heinemann. London 1924.

McToy (E.D.). *A Brief History Of The 13th Regiment (P.A.L.I.) In South Africa During The Transvaal And Zulu Difficulties 1877–8–9*. A. H. Swiss. Devonport 1880.

Molyneux (Maj-Gen. W.C.F.). *Campaigning In South Africa And Egypt*. Macmillan. London 1896.

Montague (Capt. W.E.). *Campaigning In South Africa: Reminiscences Of An Officer In 1879*. William Blackwood. Edinburgh 1880.

Moodie (D.C.F.). *The History Of The Battles And Adventures Of The British, The Boers And The Zulus Etc In Southern Africa From The Time Of The Pharoah Necho To 1880*. 2 vols. Murray & St Leger. Cape Town 1888.

Morris (D.). *The Washing Of The Spears: A History Of The Rise Of The Zulu Nation Under Shaka And The Fall In The Zulu War Of 1879*. Simon & Schuster. New York 1965.

Mossop (G.). *Running The Gauntlet: Some Recollections Of Adventure*. G. F. Button. Pietermaritzburg 1990.

Murray (Col Sir W.). *A Varied Life*. Pvt pub. Winchester 1925.

Napier (Lt-Col. The Hon. H.D.). *Letters Of Field-Marshal Lord Napier Of Magdala*. Jarrolds. Norwich 1936.

Norris-Newman (C.). *In Zululand With The British Throughout The War Of 1879*. W. H. Allen. London 1880.

_______ *With The Boers In The Transvaal And Orange Free State In 1880–81*. W. H. Allen. London 1881.

O'Connor (D). *The Zulu And The Raj: The Life Of Sir Bartle Frere*. Able. Knebworth 2002.

Pakenham (T.). *The Boer War*. Random House. New York 1979.

Parr (Capt. H. H.). *A Sketch Of The Kafir And Zulu Wars: Guadana To Isandlwana*. C. Kegan Paul. London 1880.

Peers (C.). *The African Wars: Warriors And Soldiers In The Colonial Campaigns*. Pen & Sword. Barnsley 2010.

Pollock(J.). *Kitchener: The Road To Omdurman*. Constable. London 1988.

Powell (G.). *Buller: A Scapegoat? A Life Of General Sir Redvers Buller 1839–1908*. Leo Cooper. London 1994.

Preston (A.) ed. *The South African Diaries (Natal) 1875*. A. A. Balkema. Cape Town 1971.

_______ *South African Journal Of Sir Garnet Wolseley 1879–1880*. A. A. Balkema. Cape Town 1973.

Prior (M.). *Campaigns Of A War Correspondent*. Edward Arnold. London 1912.

Ransford (O.). *The Battle Of Majuba Hill*. John Murray. London 1967.

Reade (W.). *The Story Of The Ashantee Campaign*. Smith, Elder. London 1874.

Roberts (A.). *Salisbury* Victorian Titan. Weidenfeld & Nicolson. London 1999.

Robinson (R.), Gallagher (J.) & Denny (A.). *Africa And The Victorians: The Official Mind Of Imperialism*. Macmillan. London 1961.

Sampson (V.) & Hamilton (I.). *Anti-Commando*. Faber & Faber. London 1931.

Scott-Stevenson (Mrs A.). *Our Home In Cyprus*. Chapman & Hall. London 1880.

Smith (K.). *Dead Was Everything: Studies In The Anglo-Zulu War*. Frontline. Barnsley 2014.

Spiers (E.M.). *The Late Victorian Army 1868–1902*. University Press. Manchester 1992.

_______ *The Victorian Soldier In Africa*. University Press. Manchester 2004.

St Aubyn (G.). *The Royal George 1819–1904* Alfred A.Knopf. New York 1964.

Storey (W. K.). *Guns, Race And Power In Colonial South Africa*. University Press. Cambridge 2008.

Stossel (K.). *A Handful Of Heroes: Rorke's Drift – Facts, Myths & Legends*. Pen & Sword. Barnsley 2015.

Struben (H.W.). *Recollections Of Adventures: Pioneering And Development In South Africa 1850–1911*. T. Maskew Miller. Cape Town 1920.

Thompson (P.S.). *The Natal Native Contingents In The Anglo-Zulu War 1879*. Pvt pub. Npp. 2003.

Toomey (G.E.). *Heroes Of The Victoria Cross*. George Newnes. London 1895.

Turrell (R.V.). *Capital And Labour On The Kimberley Diamond Fields, 1870–1890*. University Press. Cambridge 1987.

Uys (C.J.). *In The Era Of Shepstone: Being A Study Of British Expansion In South Africa (1842–1877)*. Lovedale Press. Lovedale 1933.

Verner (Col W.) & Parker (Capt. E.). *The Military Life Of H.R.H. George, Duke Of Cambridge*. 2 vols. John Murray. London 1905.

Vijn (C.). *Cetshwayo's Dutchman, Being The Private Journal Of A White Trader In Zululand During The British Invasion*. Longmans Green. London 1880.

Warren (Lt-Gen. Sir C.). *On The Veldt In The Seventies*. Isbister. London 1902.

Webb (C.L.) & Wright (J.B.) ed. *A Zulu King Speaks: Statements By Cetshwayo kaMpande On The History And Customs Of The Zulu People*. University Of Natal. Pietermaritzburg 1978.

Wheeler (Capt. O.). *The War Office Past And Present*. Methuen. London 1914.

Wilkinson-Latham (C.). *Uniforms & Weapons Of The Zulu War*. Batsford. London 1978.

_______ *From Our Special Correspondent: Victorian War Correspondents And Their Campaigns*. Hodder & Stoughton. London 1979.

Williams (S.). *Running The Show: Governors Of The British Empire 1857–1912*. Viking. London 1911.

_______ (W. A.). *Commandant Of The Transvaal: The Life And Career Of General Sir Hugh Rowlands VC, KCB*. Bridge Books. Wrexham 2001.

Wilson (M.) & Thompson (L. M.). *The Oxford History Of South Africa*. University Press. Oxford 1969.

Wolseley (F. M. Visc.). *The Story Of A Soldier's Life*. 2 vols. Archibald Constable. London 1903.

Wood (FM. E.). *From Midshipman To Field-Marshal*. 2 vols. Methuen. London 1906.

Wright (W.). *A Tidy Little War: The British Invasion Of Egypt 1882*. Spellmount. Brimscombe Port 2009.

_______ *Warriors Of The Queen: Fighting Generals Of The Victorian Age*. Spellmount. Brimscombe Port 2014.

Articles

Barnard (W. G.) 'The Defeat Of Chief Sekukuni'. *The Ranger* Vol. XI November 1945.

Brackenbury (Gen. Sir H.). 'The Transvaal Twenty Years Ago'. *Blackwood's Magazine* November 1899.

Kinsey (H. W.). 'The Sekukuni Wars'. *Journal of the South African Military History Society* Vol. 2 Nos 5–6 June-December 1973.

Tylden (Maj G.). 'A South African Soldier – Colonel I. P. Ferreira CMG'. *Journal of the Society for Army Historical Research* 1942.

_______ 'The Sekukuni Campaign Of November-December 1879'. *Journal of the Society for Army Historical Research* November 1945.

Theses

Barber (S. B.). *John Dunn And Zululand 1856–1883*. University of Natal 1971.

Diver (L.). *Perception Versus Reality? Newspaper Coverage On The Anglo-Zulu War Of 1879*. University of Ireland 2010.

Hook (G.). *Britons In Cyprus, 1878–1914*. University of Texas 2009.

Kilby (P.). *The Anglo-Asante War Of 1873–1874: A Narrative And Analysis*. University of British Columbia 1960.

Maggs (C.). *Sir Garnet Wolseley's Mission To Natal In 1875*. University of Natal 1982.

Smith (K.). *The Commandants: The Leadership Of The Natal Native Contingents In The Anglo-Zulu War*. University of Western Australia 2005.

_______ (K. W.). *The Campaigns Against The Bapedi Of Sekhukhune 1877–1879*. University of South Africa 1966.

Theron-Bushell (B. M.). *Puppet On An Imperial String? Owen Lanyon In South Africa 1875–1881*. University of South Africa 2002.

Thompson (W.). '*Wolseley And South Africa: A Study Of Sir Garnet Wolseley's Role In South African Affairs 1875–1877*. Vanderbilt University 1973.

Magazines & Newspapers

Cape Argus
Daily News
Daily Telegraph
Fun
The Graphic
Illustrated London News
Punch
The Standard
Natal Mercury
Natal Times

INDEX